Romans

Romans

An Exposition of Chapter 10
Saving Faith

D. M. Lloyd-Jones

THE BANNER OF TRUTH TRUST

THE BANNER OF TRUTH TRUST
3 Murrayfield Road, Edinburgh EH12 6EL

*

© Lady Catherwood and Ann Desmond 1997
First published 1997
ISBN 0 85151 737 4

*

Typeset in 10 on 12 Stempel Garamond
by Watermark
Cromer NR27 9HL
and printed in Great Britain by
the Bath Press

The sermons in this volume
were originally preached at Westminster Chapel
between May 1963 and May 1964

Contents

Contents

Contents

One

*

> Brethren, my heart's desire and prayer to God for Israel is, that
> they might be saved. For I bear them record that they have a zeal
> of God, but not according to knowledge.   Romans 10:1–2

In our consideration of this great Epistle to the Romans, we come to
the tenth chapter. This is a distinct part of that major section which
also includes chapters 9[1] and 11. In these three chapters Paul, having
completed his exposition of the Christian faith, takes up the whole
matter of the position of the Jews.

We have seen that there were two main reasons for doing that. One
was, of course, the fact that the Jews as a nation were outside the
Christian church. A small number had come in, but most were outside, whereas the Gentiles, of all people, were crowding in. The
second reason was that the fact of the Jews being outside seemed, to
some people, to raise a query as to whether the promises of God on
which the Apostle had been elaborating at the end of chapter 8 were,
after all, as certain as he had been making out.

So the Apostle takes up this matter and he deals with it in these
three chapters. In chapter 9 we saw that Paul's main teaching is that
salvation is something that is entirely dependent upon the purpose of
God. Before the creation of the world and of man, God conceived the
purpose of saving many of those who would fall and this he does in
accord with his election of them. This is found in verse 11: 'That the
purpose of God according to election might stand, not of works, but
of him that calleth.' There is therefore no more to be said. Salvation
is entirely of God. Men and women can never boast of the fact that
they have saved themselves; not even their faith saves them. It is God
who saves and the Apostle gives the bulk of chapter 9 to an exposition
and defence of that great and high doctrine.

[1] See *An Exposition of Chapter 9: God's Sovereign Purpose*, 1991

But there is another side of the truth stated in that chapter. Towards the end of it Paul refers to the fact that Jews, in contrast with Gentiles, had not obtained the righteousness of God. This was because of their unbelief. So if a man is saved, it is because God has saved him. But if a man is lost, that is to be attributed to his own rejection of the gospel and his rebellion against God's way of salvation. It is in chapter 10 that the Apostle takes up this second point. In doing so, he explains it more fully and also maintains the balance of Scripture.

Then, after Paul has finished that, which he does at the end of chapter 10, he goes back, at the beginning of chapter 11, to his main theme, which is God's purpose for Jew and Gentile. He returns to God's great plan of salvation leading up to the final consummation and closing with that tremendous apostrophe: 'O the depth of the riches both of the wisdom and knowledge of God . . .'

That, then, is the setting of this tenth chapter. You could say, looking at chapters 9, 10 and 11 as a whole, that chapter 10 is almost a kind of parenthesis. It is, as it were, an extended commentary on verses 32 and 33 of chapter 9. So the setting is most important and you notice that he starts the three chapters with the same sort of formula in which he refers to the unbelief of the Jewish people. In chapter 9, he says: 'I have great heaviness and continual sorrow in my heart. For I could wish that myself were accursed from Christ for my brethren, my kinsmen according to the flesh.' Here in chapter 10 he says: 'Brethren, my heart's desire and prayer to God for Israel is, that they might be saved.' At the beginning of chapter 11, he puts it in the form of a question: 'Hath God cast away his people?'

That is the setting. Let us now make a general analysis of the contents of the whole chapter, so that as we come to look at it verse by verse we shall be taking each portion in the light of the whole argument. I suggest, therefore, that you can subdivide the chapter like this.

First of all, verses 1 and 2, in which the Apostle again makes these loving references to his own fellow-countrymen, the Jews, and expresses his heartfelt desire concerning them.

Verses 3 and 4 are the next division. Here Paul again reminds us why it is that the Jews are outside – that it is because of their failure to understand the way of salvation and how to be right before God. It was all because of their fatal misunderstanding and misreading of the law.

[2]

The next section is from verse 5 to verse 10, where Paul gives us a comparison and a contrast between the law and the gospel as a way of righteousness. This is most illuminating. He compares and contrasts the two ways – the way the Jew was following, which is the way of the law, and the Christian way, the way of the gospel.

Then in verses 11 to 13, Paul points out that the gospel way, being what it is, is a way that is open to all – to Gentile as well as to Jew. If salvation had been by means of the law, the Gentile would be excluded, because he had not been given the law; but as salvation is not by means of the law, but by another way, then it is as open to the Gentile as it is to the Jew.

Then in verses 14 to 17 he takes that further and says that in view of this, salvation is for the Gentile as well as the Jew. The gospel is therefore to be preached to the Jew and the Gentile alike and its salvation is to be offered to the Gentile as much as it is to the Jew. Indeed, it is to be offered to all.

In the last section, verses 18 to 21, the Apostle points out that in spite of the fact that the gospel is thus offered to all, all do not believe, obey or accept it. And yet, he says, we should not be surprised at this, because it had been prophesied long before in the Scriptures.

That is Paul's method and it is very similar to the one he adopted in chapter 9. He makes his assertions and supports them with scriptural quotations. He establishes every point by some quotation from the Old Testament. He does that, not only to prove that he is right, but to bring out still more clearly the tragic blindness of the Jews, who boasted of their knowledge of the Scriptures and yet were so blind to their teaching.

There, then, is our analysis of the chapter, and you notice that, by the end of it, Paul has brought us back to exactly the same point at which he ended chapter 9. At the conclusion of that chapter he puts before us the extraordinary fact that the Jews have not believed, while the Gentiles have, and at the end of chapter 10 he says it all once more.

In other words, with this master mind of his, which always makes me think of a Beethoven symphony, he has used his usual method. At the end of chapter 9, he put a theme before us. In this chapter he takes that theme and works it out quite fully and ends by repeating it so that he can go on and take up the main argument at the beginning of chapter 11. It is indeed fascinating to watch the working of a great mind such as that of the Apostle Paul and, you see, what it really comes to is that, in chapter 10, Paul gives us the doctrine of justification by faith only – that is the big point of the chapter, which is an extended treatment of that teaching.

However, someone may well ask the question at this point: 'But why does he do that again? Surely he dealt with that doctrine in a perfect and exhaustive manner in chapters 1 to 4? Why does he come back to it?' That is a perfectly fair question, and it seems to me that the answer is this. In those chapters he put this doctrine before us in what we may call a theological manner. He enunciated great theological principles in a general and definitive way. Here, though it is exactly the same doctrine, he puts it in a more pastoral and practical manner, bringing it nearer to us. And, of course, this is something that Paul is very fond of doing. The teaching is, therefore, much more applied in chapter 10 than in chapters 1 to 4, and that, surely, is one of his reasons for the repetition.

But there is another reason for this. Paul repeats himself as plainly, as simply and as directly as he can because of his great pastoral concern for the Jews. A pastor is like a good teacher or a wise parent and one of the first things that a parent has to learn is that it is not enough to say a thing once to a child. If you love your child, and are anxious for that child to know what is right and what is wrong, you will have to say a thing over and over again, particularly if you can see that the child does not quite grasp the point. And you have certainly got to be very patient.

This is what the Apostle is doing here, and if you approach this chapter, therefore, feeling that it is rather unnecessary, then you are just admitting that you know nothing about pastoral work. You are merely a theorist, an intellectualist. You say, 'But I know all about justification. I have mastered chapters 1 to 4 – I do not need this!' But wait, and you will see, before we have gone much further, that you need it very badly.

Then, the third reason why the Apostle repeats his theme is that this matter of justification by faith only is so crucial. It is the hinge on which everything turns. This is the doctrine which led to the Protestant Reformation, and it is the essence of Protestant preaching. The whole of our salvation is bound up with our understanding of this particular doctrine. It therefore calls for continual emphasis. In various ways, we are all liable to slip back to a trust in works. We would even think of our faith as if it were a work. So we can never hear the doctrine of justification by faith too frequently and it is good that the Apostle should have given it to us once more. There, then, is our general review, a general conspectus of the teaching of chapter 10.

We are now in a position to start on our detailed analysis, and so we begin with verses 1 and 2. Here there are certain vital lessons which stand out immediately. What are they? The first is that we must learn once more the lesson given us by the Apostle's attitude towards the Jews. What a saint he was! What a man of God! What a Christian! How like his Lord and Master! Look at him, watch him. We may learn from any such great example, but this man seems to be preeminent.

What do I mean? Well, here is a man who was being reviled and persecuted by his fellow-countrymen. They had tried to kill him many times. They hated him; they abominated him; there was nothing bad that they would not say about him. And yet he bears them no malice whatsoever! 'Brethren, my heart's desire and prayer to God for Israel is, that they might be saved.' He does not bear any resentment. Indeed, I must not leave it like that, negatively, I must put that in a positive form. He has a great concern for them; he has a great longing in his heart.

Now he has said that before, has he not? He said at the beginning of chapter 9, 'I could wish that myself were accursed from Christ for my brethren, my kinsmen according to the flesh.[1] But he says it again here. When people feel things deeply, they repeat them. And here Paul gives us a glimpse into his great heart of love.

Remember, he was not always like that. At one time, he had been a very narrow Pharisee and nationalist. He is no longer that, and he shows us that still further in this interesting way. Though they have treated him as they have, and though their attitude towards him is abominable, he goes out of his way to find anything about them that he can praise. He says, 'I bear them record' – I have to acknowledge and I do so gladly – 'that they have a zeal of God.' He pays tribute to them. What an extraordinary man this is!

But we can also put that in another way. The Apostle does not attack the Jews for not believing; setting about them in order to demolish their position and establish his own case. If ever anyone had provocation to do that it was the Apostle. The position of the Jews was altogether wrong. They had misunderstood their Scriptures and they were blind. All that is perfectly true and Paul knew it. But he was

[1] For a detailed study of this verse, see *An Exposition of Chapter 9: God's Sovereign Purpose*, 1991.

[5]

troubled by their blindness and their wrongness and his greatest desire was to show them a better way.

So we must learn lessons from him because we all know someone who is in the position of the Jews. It may even be somebody who is related to us, very near and dear to us, who not only does not believe the gospel, but ridicules and blasphemes it. I wonder how we are handling such a person? I wonder what we are doing in such a situation?

So let us note the way in which the Apostle speaks about the Jews and how he responds to them. Let us try to extract a principle from what he says which relates to our day-to-day relationships with people who are not Christians. What I find in his words – and I know of nothing that is more important – is that we must learn to be objective with respect to unbelievers; we must not become emotional.

But what do I mean by that, because surely the Apostle is displaying great emotion here? I mean that while we are to feel emotion, we are not to be emotionally overcome, because if so we will soon be utterly useless with regard to helping these people. We will be irritated and annoyed by them and, the moment that happens, we will be unable to help them at all. We will feel that because they are related to us, they ought to listen to us. But they will not do this, and that makes us sensitive and on edge, and we become quite useless in our testimony. We must learn to differentiate between the persons themselves and the god of this world who is blinding their minds. They cannot help it; they are blinded by him. 'If our gospel be hid,' says Paul, 'it is hid to them that are lost: in whom the god of this world hath blinded the minds of them which believe not, lest the light of the glorious gospel of Christ, who is the image of God, should shine unto them' [2 *Cor.* 4:3–4].

The Apostle, you see, understands that. He sees that unbelievers are the victims of the devil and so he does his utmost to present the truth. He is inhibited neither by the devil's activity nor by his own emotional involvement. This is a most important thing. I must not stay with it, but I could do so very easily! Anyone who has ever practised medicine will know the importance of what I am saying. If you are handling any person psychologically or spiritually, this is one of the first rules. You are to be sympathetic, understanding, and patient, but if you become affected personally by their condition you will be reacting in a way that you should not. You must keep yourself in control. 'He that winneth souls is wise' [*Prov.* 11:30].

We all must already have found that this is particularly important when we are dealing with those who are nearest and dearest to us. It is always easier to deal with strangers, because you are not emotionally involved with them in the way that you are with a relative. So in such a situation, you must say to yourself, 'The fact that they are related to me has nothing to do with it at all.' They must not believe because they are your relatives or in order to please you! That is all wrong. No, natural relationships do not determine this matter at all, so do not let them come in. You must realise why such souls are where and as they are, and then you will be able to help them.

So the Apostle does not react violently, or with a desire to retaliate as they revile and persecute him. He says, 'Oh, they are blind! What a tragedy! My heart is breaking for them; there is nothing I would not do for them if only I could help them.' He sees the tragedy of it all and so he is able to praise their zeal, and to present the message to them again. And though he has done it before, he will go on and on doing it – anything, as long as he can bring them to a knowledge of salvation. God grant that we may all have a double portion of the same spirit! Let us be careful: sometimes we may drive people further away through our very concern for them. We need great wisdom.

But now we come to a second lesson, which is again an important one. I wonder how many of you have felt surprised that the Apostle starts chapter 10 in the way in which he does, that is, in view of the fact that it comes after chapter 9? As we have seen, the great doctrine of chapter 9 is the doctrine of God's sovereign, free predestination – unconditional election. So how many of us would have followed that with the first verse of chapter 10: 'Brethren, my heart's desire and prayer to God for Israel is, that they might be saved'?

Now what do I mean by that? Well, I want to put before you the whole question of the relationship between doctrine and practice. How many have gone wrong at this very point! And they go wrong like this: they say, 'If salvation depends solely and altogether upon God's eternal purpose of election, then there is no point in desiring or praying for the salvation of anyone, because we may be desiring the salvation of someone who has not been elected by God, and that is a very wrong thing to do. Therefore I do not pray for the salvation of anybody.' That is an argument which is often heard, is it not?

Then there is another step. If it is right to say that a person's salvation has been determined by God before the very foundation of time and the creation of the world, then it is something solely in His purpose and nothing can frustrate it. There is, therefore, no point in preaching the gospel to the lost or offering salvation to all – there is no need for evangelism. The church must spend her whole time in building up the believer and helping people to fight temptation and sin in the world, and must never be evangelistic. Many have worked it out like that; if 'what is to be will be,' and salvation is all in the mind of God, then we do nothing.

Now this tenth chapter gives the lie direct to all that. Thank God for this chapter, which condemns all such reasoning root and branch! It is all wrong. But oh, how common it has been! There are those of us who are still criticised for offering salvation to all and some of us are criticised for praying for the salvation of men and women and for feeling a great desire to do so.

But let us see how the Apostle answers all that and how terribly wrong it is. Let me show you what a perversion and abuse of glorious doctrine these deductions are. In the first place, there is the danger of being guided by our little reason, by what seems to us to be so clear and logically necessary. That is what we do and it is the cause of most of our troubles. 'If God elects, then it does not matter what I do. God will save whom He has decided to save, therefore I sit down and do nothing. I do not desire anybody's salvation; I do not pray for anybody's salvation; I do not preach the gospel, for what is to be will be.' That is what our so-called logic tells us, that is what our small minds seem to indicate to be quite inevitable and unanswerable.

But the first part of the answer to that is that we are dealing here with the mystery of the mind of God, and that mystery is something that you and I cannot understand. The fact that we think we can, proves how wrong and how foolish we are. God's ways cannot be finally understood. We want everything neat and tidy so that we can encompass it, and we say, 'If this – therefore that'! But we must not do that with Scripture. The two things are here. If a man is saved it is because God saves him; if he is lost it is because he has not believed. Paul teaches both and we must not try to get rid of either.

But that is only the first step. We must, secondly, always be careful that we are not being governed by our feelings. Rather, to put it positively, we must always be governed by Scripture and its teaching. Even if we cannot see why we should pray, because of God's election, the answer is that the Scripture tells us to do so.

So, in the third place, the Scriptures alone should be enough for us; and this one Scripture is enough, even if there were no other. If you have been feeling, because of the argument of chapter 9, 'Well,

I cannot pray for that relative of mine who is not a Christian,' here is your answer! Paul prayed for these Jews who were rejecting Christ and the gospel. If you do what Paul did, you will not be far wrong. This is Scripture, and there are other Scriptures in abundance to support it. The Apostle had a deep desire and longing for the salvation of these others.

Christianity does not make us unnatural. If you are not deeply concerned about the lost condition of anybody who is dear to you, then you are a monster! You have become lopsided and unnatural in your thinking. Of course Paul was concerned, and we are meant to be concerned. Not only was he concerned, he prayed for them: 'My heart's desire and prayer to God for Israel is . . .' He did not say, 'I do not know whether they are saved or not, therefore . . .' Not at all! He prayed for them, and he prayed with great fervency.

But there is an explanation also, and it is this: you say to yourself, 'I do not know whether that person is elect or not, so how can I pray for his salvation?' But that is the very reason why you should pray for it, because you do not know! It is because we do not know who is elect and who is not, that we should desire and pray for the salvation of all, and a preacher should offer the gospel to all and press them to accept it. I do not know, and it is because I do not know that I can offer it to all.

You see the fallacy in that simple bit of logic that I was referring to? God could quite easily save the elect without us. God could save the elect if He had chosen to do so, without preaching, without our prayers, without anything at all. 'With God nothing shall be impossible' [*Luke* 1:37]. But God has ordained that He will do His work of saving through us and by means of us. And God's way of saving people, as chapter 10 points out to us so wonderfully, is through preaching and so on: 'How beautiful are the feet of them that preach the gospel of peace, and bring glad tidings of good things!' [v. 15]. He has ordained that it should happen through someone preaching, and another hearing, and others helping and arguing and praying. So if we do not do these things, we are not adopting God's method.

I have often had people come to talk to me about this. They say, 'If God ordains everything, what is the point of prayer?' The answer to that is that it is the same God who ordains everything, who has taught us to pray. He uses means. Therefore do not try to understand, do not try to reconcile prayer with the sovereignty of God. The Bible teaches me the sovereignty of God and, equally definitely, it teaches me the duty of prayer. I hold to that doctrine *and* I pray. I am not concerned about reconciling them. I cannot. Nobody else can. I imagine that in the glory we shall be given the explanation.

So be careful that your neat little logic does not paralyse your prayer! I have known sections of the Christian church, even at the present time, where they have no prayer meetings at all. And they are great doctrinal people, followers of the Reformed faith. They hold a high so-called Calvinistic doctrine, and they do not have prayer meetings! Why not? Because they have followed their own logic instead of following the Scriptures, and that is a terrible thing to do.

But let me support all this by pointing you to the lessons of history – and history is very eloquent on this subject. The greatest evangelists this world has ever known have been men who have believed in the sovereign, free election of God. Let us not forget that! Two of the greatest evangelists that England has ever produced have been George Whitefield and Charles Haddon Spurgeon, and they both preached and believed in unconditional election. They said that no man is saved unless God has chosen him and set him apart for Himself – the doctrine of Romans 9 – yet they were two men who were indefatigable as evangelists, urging men and women to believe on the Lord Jesus Christ. The same thing can be said of others in other countries: Howell Harris and Daniel Rowland in Wales; Jonathan Edwards in America, Samuel Davies, the writer of many hymns, and David Brainerd, who evangelised the Indians. All these men held this high doctrine of election, but they were indefatigable in their evangelism and in their praying.

But here is another interesting thing. The founders of the great missionary enterprise, the modern missionary movement, were all men who held to this high doctrine of Romans 9. William Carey believed that if someone was saved it was because this was the purpose of God according to election; and yet he was, in so many senses, the father of the modern missionary movement.

And it was not only true of Carey and the Baptist Missionary Society, it was equally true of the founders of the London Missionary Society and the Church Missionary Society. Dr R. W. Dale, a Congregational minister at Carrs Lane, Birmingham, was 'a typical Arminian' who did not believe in election or predestination. Asked to preach the centenary sermon of the founding of the modern missionary movement, he was honest enough to admit that its founders all believed in the sovereign election of God, though he could not understand it.

My final conclusion is: If you find that your knowledge of doctrine paralyses you, then you can take it that you are misunderstanding the doctrine that you think you know. If your doctrine leads you to do nothing; if it does not create within you a burning desire for the salvation of the lost; if it does not lead you to pray for revival, that the lost may be saved – then you are entirely unlike the Apostle Paul, and you have not understood his doctrine. The doctrine of God's purpose according to election is not fatalism. It is not a doctrine that says, 'What is to be will be, whom God is going to save, He will save, therefore I do nothing.' Not at all! That is its very antithesis. This is certainty not fatalism! If you really believe in the sovereign election of God you will say, 'My heart's desire and prayer to God for that person is that he might be saved!'

And you will pray without ceasing for it and do everything you can to bring it about. If you do not, you are a fatalist, you are following your own logic and you are reducing men to machines. No, my friends, we are to long for the salvation of others, we are to pray for it and preach for it. And we must realise, as this chapter will tell us, that though it is God, and God alone, who always saves, men and women nevertheless have to believe. This is how Paul puts it: 'With the heart man believeth unto righteousness; and with the mouth confession is made unto salvation . . . Whosoever shall call upon the name of the Lord shall be saved' [vv. 10, 13–14]. All that is Scripture, quite as much as chapter 9. It does not reduce people to automata; it does not turn them into machines. We know what it is that makes someone believe, but God's method is important. It comes as the result of preaching and praying. Be careful, I say, lest your little understanding obtrudes itself at the centre and leads to this fatal paralysis.

Here, then, is the question: Do you believe the doctrine enunciated in chapter 9 of the Epistle to the Romans? The best way of testing whether you do or do not is this: Do you long for the salvation of others? Are you praying for it? These two things always belong together: 'That the purpose of God according to election might stand, not of works, but of him that calleth' [9:11]; and: 'Brethren, my heart's desire and prayer to God for Israel is, that they might be saved' [10:1].

Thank God for chapter 10 of the Epistle to the Romans! If Paul had only written these two verses we should thank God for them for ever.

God save us from becoming barren logicians! God save us from becoming useless intellectuals! I am not interested in the amount of doctrine you know if it means you do nothing. If you just sit down with your great knowledge, you are unlike the Apostle Paul. The real understanding of doctrine leads to a heart's longing and desire and prayer for the salvation of the lost.

There, then, is just a beginning. That is a foretaste of some of the great and wonderful things that the Apostle has to tell us in this tenth chapter, which at first sight appears to be nothing but a parenthesis. It brings the great truth down to the level of ordinary, practical application. God forbid that we should be puffed up with a head knowledge but empty in our hearts and consequently useless with respect to our fellow men and women who are dead in trespasses and sins and going to perdition.

Let our prayer always be: 'O Lord our God, we come into Thy holy presence aware of our smallness, of our folly, of our foolish pride of knowledge in particular, of our uselessness. God have mercy upon us! We do indeed thank Thee more than ever for Thy blessed Word. We thank Thee for its fulness, its completeness, its roundness. Oh forgive us that we have ever in our folly and smallness imagined that we have comprehended it and can pack it into our little understandings. God have mercy upon us! Enable us to see that we need large hearts. Oh, shed Thy love abroad in our hearts! Knowledge puffs up, charity edifies. Lord, we long for this edification, for this being built up in the faith, with knowledge and understanding but with hearts of love and a longing for the salvation of the lost.

O God, help us to see that we are meant to experience the power of the truth, that it is to move us and not merely to lie barren and useless in our minds and intellects. Oh, keep us, we pray Thee, to the simplicity that is in Christ Jesus! Make of us men and women like this Apostle Paul. O God, reveal Thyself and Thy truth to us and so fill us with Thy Spirit that we shall indeed be as He was. Shed Thy love abroad in our hearts, O Lord. Fill them until they shall be overflowing, until we shall be melted with a sense of compassion for the lost and all who have gone astray and who are hurtling to perdition. O God, may we have something of that heart of love that was in Thy dear Son, who, looking out upon the multitudes, saw them as sheep without a shepherd and had compassion upon them.

O Lord, apply Thy Word to us in the power of Thy Spirit. Hear us in this our prayer, and pardon and forgive us all. We ask it, pleading nothing save His glorious name and the merit of Him who loved us and gave Himself for us. We see that we have no plea still but the fact that He died for us and that Thou hast ever looked upon us and called us by Thy grace. Lord, have mercy upon us! We ask it for His Name's sake. Amen.'

Two

*

Brethren, my heart's desire and prayer to God for Israel is, that they might be saved. For I bear them record that they have a zeal of God, but not according to knowledge.   Romans 10:1–2

We saw in the last chapter that when we truly understand the doctrine of God's sovereignty in salvation, it is wrong to be paralysed in our evangelism. But if it is wrong to do nothing, what is right? What should we do? What should be the position of the Christian? And the answer that is generally returned, at the present time in particular, is that we should be full of zeal. But the very statement of the Apostle compels us to examine critically that position, for he tells us in the second verse, 'I bear them record that they have a zeal of God, but not according to knowledge.' So we are driven, by this statement and by the way in which Paul puts it, to examine this whole question of zeal. I hope to show you that this is a most urgent question for every one of us as individual Christians, and for the church as a whole, and that for several reasons.

The first is the alarming fact that Christians, putting it at its highest, are only some ten per cent of the population of this country – and only half of those attend a place of worship with any regularity. Not only that, but we are aware of the whole collapse of morals, and the terrible confusion in so many departments of life at the present time. The position is quite desperate and so many people, in the face of that, are tempted to say, 'We must do *something*! Surely it is better to be doing something than to be doing nothing.' Any position of desperation inevitably tends to call for action, and the more desperate the position, the more liable we are to think that anything that is being done must of necessity be right, because we are not just sitting back in a paralysed condition doing nothing at all. That is one reason why we must of necessity consider this question of zeal.

But there is another reason also. There is a great tendency at the present time to say that in the last analysis nothing really matters but *zeal* or *sincerity*. Now you will find so many saying today – and it is indeed one of the most common things that one sees in print, or hears in conversation – that, at a desperate moment like this, in this country and throughout the entire world, nothing matters but that Christian people should get together, act together and do something to stem the tide of Communism, immorality or any other 'ism' that may be threatening. People say, 'What does it matter what you believe as long as you can get hold of a body of sincere, zealous people who are anxious to do something? This is no time to be asking what they believe about this or that doctrine. When the whole house is on fire is it not ridiculous to be paying attention to particular pieces of furniture? The thing to do is to put out the fire, and not to be quibbling with one another about particular articles of the Christian faith.'

Now that is more or less what is being said by supporters of what is called the Ecumenical Movement. This is a day, we are told, when people who call themselves Christians, whatever they may believe in detail, are men and women to whom we should give the right hand of fellowship. We are to work with them; we are to stand together and do all we can in a sincere and zealous manner. 'What does it matter,' they say, 'what people believe as long as they are sincere?' They say that the curse of the past has been that many people who were so correct in their doctrine did not put into practice what they believed, and that is the cause of the present trouble. So, because of the terrible plight in which we find ourselves, the tendency now is to exalt sincerity, zeal and activity.

Then let me give you a third reason which is not perhaps quite so applicable in this country as it is in other parts of the world. In some countries, some of the most intellectually acute and spiritually discerning leaders are very concerned about this situation. In those places, in contradistinction to this country, most of the churches are full on Sundays. In the United States, for example, it is the thing to do to go to a place of worship, particularly on Sunday morning. So the churches are flourishing and prosperous. But, at the same time, crime is increasing at an alarming rate. So much so that a number of the best Christian thinkers in that country are beginning to say, 'What have we got in our churches? Is it Christianity or is it religion? Is it the Christian faith, or is it some kind of social club?'

They are becoming very concerned about this. The churches are not only full, they have all kinds of organisations and clubs and they are all thriving. The activity is quite amazing. But at long last many are asking the question: What is the value of all this? Have we a right to be complacent? They are beginning to see that you can have a so-called active church, brimming over with people and with excitement and activity, and yet your Christianity, if it is such, is not counting for very much in the life of the nation. A number of books have been written recently about this subject and there is increasing concern with regard to the whole question.

So it is in the light of all this that I call attention to this subject, but my fundamental reason for doing so is the very way in which the Apostle writes about a 'a zeal for God' which is 'not according to knowledge.' In other words, it is obvious that you can have a wrong zeal. Zeal may be mistaken and may even be dangerous.

Now if you take the long history of the Christian church, you will find that very often a wrong or a false zeal has done great harm. Take, for example, the time of the Protestant Reformation. Martin Luther, having seen the truth of justification by faith only, mainly through this Epistle to the Romans, was all along having to fight against Roman Catholicism. Quite soon, however, he found himself engaged in another battle, because certain people following in his wake, having got a taste of liberty, turned it into licence. So from there on, Luther was fighting on the one front against Roman Catholicism, and at the same time having to fight against the fanatical Protestant sects that rose up on the other side. The reason was that he could see very plainly that the excesses of the fanatics were almost a greater danger than Roman Catholicism itself. They were weakening his whole position and argument against Roman Catholicism. His heart was therefore greatly grieved by the excesses, zealous and sincere though their proponents may have been.

The same thing happened in this country in the seventeenth century at the time of the great Puritan awakening and revival. Then there were the Quakers – George Fox himself was a great and good man but there were others, men such as William Naylor, who became a quite fanatical Quaker, and rode on a horse into Bristol claiming that he was the Messiah. Fanaticism came in. And so anyone who reads the works of people like John Owen, Thomas Goodwin and Richard Baxter will know that they, likewise, were fighting on two fronts. They were not only fighting the dangerous tendencies they found in Anglicanism and in Roman Catholicism, but were having to fight radical sects that arose and constituted a terrible danger to the whole Puritan movement.

When you come to the next century, you find exactly the same thing. I have been refreshing my memory recently on certain aspects of the Evangelical Awakening in America in the eighteenth century, and the work of Jonathan Edwards and George Whitefield. I have been reminded again of the havoc that was wrought in the churches of New England by a man called James Davenport. He came in the wake of Whitefield and was a fanatic who carried everything to terrible excesses. He was full of zeal, a most sincere man, but he did great harm to the Revival in New England and caused much heart searching and trouble for Jonathan Edwards and the other godly men who co-operated with him. There is no doubt at all but that it was the fanaticism of James Davenport and his supporters which did the greatest amount of damage to that great revival. As a result, Whitefield, who had been received almost as an angel of God in 1742, when he went back to the same places in 1745 received a very cool reception and his ministry was not as effective as it had previously been. These things, you see, demonstrate the reason for examining this whole question very carefully, and if ever it was necessary to do so, it is necessary today.

Fortunately for us, the Apostle deals with this in verses 1 and 2, where we see true and false zeal depicted. How can I tell the difference? Well, in the first verse you have true zeal: 'Brethren, my heart's desire and prayer to God for Israel is, that they might be saved.' Then in verse 2 we read, 'I bear them record that they have a zeal of God, but not according to knowledge.' That is the false zeal. So let us now look at the dangers of false zeal. First of all, let us consider the heresy of setting up zeal or sincerity in the supreme position, that is the fallacy of saying that if a man is sincere or zealous, it does not matter what he believes. We have already observed how common that position is today.

Now the first reason for saying that this is wrong is that it misunderstands altogether the nature of zeal or sincerity. What is zeal? It is nothing but a form of power, a kind of motivating force. It is a measure of the energy with which a person does anything. The obvious comparison is that zeal is like fire. Fire is a form of energy and because that is what zeal is, we must never regard zeal as something in and of itself or put it into the supreme position.

We can put it in another way, like this: men and women have minds and hearts and wills. Now zeal belongs entirely to the realm of the will and, because of that, it should never be put up on its own; it should never be regarded as the supreme thing. Therefore, it is always wrong to say that if we are zealous or sincere we must be right. We cannot therefore say that doing something, anything, is better than doing nothing. It does not follow.

I could illustrate this to you in many different ways. Take, for instance, that proverb of ours which puts it so perfectly: 'Fire is a good servant, but a bad master.' There it is in a nutshell. If you control your fire you can heat your house and cook your food, etc. Fire is a most excellent servant, but let fire get in control and there is nothing but disaster. It will burn down your house; it may ruin a whole countryside; it may burn up a prairie and destroy crops. Fire was never meant to be master; it is only meant to be a servant. And that is something which is true with regard to zeal or sincerity, and it is the answer to this whole argument which says that at any rate we must do *something*.

In fact, zeal and sincerity are neutral in and of themselves. They are never meant to be in the most prominent position. Indeed, I can go further: zeal is quite often a matter of temperament. There are some people who are more zealous than others, while there are some who are lethargic and phlegmatic. They do their work, but they do it in a quiet way. The others are full of energy and power but it is no credit to them, they are born like that! People do not realise that; they think they are zealous because they are Christians. It is a very subtle point and that is why we must go on with this examination.

Secondly, you will find, I think almost invariably, that zeal is one of the most prominent characteristics of people who belong to the cults. Do you not find them coming round to your door on Saturday afternoons, selling books? Are Christian people as zealous as that? Here are people who give their time, energy and money to the propagation of what they believe; they make great sacrifices for it. The Communists give up their time, and even risk losing their jobs, as they quietly try to change society with what they call 'cellular infiltration'. The Japanese in the war were ready to sacrifice their lives for the sake of their emperor. These are illustrations of the lengths to which people will go for their beliefs.

But there is yet another argument at this point. The Apostle tells us here that it is actually possible for people to have a 'zeal of God' and still to be wrong, tragically wrong. This is not merely a question of temperament or of being a zealous member of a cult. Men and women can have a zeal *for God* and still be totally wrong. That, Paul says, was the trouble with the Jews. But listen to our Lord putting this in some terrifying words in Matthew 23:15 about the Pharisees: 'Woe unto you, scribes and Pharisees, hypocrites!' – notice – 'for ye compass sea and land to make one proselyte, and when he is made, ye make him twofold more the child of hell than yourselves.' That is zeal – compassing sea and land to make one convert, one proselyte. There was no end to their zeal.

The Apostle Paul makes exactly the same point in Galatians 4:17–18, where he is dealing with the Pharisees and others among the Jews, who were opposing his work: 'They zealously affect you, but not well; yea, they would exclude you, that ye might affect them. But it is good,' says the Apostle, 'to be zealously affected always in a good thing.' He is again paying tribute to their zeal. They were most sincere and thorough-going in their endeavours to influence the Galatians, but they were all wrong; they were zealously affecting them, but in a bad, not a good, cause.

Furthermore, we are reminded in Acts 26:9–11 of how this was once true of the Apostle Paul himself: 'I verily thought with myself, that I ought to do many things contrary to the name of Jesus of Nazareth. Which thing I also did in Jerusalem . . .' There was never a more sincere man than Saul of Tarsus. 'I punished them oft in every synagogue, and compelled them to blaspheme; and being exceedingly mad against them . . .' – you cannot have greater zeal than that! – 'I persecuted them even unto strange cities.' And you remember how, setting out on that famous journey from Jerusalem to Damascus to persecute the Christians there, he went 'breathing out threatenings and slaughter'. Was there ever a more zealous, sincere person than Saul of Tarsus going down to Damascus? But he was altogether wrong, absolutely mistaken.

He refers to this again in Philippians 3:6, saying of himself: 'as touching the law, a Pharisee; concerning zeal, persecuting the church; touching the righteousness which is in the law, blameless' [vv. 5–6]. But he came to see how tragically wrong he was, and so he constantly made this point, in his teaching, later on. In 2 Timothy 3:6 he put it like this: 'For of this sort are they which creep into houses, and lead captive silly women laden with sins, led away with divers lusts, ever learning, and never able to come to the knowledge of the truth.' In 2 Timothy 4:3, he wrote: 'For the time will come when they will not endure sound doctrine; but after their own lusts' – here is the zeal – 'shall they heap to themselves teachers, having itching ears; and they shall turn away their ears from the truth, and shall be turned unto fables.'

You can see, therefore, from the Apostle's teaching and experience, that you can even have a zeal for God, and yet be altogether wrong. From this there is only one conclusion to draw: zeal must always be tested and examined. You do not say, 'What a wonderfully zealous man that is! He must be right because he is so zealous. How sincere he is. Who am I to question him?' That is a most dangerous thing to say. All the teaching of our Lord and the Apostles in the New Testament urges us to be careful, to be warned. The whole case of the Jews is a standing warning against trusting in 'a zeal of God, but not according to knowledge'.

So my second main heading is: What, then, are the characteristics of false zeal? If I have got to examine zeal, because zeal itself is morally neutral and there is a false as well as a true zeal, how can I test whether my zeal is true or false? Here are some tests which must be used together and not individually, as if any one were adequate by itself.

First, there should always be a query in our minds if our zeal has been imposed upon us by somebody else and we are just conforming to a pattern. That is, of course, always a characteristic of the cults. A case is put before you, and if you are persuaded you take it up, becoming one of them and you begin to be exactly like all the rest. That is a zeal that is imposed upon you.

Secondly, if it is a zeal that has to be whipped up or organised or kept up, that is good presumptive evidence that it may well be a false zeal, particularly if the stimulus always has to come from other people.

Another very important point is this, my third test: if you find that you put greater emphasis upon *doing* than upon *being*, it is always an indication that you should be careful. If you are more anxious to do things than to be a saint, you had better examine your zeal again. False zeal always puts its emphasis upon the doing; it is not very interested in being, hence its danger.

The fourth test is that in false zeal it is the activity, rather than the truth, which is always very prominent, and at the centre of the life. The thing you are struck by all along is the energy that is displayed, rather than the truth which the people claim to be representing. In other words, in false zeal there is always a tendency to overdo things, an element of excess. The activity is more in evidence than the teaching which has called forth the activity.

In the fifth place, when methods, organisation and the machinery are very prominent, it is good presumptive evidence that it is a false zeal.

As my sixth test I would group a number of things together under the heading of *carnality*, and by that I mean the flesh. In false zeal there is always this carnal element, and it shows itself quite often by a kind of lightness of spirit, at times almost a frivolity. Alas, this can sometimes be seen in religious meetings. There is a lightness, a joviality and a kind of superficiality. You cannot imagine such things anywhere near the Apostle Paul or any other of the Apostles, or anywhere near our blessed Lord Himself. But you get it in many meetings. They are very zealous – I am not querying their zeal, I am granting it, and their enthusiasm – but they always overdo it, and there is this light touch about it. Indeed, on some occasions I have had to remind myself that I am in a religious meeting. The spirit I have felt present has been the spirit of a cricket or football team, some worldly entertainment, and yet the people were absolutely sincere! But there was no sense of awe, no sense of God, no sense of holiness, no sense of reverence. Everything was bright and breezy, carried along with great verve and wonderful organising power. I say that these are indications of carnality and not of true zeal.

So you can add to that: false zeal may be found whenever there is a good deal of excitement – and this is still under the heading of carnality – because excitement is generally of the flesh. And, if there is an element of self-confidence and of assurance and of being in control of the situation, you can be quite certain it is false zeal. I do not care how zealous or sincere a man may be, if he gives the impression that he is self-confident and assured, I am suspicious of his zeal. And if there is any hint at all of his being proud of himself, it is still worse.

We go on to the seventh test. False zeal dislikes being questioned. It resents enquiry. It says, 'Can you not see that I am zealous? I am enthusiastic, I am sincere. I want to do it.' But you say, 'Still, let us make sure, because of the teaching of the Scriptures.' But no, it is impatient of all that, it wants to get on with things, it must be doing something. It is impatient of any examination, and that is surely a very bad sign.

Eighthly, when zeal shows an impatience with teaching, the

situation is still worse. 'They have a zeal of God, *but not according to knowledge.*' They do not want the knowledge, says Paul, they have rejected it; they are not interested in it. They must get on with things, and they do not want to be taught. That is the spirit of the false zeal.

The ninth test is fanaticism! Intolerance! False zeal is concerned primarily with the success rather than the truth of what it is propagating.

So I put as my tenth test, a lack of balance. You will generally find that people who are animated by a false zeal see one thing only, one aspect of the truth only, and they are not interested in anything else. It may be evangelism only; it may be Calvinism only; it may be Arminianism only; it may be prophecy only. This is the one thing, and with all their might and main they press this one thing and are not interested in anything else. That is always a fatal sign. That has always been the trouble with heretics. They are men and women who have lost their balance. They have become so absorbed by one thing that they see nothing else, and they so press this one thing that not only do they lose their balance, this 'one thing' becomes a lie. It is blind zeal, and zeal can be blinding.

So if there is any evidence of a lack of balance, if the fulness of the truth is not being presented, if the whole counsel of God is not being dealt with, and there is a constant hammering away on the one thing, then it is false zeal. False zeal is not interested in learning or doctrine; it is not interested in theology – it 'must get people saved' and nothing else. Or there are those who are not interested in getting people saved, but in their one particular aspect of doctrine and they are always on about that. You are certain to find it whenever they speak or write, it always comes out. That, too, is a false zeal, it is a lack of balance. And, of course, if you see any lack of balance between doctrine and life, between what people believe and teach and the way they live, that is, of necessity, proof positive that they have a false zeal.

So the last test – the eleventh – is this: men and women who have a false zeal are always restless people, and they are restless because they are living on their own activity, their energy, their enthusiasm and their own sincerity. That will never give them peace. And these people show it, of course, in this way: if they are taken ill and cannot do things, they become depressed, they are unhappy. They then realise that they have been living on their own activity.

God knows, I am preaching as much to myself as I am to you. I have known preachers, alas, who have lived on their own preaching.

I have seen some tragedies. I have seen old men, who have been a lifetime in the ministry, unhappy when they could no longer preach. They were not unhappy because they could not preach, but they were unhappy in themselves. They had been living on their preaching instead of living on the Lord and on the truth. It is a terrible danger for any man in the ministry. It is a danger for anyone who is active in the Christian life. Let us be certain we are not living on our own activities, because if we are, we have a false zeal. It is of no value. We can be indefatigable and assiduous; we can really give ourselves, but it is all wrong if it leaves us restless and lost when we can no longer be active.

There, then, are some of the more important tests by which you can discover whether your zeal is false or not.

But let me turn to the other side – what are the characteristics of a true zeal? The answer is, of course, that it is more or less the exact opposite of what I have been saying. But let me put it like this. A true zeal is never a zeal that is put on. It is not put on you by anybody else, nor is it put on you by you yourself. If you have a true zeal, you do not have it because you have been told it is the thing to do when you join this church, or this society, or whatever it is. If you are showing this zeal simply because it is the thing to do, it is probably false. But that is never the case with true zeal.

Secondly, true zeal is always the result of *being*. Men and women who have a true zeal have it because they are what they are; they have it because they have grown in grace, and in sanctification; they act because of what they are.

Or, thirdly, putting it still more specifically and in terms of our text, true zeal is always the outcome of knowledge. Now the Apostle has already put this wonderfully for us in Romans 6:17, where he says, 'But God be thanked, that ye were the servants of sin, but ye have obeyed from the heart that form of doctrine which was delivered to you.' Did you notice the order? He actually puts the *obeying* first, but in practice the obeying was the last. 'You were the servants of sin' – what has happened to them? Well, the first thing was that 'a form of doctrine was delivered you'. The gospel was preached to them, and they received it and believed it with their minds.

But it was not only in their minds, the heart was involved; they were moved by it. And because of that, they gave it obedience, their will came into action. But that was the order: they received with the mind, and it moved the heart, and then the will to action – and that is always the true order! The trouble with a false zeal is that it puts the will first and is not even interested in the heart or the head. The man who says, 'Nothing matters but doing something', is dismissing both of these; to him activity alone is important.

That is always the danger of activism. It does not know what it is doing, it is not even interested in what it is doing. Doing, that is the thing! And it rushes on in its headlong, blind manner. The right order is – the mind, the heart, the will. The man who has the true zeal knows what he is doing, and he knows why he is doing it; his zeal is 'according to knowledge'.

So the fourth test is that it is a deep zeal, not a superficial one. It is not spectacular, not showy. You get a much bigger blaze if you put a match to paper than if you put it to wood, but it is soon over. The wood is not so instantly spectacular but you get a better fire; it lasts longer and it does more useful service. There is a depth about the true zeal, and there is a control about it. As we have seen, if zeal is in control, it is like fire, which is a bad master. But when zeal is controlled by knowledge, it is as it should be, the true zeal.

And therefore it follows that there are certain characteristics which, once more, are the exact opposite of carnality. The man with a true zeal is never self-confident. Never *self*-confident! He is always reverent; he does not get excited in a false sense; he is a man who depreciates himself. The Apostle Paul says to the Corinthians that when he went among them, he did so 'in weakness, and in fear, and in much trembling' [*1 Cor.* 2:3]. Paul trembling! Apprehensive, fearful, nervous, as it were. How different that is from the false zeal, with its confidence, and assurance, and assertion that it is the 'master of the occasion'!

Paul was greatly used by the Lord; he says in 1 Corinthians 15:10, 'I laboured more abundantly than they all' – but wait a minute – 'yet not I, but the grace of God which was with me.' The Corinthians despised Paul because he was not boasting about himself. Some of the false teachers were boasting about themselves, they were commending themselves, as Paul says in 2 Corinthians 3:1. And because Paul was a humble, modest man, who did not advertise what he was doing, they said that he was a nobody! 'His bodily presence is weak, and his speech contemptible' [*2 Cor.* 10:10]. What did he do? Well, says Paul, if you want to know, 'By the grace of God I am what I am . . . I laboured more abundantly than they all: yet not I, but the grace of God which was with me' [*1 Cor.* 15:10].

What is the motive that animates true zeal? It is certainly not just to be busy, and to do things, and to get results. It is the glory of God! 'The love of Christ constraineth us' [*2 Cor.* 5:14]. That is it! Paul has true zeal, not because he is an active fellow, and full of enthusiasm and energy, no, not that, but because of the glory of God! The love of Christ! His concern is about the condition of the lost; he sees their destiny, he sees them as hell-bound sinners. He does not talk glibly, lightly, about souls being saved. He realises the condition of the lost and he is desperate. It is serious; it is alarming; it is terrifying. And that is why he is engaged as he is.

So he is not simply anxious that people should 'decide for Christ'; he wants them to come to what he calls 'a knowledge of the truth'. He is not interested in superficial results, but he is very concerned that men and women should have the knowledge that will save them from hell, bring them to see the glory of God and make them heirs of eternal bliss. Those are his motives.

So ultimately it comes to this: the man who is animated by a true zeal, however successful he may be, is never elated or excited by his own success. He is a man who has taken to heart the words that were uttered by our Lord Himself to the Seventy. When He sent them out to preach and to cast out devils, they were so successful that they came back full of excitement and they said: 'Lord, even the devils are subject unto us . . .' And our Lord looked at them and said, 'In this rejoice not, that the spirits are subject unto you; but rather rejoice, because your names are written in heaven' [*Luke* 10:17–20].

And that is the position of men and women who have this true zeal. They thank God that they have been used, and that God has deigned to bless their puny efforts. But they rejoice not because of the results they have had, but that their names are written in heaven. So at the end of their life they can say with the Apostle Paul: 'I am now ready to be offered, and the time of my departure is at hand. I have fought a good fight, I have finished my course, I have kept the faith: henceforth there is laid up for me a crown of righteousness, which the Lord, the righteous judge, shall give me at that day: and not to me only, but unto all them also that love his appearing' [*2 Tim.* 4:6–8].

That is what Paul is interested in! With all his phenomenal success, this is what he says: 'That I may know him, and the power of his resurrection, and the fellowship of his sufferings, being made conformable unto his death; if by any means I might attain unto the resurrection of the dead. Not as though I had already attained, either were already perfect: but I follow after, if that I may apprehend that for which also I am apprehended of Christ Jesus' [*Phil.* 3:10–12]. That is the man with the true zeal. His desire is not primarily to be successful but to know the Lord and to be like Him, and to apprehend Him with a greater fulness. That is a most wonderful test!

Now, finally, a question. What is the effect of all this upon you? Is it that you are so afraid of a false zeal that you do nothing at all? If it is, I have spoken in vain. If you are so afraid of a false zeal that it paralyses you, you are the very antithesis of Paul. You have not understood the truth. A knowledge of the truth always moves the heart and moves the will. If it is only in your mind, examine yourself; there is something wrong with you. If the knowledge of the truth has not moved you, has not engaged your emotions, has not made you do something, then you have not known the truth properly. When men and women really know this truth they say, 'We cannot but speak the things which we have seen and heard' [*Acts* 4:20].

When the early Christians, the ordinary people, were scattered out of Jerusalem by persecution, 'they . . . went every where preaching the word' [*Acts* 8:4], not in pulpits, but by telling everybody whom they met. Why? Well, it was so wonderful, it was so glorious, it had done so much for them that they were anxious for everybody else to have it. In any case, the Apostle Paul teaches us in Romans 12:11 that we must not be 'slothful in business'. Rather, we must be 'fervent in spirit; serving the Lord' – not a false but a true zeal. He is not writing to apostles but to ordinary church members. Are you fervent in spirit? Are you moved by what you claim to believe? Do you really believe it?

If you do, you know that everybody who does not believe it is going to hell. And can you be passive and quiet and paralysed and say and do nothing? How often do you take strangers to your place of worship that they may hear the gospel? To what extent are you concerned about the souls of the lost? How can people believe this gospel and not be concerned about those who do not? How can they sit down feeling their own pulse, worrying about their own temptations and sins and problems, and have no concern about the lost? It must be that they do not know the truth, that is their trouble. Those who know the truth must be 'fervent in spirit; serving the Lord'.

Now I am not just asking you to get up and do something; what I am saying is that if you are paralysed and are doing nothing, then you need the Holy Spirit. You cannot make your own spirit fervent. If you try to do so it will be a false zeal. The Holy Spirit alone can make people truly fervent. It is the fire from the altar of heaven that alone can burn in the heart and give us a concern for the lost, and make us do something about them. That is what you need. You need a baptism of the Spirit of God, you need the fire of the Spirit! And you should give yourself no rest and no peace until you have it.

Three

*

For they being ignorant of God's righteousness, and going about
to establish their own righteousness, have not submitted themselves unto the righteousness of God.   Romans 10:3

We have, so far, been dealing with the first two verses, and have seen
that certain general lessons are taught there by the Apostle. These not
only concern his contemporaries, the Jews, but are of universal application in the life of the church up to the present time.

We have seen that the Apostle's particular concern here is to
explain why the Jews were, in the main, outside the Christian church,
whereas the Gentiles had been coming in. The general trouble was
that the Jews had a zeal for God but it was 'not according to knowledge'. Now the word that Paul uses here which is translated
'knowledge' is very interesting. It is the strongest word used in the
Scriptures with regard to knowing. It does not merely mean a general
acquaintance with something. It goes beyond that. It means a full, a
correct, a precise and a vital knowledge, and the trouble with the
Jews, says the Apostle Paul, is that they lacked it. And there is one
further idea in the word. It refers to a knowledge which has been
arrived at as the result of a good deal of investigation and effort. So
then, Paul says, the Jews lacked that full apprehension, that certain
knowledge which is the result of a careful and a thorough examination of a teaching. They had a zeal, but not such a knowledge.

Here, then, Paul again puts before us a most important principle,
which is that an exact knowledge of the truth is essential to salvation.
The Jews had not got it, so they were outside; they were lost and he
prays and longs for their salvation. Now this matter of knowledge is
most important. I am of the opinion that the greatest danger confronting the Christian church and every individual Christian at this
moment is to fail to understand and appreciate the absolute necessity

of a precise, clear knowledge of the truth. I say this because we are living in days when there is a powerful reaction against all this.

We are living in an age that dislikes precision and definitions. It is an age that is anti-theological, anti-doctrinal and which dislikes propositions and exact knowledge. It is a lazy age in every respect, a sentimental, sloppy age, an age that wants entertainment and dislikes effort. In the whole of life today the principle is 'something for nothing'. We are ready to take but we are not ready to work; we are not ready to give ourselves. It is true all round and it accounts for most of our problems. It is particularly true in the realm of the Christian church. We must therefore deal with this very carefully.

This tendency shows itself in many ways which are generally very plausible. One way is to say that Christianity is something that is so wonderful that it cannot be defined, that it baffles analysis or any attempt to state it in propositions. I am sure you are familiar with that particular view. People say you might as well try to dissect beauty, or an aroma, as to define the Christian faith. It cannot be done, they say. You experience it – marvellous and wonderful! But if you try to analyse it, then you destroy it, there is nothing left. You must not bring the rude hands of analysis here.

Another way in which it is put is this: that Christianity is only a matter of one's spirit. What makes us Christians is our spirit, and if we have an appropriate spirit, then we are Christians. Christianity is an attitude, a view of life, a general statement concerning our personality and our being. There was a slogan not so long ago which said, 'Christianity is caught, not taught'. You catch the spirit. You feel it in the meeting and you get it. But what is it? Well, you do not know, but that does not matter. You have got it! That is the great thing and you feel much happier and much better than you did before.

Then a third way in which it is put is this: that after all what matters is our general reaction to the person of our Lord Jesus Christ. Now this is one of the most popular views of all. People say, 'You read the Gospels and there you see this portrait of Him and, as it were, you meet Him. Now what decides whether you are a Christian or not is this: Do you like Him? Do you want to be like Him? Do you try to imitate Him? What is your reaction to Him?' You must not come and dissect, and bring your propositions and your theology and say you have got to believe this and not believe that. What matters is your total response to Him, and if you react favourably to Him, then you are a Christian.

The fourth way is the approach that describes Christianity in terms of *living*. What does it matter what people believe as long as they are living good, Christ-like lives, as long as they are generous, ready to make sacrifices, ready to help others, and concerned about the uplift of the race? That is what makes people Christians.

Now this dangerous attitude takes one other form. I put this in a category on its own because I am beginning to think that in some ways it is the most subtle form of all among evangelical people. It is the tendency to estimate whether or not people are Christians, not by what they actually say about their beliefs but by what you feel about them. Now, I do want to make this clear, because I have encountered it a great deal. We attach greater importance and significance to this 'feeling' that we may have about them than to the very words that the people themselves use about the Christian faith.

I want to give an example or two of this, because I confess that I am becoming alarmed about it; indeed, I am almost discouraged because it seems to me that if we proceed much further along this line, the evangelical faith is going to disappear. Let me give you an illustration. On a visit to London some years ago, I went into a certain bookroom which was managed by an evangelical organisation in one of the major Christian denominations. To my astonishment, I found that they were selling there a second-hand book by a man who was notorious at that time. He was no longer alive, but he had written this well-known book about Christianity in which he virtually denied all the cardinal articles of the Christian faith. As I was looking round, the secretary of this society came to speak to me, so I called his attention to this book and expressed my amazement.

'Ah,' he said, 'wait a minute. You know, we must be very careful.'

'What do you mean?' I asked.

He said, 'Have you ever met this man?' and when I told him I had not, he replied, 'Well, I have. I stayed with him a few months back. I was on deputation work and he entertained me for the night, and the next morning we went into a little chapel attached to his house where he took family prayers. And you know, I don't think I have ever been in such a spiritual atmosphere. It was a blessing to my soul to hear him taking family prayers on that occasion.'

'Yes, but my dear sir,' I said, 'what does he say in this book?'

'Oh, I know that,' he said, 'but you see, if you had heard him taking those prayers! I have never known a more devout man. I have never been in a more devotional atmosphere.'

My reply was this: 'But I don't care what you felt. This is what the man says about the Lord Jesus Christ and His work and it is a denial of the Scriptures!' But I found it very difficult to persuade him.

Then recently, a speaker was about to give an address on a certain religious book which had achieved some notoriety, and he prefaced his remarks by saying something like this. 'Now I am going to criticise this book, but I must say this. A friend of mine who saw this man on television said to me, "If ever I have looked at a born-again man there he was."'

You see, he was suggesting that what is said in the book does not matter! Though the writer denies the teaching of the Scripture and the creeds of his church, though he denies the being of God, the deity of Christ, and all the essentials of Christianity, in spite of that, what is being put first is our subjective feeling – 'The man looks to me to be a born-again man.' So – in spite of what he says in his book – 'I therefore have a feeling, somehow, that the man is all right after all'!

This is happening in other ways, too. A few years ago there were various campaigns at which all kinds of people had come together who had never been together before. And evangelical Christians were saying, 'You know, these others are such nice people, they are much nicer people than we ever thought.' Why they should ever imagine that people who are wrong in their doctrine are of necessity not nice I do not know! But the argument had reached the point at which it was being said that, because they were so surprisingly nice, it did not matter very much, after all, that they were so wrong in their doctrine.

Or, to give one final illustration, I once had a lengthy discussion with an evangelical Christian in which I asked him why he had used a certain man in connection with his work. 'Well,' he said, 'I know what you mean, I know what he has written in his books, I know what he preaches, but I have got to be honest. I find that I can have more fellowship with him than I can with many conservative evangelical Christians.'

I said, 'What you really mean, of course, is that he is a nicer man by nature than many evangelical Christians. But,' I went on, 'you must not call it fellowship. You find that he is more affable and that you can get on more easily with him. But that is not spiritual fellowship!'

Now that is the kind of thing that is being said at the present time. It does not matter what people may teach. Though they may deny the very essence of Christianity, if I like them, if I am attracted to them, if

I can talk easily to them, then that is what counts. It is what they are that is important and thus they make an appeal to you.

Here, then, is the very thing to which our attention is being drawn by this statement of the Apostle Paul. So what do we say about this modern tendency? Here is the answer.

First, that Christian people are mistaking natural qualities, niceness, a cultural veneer or politeness, for true Christian grace. It seems that we are no longer capable of differentiating between the two. How often today is affability mistaken for saintliness! 'What a gracious man he is,' they say. What they really mean is this: he never criticises and he agrees with everybody and everything. I know of nothing more dangerous than that. These so-called gracious men are, of course, altogether nicer than John the Baptist or the Apostle Paul! I do not hesitate to go further – they are very much nicer than the Lord Jesus Christ Himself, who denounced the Pharisees! Affability is not saintliness. A mere intellectual, moral flabbiness, is not synonymous with graciousness and with the possession of grace!

Secondly, the fact that people are devout tells us nothing about the truth of what they believe. There are very devout Jews, devout Muslims, devout followers of Buddha, Confucius, and so on. A devout attitude in and of itself tells us nothing.

Thirdly, the moment we begin to talk in these terms, it means that we have abandoned all objective standards. We are now judging only by our own subjective feelings, by our impressions and reactions. Is there anything so dangerous?

Fourthly, and much more important, it is a complete denial of what the Apostle is teaching at this very point, and indeed in the whole of his Epistle. The Jews, he says, are lost and they need to be saved. Why? Because they are lacking in exact knowledge of the truth. This is the reason for their condemnation. So we must never put anything before exact knowledge. It is the most important thing of all.

My fifth argument is this: to speak like that is a violation not only of what the Apostle teaches here, but also of the whole of the New Testament teaching with regard to the way of salvation. What does it teach? Well, it talks about coming 'unto the knowledge of the truth' [1 Tim. 2:4]. Everything in the New Testament is put in terms of truth. What is preaching? Preaching is a proclamation of the truth. And it is an exact proclamation. Preaching is not talking about a vague feeling, but is the presentation of a message, of a case. Preaching is something that is reasoned and argued from the Scriptures. It is truth, and therefore it must always be in the first position.

The Apostle says this clearly and specifically in 1 Timothy 2:3–5: 'For this is good and acceptable in the sight of God our Saviour; who will have all men to be saved' – he means all types and kinds of men – 'and to come unto *the knowledge of the truth*'. That is salvation, this exact knowledge of the truth. 'For there is one God' – there it is! – 'and one mediator between God and men, the man Christ Jesus.' There is the truth specified. And yet the whole tendency today is to say, 'It doesn't matter!'

Furthermore, this is a truth that can be defined in detail, indeed, it must be defined in detail. The first chapter of Galatians brings out this point. 'I marvel that ye are so soon removed from him that called you into the grace of Christ unto another gospel: which is not another...' [*Gal.* 1:6–7]. But how can Paul say that? You can only make a statement like that if you know what the gospel is. There must be some objective standard, and he says that these people have departed from that. They say they are preaching a gospel. But it is 'not another', he says, there cannot be, this is the one and only gospel.

In other words, you can tell whether a man is preaching the gospel or not, or whether he believes the gospel or not, by what he says! It does not matter what he is in his appearance or in his personality – what does he *say*? Is it the gospel, or something that is passing as gospel, which is not the gospel? Then Paul makes it still more explicit: 'But though we, or an angel from heaven, preach any other gospel unto you than that which we have preached unto you, let him be accursed' [v. 8]. Could anything be plainer or stronger?

Or take it again in 2 Timothy 2:7–8: 'Consider what I say,' says the Apostle, 'and the Lord give thee understanding.' That is what people need; it is *understanding*. Get rid of this sloppy sentimentality that talks about 'niceness' and lives on its feelings. 'Remember,' he says, 'that Jesus Christ of the seed of David was raised from the dead according to my gospel.' What did he mean by *my gospel*? Well, he goes on to tell us. He contrasts it with the false teaching in which some people were indulging. They taught that 'the resurrection is past already' and they 'overthrow the faith of some' [v. 18].

I once read a printed sermon on Paul's words, 'my gospel', in which the preacher put forward this erroneous view. He said, 'The Apostle says, "*My* gospel", and the question for you, friends, is: Can you say, "*My* gospel"? Of course, it may not be mine, it may not be somebody else's, but the whole point is, can you say, "My gospel"?'

The whole purpose of that sermon was to show that the Apostle
did not mean to suggest that he was right and everyone else was
wrong. The preacher argued that such a thing would be unthinkable
for a Christian man to say. What Paul meant, said this preacher, was
that he had not got a second-hand faith but had found something
which had made all the difference to *him*, and all he was concerned
about was that everybody else should have something that made all
the difference to them – something about which they could say 'my
gospel'. It would not be the same thing in every case, of course. It
would be one thing for one person and another for someone else. One
would believe in the deity of Christ, and another would not; one
believes that Christ bore his sins and was punished, someone else
believes He was just dying the death of a pacifist. But what does it
matter? We all get a good deal out of that death. '*My gospel*'! And this
is, of course, nothing but a complete denial of what the Apostle was
teaching!

The Apostle's case was always this: there is only one gospel. It had
been committed to him and he preached it. Any departure from it was
a lie, and whoever preached a lie deserved to be 'accursed'. And, of
course, this teaching is not confined to the Apostle Paul. In Jude 3, we
read this: 'Beloved, when I gave all diligence to write unto you of the
common salvation, it was needful for me to write unto you, and
exhort you that ye should earnestly contend for the faith which was
once [and forever] delivered unto the saints.' The faith is something
that you can contend for and if you do not know what it is, or if
people can believe what they like, then you cannot contend for it. The
New Testament denounces heresies; and there would never be such a
thing as a heresy if you did not have a truth that can be defined and
stated in the form of propositions. So this modern idea which puts
personality, or niceness, or 'what I feel' about a person, before exact
propositions and definitions, and precision in knowledge, is a denial
of the whole of the New Testament teaching.

But still further: the Bible teaches us that continuation in the
Christian life is always as the result of truth, and knowledge of truth.
Our Lord prayed in His high-priestly prayer: 'Sanctify them through
thy truth: thy word is truth' [*John* 17:17]. Or take what He said on
another occasion to those Jews who believed on Him, 'If ye continue
in my word, then are ye my disciples indeed; and ye shall know the
truth, and the truth shall make you free' [*John* 8:31]. It is the truth,
not feelings, that makes you free!

My final argument is this. The Apostle Peter, in the third chapter of his First Epistle, verse fifteen, says, 'be ready always to give an answer to every man that asketh you a reason of the hope that is in you with meekness and fear.' A man comes to you and says, 'Look here, why are you a Christian?' He wants you to give an explanation. If you adopt this modern teaching, all you can say is this: 'Well, I don't know that I can tell you but I just feel like this. I began to feel like this suddenly in a meeting, and I am glad to say that I have been feeling like this ever since. It is a wonderful feeling, though I don't know what it is.'

Then the man says, 'What is this "hope" you have?'

'Well,' you reply, 'I don't know, I am just hopeful, that is all. I have taken a more optimistic view of life ever since I had this wonderful experience and I feel happier and bright and cheerful.' You cannot give him *a reason*. In that case, says Peter, you are no use to him; he will now, poor fellow, try to get this 'feeling' that you have had and he will go the round of meetings hoping that he is going to get it. That is not the way, says Peter. Give him a *reason* for the hope that is in you. And that means a detailed knowledge of the truth.

I am not saying, of course, that a Christian is someone who has a complete understanding about the whole of the Christian faith. Of course not! Nobody has that. We are all still learning. All that I am saying is that there must be a clear understanding about an irreducible minimum. You cannot be a Christian at all unless you have that. I am not, in other words, saying that we must turn this gospel into a requirement, and that unless we all agree in every detail about prophecy, or the mode of baptism, or many other subjects, that we are not Christians. That is sheer legalism! There are many people who have fallen into that error.

But that is not the danger today! The danger today is that we are so afraid of legalism that we have become utterly nondescript. We have knocked down all the barriers and the signposts; anything is all right. We are a happy lot together and we have a wonderful spirit. Roman Catholics are suddenly now changing. Everything is marvellous. We are going to have a great universal church and there will be no more trouble.

But that is the very opposite of the New Testament teaching. No, I am not arguing for a legalistic precision. All I am arguing for is what the Apostle Paul is putting before us here in Romans 10:3. These Jews, he says, are outside because they have not got this exact knowledge that saves! There are implications and aspects of this great truth about which we cannot and must not speak dogmatically. But about the thing that saves us we must be as dogmatic as we can be. This is absolutely essential to salvation.

The Apostle's whole point is that the Jews are lost, and he is anxious about them, concerned for them and praying for them. They are in that position for one reason only – their lack of a precise knowledge as to the way of salvation. Therefore I do not hesitate to say that if you tell me that such an exact knowledge is not essential, that people can be Christians without it, then I say that you are denying the New Testament gospel. I do not care what experience they have had, how much better or nicer they are than they once were – I am not interested. Men and women are saved by coming to a knowledge of the truth!

The Apostle says all that to us in this word 'knowledge'. But in verse 3 he works it out in detail, and he has three things to say about the Jews. The first is that they were 'ignorant of God's righteousness'. That is the first respect in which this lack of knowledge caused their condemnation. Now what does Paul mean here by the term 'God's righteousness'? There is a slight difficulty about this. It is not important ultimately, but we must look at it in order to get our minds clear. There are two views.

Most of the commentators are agreed in saying that by 'God's righteousness' Paul means the righteousness that God has prepared for, and gives to, the Christian. They say that it must be that because of what Paul says at the end of the verse: 'They being ignorant of God's righteousness . . . have not submitted themselves unto the righteousness of God.'

Now there is no doubt about the meaning of 'the righteousness of God'. It means that they have not submitted themselves to the righteousness that God has prepared and gives, about which Paul has spoken in chapter 1:17 – 'the righteousness of God revealed from faith to faith'. So, the commentators say, it must have that meaning at the beginning of 10:3 also, because if it does not, then the Apostle is using the same word in two different senses in the same verse.

If that view is correct, the Apostle is saying that these people are lost because they have a great zeal but it is not according to knowledge. They do not know about the righteousness that God has provided and have not submitted to it. Instead, they have gone about to establish their own righteousness. That is the commonly accepted interpretation.

But with considerable trepidation, because of the authorities, I feel constrained to say that even if I do accept that, I cannot accept it as being the total or indeed the adequate explanation of this term. What, then, does it mean? Well, I suggest it means the righteousness that God demands of me. Paul is saying that they were ignorant of this righteousness that God demands. Why do I say that? Partly because, taking the other view, Paul is guilty of tautology, and he is not normally guilty of that. So it seems to me that in order to show how the argument advances here we must accept this second interpretation.

But there is an even stronger argument. What was the main trouble with the Jews? Well, our Lord Himself has answered the question for us. It is to be found in Matthew 5:20, part of the Sermon on the Mount: 'I say unto you, That except your righteousness shall exceed the righteousness of the scribes and Pharisees, ye shall in no case enter into the kingdom of heaven.' And then He goes on to interpret what He means by that. The whole trouble with the Pharisees was that they had misinterpreted the Old Testament teaching about the righteousness that God demands. That is what the Sermon on the Mount deals with, especially in chapter five: 'Ye have heard that it was said by them of old time . . . But I say unto you' [see, for example, vv. 21–22, 27–28, 31–32].

The Pharisees rejected Christ because they had misunderstood God's real demands, the demands of God's law, the demands of God's righteousness. So in the Sermon on the Mount our Lord preaches to them on the meaning of the law that was given through Moses, and what He keeps on saying to them, in effect, is this: 'You have misinterpreted it. You are taking it only in the act, but God means it in the spirit, in the mind, in the heart. You say, "I have not committed adultery." I ask you, have you looked at a woman to commit adultery in your imagination? If you have, you are guilty.' And so on with murder and all the rest.

In other words, our Lord's whole case against the Pharisees and scribes was that they had got muddled about the meaning of God's demands upon them in terms of righteousness. There are many examples of this very thing in the Gospels, for instance, what the Lord said about the support of parents in Matthew 15:3–9 and about tithing in Matthew 23:23–28. The final proof of this is the famous case of the Pharisee and the publican: 'Two men went up into the temple to pray; the one a Pharisee, and the other a publican. The Pharisee stood and prayed thus with himself, God, I thank thee, that I am not as other men are' [*Luke* 18:10–11]. Here is the picture of a man who thought that he had completely satisfied the demands of God.

So I argue that when the Apostle says in Romans 10:3 that the Jews were ignorant of God's righteousness, he means that they were entirely ignorant of what God really was demanding of them.

This leads us to the word *ignorant,* which is a most interesting word. It implies that they had some knowledge. Paul does not say that these Jews were completely ignorant about the righteousness of God. No. Their trouble was that they knew something about it but they did not have an exact knowledge of it. In other words, 'ignorance' here is the exact opposite of the full and precise knowledge of verse 2.

You see, you can have a certain amount of knowledge, but it is not enough. You must have precise knowledge. The Jews had *a* knowledge. But they were ignorant! It was not a full knowledge but was partial and vitiated. That again, of course, was the trouble with the Pharisees and was it not also the trouble with the Apostle Paul himself before his conversion? Take Philippians 3:4–6: 'Though I might also have confidence in the flesh. If any other man thinketh that he hath whereof he might trust in the flesh, I more: Circumcised the eighth day, of the stock of Israel, of the tribe of Benjamin, an Hebrew of the Hebrews; as touching the law, a Pharisee; concerning zeal, persecuting the church; touching the righteousness which is in the law, blameless.'

That is what Paul used to think. He really did believe, like all the Pharisees, that he had fulfilled the law of God, and was absolutely blameless. So what was his trouble? It was that he had a knowledge of the law but not an exact knowledge. It was all right up to a point, but then he ruined it all by misinterpretation. He himself was a perfect illustration of the very thing that he says here.

And then 1 Timothy 1:13, where Paul expresses amazement that he is in the ministry. He recalls that he 'was before a blasphemer, and a persecutor, and injurious', but he 'obtained mercy because,' he says, 'I did it ignorantly in unbelief.' And when he says that he was ignorant he does not mean that he knew nothing. He was a Pharisee, he knew a great deal about the law and the Scriptures. But, he says, 'I did it ignorantly.' Yes, it is exactly the same word.

The Apostle's own experience, therefore, and that of all the Pharisees, I think confirms this exposition that I am putting before you. The whole trouble with the Jews was that they thought that they knew what the law of God demanded. But they did not. Their knowledge was so imperfect that it had become a lie, and it was standing between them and the knowledge of salvation in and through our Lord and Saviour Jesus Christ.

So you see the point at which we have arrived. This precise knowledge is absolutely essential. Not only must you have knowledge, you must have precise knowledge. Ignorance (a little knowledge) is the enemy; it is the cause of the lost condition of Paul's fellow-countrymen, the Jews. May God once and for ever rid our minds of this dangerous, terrible tendency to discount exact knowledge, definition, propositions, doctrine and theology.

And may the Lord help us to see that what passes as charity is at the expense of denying precise knowledge of the truth and is not charity but laxity. Ultimately, it is a betrayal and denial of the truth of God.

Four

*

Brethren, my heart's desire and prayer to God for Israel is, that they might be saved. For I bear them record that they have a zeal of God, but not according to knowledge. For they being ignorant of God's righteousness, and going about to establish their own righteousness, have not submitted themselves unto the righteousness of God. Romans 10:1–3

We have been examining these three verses in some detail because they are, of course, one of the crucial statements in this great Epistle and a very vital part of the Apostle's whole argument. At this point, we are particularly concerned with Paul's emphasis upon lack of knowledge, and we are emphasising that because it is the sole explanation of the condition of the Jews at the Apostle's time and even up until today.

Secondly, lack of knowledge has continued, throughout the centuries and up to the present, to be the main stumbling-block to all people and especially to those who are pharisaical by nature, by which I mean people who take their religion seriously and who are concerned about pleasing God.

My third reason for emphasising all this is the present, foolish tendency in the church to decry definitions and an exact knowledge of what we believe. This even afflicts evangelical people.

Then the fourth, and the greatest reason of all, for emphasising this point is that it relates to the only way of salvation. There is no other. We are saved by 'coming to a knowledge of the truth'; so that if we have not got that knowledge, we are not saved.

Now this has always been the great matter, and history proves that abundantly. This was the grand discovery that was made by Martin Luther, the thing that led to the Protestant Reformation; and this was the very thing also that led to the great Evangelical Awakening and Revival of two hundred years ago.

We are, therefore, considering the ways or the respects in which the Jews were ignorant. That was their trouble, says Paul, they were lacking in this knowledge, were ignorant at the vital point. And we have already seen one respect in which they were ignorant, and that was that they were 'ignorant of God's righteousness', which I interpreted as meaning 'the righteousness that God demands'. They were ignorant of what the law of God really demanded, and because of that they went wrong elsewhere.

But the ignorance of the Jews did not stop at that point, so we go on, in the second place, to point out that they did not know that the righteousness of which they boasted so much, and which they had been building up, was simply *their own* righteousness. 'Going about,' says Paul, 'to establish their own righteousness.' That is the emphasis, and it is a most important point. This was the very essence of the tragedy of the Jew. The Jew, and particularly the Pharisee, was so pleased with himself. He looked at the others – Gentiles – as 'dogs', 'lesser breeds without the law'. They had not got the oracles of God; they knew nothing about the righteousness that God demanded. There they were – pagans!

But the Jews had got the Scriptures. They were godly, they were righteous; and they were very proud of their own righteousness. But the trouble was that they fondly imagined that by working up this righteousness and amassing it, they were pleasing God and were satisfying God's holy and righteous demands. That was their whole tragedy. They really were very pleased with themselves, and they were resting in their self-righteousness and their self-satisfaction.

Now the Apostle uses a very interesting word here and it is most important in this whole connection. 'They,' he says, 'being ignorant of God's righteousness, and *going about* to establish their own righteousness . . .' 'Going about' is a strong word. It does not only mean that they were seeking righteousness. It does mean that, but it carries the notion of a strenuous effort and toilsome labour. You can see it, can you not, in the very word 'going about'? 'Fussing about', if you like. As Martha was 'cumbered about', 'troubled with many things', and not the 'one thing needful' [*Luke* 10:38–42]. There they were – 'going about'.

The same thought is seen in our Lord's condemnation of the Pharisees who, He says, 'compass sea and land to make one proselyte' [*Matt.* 23:15]. And that is the characteristic of this false view – it involves toil, labour, great endeavour. And Paul grants the Jews that

[41]

they have a zeal for God, and that they really are working very hard in order to amass this righteousness which they think is going to satisfy God. They 'go about' to do it.

I must refer at this point to a notable example of this very thing. If ever a man went about to establish his own righteousness, it was John Wesley![1] There he was, a very brilliant man, doing well in his career in Oxford, and a fellow of his college. But even while he was there he was not satisfied. With his brother and others he formed the Holy Club: 'going about to establish their own righteousness'. They gave alms to the prisoners in the prison; they spoke to them and preached to them. But even that was not enough. Wesley had to make himself righteous with God, so he gave up his fellowship, his brilliant prospects and opportunities, crossed the Atlantic – it was something to cross the Atlantic two hundred years ago! – and preached to natives in Georgia in America.

And what he was trying to do was to put himself right with God. He believed that he had to make himself righteous. So he went back and forth to America trying to do it. What a perfect picture that is of this 'going about'.

The same thing had happened to Luther two hundred years earlier. He was there in his cell, fasting, sweating, praying, 'going about to establish his own righteousness'. It is astounding to contemplate what people are prepared to do in order to work up this 'righteousness'. There have been notable examples of self-sacrifice; men and women have given up great prospects and they are praised, they gain great adulation, and people say, 'What fine Christians!' But the whole time they are simply going about to establish their own righteousness.

At the beginning of 1 Corinthians 13, you find another statement of it. What sacrifices men and women are prepared to make – even their own lives – in order to establish their own righteousness before God! And, again, it is summed up perfectly in the introduction to that parable of our Lord's on the Pharisee and the tax-collector. 'He spake this parable unto certain *which trusted in themselves that they were righteous*' [*Luke* 18:9]. But here in Romans 10 the Apostle shows us so plainly that it is of no value at all, and he does it in these words, 'their own righteousness'. For that is what it is, and nothing else, so let us look at it.

---

[1] This lecture was given on May 24th, 1963 – the anniversary of Wesley's experience.

Why does he say that it is *their own* righteousness? Well, the first answer is that it was not the righteousness that God demands. Here they were, working very hard at it, but it did not happen to be what God asked of them. And this, of course, is the main problem that confronts all of us who have to preach the evangelical gospel. The main heresy is still justification by works. 'What I say,' says the average person, 'is that if you are living a good life, if you are doing good, if you are attending a place of worship, that is what God wants of you.' But it happens not to be the truth! It is not what God asks. But people think it is. If only you do these things, they say, you are a Christian.

To this there is only one reply – Who told you so? On what authority are you making that statement? It is not what God demands. We saw in the last chapter that what God demands of us is not a bit of morality and decency and goodness. No, what God demands is this: 'Thou shalt love the Lord thy God with all thy heart, and with all thy soul, and with all thy mind, and with all thy strength: this is the first commandment. And the second is like, namely this, Thou shalt love thy neighbour as thyself' [*Mark* 12:30–31]. That is God's demand. Not what you and I think, not what the world thinks, not what the church so often thinks. That is *man's* idea, not God's.

The second way of showing that it is nothing but their own righteousness is to demonstrate that it is based, of course, on a completely false view of human sin. You see, it rests on the supposition that we are capable in ourselves of pleasing God; that by putting our backs into it, by 'going about', we can produce a righteousness that will satisfy God. Is that not what you find most people believe today? They say, 'You do this, that, and the other and you are all right with God.' In other words, you can do it, you are capable of doing it.

But then you say, 'What about Jesus Christ?'

'Ah, well,' they reply, 'He came to give us an example, that is how He helps us. An example is always helpful.' So what you must do is 'imitate Christ'; live like Him; make sacrifices as He did. But *you* are doing it! Of course you are capable of doing it! They do not like the doctrine of sin, and if you mention original sin they will hold up their hands in horror – 'Fancy believing in that!' Human nature is not fallen, it is essentially good. Men and women are not sinful, they do not need to be born again. They just need to put their backs into it and that is all – they can do it.

So this whole notion of justification by works, or, to put it in other language, the view that men and women can make themselves righteous in the sight of God, is a complete denial of the great biblical doctrine of the fall, and of our total inability to justify ourselves before God. It denies that completely. It acts on the assumption that people can make themselves Christians and that they really can satisfy the demands of God.

The third objection is that, of course, it inevitably leads us to something which is, of all things, most hateful in the sight of God, and that is self-righteousness. Nothing is so condemned in the New Testament. That is why our Lord spoke that parable of the Pharisee and the tax-collector. There He gives you a picture of this proud, self-satisfied man who does not ask for anything – he has no need to. He simply thanks God that he is what he is, and that he is so much better than the tax-collector. That is complete self-satisfaction and self-righteousness and our Lord condemns it in the plainest manner possible.

But then, of course, He condemns it still more explicitly, not by a parable but in his denunciation of the Pharisees in Matthew 23:5–7: 'All their works they do for to be seen of men.' The Pharisees were the leaders, the religious teachers. They fasted twice a week, and gave a tenth of their goods to the poor. They were not merely talkers, they really put it into practice. But this is what He says: 'All their works they do for to be seen of men'. It is the most severe denunciation of any type of person that you will find anywhere in the whole of the Bible. Our Lord denounces them for this self-righteousness, which is the most hateful thing of all in the sight of God.

And then, in the fourth place, we see the utter uselessness of this righteousness that they produce, in that it ignores completely what God has said about it, and what our Lord, especially, has said about it. Now Paul himself has already said a great deal about this in the third chapter of Romans. The thing is so plain, it is astounding that anybody can miss it. In Romans 3:19–20, Paul says, 'Now we know that what things soever the law saith, it saith to them who are under the law: that every mouth may be stopped, and all the world may become guilty before God. Therefore by the deeds of the law there shall no flesh be justified in his sight: for by the law is the knowledge of sin.' Then in verse 23: 'All have sinned, and come short of the glory of God.'

Now that is the teaching of the Scriptures, that is what the law says so clearly. As Paul puts it again in Philippians 3:7–8, 'What things were gain to me, those I counted loss for Christ. Yea doubtless, and I count all things but loss for the excellency of the knowledge of Christ Jesus my Lord: for whom I have suffered the loss of all things, and do count them but dung, that I may win Christ.'

So there it is in the words of the Apostle, but our Lord had taught the same thing: 'Blessed are the poor in spirit' [*Matt.* 5:3]. But, you see, people who believe that they can put themselves right in the sight of God by their works are not poor in spirit. They are proud of themselves, as the Apostle was before his conversion, as our Lord depicted the Pharisees. 'What you need,' they say, 'is not poverty of spirit but self-confidence, a belief in yourself, a belief that you can do it. Set out to imitate Christ, you have it in you.' This is the opposite of being 'poor in spirit'.

You find the same thing again, in another form, in Matthew 9, when our Lord says quite plainly, 'I am not come to call the righteous, but sinners to repentance' [v. 13]. 'They that be whole need not a physician, but they that are sick' [v. 12]. The reason why the Pharisees did not believe in Him was that they thought they were whole and did not need a physician! That is why He infuriated them – He made them see that they did. And they hated that. They felt they did not need rebirth; they did not need Him to die because they were already satisfying the demands of God.

And then, of course, our Lord put it like this in a terrible phrase in Luke 16:15: 'Ye are they which justify yourselves before men; but God knoweth your hearts: for that which is highly esteemed among men is abomination in the sight of God.' There you are, look at this great mound of righteousness that the Pharisees had built up: 'That is what I have done. Look at my deeds, look at my good life, look what I have sacrificed, look what I am giving away . . . there is my mound of righteousness.'

And our Lord's comment upon it is that it is nothing but 'abomination in the sight of God'. 'All our righteousnesses,' says Isaiah, 'are as filthy rags' [*Isa.* 64:6]. The Old Testament had already said it – our Lord repeats it. It is useless; it is valueless. Our best deeds are impure, polluted, unworthy. Any man who talks about his goodness and his righteousness has completely misunderstood the whole of the biblical teaching. His words are abomination in the sight of God, who does not see as man sees nor judge as man judges.

So then the end of all that is that these tragic Jews were ignorant of the fact that having gone about and expended so much energy and labour, they had succeeded only in pleasing themselves; they had not pleased God at all. They had established their own righteousness and nothing more. They were like a man entering a competition. He has produced his work and he is tremendously pleased with it. Then the day comes for the competition to be judged and the man goes forward with great confidence, only to find that his composition has been excluded. It does not have a single mark. Why? Well, the foolish man had not read the syllabus carefully. He had certainly given a lot of time to this thing, he had shown considerable cleverness and ingenuity, but his entry was not what the adjudicators had asked for. It is disqualified. He has pleased nobody but himself.

In the words of our Lord Himself, 'Not every one that saith unto me, Lord, Lord, shall enter into the kingdom of heaven; but he that doeth the will of my Father which is in heaven. Many will say to me in that day, Lord, Lord, have we not prophesied in thy name? and in thy name have cast out devils? and in thy name done many wonderful works? And then will I profess unto them, I never knew you: depart from me, ye that work iniquity' [*Matt.* 7:21–23]. He does not dispute the facts that these people put forward – they have done all these things. All He says is, 'I am not interested, I never was.' He will have nothing to do with them. There they are, very pleased with themselves, and expecting the chief place but are excluded. 'Going about to establish their own righteousness' – that is all it is.

And that is the whole tragedy in the world today. That is precisely what is being believed, alas, in the church as well as outside it: that Christianity is an encouragement to people to produce their own righteousness. And at the end it will all be utterly useless, our Lord will disown it. Though we say, 'Lord, Lord,' it is of no value. It is not the righteousness that He demands; it is not the righteousness that can satisfy Him; it is useless.

So that brings me to the third and last respect in which they were ignorant, and it is this: they were ignorant of God's way of righteousness and of salvation. 'They being ignorant of God's righteousness, and going about to establish their own righteousness, have not submitted themselves unto the righteousness of God.' Now this is the final tragedy, you see. It is the result of the two previous forms of ignorance. These things, of course, interact. If they had known what God really demands they would never have been foolish enough to go about to try to establish their own righteousness. They would have realised from the beginning that it could not be done. And then, because they thought they were satisfying God, they did not listen to the demands of God's righteousness. They were prejudiced against it and rejected it, even as the Pharisees rejected our Lord, His teaching and all that He had to offer.

And it is still the same, as it has been throughout the running centuries. The last people to believe the gospel, and to be saved, are always those who think that they can save themselves. Our Lord looked at the Pharisees, who were good, moral, godly, religious people, and said this terrible thing, 'The publicans and the harlots go into the kingdom of God before you' [*Matt.* 21:31]. It has always been true. There is no greater sin than the sin of the Pharisee, the sin of self-righteousness. It is, of everything, the thing that most blinds a man to the glory of the gospel. It sounds as if the gospel puts a premium on sin, but it does not. What the gospel does is to show the horrible, terrible danger of self-reliance, self-justification, self-righteousness. 'The publicans and the harlots' – the complete outsiders, the most hopeless in society – actually did go into the kingdom before the others. Why? Because they were more ready to admit their need; they were more ready to acknowledge their own utter helplessness and hopelessness.

Now the Apostle says that this ignorance of God's righteousness was utterly inexcusable because it is taught in the Bible from beginning to end. Look how Paul puts it in Romans 3:21: 'But now,' he says, 'the righteousness of God without the law' – apart from the law – 'is manifested, being witnessed by the law and the prophets.' That, he says, is what makes the Jew so utterly inexcusable. The Jew boasts about his knowledge of the Old Testament, and yet his very Old Testament is the thing that tells him about this way of God's righteousness. The Jew had not understood that. He had completely misunderstood the whole of the Old Testament; he had mis-understood the meaning of the law. We have looked at that. The Jew thought that when God gave the law He said, 'Now keep this law and you will be right in my sight.' Whereas God had given them the law to show them that they could not do that!

It was exactly the same with the prophets. The prophets pointed to the coming of a Deliverer because they could not deliver themselves. Indeed, that is even found in the law – the lamb offered, the burnt offerings and sacrifices. What are they for? They are my schoolmaster to bring me to Christ; they point to the great antitype that is coming. So the law and the prophets witness to salvation in Christ. The Jews were without any excuse at all.

God's method of salvation is always of grace. In chapter 9 the Apostle has proved that to the hilt by his many quotations from the Old Testament. 'For the children being not yet born, neither having done any good or evil, that the purpose of God according to election might stand, not of works, but of him that calleth' [v. 11]. It had always been so in the Old Testament, of which the Jews were so proud, and yet they had not seen it. They were entirely without any excuse. The Old Testament condemns them; the coming of Christ, His teaching, His death upon the cross and His resurrection condemns them still more. Then on top of it all there was the preaching of the Apostle. And yet in spite of everything, the Jews persisted in their rejection of the gospel and its way of salvation: there was no excuse for them.

And there is, likewise, no excuse for anybody in any country whatsoever who has ever read the Bible. The Old Testament alone is enough to condemn those who think they can make themselves Christians or who think they can satisfy God. The Old Testament tells them that it is wrong, that it is impossible. The New Testament – why, it tells them nothing else! The gospel – the good news – in itself tells them that it is useless to attempt anything else. They talk about being Christians, and yet the whole time they mean by that, living a good life in order to be right with God. It is almost incredible! There is only one explanation – it is the devil! 'If our gospel be hid, it is hid to them that are lost: in whom the god of this world hath blinded the minds of them which believe not, lest the light of the glorious gospel of Christ, who is the image of God, should shine unto them' [2 *Cor.* 4:3–4].

But not only is it inexcusable, it is utterly ridiculous. Let us work it out. What were these Jews ignorant of? And all these modern people who still believe that they make themselves right with God and make themselves Christians, what are they ignorant of? Well, the first thing is that they are ignorant of the fact that God Himself has provided the very righteousness that He demands. Is that not the whole message of salvation? 'For I am not ashamed of the gospel of Christ: for it is the power of God unto salvation to every one that believeth; to the Jew first, and also to the Greek.' Why? Well – 'For therein is the righteousness of God revealed from faith to faith: as it is written, The just shall live by faith' [*Rom.* 1:16–17].

That is why Paul is so proud of the gospel. This is the good news that God Himself has provided for us the very righteousness that we

need. What good news it is! It is especially good for those who have
been trying to work up a righteousness that is adequate. God provided a sacrifice for Abraham instead of Isaac, and there we see the
gospel. Abraham did not need to offer Isaac. You do not need to offer
your Isaac. God offers His own Son! God provides the sacrifice; God
provides the way of salvation.

Secondly, the Jews were ignorant of the fact that God offers us this
righteousness as a free gift, and we shall go on to consider how He has
done this. But here I am simply emphasising that there is a righteousness from God – 'They being ignorant' of the righteousness that God
has made, that He has provided, that He is offering as a free gift.

And, thirdly, they were ignorant of the fact that you do not need to
'go about' in order to get righteousness; you just submit to it. Going
about to establish your own righteousness is condemned completely
and utterly by the gospel. Paul says: 'But God, who is rich in mercy,
for his great love wherewith he loved us, even when we were dead in
sins, hath quickened us together with Christ . . . For by grace are ye
saved through faith; and that not of yourselves: it is the gift of God:
not of works, lest any man should boast' [*Eph.* 2:4–9].

'Not of works'! Do not trouble any further. Do not 'compass sea
and land', do not give up this and that. It is of no use to you. Stop! 'By
grace are ye saved!' No 'going about' here! But what then? Well, as
the Apostle puts it here: 'They going about to establish their own
righteousness, *have not submitted themselves*' – the opposite of
'going about' is 'submission' – 'to the righteousness of God.' This is a
military term. A man who joins the army has to submit himself to the
rules and regulations. It does not matter how much of an individualist
he is, if he goes on speaking his own ideas he will soon be punished.
He must obey orders. So he submits to the rules and regulations, to
the discipline. He is no longer his own master; he has handed himself
over.

And that is precisely how we are saved. We submit ourselves 'unto
the righteousness of God'. The Jews would not do that because they
thought they had got their own. But you cannot be saved, says Paul,
until you submit yourself unto the righteousness which is provided
by God. It means to give in, to surrender. It means that you stop
saying, 'I am going to do this and that, then I shall be a Christian, then
I will satisfy God.'

No, you do nothing. You admit that you are in a state of utter
condemnation; you admit that all your 'righteousnesses are as filthy

rags' [*Isa.* 64:6]. You stop arguing and trying to justify yourself – 'But I don't see . . .' You stop all that. You say, 'It is absolutely right. I thought I was good, but I find I am not.' You stand before God and His holiness, and you admit your vileness.

> *Just and holy is Thy name:*
> *I am all unrighteousness.*

You say,

> *Vile, and full of sin I am.*
> Charles Wesley

Have you said it? Have you submitted to that? That is the verdict of the gospel and of the Bible upon you.

'What!' you say. 'But I have always lived a good life.' But if you say that, you have not submitted, you are still standing up, and defending yourself. Until you have seen your vileness and have admitted it, you have not submitted. You must admit the condemnation; you must go further and confess that you are completely incapable, completely helpless. Oh, you must learn to say with Augustus Toplady,

> *Not the labours of my hands*
> *Can fulfil Thy law's demands.*
> *Could my zeal no respite know,*
> *Could my tears for ever flow,*
> *All for sin could not atone.*

You must admit that. You must believe it and feel it and know that it is true. And then you look up and say,

> *Thou must save, and Thou alone.*

You accept God's way. This is His way in Christ:

> *Foul, I to the Fountain fly;*
> *Wash me, Saviour, or I die!*

That is submission! No defences, no arguments, no attempts at self-justification. You see that God's way is this that He has provided. You see that there is no other, and you gladly and willingly yield yourself to it and thank God for it. But here is the test: you do it at once! If you see that it is altogether of God and nothing in you, then what is the point of delaying? What is the point of doing anything? Nothing that you can do is of any value, so you believe it now and you say,

> *Just as I am, without one plea,*
> *But that Thy blood was shed for me,*
> *And that Thou bidd'st me come to Thee,*
> *O Lamb of God, I come!*

> *Just as I am, and waiting not*
> *To rid my soul of one dark blot;*
> *To Thee, whose blood can cleanse each spot,*
> *O Lamb of God, I come!*

Charlotte Elliott

The moment men and women see this, they do it at once; and if this element of immediacy is not there, there is some misunderstanding somewhere. It is a righteousness provided by God. It is a free gift, and all I do is to hold out my hands to receive it; nothing else. Just as I am, without a moment's delay.

My dear friend, do you know that your sins are forgiven? Do you know that you are a child of God? Trust utterly, only, entirely to Him; submit yourself just as you are to God's way of righteousness and of salvation, and do not rest satisfied until you have the witness in yourself. Have you got it? Are you rejoicing in it? This is true Christianity.

Five

＊

For Christ is the end of the law for righteousness to every one that believeth.   Romans 10:4

These great words are connected with what precedes them. Paul has been explaining why the Jews, as a nation, were outside the Christian church. It was because of their ignorance, which means their lack of precise knowledge. We have been tracing the forms which this ignorance took and still takes and, in this fourth verse, Paul sums up all that he has been saying and adds to it. The real trouble, he says, with the Jews – and this he introduces with the word 'For' – is that they were ignorant of the truth concerning our Lord and Saviour Jesus Christ.

So you can take this verse as a fourth respect in which they were ignorant or you can take it as a summing up of all that has gone before, as if Paul were saying – 'All this really amounts to the fact that they are ignorant of the truth concerning the Lord Jesus Christ and His work.' And as that truth concerns the way in which God has provided His righteousness, ignorance of it is, of course, particularly fatal. That was the whole tragedy of the Jews as depicted in the New Testament.

In the Gospels we see the religious leaders of the Jewish people arguing with our Lord, failing to recognise Him and eventually persuading the people to cry out, 'Away with him! Crucify him!' It was because they did not recognise Him that they rejected Him, and that is why they were therefore missing the blessings of salvation that God had sent in Him. And it was the same with the Gentiles who refused Him. They did not recognise the Lord of glory, for had they done so they would never have crucified Him. This ignorance is therefore a very crucial matter.

In a sense, this is still the cause of man's trouble. The rejection of the gospel is ultimately due to the fact that men and women do not realise and appreciate the truth of this one glorious verse, which is a summary of the whole Christian message – that 'Christ is the end of the law for righteousness to every one that believeth.' Indeed, I make bold to call this verse 'The Christian's Charter'. Here is the verse that sets us at liberty. It delivers us from every kind of bondage and sets us free.

Here, then, is the great word which should thrill the heart and move the emotions of every true Christian. If the mere reading of this verse does not make you want to praise God and to thank Him, then I think you had better look again at the foundations of your faith. There is no more glorious statement in the whole of the Scripture than just this; and therefore our reaction to it proclaims exactly what we are.

You can divide up this verse into the certain general truths that it puts before us, and then into the particular statements that it makes. So let us begin with the general truths. In the first place we are reminded that the Jews, whatever might be wrong with them, were absolutely right in realising the seriousness of the law and its demands. They made a great deal of the law; they boasted that it had been given to them and that the Gentiles had not got it. And they were quite right! It was most important. In a sense, nothing in the Old Testament is more important than the giving of the law, through Moses, to the children of Israel, and it is vital that we should realise that.

The Jews realised that they could not stand before God without keeping the law. We have seen that they misunderstood the law and that they were foolish enough to think that they could keep it. But at any rate they could see that it had to be kept, and that there was no possible righteousness before God except in terms of keeping it. This verse underlines that and re-emphasises it and today we must realise the same thing. Our main problem is not our particular sins. The main problem of every person born into this world is the problem of his standing before God.

Now many people are not aware of that. They are troubled by particular sins and failures, and they think that if they were delivered from these things, then they would be perfect and all would be well. So the great business of preaching is, in a sense, to show everybody that all have to stand before God, and that all will be judged in terms of the righteous demands of the law. Though you may not be guilty of many sins, and though you may be delivered from particular wrongdoings, it does not help you at all because we are not judged in terms of particular sins but in terms of the righteous demands of the law of God. And, as James reminds us, if a man fails in any one point of the law, he has failed with regard to it all [*Jas.* 2:10].

A second general point is that any teaching concerning salvation which does not express itself in terms of the demands of the law of God is a false teaching. This, again, is a most important point. There are many such false teachings with which you are familiar. Many people teach salvation solely in terms of the love of God. They talk about nothing but God's love, and their message is that however much you may have sinned it does not matter, because God loves you and it is this love which gives you your salvation.

Or they put it in terms of the love of our Lord and Saviour Jesus Christ. They teach that He came into the world to tell men and women about the love of God and the trouble with people is that they do not know how much God loves them. The problem, they say, is entirely on our side. Here is God loving everybody, ready to forgive everybody, but people are unhappy because they do not realise it. So the preaching of salvation, according to them, is just the making known of that fact, and we only need to come to a realisation of it.

Now this verse is sufficient in and of itself to show that such teaching is not only wrong, but it is dangerously and tragically so. There is no more misleading teaching than that. Any teaching concerning salvation must be put in terms of the demands of the law. 'Christ is the end of the law for righteousness to everyone that believeth.' So if our notion of salvation is not in terms of the satisfaction of the law of God, it is wrong.

Those who know the Epistle to the Romans should be in no trouble about this. The Apostle has already told us this very clearly in chapter 3:24–26, where he describes the way in which God saves sinners through the Lord Jesus Christ as being in keeping with the righteous demands of His law. He then asks, in verse 31, 'Do we then make void the law through faith? God forbid: yea, we establish the law.' So any teaching, or any thinking, about salvation which does not put it in terms of satisfying the law of God is completely false and is to be rejected as being of the devil himself. All this comes out, in a general manner, in this fourth verse of the tenth chapter.

And then our third general point is the absolute centrality of the person and work of the Lord Jesus Christ. *Christ* is the end of the law: this Person! And once more, therefore, we have to be very clear about certain things. You see, the whole trouble with the Jews was that they did not recognise Him and they did not see the crucial nature of His work, of His death upon the cross; that is why they were not saved. They believed in God, they believed in the love of God and in the forgiveness of sins, but they were not in the kingdom. Why not? Why were they lost? It was because they had failed to realise the absolute necessity of this Person and of what He had done.

So, you see, the Apostle emphasises this, and it is as important today as it was in the first century. There are many people today who regard themselves as Christians, who say they believe in God and that He loves them, and who are concerned about being blessed by Him – and yet they never mention the Lord Jesus Christ at all! They say you can go to God and listen to Him and get guidance and many other things from Him but, quite literally, they do not mention the Lord Jesus Christ. But that is a denial of the whole of the Christian gospel! Christianity is Christ. Without Him there is no Christianity; without Him there is no gospel, there is no salvation! *Christ* is the end of the law. So again we must test any idea of a relationship to God, or blessings from Him, or any teaching about His love or anything else, we must test it all with this vital test of the place and the importance of the Lord Jesus Christ, the Son of God.

But we must go even further. It is not only His Person that is included but also His work. It is the Lord Jesus Christ in relation to the law of God. That is the crucial point in this whole matter of salvation. Now here again, there are many people who say, 'Yes, we agree, we believe that Jesus Christ is the Son of God.' They are interested in Him as a person and in His teaching, but when you come to His death upon the cross, they are not interested. To them His death was a tragedy, a mistake, it was men doing a wicked, senseless thing, but it is not vital to their position. They do not see that had He not died, there would be no salvation.

Now this verse condemns them. All ideas about Christ, His Person and His work and our relationship to God, are erroneous if they bypass the death upon the cross. Such ideas are a lie; they are not the Christian gospel. These, then, are some general points that stand out on the very surface of this glorious statement in the fourth verse.

But now let us look at it in a more detailed manner. The Apostle says, first of all, that 'Christ is *the end of the law* for righteousness'. What does he mean? This, too, is a most important question, and we must be very careful with it. There are those who misunderstand this verse and think that it is telling us that the law has been done away with. They say that God gave the law under the Old Testament dispensation, but that once Christ came, the law was finished; it no longer applies. But that, again, is a very serious error. This verse does not mean that.

In Matthew 5:17–18, we have our Lord's own word with regard to this: 'Think not that I am come to destroy the law or the prophets: I am not come to destroy, but to fulfil. For verily I say unto you, Till heaven and earth pass, one jot or one tittle shall in no wise pass from the law, till all be fulfilled.' Now that, surely, should be enough in and of itself. The law of God which He gave to the children of Israel through Moses is a permanent expression of God's holy character and of what God expects from men and women. The law is not temporary; it is eternal. The law is still the expression of how God would have men and women live in this world.

Back in the second chapter,[1] the Apostle makes a great point of this and he shows that everybody has to face this law of God. He says that the Jews had the law given to them explicitly, but even the Gentiles, who had not received it in that explicit manner, have an awareness of its requirements written in their hearts: 'For when the Gentiles, which have not the law, do by nature the things contained in the law, these, having not the law, are a law unto themselves: which shew the work of the law written in their hearts, their conscience also bearing witness, and their thoughts the mean while accusing or else excusing one another' [*Rom.* 2:14–15]. So everybody is subject to this law, both Jews and Gentiles. The law is God's expression of His holy character and shows what He expects from the human race. So we must never say that the law has been abolished by the coming of our Lord and that God no longer demands that it be kept. He does. He demands it still of everybody. There is no greater error than to set law and grace in opposition.

There is a teaching which says, 'We are no longer judged by the law; we are simply judged by whether we believe in the Lord Jesus Christ or not.' That is not true: we are still judged by the law of God. That is the eternal standard of judgment and always will be. Indeed, we must go further and say that even though we become Christians we do not say farewell to the law, we must still keep it. It still makes

---

[1] For a full exposition, see *An Exposition of Chapters 2:1 – 3:20: The Righteous Judgement of God*, 1989.

its demands and shows the kind of life which we should be living.

And one of the purposes of salvation is to enable us to live a life such as is demanded by the holy law of God. It is a very dangerous teaching which says that the Christian now has a lower standard. There are many who hold that view. They say, 'Law has gone; we are under grace now; and because we are under grace the standard is lowered, we are forgiven, it does not matter what we do.' But that is sheer Antinomianism, which is a terrible sin. Christ did not die in order to lower the standard. That is not what He has done at all, as I shall show you. The standard remains; the gospel has not made things easier with regard to the demands of the law. They are there, they are absolute and eternal. Christ is not the end of the law in the sense that He has done away with it.

How, then, is He the end of the law? The answer is in the Sermon on the Mount. Christ is the end of the law in the sense that He has fulfilled it for those who believe in Him. He is the end of the law in that He carried out the dictates of the law perfectly in every respect. All it calls for in terms of righteousness before God, Christ has accomplished.

How did He do so? Well, this verse is a great summary of Christian doctrine. The whole gospel is in it. He began by being 'made of a woman', He was 'made under the law' [*Gal.* 4:4]. He did not come into the world as God; He came into the world as God-Man. He took human nature; He was born of a woman. Yes, He put Himself under the law. He was subject to its demands. His incarnation was a part of His fulfilling of the law. He could not have done so unless He had taken on our nature. He could not be our representative unless He was one of us and so you have the incarnation and the virgin birth.

The second great step is when He was baptised. He went to John to be baptised and John said, in effect, 'No, no, I do not baptise you, you baptise me!' And our Lord said, 'Suffer it to be so now: for thus it becometh us to fulfil all righteousness' [*Matt.* 3:15]. What was He doing? He was again identifying Himself with us. Here was the taking up of His work as the Messiah and the Saviour; He was putting Himself into our position. He was under the law and He was iden-tifying Himself with all the demands that the law makes upon us. So the baptism is of crucial importance.

Then, He went on to live a life of perfect obedience to the law of God. The law made on Him all the demands that it makes on us, and He satisfied every single one of them. He never broke the law in any respect. He carried out every jot and tittle absolutely perfectly. All the demands of the law He satisfied in His positive life of obedience.

But He did not stop at that. He went to the cross. He set His face steadfastly to go to Jerusalem. Why? Because the demands of the law upon us have got to be met. We are guilty before the law and the law demands punishment. So in order to fulfil completely the demands of the law He did something about our guilt, about the condemnation of the law on our transgressions. And there on the cross He 'bare our sins in his own body on the tree' [*1 Pet.* 2:24]. He received the punishment decreed and meted out by the law upon human sin. He received what the guilt of our sin demanded from the law. The vials of God's wrath were poured out upon Him there on the cross. And so you see that it was in this way that He became 'the end of the law'; He carried out its ultimate demands.

How am I sure that the law's demands were fulfilled? The resurrection is the answer. In Romans 4:25, we read: 'Who was delivered for our offences, and was raised again for our justification.' He completely fulfilled and satisfied every single demand of the law in every conceivable respect. He ascended to the Father. He presented His blood in the presence of the Father. It was accepted. He is seated at the right hand of God in the glory everlasting.

That is how He is the end of the law: not by doing away with it but by giving a complete answer and satisfaction to it. That is what He meant by saying on the cross, 'It is finished' [*John* 19:30]. That is the meaning of the word. He has satisfied every single demand.

So, you see, this is the way of salvation. The law comes to us and says, 'Unless you produce the righteousness that I demand, you are damned, you are lost.' But Christ has done it for us! The law has nothing against us. He gives us His own righteousness; God the Father gives us the righteousness of His own Son. 'God was in Christ, reconciling the world unto himself, not imputing their trespasses unto them'. Instead, He has imputed them to Him – 'For he hath made him to be sin for us, who knew no sin; that [in order that] we might be made the righteousness of God in him' [*2 Cor.* 5:19–21]. So He is 'the end of the law for righteousness' in that way, and in that way alone. That is the first particular statement.

But come to the second statement: Christ alone is the end of the law for righteousness. This is equally important. In the first statement we put the emphasis on 'the end of the law'. Now we put it on Christ – '*Christ* is the end of the law for righteousness'; nobody else. In chapter 3:19–20 the Apostle gave us abundant evidence of the fact that nobody else could possibly do this by saying that the law silences everybody and renders them guilty before God.

No man or woman can keep the law. No-one has ever done so. 'All have sinned, and come short of the glory of God' [*Rom.* 3:23]. We have it again in chapter 8, verses 3 and 4. And what all that means is that the whole of humanity fails to keep the law of God. Adam was the first to fail, and all his progeny failed after him. 'There is none righteous, no, not one' [*Rom.* 3:10]. So, it is Christ alone who is the end of the law because it is Christ alone who fulfils it and satisfies its every demand. That is why He is absolutely essential. That is why God did not create a second man like Adam. Adam, the first, was perfect, but he could not keep the law; he failed. If God had created another Adam, he, too, would have failed in exactly the same way. The devil is too strong. There is only one way of salvation – God must become flesh.

And God did become flesh! The incarnation is an absolute necessity. Christ came into the world because He had to. 'The Son of man is come to seek and to save that which was lost' [*Luke* 19:10]. No man can save himself and no-one can save anybody else. Even a new, perfect man could not save himself: he would fall. There is need for someone stronger. And someone stronger has come! The second Person of the blessed Holy Trinity was the one who was born as the babe of Bethlehem. Man is not enough. We must have a God-Man before we can have deliverance and salvation, and He has come!

This is where it is so tragic. People talk about being related to God, loving God and having God's love and forgiveness, yet they never mention the Son of God or His death. But there is no salvation apart from Him. 'There is none other name under heaven given among men, whereby we must be saved' [*Acts* 4:12]. 'I am the way, the truth, and the life: no man cometh unto the Father, but by me' [*John* 14:6].

The thing is obvious. The moment you bring in the law – and it is because of their failure to do this that people do not see the need of the Lord Jesus Christ – and the moment you realise the demands of God's holy law upon you, you not only see your own helplessness, you see that nothing but a God-Man can deliver you; He is essential to our salvation. So the second statement the Apostle makes is that Christ alone is the end of the law for righteousness. He is unique. Without the incarnation, without the perfect life, without the atoning death, without the resurrection, there is no salvation: none at all.

And that brings us to the third statement made by the Apostle, which is that Christ is the end of the law for righteousness '*to every one that believeth*'. And to nobody else. Christ is the end of the law only for those who believe. Now here is something else that needs to be emphasised at the present time. You see, this one verse answers all modern heretics and blasphemers. Universalism is not taught in the Bible, yet today people believe that everybody is going to heaven in the end. So the business of the church is just to tell everyone that God loves them; it is to proclaim the universal fatherhood of God and the universal brotherhood of man! Universal salvation! They do not believe in the wrath of God; they do not believe in law or in judgment; they do not believe in hell. No, we are all going to be saved.

But, 'Christ is the end of the law for righteousness to every one that believeth' – but to nobody else. That is why Paul was worried about his fellow-countrymen. That is why he could almost be 'accursed' for them [*Rom.* 9:3]. He had a continual sorrow in his heart with respect to them. Why? Because they were lost and damned; because they were going to hell. So he says, 'My heart's desire and prayer to God for Israel is, that they might be *saved*.' He does not say, 'that they might know that God loves them and that all is well with them'. No; they needed to be delivered because they were lost.

But we are taught this universalism today, and it not only denies the doctrine of the Apostle Paul, it denies the specific words of the Lord Jesus Christ Himself in one of the most exalted statements we have from His lips – His own prayer to God as recorded in John 17. Take the second verse: 'As thou hast given him power over all flesh, that he should give eternal life to as many as thou hast given him.' You see, it is not to all but 'to as many as thou hast given him'. Verses 6, 9–11, 20 and 24 all teach the same truth. Christ is the end of the law for righteousness to you: but only if you believe.

And that means that you realise that you are utterly condemned by God's holy law. It means that you recognise that all your goodness is vile, that all your righteousness is as filthy rags and as dung. You have no hope and no standing whatsoever, though you may be the best, the most moral, and the most religious person in the world. Those who believe are those who submit utterly to Him and to His way, and who rely upon the Lord Jesus Christ alone.

'Christ is the end of the law for righteousness to every one that believeth.' Such people not only believe that, they also give proof that they believe. 'If any man will come after me, let him deny himself, and take up his cross daily, and follow me' [*Luke* 9:23]. This is not a 'believism' that merely mouths the words, 'Yes, I believe.' It means believing from the heart, as we will see later on in this tenth chapter. It is a genuine belief held by men and women who give proof of it by denying themselves, taking up their cross and following after Christ, living this life of righteousness which He has made possible for them. So there we have it all: '*Christ* is the *end* of the law *for righteousness to everyone who believes.*'

So what does this mean for us? Well, the moment you believe in Him, all that He is and all that He has done on your behalf become true of you. The Apostle has already told us this, particularly in chapter 6. He introduces it in that great fifth chapter[1] where he talks about our union with Christ and shows how we are in Christ and no longer in Adam. He goes on to say in chapter 6,[2] 'Know ye not, that so many of us as were baptized into Jesus Christ were baptized into his death? Therefore we are buried with him by baptism into death: that like as Christ was raised up from the dead by the glory of the Father, even so we also should walk in newness of life. For if we have been planted together in the likeness of his death, we shall be also in the likeness of his resurrection' [*Rom.* 6:3–5].

If you are a believer in Christ your 'old man' was crucified with Christ there on the cross on Calvary [v. 6]. You need not try to crucify your old nature, it has already happened! What happened to Christ has happened to you. As a result, you have died to the law. In Romans 6:14 we read: 'Ye are not under the law, but under grace.' That does not mean that the law is done away with, but that we are not under it in the sense that it is demanding the impossible from us and condemning us. No, we are under grace. We are forgiven completely; we are justified absolutely. We are reconciled to God in Christ. God is our Father. He has adopted us into His family and given us 'the Spirit of adoption' [*Rom.* 8:15]. We are 'well-pleasing in his sight' [*Heb.* 13:21]; we are 'alive unto God' [*Rom.* 6:11]; risen with Christ in a new realm. At this moment we are seated 'together in heavenly places in Christ Jesus' [*Eph.* 2:6].

Not only that, we are eternally secure. 'There is therefore now no condemnation to them which are in Christ Jesus' [*Rom.* 8:1]. There never can be any. That is the opening statement of chapter 8 and we

---

[1] See *An Exposition of Chapter 5: Assurance*, 1971.
[2] See *An Exposition of Chapter 6: The New Man*, 1972.

have seen[1] how that great chapter closes with nothing being able to separate believers from the love of God in Jesus Christ. Christ is the end of the law; there is no condemnation, there never can be. He has dealt with it and I am in Him, and being justified, I am as good as glorified.

That, then, is what this great and glorious verse tells us. The tragedy of the Jews was that they did not know this. Are you clear about it? Do you realise that this is the charter of your salvation, the charter of your deliverance? Let every demon in hell, and Satan himself at their head, rise up and try to condemn you. Answer him! They say, 'The law demands this; God is holy, here are the demands. . .'

'Quite right,' you say, 'but Christ is the end of the law to me because I believe in Him – He is my righteousness.'

[1] See *An Exposition of Chapters 7:1 – 8:4: The Law, Its Functions and Limits*, 1973.

Six

*

For Moses describeth the righteousness which is of the law, That the man which doeth those things shall live by them. But the righteousness which is of faith speaketh on this wise, Say not in thine heart, Who shall ascend into heaven? (that is, to bring Christ down from above:) or, Who shall descend into the deep? (that is, to bring up Christ again from the dead.) But what saith it? The word is nigh thee, even in thy mouth, and in thy heart: that is, the word of faith, which we preach; that if thou shalt confess with thy mouth the Lord Jesus, and shalt believe in thine heart that God hath raised him from the dead, thou shalt be saved. For with the heart man believeth unto righteousness; and with the mouth confession is made unto salvation.

Romans 10:5–10

We come now to this subsection of the tenth chapter and if we are to understand what these verses mean, it is absolutely essential that we should remind ourselves of the context. You notice that we have in this chapter a succession of uses of the word 'For'. The second verse begins with it, and so do the third, the fourth and the fifth. This is indicative of the fact that the Apostle is arguing. He is tracing the logical steps in an argument, and therefore as we take up the 'For' at the beginning of verse 5, it is obvious that we will not be able to understand its meaning unless we are aware of the connection.

In order to do that, let me again remind you that the Apostle's theme in chapters 9, 10 and 11 of this Epistle is the position and the condition of the Jews. By the end of chapter 8, he had outlined the great plan of salvation and shown it in all its fulness, but a question seemed to arise: If salvation is the result of God's purpose, then what about the Jews? It is clear that they had been brought into being as a part of the purpose of God and yet nothing was more evident than the fact that they were, at that time, rejecting the gospel, while the Gentiles, on the other hand, seemed to be receiving it with great alacrity.

[63]

Here was something which, on the surface, seemed to indicate that the purpose of God had failed – had 'fallen down', as the Apostle puts it. So Paul takes the matter up and you remember all that we saw in studying chapter 9.[1]

Paul says that the purposes of God have not failed, in spite of Jewish unbelief. The mistake, of course, was to assume that it was God's purpose to save everybody who belonged to Israel. That was the cardinal error. So Paul gives us that great statement: 'They are not all Israel, which are of Israel' [9:6]. There was an Israel within Israel, and it was only that inner Israel that God had ever purposed to save. This He had done throughout the centuries, and He was still doing so.

That led Paul to say that salvation is entirely a matter of God's free, sovereign choice and to establish that in great detail. Nevertheless, it is equally true to say that if a man is not saved, it is because of his own rejection of the gospel which is offered to him.

So Paul says those two things in chapter 9. He gives most of the chapter to salvation, emphasising the free, sovereign, electing grace of God. But towards the end of the chapter he brings in the other element of condemnation and says that it is entirely the result of mankind's rebellion against God and refusal of salvation. At the end of the chapter, Paul shows that this is in particular the case with regard to the Jews. So he sums it all up in verses 30 to 32 of chapter 9.

This is such an important matter that the Apostle obviously feels that he must elaborate it, so he takes it up in this tenth chapter. Indeed, as we have seen, this chapter is, in a sense, a parenthesis in which the Apostle expounds and explains more fully this tragic error on the part of the Jew. Then when he comes to the beginning of chapter 11, he takes up his main theme again, which is the place of the Jew in the purpose of God, and he arrives at his ultimate conclusion at the end of chapter 11.

We have been looking in detail at verses 1–4 and come now to the beginning of this fifth verse where Paul carries on the argument. In this subsection, verses 5–10, he drives home the point which he has made in a summary manner in verses 3 and 4. He just stated it there, but now he wants to establish it. He does so by making a comparison between the law and the gospel as ways of righteousness and salvation: 'Moses describeth the righteousness which is of the law . . . But the righteousness which is of faith speaketh on this wise . . .' In verse 5

[1] See *An Exposition of Chapter 9: God's Sovereign Purpose*, 1991.

he states what the law says, and in verse 6 what the righteousness of faith says. And he does this in order that he may expose, once and forever, the error of the Jews and of all who are in a similar condition.

This is a most important matter for us, not merely that we may understand the whole case of the Jews in the time of the Apostle Paul, but because it is something that is always important. It is an absolutely basic point which – more, perhaps, than any other – has been a stumbling block to men and women throughout the running centuries. It is just this question: How shall a man be just with God? How are we saved?

This was the great problem that came into such prominence at the Protestant Reformation. It was, indeed, the thing that made the Reformation. This doctrine had been hidden for so many centuries by the Western, the Roman Catholic Church, and in exactly the same way by the Eastern Church – the so-called Orthodox Churches. But Luther suddenly had his eyes opened, and he discovered this great thing: 'The just shall live by faith.' It revolutionised his life and he began to preach it. It produced a revolution in the church and Protestantism came out of the darkness.

The question is as urgent today as it has ever been, because the tendency to believe in justification by works is, perhaps, greater today than it has been since the end of the fifteenth century. This is the very essence of the modern problem. People who talk vaguely about all Christians being united do so because they are discounting this vital principle. So there is nothing that we must consider more carefully than this doctrine which is here put before us.

Now the Apostle has dealt with it several times already in this great Epistle, but he comes back to it. Why is this? Because he feels he *must* come back to it. He is not only concerned about the Jews – he is very concerned about them and will do anything, repeating himself as often as he can, if that will open their eyes – but he is not only concerned about them, he is also concerned about all others. There is always a tendency to slip back to dependence on works, and one can do nothing more fatal. If we are not right about that, then we shall be wrong everywhere. And this has been, throughout the centuries, one of the greatest causes of confusion.

So the Apostle takes it up again, and here he really does deal with it for the last time. He exposes it, and he does so in a very dramatic manner by putting up two speakers, as it were. Let the righteousness which is according to the law speak. Then let the righteousness which is according to faith speak. He personifies these two ways of salvation in order that the issue may be made abundantly clear to the members of the church in Rome, to the Jews in particular, and to all who subsequently read what he says. In these verses, therefore, we have one of the Apostle's great summaries of this doctrine of justification by faith only.

So let us look at what he says, but before we do that let me ask a question. Are we clear about justification by faith only? Are we free from any tendency to go back to works? Is there some small part of us that is relying upon anything we have ever done or thought or said or experienced? Because if we are basing our acceptance with God even to the slightest extent upon any one of those things, we have slipped back. To use the phrase that Paul uses in Galatians 5:4, we have 'fallen from grace', which does not mean that we have actually fallen from grace but that we have fallen from it in our thinking; we have gone back to justification by works. Our experience shows us that we are constantly doing so, and thus we become miserable.

I have often put it like this: If, when you happen to fall into sin, you have a feeling that, because of that sin, you are not a Christian at all, and never can have been, then you are still thinking in terms of justification by works. If you can be filled with doubt when you fall into sin like that, or when something else happens to you; if you feel any kind of uncertainty about your salvation because of some inadequacy or deficiency in yourself – if that makes you doubt whether you are a Christian at all – then you have reverted in your thinking to justification by works. Never in any way must our salvation be based upon anything in us. It is entirely in the Lord Jesus Christ.

So the Apostle wants to settle this matter once and for all, and he takes it up like this: Come along, he says, you people who want to justify yourselves by works, let us consider the position. 'Moses describeth the righteousness which is of the law, [in this way] That the man which doeth those things shall live by them.' Paul is quoting Leviticus 18:5 and it is important that we should be clear about this great statement.

Notice that although the Apostle here says that 'Moses describeth the righteousness which is of the law,' he is not saying that we have a description given by Moses. Often the Scripture uses the words 'Moses says' when it is referring to one of the five books of Moses, and that is precisely what the Apostle is doing here because it was God Himself who said this. We are looking here at God's own pronouncement with regard to this whole matter of keeping the law.

So the Apostle is saying here, in effect, 'If you really want to try to justify yourselves by keeping the law, if you really think that you can make yourselves right with God and become God's children as the result of your actions, then let us start by considering what God Himself has to say about it.' Now that is the important point. The trouble with people who resent the doctrine of justification by faith only is that they have never realised what they have to do. It was also the trouble with the Jews.

The first point which we make is this: It is *God* who decides what we have got to do; we do not decide. It is the commandment of God. That is the standard. The problem is, 'How can a man be just with God?' And the obvious place to start is with the question, 'What does God say about it?' And in these verses the Apostle reminds us of what God did say. He gave His commandments, and when He had given them He said, 'The man which doeth those things shall live by them.' We are told, therefore, that we must keep God's commandments.

What are they? Well, they are in essence the Ten Commandments. God made His demands in an outward, explicit manner through Moses. He said: Now, you are about to be led into the land which you are to possess and this is the kind of people I want you to be, and this is the way in which I would have you live.

So there are God's demands, which are perfectly clear. We have them in that twentieth chapter of Exodus and they are very specific. They start with God and our relationship to Him, our worship of Him and our observance of His day. Then we have the negative injunctions, and let us never forget that the final one deals with the whole question of coveting: 'Thou shalt not covet thy neighbour's house, thou shalt not covet thy neighbour's wife, nor his manservant, nor his ox, nor his ass, nor any thing that is thy neighbour's' [*Exod.* 20:17]. No coveting! That is God's commandment, God's law, God's demand which He makes upon us.

But let us remember that our blessed Lord and Saviour interpreted that law more fully for us. The Sermon on the Mount is nothing but an exposition of God's law, and you remember how our Lord there puts such an emphasis upon this element of coveting, and thereby exposes the error of the Pharisees. And Paul has already told us himself that when he really understood the meaning of the law, he saw what an utter failure he was. In Romans 7:7 he says: 'What shall we say then? Is the law sin? God forbid. Nay, I had not known sin, but by the law: for I had not known lust, except the law had said, Thou shalt not covet.' The moment he understood that, he saw the falseness of his whole position.

There, then, is the first thing – God's demand. Before we begin to do anything, is it not the essence of commonsense to ask: 'What have I got to do?' But people do not do this, of course. They immediately rush to do certain things that they are interested in. But we need to know what it is that God demands of us.

Then the second element is this: God requires us to keep this law. Why do I emphasise that? Well, it is emphasised in verse 5: 'The man *which doeth* those things shall live by them.' Those who remember our consideration of the second chapter of this great Epistle[1] will recall that the Apostle there makes a very great point of this in order that he may convict the Jews, because, as he points out, it is not the mere possession of the law that matters, but the carrying out of it. The Jew tended to say that God had given him the law, and had not given it to the Gentiles, and because of that, and that alone, he was made right with God and a child of God. But Paul says it is not that at all. He says: You do indeed have the law, but the whole question is, have you kept it? You not only have the law, you have also heard it and you boast of that; but, he reminds them that it is 'not the hearers of the law [who] are just before God, but the doers of the law shall be justified' [*Rom.* 2:13].

Now there again is a vital point. We all tend to think that as long as we know what is right, then somehow or another we are *doing* it. But that is not so. Mere knowledge, mere religious interest which others do not have, does nothing for us at all. There are people in the world today who do not recognise the category of morality, but the mere fact that we do, does not make us moral. That comes from keeping the moral code.

Now this is the whole trouble with what is called Antinomianism; that people know the law but they do not keep it. In these verses the whole emphasis is upon the doing and the keeping. 'Not the hearers of the law . . . but the doers of the law.' The Jews were boasting, 'We have the oracles of God, those Gentiles have not; they are dogs, they are outsiders.'

What matters, says Paul, is: Have you *kept* the law? If you have

[1] See *An Exposition of Chapters 2:1 – 3:20: The Righteous Judgement of God*, 1989.

not, it makes it worse for you rather than better. If you do know what is right, why have you not done it? It is a matter of doing.

But we must add even to that. Not only do we say that the law must be kept, but the *whole* of the law must be kept. This is not my idea, this is what the law itself says. The Apostle Paul puts this quite clearly in writing to the Galatians: 'For as many as are of the works of the law are under the curse: for it is written, Cursed is every one that continueth not in all things' – not some things – 'which are written in the book of the law to do them' [*Gal.* 3:10]. That is the emphasis.

But then James in his Epistle is still more explicit and makes it as clear as it can ever be made: 'Whosoever shall keep the whole law, and yet offend in one point, he is guilty of all. For he that said, Do not commit adultery, said also, Do not kill. Now if thou commit no adultery, yet if thou kill, thou art become a transgressor of the law' [*Jas.* 2:10–11]. That is what the law says. You have got to keep the whole of the law. Even if you can prove that you have kept ninety-nine point nine per cent of it, it does not save you. If you have broken point one per cent, then you have failed in the lot. Any part of the law that is broken puts us under God's condemnation.

Now this is something that we all tend to forget. We assume, as James puts it, that if we keep one commandment we are all right. But, he says, what about the others? It is the same God who has given all of them, and He does not say that this is important and that is not. Every one of God's commandments is of vital importance, and it does not matter how perfect you may be, if you fail at one point, you have failed in it all.

So our Lord in His summary of the law puts it like this: 'The first of all the commandments is, Hear, O Israel; The Lord our God is one Lord: and thou shalt love the Lord thy God with all thy heart, and with all thy soul, and with all thy mind, and with all thy strength' [*Mark* 12:29–30]. It is totalitarian; nothing may be kept back. If you do keep anything back it is an insult to God. In His law He demands a total allegiance, the whole person – heart, soul, mind and strength. 'And the second is like, namely this, Thou shalt love thy neighbour as thyself.' That is the law of God. That is what God demands of us.

And then the other thing that is emphasised here, of course, is that it is you and I who have to keep it. '*The man* which doeth these things shall live by them.' It is each individual person who has to do it. Each of us is given the commandment and is given nothing else. Help is not given, nor is strength. Someone comes forward and says, 'I want to know what I am to do. I can justify myself before God. By putting an effort into it, by exercising my will-power, I can make myself a Christian. I can deliver myself from the guilt and the condemnation of the law.'

Very well, says the law, here is the answer. This is what you have to do. Unaided as you are, you have got to do it. The law puts forward its demands squarely and honestly.

There, then, is the exposition of the demands of the law, and what the law says to us is that if we keep these commandments we are just with God. 'The man which doeth these things shall live by them.' He shall live in the sense of being saved, in the sense of having eternal life. Live this kind of life and you are saved. That is what the law says.

Now when you hear that, the question that obviously must arise in your minds at once is this: How could the Jews ever have misunderstood that? The Apostle is quoting from the Old Testament where it is repeated many times and expounded by the prophets; it is perfectly clear. Here were Jews who had been brought up on their Scriptures. They read them and heard them read aloud. They studied them; they boasted of them and they rejoiced in them. So how could they have gone wrong? And in particular, what about the Pharisees? The Pharisees were the experts on the law of God, and gave their time to studying it. That was their great interest in life. How could they have gone wrong?

That is a most important question, because, you see, the same question still has to be asked. Here it is put in modern form. How does it come to pass that any man or woman with an open Bible could still go on saying, 'I am a Christian because of the good life I live'? Or, 'I am a Christian as the result of the good I do, and the sins that I do not commit.' How is it possible that anybody could still think that and believe it and rest upon it, and be annoyed when the preacher of the gospel says, 'That is no use to you at all because you need to be born again and Christ has to die for you'?

And the answer is given us in the Bible itself. Our Lord gives it in the Sermon on the Mount. That great section in Matthew 5, from verse 17 to the end is nothing but an exposition of that one thing. 'Ye have heard that it was said by them of old time . . . but I say unto you . . .' And there our Lord expounds the real meaning of the law.

The Pharisees said, 'I have never committed murder.'

'Haven't you?' says Christ. 'What have you said about your brother?'

'I have never committed adultery,' says the Pharisee. 'Haven't you?' is the answer. 'Have you ever looked with lust . . .?' That is the whole argument. Our Lord also brings out this element of coveting in the spirit, in thought. 'God which seeth in secret,' says our Lord. God reads the heart. So our Lord expounds the law in that way in the Sermon on the Mount.

But elsewhere our Lord does more, and it is important that we should realise this. Matthew 15, and the parallel passage in Mark 7, is so explicit. This is a most important passage. Quoting from Isaiah, Jesus exposed the hypocrisy of the Jewish teachers, saying: 'This people draweth nigh unto me with their mouth, and honoureth me with their lips; but their heart is far from me. But in vain they do worship me, teaching for doctrines the commandments of men' [*Matt.* 15:8–9].

There it is; that is the one explanation. That was the whole trouble with the Pharisees and with all the Jews who listened to their teaching. They had a zeal for God, and they were setting out to establish their own righteousness in the sight of God. What was their mistake, then? It was that though the law of God was there and open before them, they did not look at it but at their teaching about it. They looked at their own refinements and comments upon it – and that is precisely what is still happening in the Christian church. That is why men and women still fall into this trap and this error of justification by works. They really do not look at the Bible and listen to what it says; they say what *they* think. They substitute the traditions of men for the law of God. This is amazing, but it is still happening, as it has happened throughout the running centuries. The law of God is there, plain and open before them, yet men and women do not take it as it is.

And so the Pharisees had reconstructed the law of God. There were higher critics then, too, you see! That is the whole trouble with the higher critic. He says he starts with this, yes, but then he changes this and that; he modifies it and accommodates it until in the end it is something entirely different. On the surface it seems to be the same thing. Some of the same terms are still used. But it has been changed. It is no longer God's Word, it is what the critic thinks, what *he* says. And what the Pharisee said was, 'If you have not actually murdered a man you are not guilty of "Thou shalt not kill". If you have not actually committed physical adultery you are all right.' But it is not all right, as our Lord points out. And the same is true of coveting! That is where Saul of Tarsus, this Apostle Paul, had gone so tragically astray: he had not realised the inwardness of sin, as he tells us. But the moment he saw it, he saw how lost he was.

The tragedy is, therefore, that instead of facing what God really says, men and women substitute what they think. And so you get your modern man and woman saying, 'What I say is this: people who do their best or who are out to improve the world; people who are trying to lead a straight and a moral life, whether they believe in Christ or not, they are Christians; they are right in the sight of God.' But the question to ask is: Who told you so? Is that what God says?

We must start by considering what God Himself says. It is not what people think, no matter who they are. If you have all the bishops in the universe preaching justification by works, it does not matter at all. This is not what God says, and they are wrong! And we must not be afraid of saying so. They will say that we have a wrong spirit. We will say that something worse is true of them: they are liars and blasphemers who are substituting their own thoughts for God's plain, explicit commandment.

You see how far astray we have gone at the present time with all this niceness, and these warnings that we must not criticise. We *must* criticise! This is a doctrine that leads to hell and to damnation! It is a denial of the doctrine of God and of His dear Son.

So we can sum it up like this: our Lord said to these Pharisees, 'Ye are they which justify yourselves before men; but God knoweth your hearts: for that which is highly esteemed among men is abomination in the sight of God' [*Luke* 16:15]. And that is still true! The world will praise you if you try to justify yourself by your works; it is doing so. It praises men and women as great Christians who deny the very elements of the Christian faith. But that which is highly esteemed among men is abomination in the sight of God. God demands an absolute obedience, one hundred per cent obedience to His law. Over and above what I must not do and what I must do, He says that I must have 'clean hands, and a pure heart'. 'Who shall ascend into the hill of the Lord? . . . He that hath clean hands, and a pure heart' [*Ps.* 24:3–4], a heart without a speck or a spot in it. Or as David puts it in Psalm 51: 'Thou desirest truth in the inward parts' [v. 6].

If, then, you think you can save yourself, that is what you have to do. You must keep the Ten Commandments perfectly; you must have an absolutely clean, pure heart. You must have truth in your 'inward parts'. That is what you must do. 'The man that doeth those things shall live by them.' Do you still think you can do so? No, it is an utter impossibility.

Can you not see that the law was never meant to be a way of salvation? It was given that men and women might be condemned – the Apostle has already told us that in chapter 4, where he says, 'The law worketh wrath: for where no law is, there is no transgression' [v. 15]. He says the same thing in chapter 3:20: 'Therefore by the deeds of the law there shall no flesh be justified in his sight: for by the law is the knowledge of sin.' It was never meant to save, it was never meant but to bring home the knowledge of transgression and to establish guilt. That was its one and only purpose.

Or listen to something still more explicit said by the Apostle in 2 Corinthians 3. He describes the law as 'the ministration of death' and 'condemnation'. And, you see, the moment people realise the truth about God's law, they stop thinking that they can justify themselves or put themselves right before God. Do you want to know what the law is like? Well, here it is given in a tremendous description by the author of the Epistle to the Hebrews. 'Ye,' he says, 'are not come unto the mount that might be touched' – this is, the giving of the law of God – 'and that burned with fire, nor unto blackness, and darkness, and tempest, and the sound of a trumpet, and the voice of words; which voice they that heard intreated that the word should not be spoken unto them any more: (For they could not endure that which was commanded. And if so much as a beast touch the mountain, it shall be stoned, or thrust through with a dart)' [*Heb.* 12:18–20].

Have you ever felt that about the law? Have you ever asked that it should not be spoken to you any more? Have you felt that it is unendurable because of its exalted and impossible demands? If you have not, you have never seen the law, you know nothing about it. But that is the law. And when men and women truly realise its terms and demands, and hear it saying to them, 'If you keep that, it will justify you; the man that doeth these things shall live by them,' then they say, 'What am I to do?' They feel like Paul when he cried, 'O wretched man that I am! who shall deliver me?' [*Rom.* 7:24]. They are terrified, and filled with alarm, as those children of Israel were at the giving of the law on mount Sinai. Then they cease to attempt to save or to justify themselves by keeping the law, and are delighted and thankful to listen to what the righteousness which is of faith has got to say; and so they become saved men and women.

[73]

The trouble, then, with the Jews was that they had never faced what the law actually said about this question of righteousness. I trust that none of you are guilty of that ancient error of the Jews. If you are still not convinced, I ask you to go back and read Exodus 19 and 20, and the other statements that we have considered together. Face the demands of God and realise what you have got to do. Stop saying that it is enough if we are good and moral and pay our dues as we should. That is what *you* say, that is what the newspapers say, that is what an apostate church says. But it is not what God says. Be wise, start by asking this question: What does God demand of me? And the moment you realise that, then you will be ready to say,

> *Foul, I to the fountain fly;*
> *Wash me, Saviour, or I die!*
> Augustus Toplady

Seven

*

For Moses describeth the righteousness which is of the law, That the man which doeth those things shall live by them. But the righteousness which is of faith speaketh on this wise, Say not in thine heart, Who shall ascend into heaven? (that is, to bring Christ down from above:) or, Who shall descend into the deep? (that is, to bring up Christ again from the dead.) But what saith it? The word is nigh thee, even in thy mouth, and in thy heart: that is, the word of faith, which we preach; that if thou shalt confess with thy mouth the Lord Jesus, and shalt believe in thine heart that God hath raised him from the dead, thou shalt be saved. For with the heart man believeth unto righteousness; and with the mouth confession is made unto salvation.

Romans 10:5–10

When we began our consideration of this subsection, I emphasised the importance of bearing the context in mind. The Apostle is dealing here with the question of why the Jews are outside the kingdom of God. He says that it is all due to the fact that, having misunderstood the meaning and the purpose of the law, they had misunderstood the true way of salvation. The Apostle now wants to deal finally with this subject. You see his method? He is not content merely with throwing out statements. The Apostle was a preacher and the business of a preacher is to drive his points home; that is why he must repeat himself, and go on repeating himself. I am reminded of the story of an old preacher who had preached the same sermon on many occasions. A young man who had heard this sermon five or six times went to him and said, 'You know, I have heard you preach that sermon five or six times before'.

'What about it?' said the old man.

'Well,' he replied, 'I was just beginning to wonder . . .'

'Now, my friend,' said the preacher, 'have you put it into practice yet?' And as the young man could not reply with confidence that he had, the preacher said, 'Then I shall go on preaching it to you!'

Now that is the very essence of preaching. These things are not to be considered intellectually, they are to be applied, and the business of the preacher is to make them plain and unmistakeable. The Apostle, of course, is very concerned about his fellow-countrymen. He said so at the beginning of this chapter, as he had said it at the beginning of the previous one. He is in distress about them. Their predicament is so plain to him, how is it that they cannot see it? So he keeps on saying it and now he puts it in a new way.

He says, 'Look here, this is a tragedy!' And he dramatises it, using the two main ways in which people think about salvation. The trouble with the Jew was that he thought of righteousness in terms of keeping the law as given through Moses. On the other hand, the gospel way is the way of faith. The choice is always either justification by works or justification by faith. And the Apostle now personifies these ways. He says: This is what justification by works really means; this is what justification by the law has got to say to you. And then he says: But the righteousness which is of faith (justification by faith) speaks like this . . .

So Paul puts up two speakers, two preachers, and says: How can you possibly go astray if you realise what these two preachers are saying to you?

Now we have considered the first preacher – the preacher of the law. 'Moses describeth the righteousness which is of the law, [in this way] That the man which doeth those things shall live by them' – and we have seen what that meant. This preacher leaves us in a state of complete hopelessness and helplessness. If people who think that they can make themselves Christian only realised what they have got to do in order to bring that about, they would never think that again. The trouble with them is that they put up their own little standard; they have never considered God's standard.

Apart from anything else, that is what makes people who think that their good lives are sufficient, so foolish. Once they realise what God asks them to do, they will soon realise that they cannot do it. That was the experience of Martin Luther before his eyes were opened to the truth. Trying to keep God's law is a way of despair, of hopelessness; it is a way of death. The Apostle has already called it 'the law of sin and of death' [*Rom.* 8:2]. Hopeless!

But, thank God, we can listen to the second preacher. 'But,' he says – and thank God for this contrast – 'the righteousness which is of faith speaketh on this wise ...' Listen, Paul says, to this second preacher. Having been rendered utterly hopeless by the first, listen to the second and to what he has to say to you.

And so Paul once more sets out the case for justification by faith only, referring to 'the righteousness which is of faith' – an expression which has often caused a great deal of difficulty. Although its meaning is not straightforward, yet I think that if we take the words in their context, they are not as difficult as some of the commentators tend to make out.

The problem is due to the fact that although the Apostle clearly had Deuteronomy 30:11–14 in mind, he did not make an exact quotation from that passage. Difficulties arise either because people think that he is quoting or because they misunderstand his object in using these words. The key to understanding what Paul is saying is as follows. The words – 'Say not in thine heart, Who shall ascend into heaven? ... or, Who shall descend into the deep? ... The word is nigh thee, even in thy mouth, and in thy heart' – are words that were spoken by Moses. They were spoken by Moses in exactly the same way as the words which Paul quotes in verse 5 were spoken by him: 'That the man which doeth those things shall live by them.' There, as we saw, the Apostle is quoting Leviticus 18:5. Here he has in mind Deuteronomy 30. But the significant difference is that he does not refer to Moses here. In verse 5 he says, 'Moses describeth ...' but here he does not say that. He simply says, 'The righteousness which is of faith speaketh on this wise.'

What, then, is he saying? Well, people have gone astray because they have omitted to notice the point I have just made. They have said that the Apostle is saying: In the statement of Leviticus 18:5 Moses tells us about the way of righteousness by the law, whereas in Deuteronomy 30:11–14 Moses is giving us a description of the way of righteousness by faith. So that Moses has made the two statements, and Paul is contrasting the one with the other.

Now many commentators have said that, among them John Calvin, so we cannot dismiss this point, but must regard it as worthy of our respectful consideration. But I want to suggest that it is an entirely wrong exposition, and I do so for two main reasons. One is, as we have seen, the very form of words which Paul uses. If he were still quoting Moses and Moses' opinion as to the way of righteousness he would have said so – 'Moses says this; Moses also says that.' But Paul does not do that. He says, 'Moses says this ... the way of righteousness by faith says that.' That is one reason.

And the second is this: in Deuteronomy 30, Moses is still talking about the law, and he is talking about keeping it. He is really saying exactly the same thing as he said in Leviticus 18:5. Notice the emphasis upon the doing, and upon what happens if you do not do this. He even says explicitly that he is talking about the law which has been given. Therefore we cannot accept this suggestion that here the Apostle is quoting Moses' opinion with regard to the two ways.

So what is Paul doing here? Why does he refer to these words in Deuteronomy 30 at all? It seems to me that the explanation must be this – and it is the explanation that has been adopted by many other commentators throughout the centuries – the Apostle is borrowing the words of Moses in order to present us with a statement of the way of justification or righteousness by faith. He has got this idea, he knows what he wants to say, and he thinks of Moses' words there in Deuteronomy 30, and he says: Now this puts the thing very perfectly. So he quotes the words. He does not even quote them exactly, there is a variation, but he uses them in order to convey his teaching and the point that he is anxious to make.

Now this is something that the Apostle does quite often. I suggest that he does very much the same thing in verses 18 and 19 of this same chapter, as we shall see. Preachers do something similar from time to time. Indeed, it is something that we all do in general conversation. A man may be anxious to make a point and as he is speaking he suddenly remembers something that Shakespeare said. So he makes his point, not by using his own words, but by quoting Shakespeare, because the form of words used by Shakespeare in that particular case, which may not be absolutely relevant to his point, conveys his idea. And that is what the Apostle is doing on this occasion.

This, then, is what he is saying: What was the main object of the words used by Moses, especially in verses 11 to 14, 'Say not in thine heart, Who shall ascend into heaven? . . . Or, Who shall descend into the deep?' and so on? Well it is perfectly clear that that is just Moses' very forcible way of bringing out his point. He is addressing the children of Israel at the end of his life. It is the Deuteronomy, the second giving, as it were, of the law. He is now at the end of his address and he is driving the point home. He ends by saying, 'See, I have set before thee this day life and good, and death and evil' [*Deut.* 30:15] – the two possibilities, these two ways.

And then Moses says – and this is the point made here: Now you cannot say that you did not know; you cannot say that God is unfair or that you are left in a position with something extremely difficult to find out. No, he says, it is not like that. The thing has been put before you so plainly and so clearly, 'The word is very nigh unto thee, in thy mouth . . .' It is there, it is right in front of you, so that you have no excuse at all and you cannot say that you did not know what you were being called upon to do.

And I suggest that Paul takes up that idea, and says, in effect, 'Now the righteousness which is of faith has this characteristic, that it is there right before you, perfectly plain and clear.' That is what he is conveying at this point, and I want to work this out with you. You notice the slight variation in the language used? The Apostle does not say, 'Who shall go over the sea?' as you have in Deuteronomy 30:13; he says, 'Who shall descend into the deep?' But of course it makes no difference. The sea is deep; it was regarded as unfathomable, and so the whole notion of the sea became almost synonymous with the idea of depth, and that idea, in turn, carried the idea of hell, the depth of hell, the abyss.

So the Apostle just takes the language and modifies it to that extent in order to bring out his teaching so that instead of talking about 'crossing the sea', he talks about 'going down to Hades', as it were, in order 'to bring up Christ again from the dead'. But that does not make the slightest difference, indeed, it enforces my exposition that the Apostle is taking the language and using it in a general sense to convey this one big point.

So Paul is anxious to show the contrast between the way of righteousness by faith, and that other attempt to get righteousness by means of the law. The trouble with the latter was that it was not only extremely difficult, it was impossible. 'But,' he says – here is the contrast – 'the righteousness which is of faith speaketh on this wise.' It is not like that other at all! So what does it say? It says: Do not begin to say – 'Say not in thine heart, Who shall ascend into heaven? (that is, to bring Christ down from above:) or, Who shall descend into the deep? (that is, to bring up Christ again from the dead.) But what saith it?' – and so he continues.

Now you notice that some of these words are in brackets, and that is where people have got into difficulty. You see, the Apostle is really anxious to state the gospel and therefore he borrows this pictorial language from Moses and the book of Deuteronomy, but he makes it clear that what he is really talking about is the Christian gospel. And we should not have been misled into attributing the whole thing to Moses. Paul, by putting this exposition of what he is saying in terms of our Lord, is clearly saying that it is not Moses who is speaking now. 'I am borrowing his language,' he says in effect, 'to show you what the preaching of the gospel says.'

What, then, does it say? The first point is this – and these are the things for which we should thank God – there is no difficulty about knowing what the way of salvation is. Nobody has the excuse today of saying that they do not know it, because it has been made perfectly clear. Or we can put it like this: there is no need to investigate, there is no need to set out on a voyage of discovery or some great quest, for it is all here.

You see the relevance of all this? It was important then, it is important now, it has always been important. There are many people today who think that the Christian is someone who has set out on a great quest for truth and for reality. To them, that is Christianity. I remember reading a book by a well-known American author, a Quaker. He took this view and it is typical of the Quaker teaching. He said, 'If somebody came to me and offered me on the one hand, the thrill and the excitement and the pleasure of the quest for truth, and on the other hand, truth itself, and a knowledge of truth, I would, without any hesitation, choose the first.' But here is the lie direct to that. Do not say that, says Paul. You need not start off with your heroics, climbing into the heavens, going down into the depths, to find truth; there is no need to.

You see how important this is? Some of the most popular books today are those which say, 'We have got to have a new truth for this century. Man in the atomic age, scientific man, has grown up, come of age. We must set out to discover truth, the truth that is adequate for people today.' And the answer is, 'Say not in thine heart, Who . . .' There is no need for you to do anything, it is all here, it is all available. That is what Paul is saying. There is no difficulty. We are not, as Christians, here to exhort one another to seek for the way of salvation and of truth, there is no need for us to search at all. A revelation has been given. It is not a quest, not a voyage of discovery, it is not research – it is here, it is given. That is the first thing.

But then, secondly, Paul rejoices in the fact that the way of salvation is not impossible. The other was impossible. The moment you realise, as I say, what it asks of you, you realise you cannot do it. But this is not an impossible way, and Paul puts it in this extraordinary manner. If you and I had to go up into the heavens in order to get it, or if we had to go down into the abyss to bring it up, then it would be impossible. But, he says, you must not say that, there is no need to do all that; it is not impossible.

And, of course, Moses' language is most appropriate to bring out this point, because there are people who really do make the Christian salvation impossible by saying that you have got to go up or down. Interestingly, these are the very terms they are using today – you see, the Bible is always contemporary and up to date! God is 'depth' we are told – 'the ground of Being'. The man who has discovered depth in himself discovers God. And that is the very thing we are told here that we must not be doing! No, we need not move from where we are; it is not 'impossible'.

Let me make this quite clear. There is no need, as I say, for us to feel that we have now got to set out on this great endeavour, and that the truth is always there somewhere in the distance. The Apostle has already said that: 'They being ignorant of God's righteousness, and *going about* . . .' – you remember how we interpreted that – all this 'going about', this tremendous effort here and there with a number of people researching in different directions. Then you try to get all the data together and collate it to see if you can find some sort of solution. It is all a denial of Christianity; it is all wrong. The very attempt is already a proof that such people have not understood the gospel.

In the book of Job there is a wonderful illustration of all that I am trying to say, and all that the Apostle is saying here. It is that great twenty-eighth chapter on the search for wisdom. It puts it all very plainly and I would urge you to read it all for yourselves. Let me just quote the opening and conclusion of it. It begins: 'Where shall wisdom be found? and where is the place of understanding? Man knoweth not the price thereof; neither is it found in the land of the living.' It concludes: 'God understandeth the way thereof, and he knoweth the place thereof. For he looketh to the ends of the earth, and seeth under the whole heaven' [vv. 12–24]. Then he ends, 'And unto man he said, Behold, the fear of the Lord, that is wisdom; and to depart from evil is understanding' [v. 28].

You see, you may have set out on this great quest for wisdom, but you need not have moved an inch. The thing is essentially simple – 'the fear of the Lord' – that is all you need; and you will be given it. And Paul's statement here is very much the same idea. Salvation is not something that you and I have to search for.

And, thirdly, the way of salvation demands no effort on our part because it is provided by the Lord Jesus Christ. Paul puts this at the end of verse 8: '. . . that is, the word of faith, which we preach,' going on to unfold that in its relationship to believing on the Lord Jesus Christ.

So I would put it as a principle like this. This is the way of salvation. Thank God, says the Apostle, and listen to what it says. You do not have to indulge in these heroics, either mentally, or in your works and your behaviour. Why not? Because it is all provided by the Lord Jesus Christ.

We do not have to provide the Saviour. We do not have to 'ascend into the heavens' to bring down the Saviour, neither do we have to 'go down into the abyss' to bring Him up again from the dead. Secondly, we do not have to struggle to find Him or to lay hold upon Him, though there are many, as I shall show you, who try to do that. They say, 'Yes, the Lord Jesus Christ is the Saviour, but how can I get hold of Him? What a tremendous task it is. I have got to climb up into heaven or go down into the deep to lay hold of Him.' But there is no need to do all that, says the Apostle. The Saviour is not difficult to find. He is not somewhere far away. He is with you, He is at hand, wherever you are He is there.

Why are we so sure of this? The answer, according to Paul, is that there is no need for you to go up into the heavens to drag the Saviour down, because the Saviour came down Himself. 'When the fulness of the time was come, God sent forth his Son, made of a woman, made under the law . . .' [*Gal.* 4:4]. This is how 'the righteousness of faith' speaks. He has come down, and those who try to climb into heaven when He has come down are fools. They cannot do it, to start with, but they should not even try it. 'The Word was made flesh, and dwelt among us' [*John* 1:14].

Not only that, you need not go down into the depths to try to bring Him up again from the grave. Coming into this world, and bearing our burden, cost Him His life and He was buried in a grave. You say, 'He has been defeated, He is finished . . . If only He could have conquered!' But you need not say that. He *has* conquered. He has come up from the dead. We do not have to bring Him up, He has done everything Himself, everything that is necessary for us.

That is another way of saying what Paul has already said in verse 4: 'Christ is the end of the law for righteousness to every one that believeth.' Man has failed to keep the law; man at his best has failed to keep it; we need somebody more than man to keep the law. Where can I find Him? You need not go searching, my friend. He has come! The only one who has ever kept the law has already done so. Yes, but there was the penalty of the law, which is death. It is all right; He paid that penalty, and He proved that the payment was sufficient by rising again from the dead. So you need do nothing at all. It has all been done.

Not only that; there is no difficulty about knowing how He has done this. It has been preached, says the Apostle – 'that is, the word of faith, which we preach'. As Paul puts it in that extraordinary phrase in Galatians 3:1: 'O foolish Galatians, who hath bewitched you, that ye should not obey the truth, before whose eyes Jesus Christ hath been evidently *set forth*, crucified among you?' – patently or clearly set forth among you. And Paul has the same thought here: he preached 'Jesus Christ, and him crucified' [*1 Cor.* 2:2].

There is no difficulty about discovering the way of salvation in Christ Jesus, the gospel is full of it. It says that He had to take on human nature, otherwise He could not represent us. It says that He had to live a life of perfect obedience to the law, in order to satisfy that law which we had broken and which condemns us. It says that He must pay the penalty – the penalty is death – and He has done so. This is the preaching of the gospel, 'the word of faith, which we preach'. There is no difficulty about it. You see, it is men and women who make the difficulties, it is they who make it sound involved and difficult. The gospel itself is essentially simple: 'The word is nigh thee, even in thy mouth, and in thy heart.'

So that we put it, finally, in this way: that we are not called upon to make some impossible effort of understanding. We are not saved by our understanding but by a simple trust in, that is an abandonment of ourselves to, the Lord Jesus Christ. In other words, this is salvation for all, for anybody who believes, however ignorant, they may be. It does not matter at all. It is not our intellectual understanding that saves us, otherwise we would be saved by works. It is our simple trust in the word preached.

Now that is the message of the gospel, says Paul, that is 'the word of faith, which we preach'. It was the old message preached to the Philippian jailor: 'Believe on the Lord Jesus Christ, and thou shalt be saved, and thy house' [*Acts* 16:31] – and Paul and Silas explained to him the word of the Lord. He was not a man of great intellect or of understanding but he was able to believe. In Mark 12:37, we read of

Jesus Christ, 'The common people heard him gladly.' 'The word is nigh thee.' It is simple. It does not demand some great effort, up into the heavens or down into the depth . . . No; a little child can believe it, a child can be saved. The way of salvation is as simple as that. It is a simple belief and trust in the Lord Jesus Christ, the Son of God.

So, then, you see how the Apostle has contrasted the two ways of salvation. The first is involved, difficult, and in the end, impossible. This one is simple, plain, done for us, requiring only faith – it is all of grace by faith.

Now that is the Apostle's message. But I must apply this. The Apostle applied it, and so must we. This chapter 10 of Romans is not something theoretical or academic. We are not simply considering this as though it were a lesson in literature – giving an alternative translation or analysing it. No, this is to be applied, and with urgency, because this old misunderstanding still persists.

The application was first of all to the Jews at that time, and it is still true about them. They rejected the gospel because they thought they could justify themselves by keeping the law and attain righteousness in that way – and they were altogether wrong. They had misunderstood the purpose and function of the law; they had never realised what it demanded; they had substituted their own standards and their own interpretations, which, as we have seen, were altogether wrong. But the tragedy is that they preferred to try that and fail, rather than to accept this offer which told them that all had been done in the Lord Jesus Christ, and that they could have righteousness as a free gift. Their pride was such that they preferred to rely on their own efforts and fail, rather than admit that they were paupers and receive salvation as the free gift of God's grace. That was the trouble with the Jews.

But it is still the trouble with all who refuse to believe the message of justification by faith only. It is still the position of all those who trust to their own works and their own activity. It is also the trouble with those who regard our Lord as but a teacher and an example to follow. They have never realised what they are saying. How easy to say, 'I am going to follow Jesus'! Follow Jesus? If you stop and think what He did, who He was and what He was like, then you will not move a fraction of a centimetre in an attempt to follow Him. You cannot follow Him, and it is only blindness that makes men and women talk about doing so. No, He is the *Saviour,* not the example.

But sin can be much more subtle – and I do want to emphasise this.

There are very subtle denials of this message. The two I have referred to are open and obvious. The case of the Jews is a very obvious one, so is that of all people who think that a bit of morality is the same as Christianity. Those who say that they can make themselves Christians – well, there is no difficulty about them, they are altogether wrong; they have not started seeing the gospel at all! Those who think that being members of churches, and being nice and good and moral and unlike the people you read about in the newspapers and see on the television – those who think that that makes them Christians, well, they so obviously and completely misunderstand the gospel that there is no difficulty. But there are others who are much more subtle, people who do subscribe to the essential Christian doctrines, but who nevertheless do violence to this particular teaching.

What sort of people are they? Let me put first the mystics. What is their teaching? Well, some of the mystics have believed all the great doctrines of the Christian faith with respect to our Lord, His Person and His work, but, having done that, they then put it all on one side and set out to save themselves. They say that what they want is to arrive at the knowledge of God: 'Blessed are the pure in heart: for they shall see God' [*Matt.* 5:8]. So they embark on what is called 'the mystic way'. It is the way of self-denial, the way of trying to find 'the God that is in you', the negative way, 'the dark night of the soul', and so on. Books and manuals have been written about this mystic way, telling you what you have got to do. It will involve, perhaps, a good deal of fasting. It will involve regular prayers at given times, and other acts of self-denial to make you thus die to everything, and die to yourself, until you enter into a completely negative state, and so reach 'the stage of contemplation'. If you read the works of the mystics, you will see what is involved in it all.

And that is a complete denial of all that Paul says here. The mystic is someone who ascends into heaven, or tries to, and attempts to go down into the abyss. Mystics make this tremendous effort. But the answer to them is, 'Say not!' Stop! 'The word is nigh thee, even in thy mouth and in thy heart.' So here there is a condemnation of mysticism, because ultimately the mystic is trusting to his own efforts. Now mystics are very honest and sincere, and they make tremendous efforts. But the answer to them is this: It is all unnecessary. 'Believe on the Lord Jesus Christ, and thou shalt be saved.' Paul and Silas did not say to the Philippian jailor, 'Look here, we will set you off on the mystic way; you can start now but it will involve this, that and the other, and you must go on and on. . .' Not at all! 'Believe, and thou shalt be saved.' And he was, and he rejoiced immediately with all his house. That is 'the word of faith, which we preach'. That is the Christian message.

Then there are others who are as guilty as the mystics. The gospel is always contemporary; and the second error, or misunderstanding, of this text, is, of course, the teaching of the Roman Catholic Church. It was when he discovered their error and saw this, that Martin Luther was saved and was filled with a spirit of rejoicing, and the Protestant Reformation broke forth. The teaching of the Roman Catholic Church has been a denial of these verses that we are examining together, and it is still a denial. The Roman Catholic Church may allow certain parts of the Mass to be said in English, and may make some slight alterations in the liturgy, but it has not changed the doctrine, and is not proposing to do so. I will go further, it cannot do so! It would cease to be the Roman Catholic Church if it did.

What do I mean by that? Well, Paul writes that the 'word of faith, which we preach' says that you need not go up into the heavens to try and get hold of Him, or down into the depths . . . He is with you, He is at hand, He is here. Turn to Him where you are, believe in Him and you are saved. No, says Roman Catholicism, the Lord Jesus Christ is very remote. He is the Lord! He is far away in the glory, so that we need somebody to help us to get to Him. Who can we get? Ah! . . . His mother! Now I am not caricaturing their teaching; that is precisely what it is. They say, 'She is a woman, she is tender, she understands us, and she will have influence with Him. Let us ask her to help us.' You see, they put her between Him and us! He is so far away in the heavens that they banish Him, and say that Mary is necessary first.

So in many Roman Catholic churches you see Mary and, somewhere behind her, there He is on the cross! Or look at their pictures. Very often Jesus is represented as a baby; He is either that or someone who is far removed! Mary is always central and prominent. And this is an utter denial of Paul's teaching. We do not need her. Nor do we need the saints. There is no need to pray to them, or to borrow merit from their works of supererogation. And there is no need for the church, there is no need for a priesthood, there is no need for sacraments! The Roman Church says all these things are essential to salvation. It says that the sacraments of Baptism and the Lord's Supper are absolutely essential. It says His body is in the bread! You have got to eat of Him literally, and the Church alone can administer this sacrament; the priesthood alone can work this miracle.

Not only that, Roman Catholics say the church alone can expound the Scriptures. Nobody else can understand the teaching. You must not say, 'The word is nigh thee, even in thy mouth, and in thy heart'; you must not say that the Scriptures are not difficult. They are so difficult that only the church can expound them – and you must take her tradition in addition to the Bible. You have also got to do penances, and make great sacrifices. And you need the sacrament of extreme unction at the end, otherwise your whole destiny will be doubtful. It is a tremendous problem, it is an awful problem, this problem of salvation! Notice, it is the exact opposite of what the Apostle tells us! That is why we are going into all this so thoroughly.

Do not be misled, dear Christian people, by niceness. Realise what the teaching is, what Roman Catholic doctrine says, and you will see, as Luther saw, that it is a denial of the plain teaching of the Scripture. It had held him in darkness, in bondage and in misery. This 'But!' in verse 8 is not there in their teaching; they do away with it. They make the Christian faith difficult. It is as difficult as the law was.

And to be perfectly fair, let me end by saying that there are those who make it difficult from a purely intellectual standpoint, and this includes many Protestants. I say once more that the most ignorant, the most illiterate, and the most benighted can believe this message, and be saved by it in a second. That is the whole basis of missionary work. What is the point of sending missionaries to remote places if salvation comes from the intellectual apprehension of doctrine? It does not! You are not saved by a knowledge of doctrines! You are saved by the Lord Jesus Christ and what He has done on your behalf. Let us be very careful, therefore, that with a kind of false intellectuali-sation, or intellectualism, we again turn this word that is 'nigh thee, even in thy mouth, and in thy heart', into something extremely difficult, which only the great brain of the theologian can understand.

Now this is the 'beginning' of salvation. This is what the Apostle is dealing with. I know that when we come on to other aspects we need all the ability we have, but even that will not help us without the Holy Spirit. But for this initial step, it does not matter what we are, nor how good our brain, nor how small our brain; it does not matter at all. 'By grace are ye saved through faith; and that not of yourselves: it is the gift of God' [*Eph.* 2:8]. Let us therefore be careful, even as Protestants, that we do not turn this, which is no longer difficult and impossible, into something which *is* difficult and impossible. Let us realise that the word of faith which is preached is a word which is nigh us, and even in our mouth. There is nothing we have to do but believe, as the Philippian jailor did. Let us never forget that 'the common people heard him [Christ] gladly'. Let us never forget what the Apostle says to the Corinthians: 'Ye see your calling, brethren, how that not many wise men . . . are called' [*1 Cor.* 1:26]. Thank God! We do not have to drag Him down or lift Him up. He has done it all! He has come; He has done the work; He has risen again. So that all you and I have to say is,

> *Just as I am, without one plea,*
> *But that Thy blood was shed for me,*
> *And that Thou bidd'st me come to Thee,*
> *O Lamb of God, I come!*
>
> Charlotte Elliott

I do not understand fully – 'Many a conflict, many a doubt'. It does not matter. Go as you are, cast yourself upon Him, and He will receive you. Oh, the tragedy that the Jews were rejecting this and attempting the impossible! How monstrous, how foolish, how blind!

But what of us? The word of the gospel is this:

> *Only believe, and thou shalt see*
> *That Christ is all in all to thee.*
>
> John Samuel Bewley Monsell

'Only believe'! Though you have been at the very jaws of hell, and though you are the vilest of sinners, though you have no intellect, no brain – nothing – believe on the Lord Jesus Christ *now*, and you shall be saved now. That is all! You believe this word. Salvation is by faith! Justification is by faith, and by faith alone.

Eight

*

That if thou shalt confess with thy mouth the Lord Jesus, and shalt believe in thine heart that God hath raised him from the dead, thou shalt be saved. For with the heart man believeth unto righteousness; and with the mouth confession is made unto salvation.   Romans 10:9–10

These verses obviously follow from what has gone before. The Apostle has been holding before us a comparison between an attempt to gain righteousness by the law and that which is obtained by faith. We have seen that he contrasts these two ways in order to show that the first is hopeless because keeping the law is impossible, but that the second way is plain, clear and essentially simple. So Paul's fundamental statement is that salvation is entirely by faith. And 'the word which we preach' – that is, the gospel – is a proclamation of that fact.

Now this, of course, has been the great theme of the entire Epistle. The Apostle announced it at the beginning, in chapter 1:16–17. He is 'not ashamed of the gospel of Christ,' he says, because 'it is the power of God unto salvation to every one that believeth.' And now Paul is really saying that again. He tells us that the only way for anyone to be righteous before God is to believe what God has provided in the Lord Jesus Christ. That is the content of 'the word of faith'. So having stated that as a principle, Paul proceeds to set it out in detail in these two verses that we shall now examine. The first word in verse 9 – 'that' – we can perhaps translate by the word 'because'. By doing so, the 'nearness' of the truth to be believed and confessed is highlighted.

We are, then, once more face to face with one of the great statements of the Christian gospel. Here it is put before us from both the theoretical and the practical standpoints, and as we look at it we shall be testing our own profession. This great statement which we are considering is at one and the same time not only a statement of what gospel preaching is – we are not only reminded of what is to be preached – but also of what is to be believed. It is, therefore, a very thoroughgoing test of whether we do truly believe and of whether we really are in the faith or not. That is the value of those great statements of the gospel which the Apostle gives us here and there in all his Epistles.

In other words, the Apostle Paul is giving us a definition of saving faith. And there is nothing more important than that we should be absolutely clear as to what it really is. The verses can be divided up quite simply. We must consider first of all the *content* of saving faith, and then its *character* because the Apostle's words deal with both aspects quite plainly.

Before we take up the first of these matters, there is a mechanical point which we must deal with. In these two verses Paul reverses the order of what he is saying. In verse 9 confessing with the mouth precedes believing in the heart, whereas it is the other way round in verse 10. But there is no great difficulty about this change. The explanation is as follows.

Verse 9 is written from the standpoint of a man making a statement about himself as a Christian. It begins therefore with confession. Verse 10 adopts the standpoint of how the man is ever able to speak as he does, and so the believing is the thing that comes first. Psalm 116:10 puts it perfectly: 'I believed and therefore have I spoken'. The same is found in the Gospels: 'For out of the abundance of the heart the mouth speaketh' [*Matt.* 12:34].

So having dealt with that, we come to the subject of saving faith and consider its content. We are given a wonderful summary of it here. I venture to suggest that there is perhaps nothing more important for any of us than just this very matter. There is certainly nothing in the realm of the church that is more important in these days, and it therefore becomes equally urgent in the world. Because the world knows nothing, it listens to the preaching of the church, and if the world is confused – as it is – it is because the church to which it is listening is confused. So from every standpoint this is indeed a crucial statement.

You notice that I put the *content* of saving faith as my first heading. This is where this whole subject becomes so relevant at the present time. What is it that Christians believe that makes them Christian? Well, you see at once that it is not some general ideas and notions about life and how it should be lived. It includes that, but only as the outcome of what the Apostle puts before us here.

This is a point at which so many go astray. They think that you can have the implications of the gospel without knowing what the gospel itself is. There are many people, for instance, who are very concerned at present about the moral state of their country, and they feel very strongly – and rightly so – that something must be done about it. But the whole question is this – *what* is to be done about it? The fact that you are concerned about the moral state of your country does not mean that you are of necessity a Christian. *Christian* concern about this and proposals with respect to it are distinctive and special.

One of our troubles today is that people imagine that anyone who is concerned about moral conditions must be a Christian. They have even used this very argument. 'That man,' they say, looking at a political leader, 'is concerned about moral conditions and he is speaking out about them: he must be a Christian.' Well, he may be, but it does not necessarily follow.

No, the content of saving faith is not general ideas about life and moral ideals and behaviour. It includes those things, but when the Apostle is giving us a summary of the content of the Christian faith, that is not how he puts it, and so we must never put it like that either.

Then there is a second negative that we must stress, particularly in this connection, because there are those who say that what makes a person a Christian is experience and nothing else. There was a discussion of this very matter on the television recently and the man who put this point perfectly, it seems to me, was a man who told us that he was not a Christian believer at all but a philosopher. The discussion was on the idea that you must have a new theology in almost every age, an idea about which a notorious book has been written.[1] Now this non-Christian philosopher so rightly put it like this: 'The trouble with this man, this bishop, in his book is that he does not recognise such a thing as objective truth; to him nothing matters but experience.'

And that is what many are teaching. They say that we must not think of God as personal; we must not think of Him as 'up there' or 'out there'. So, what is God? 'Well,' they say, 'God is wherever you find love, or a deep view of life. Whenever you experience something that speaks to you in the depth of your being and makes you think of life and yourself and everything in deep terms, that is God.'

They also say that you do not go to church to find God, but you go out among people who do not believe anything at all, and

[1] J. A. T. Robinson, *Honest to God* (London: SCM Press, 1963).

[91]

suddenly you find that they are kind and gentle to one another and are ready to help one another. Now that, they say, is God, because that is the expression of love, and that expression of love is God. And those people who appreciate this, and who are concerned about it, they are Christians.

So you see that what ultimately decides whether men and women are Christians or not is nothing but experience. There is no objective truth at all. According to this teaching, Christianity is purely a question of your own experience, and your feelings and of all that happens to you. Of course there is nothing new about all this, but I have to refer to it because it is given such publicity, and some people are foolish enough to think that it is new and wonderful, and that modern people can no longer believe what has always been believed, and so on! This experience of yours is your contact with God. That is God – depth! Love! And you will find this in ordinary life, among men and women who may never darken the doors of a place of worship and who do not claim to believe anything in particular. But that, they say, is the essence of Christianity!

Compare all that with what we have here and you will see the contrast. Christian faith has content! Here it is: 'That if thou shalt confess with thy mouth the Lord Jesus, and shalt believe in thine heart that God hath raised him from the dead . . .' – that is it, that is the content – 'thou shalt be saved.' So this modern idea of bringing Christianity up to date is not only not Christianity at all, it is a complete denial of it. It is a denial of the very essence of the Christian faith as it is defined here by this great Apostle, and as it has been defined in the creeds and confessions of the Christian church throughout the centuries. In the past, heretics were condemned by the church and excommunicated. And it is because the church does not do the same thing today, that she is in such a parlous, helpless and useless condition.

So we must put it like this: whatever else the content of the Christian faith may be, it is objective truth. That is the starting point. It is what Paul emphasises. But what is it about? It is about *Jesus*, a person who belongs to history. 'If thou shalt confess with thy mouth the *Lord Jesus* . . .' It is about this Person. So if you describe Christianity without mentioning Him, you are not describing Christianity, whatever else you may be describing. This is almost incredible, is it not? But here we see the wiles of the devil, that people can talk about Christianity and not mention the name of our Lord at all. But He, says Paul, is the very word which we preach; He is the essence of Christian faith; He is the content of our whole position.

So the Christian faith is about this Person, who He is, what happened to Him, and the meaning of it all. That is the content. The Christian faith is centred on the Lord Jesus Christ. It would not be called *Christian* otherwise. He is not incidental to the Christian faith; a helper of it. He is essential to it; there is no Christian faith without Him! Take Him out and you have nothing left. It all depends upon Him and upon Him alone. He is the beginning and the end, the Alpha and the Omega, the first and the last. 'Other foundation can no man lay than that is laid, which is Jesus Christ' [*1 Cor.* 3:11]. There is no other.

Now that is what the Apostle is telling us here, and you notice that he puts two things in particular before us about this Person, Jesus of Nazareth. The first is that He is Lord! And the second is that God raised Him from the dead. Those are the two absolute essentials to the Christian faith. There is no salvation unless we are clear about them. And, of course, when you read the Acts of the Apostles, you find that those are the two things that the Apostles preached at the beginning – 'Jesus and the resurrection' [*Acts* 17:18] – the two things we have here.

The first statement, then, is that 'Jesus is Lord'. We must be careful to observe that though this became a password in the early church, it is infinitely more than that. It is a tremendous, a staggering statement which along with the reference to His resurrection, sums up the whole of the Christian faith.

'The Lord Jesus' – what does that mean? Well, the word translated 'Lord' is used in the Greek translation of the Old Testament to stand for the Hebrew word 'YHWH' (Jehovah)[1] – the name by which God wished to be personally known. We are told in the early chapters of the book of Exodus that God had not previously manifested Himself by this name as He would by means of the deliverance of His people from Egypt. Through the meaning of this name He committed Himself to them as the 'I am that I am' – the covenant keeping God [*Exod.* 6:2–4].

Now the Jews regarded this name of God as being so wonderful, so

---

[1] Old Testament scholars have constructed the word 'YAHWEH' from the consonantal form 'YHWH'. This is no more than an educated guess at how the word was to be pronounced.

glorious, that they were afraid to use it and they avoided doing so by substituting other words. When they came to translate the Hebrew Scriptures into Greek (called the Septuagint translation), they translated *YHWH* by a Greek word meaning 'Lord'. Paul uses that same Greek word in verse 9. So this statement, 'If thou shalt confess with thy mouth the Lord Jesus,' means, 'If thou shalt confess with thy mouth that Jesus is Jehovah [*YHWH*]! Jesus is the Lord God Jehovah!' This means, of course, as we know from the rest of the New Testament, that he is asserting in the strongest manner possible the unique deity of our blessed Lord and Saviour.

Let us analyse this further and consider what this means. The Apostle is saying that those who confess with their mouth that Jesus is Lord, Jehovah, God, and believe that Christ, this Jehovah, has been raised from the dead, they are the men and women who are saved. These are the points, you see, by which we test ourselves. To say that 'Jesus is Lord' is to make a statement about His Person. You are here stating what you believe concerning who He is. You say, 'My faith rests upon Jesus, Jesus of Nazareth, but I say that He is God, He is Jehovah.' This is the Christian confession.

Now the Apostle, of course, has told us this at the very beginning of this Epistle and also at the opening of chapter 9, where he says of Christ that He is over all, 'God blessed for ever'. This is the great statement, of course, of the whole of the New Testament; indeed, it was really written in order to assert and to establish this very point. I think that we often fail to understand many of the things that we are told in it because we forget that. The Gospels and the Epistles were written to establish and confirm the faith of the believers.

False gospels were being written which were saying fantastic and inaccurate things while, ostensibly, teaching what was true about the Lord Jesus Christ. Not only that but the world's religions and philosophies were infiltrating the church. The result was that the believers were disturbed and confused and the message of the church to the world was becoming confused. So these documents which we call the New Testament were primarily written to correct that, to show that the apocryphal Gospels and other writings were false. They were misrepresenting the truth concerning our Lord and His great salvation, and must not be believed.

A classic example of this is the Gospel of John, who wrote in order to make certain to his readers, and to remind them, that Jesus is the Son of God, and that 'believing ye might have life through his name'

[*John* 20:31]. Then in his First Epistle, he wrote to prove that our Lord was also truly man.

But of course the most wonderful statement about Christ is to be found in the Epistle to the Colossians, in the first chapter. That teaching was very important at the time, and it is equally so today. This idea that the New Testament is out of date is just sheer rubbish! What is the real problem in the Christian church today? I would say it is the Colossian heresy. False teachers had been going round saying, 'Oh yes, Jesus was very wonderful; He is a great help in coming to God. But He is not the only one. There are all sorts of angels and supernatural powers that come between us and God and help us to get to Him . . .'

Not only that, but they taught a kind of mysticism, exactly as is being taught today. There was, therefore, a danger that the people in Colosse could be in a great muddle with regard to the gospel which they believed. So the Apostle wrote to them. He begins by thanking God for their faith and love and refers to 'the word of the truth of the gospel', implying that there are *false* gospels. In the second chapter he becomes quite specific, warning Christians against being misled. 'Beware,' he writes 'lest any man spoil you through philosophy and vain deceit, after the tradition of men, after the rudiments of the world, and not after Christ.'

Now that is so relevant to the situation today. People are saying, 'Well, of course, we are in the twentieth century and we are in the age of the splitting of the atom. We now think in scientific terms and categories. People no longer believe in the supernatural or the miraculous and even the whole notion of personality is vague. We must not speak like that any longer; we must restate the Christian faith in terms that modern men and women can follow.'

But that is just philosophy. Let us remind ourselves that Paul states the truth about the Lord. He presents Him as the One 'In whom we have redemption through his blood, even the forgiveness of sins' [*Col.* 1:14]. So who is He? He is 'the image [the exact likeness] of the invisible God' – that is who Jesus is. You see, Christianity is all about this Person. It is not about that nice feeling you get; it is not about a sense of love, or kindness, or goodness; it is not your objection to the immorality of others and your desire to do good.

No, it is about this Person by whom 'all things' were 'created, that are in heaven, and that are in earth, visible and invisible, whether they be thrones, or dominions, or principalities, or powers'; and for whom 'all things were created'. 'He is before all things, and by him all things consist. And he is the head of the body, the church: who is the beginning, the firstborn from the dead; that in all things he might have the preeminence. For it pleased the Father that in him should all fulness dwell' [*Col.* 1:16–19].

What a statement! What does it mean? Before we come to its interpretation, I want you to carry in your minds a similar statement in the first three verses of the Epistle to the Hebrews. By the way, why was that letter ever written? Before you read a book of the Bible always ask the question: Why did the author ever write it? How can you find out? You can find out by reading what he wrote. Listen to him: 'God, who at sundry times and in divers manners spake in time past unto the fathers by the prophets, hath in these last days spoken unto us by his Son, whom he hath appointed heir of all things, by whom also he made the worlds; who being the brightness of his glory, and the express image of his person, and upholding all things by the word of his power, when he had by himself purged our sins, sat down on the right hand of the Majesty on high.' Then he goes on to show our Lord's superiority to the angels.

Why did he write this? In a way, he has already given you the answer by plunging straight into a statement about the Lord. He was writing to Hebrew Christians, people who were beginning to become shaky in their faith. People had said to them, 'You were fools. You left your old religion, the religion of your fathers which has stood the test of centuries, you left all that and believed this new teaching about this Jesus . . .' And they were being shaken. So this man wrote to say, in effect, 'Your whole trouble is due to the fact that you do not realise, as you should, who this Jesus is.' So he makes his declaration at the beginning. He says: He is God's Son. He is, 'the brightness of his glory, and the express image of his person'. That is precisely why he wrote his letter. Those Hebrew Christians were wondering whether Christianity was true. Why? Because they were not clear about the greatness of Jesus Christ. This is the great essential. There is no Christianity without Him.

Those, then, are the major New Testament statements; let me try to summarise them. We are told by the Apostle in Colossians 1:15 that He is 'the firstborn of every creature' – which means that He has the primacy over all created things. A better translation would be, 'born before all created things'. In other words, He was not created but was born before anything was created. He is the One who has priority over all creation. Now it must mean that, because Paul goes on to say in the sixteenth verse, 'By him were all things created.' He is the 'firstborn' before all creation. He is the only One who is born of God; God's only begotten Son.

Then it is through Him that everything was created. We find that in the first chapter of John's Gospel where 'The Word' implies priority and sovereignty. He existed before all created things, and everything was therefore created by Him and through Him.

And then there is that tremendous statement in the nineteenth verse of Colossians 1: 'It pleased the Father that in him should all fulness dwell.' The sum total of all the divine attributes and powers are in Him: 'all the fulness'. You also find it in Colossians 2:9: 'In him dwelleth all the fulness of the Godhead bodily.' It is all there. Jesus is Lord! This Jesus! That is what we believe. This is the confession that we make with our mouth.

But, you notice, this lordship includes other things also. In His essence He is the eternal Son of God. But look at His relation to the universe. This helps you to understand His lordship: 'By him were all things created . . .' We find the same in John 1:3, and in Hebrews 1:2. And in Colossians 1:16 we read: 'For by him were all things created, that are in heaven, and that are in earth, visible and invisible, whether they be thrones, or dominions, or principalities, or powers: all things were created by him, and for him.' There is nothing in existence that was not created by Him – not a single thing. 'Without him was not any thing made that was made.' And in the first chapter of Hebrews the writer is concerned to show that even the angels in all their glory are but created beings, created by Him. He is above them all and over them all; they are but His 'ministering spirits'.

And the Apostle puts it still more plainly in Colossians 1. He says: I do not care whether they are in heaven, whether they are on earth, whether they are visible or invisible, spiritual or material; thrones, dominions, principalities, powers, everything has been created by Him, and, still more interesting, 'for him'. We can put it like this: this universe, the whole cosmos, is the Father's gift to His only begotten Son. It was created for Him, for His pleasure, that He might be Lord over it all. 'Jesus is Lord'!

But then there is this other statement, which is still a part of the definition of his lordship. 'By him all things consist' [*Col.* 1:17], which means that He holds everything together. Now Hebrews 1:3 is a good commentary on this: 'upholding all things by the word of his power.' Here Paul uses the word *consist*, which is a most interesting term. It means that everything coheres, if you like, everything hangs together. It is a way of expressing unity and solidarity. It indicates order and arrangement. What makes this universe a cosmos, rather than a chaos, is that the Lord Jesus Christ is holding it all together.

Now we notice the order and arrangement in nature, do we not? We see cause and effect. The astounding thing is that everything does hold together, and what we are told is that it is He who does it. If he stopped, everything would disintegrate. There would be an end, chaos. He – Jesus, this Jesus of Nazareth – He is Lord, and a part of His lordship is that He is the principal, as it were; it is His power that holds everything together.

And another word which we must use is this: He is the *heir* of all things. It is again found in Hebrews 1: God 'hath in these last days spoken unto us by his Son, whom he hath appointed heir of all things' [*Heb.* 1:2]. This is a part of His lordship. The heir is the one who will enter into an inheritance; well, He is the heir of the whole universe. Jesus is Lord! That means, remember, that this whole universe belongs to Him; the Father has given it to Him.

And the last thing is this – and it is something very special, it is an important aspect of His lordship – it is through Him and by Him that God is going to restore this whole cosmos to the condition in which it was originally, when God made it, and from which it has fallen as the result of sin. This is taught in Ephesians 1:9–10: 'Having made known unto us the mystery of his will, according to his good pleasure which he hath purposed in himself' – then notice this – 'That in the dispensation of the fulness of times he might gather together in one all things in Christ, both which are in heaven, and which are on earth; even in him.' So whatever way you look at the universe and the cosmos, including men and women, it all speaks of the Lordship of Jesus. It is through Him and by means of Him that God will again 'head up' everything in a great eternal unity.

The effect of sin has been disintegration, differences, quarrels, wars, bloodshed, rivalries, all that we see so plainly in this modern world. But God had made the universe perfect, it was paradise, there were none of these warring elements, everything was one, it was a glorious unity, and everything ministered to the glory of God. And the whole message of the gospel – 'the word of faith, which we preach' – says primarily this: that God is going to restore again this great unity to the whole cosmos, and He has done it and He is going to do it finally and fully through this Person, Jesus, so that He is to be 'the Lord' over all in this absolute sense. Then this glorified, unified cosmos He will hand back in its utter perfection to God the Father, who made it for Him and gave it to Him; and made it in Him and through Him.

What a subject! Jesus is Lord! That is what we believe, that is what we are here for, that is what we proclaim to the world. There is no Christianity apart from this. But this is only the beginning – I have simply stated it in its ultimate sense. We must go on to work it out still more fully and in yet greater detail.

Nine

*

That if thou shalt confess with thy mouth the Lord Jesus, and shalt believe in thine heart that God hath raised him from the dead, thou shalt be saved. For with the heart man believeth unto righteousness; and with the mouth confession is made unto salvation.   Romans 10:9–10

We have described these verses as a definition of saving faith. Nothing is more important than that we should be clear about this, for we are undoubtedly having to fight all over again the great struggle of four hundred years ago, fought by Martin Luther and those who came after him, for the doctrine of justification by faith only. It is being questioned on all sides, and I believe the whole state of the Christian church at the present time is very largely due to that. There is no chapter that is more relevant to the present condition, therefore, than this tenth chapter of Romans. With these things in mind, we have divided the matter up like this: the first heading is the *content* of saving faith. We will go on to consider its *nature*, and finally the *proof* of it.

So we are looking now at the content of this faith, and I must emphasise again that the Scripture always starts with truth, not experience. The first thing that Christians must therefore be clear about is what they believe. Many have gone astray at this point and have tended to put experience first. I will never forget the occasion back in 1935 when I had the privilege of addressing a Summer School of ministers. We met together in an Oxford college, and after I had preached on the Monday night, we had a discussion later on in the evening. I remember the discussion very well because there were a number of evangelical men there and also a number who were not. Those who were not evangelical were arguing in terms of science and philosophy and so on while the evangelicals were tending to answer by saying: 'Well, say what you like, you cannot rob me of my experience,' and they thought that that was a wonderful defence of the Christian faith!

To their astonishment, I had to correct them quite as much as the others. I tried to point out to them that if you once take up the position that truth itself does not matter, and that you do not care what science or philosophy may say, or indeed what anything else says, because nothing can rob you of your experience, then how are you going to answer the people who belong to the cults? They say exactly the same thing. That is what the Christian Scientist says: 'I am not interested in your arguments, all I know is that since I have believed this I have been absolutely different. I have found happiness where I used to be miserable; I have power where I used to have no power; and I have physical healing where I used to be ill.' Experience! If that is the only argument there is no answer to the cults.

But, still more serious, there is no answer to the psychologists. They are very ready indeed to explain away your experience. No, we must put the truth first, and experience only comes second. Our position does not depend upon what has happened to us, nor upon our feelings; it depends upon certain great objective truths and facts. So the Apostle here reminds us of this by saying, 'If thou shalt confess' – not that you have a changed life or that you are a different person from the person you were, but – 'If thou shalt confess with thy mouth the Lord Jesus, and shalt believe in thine heart that God hath raised him from the dead, thou shalt be saved.'

So, you see, our position is not based upon our experience or ideas about moral improvement. Our whole position depends upon this one Person, this historic Person, Jesus of Nazareth, and what He has done on our behalf. Our faith is centred on Him. The whole content of the apostolic message was concerning Him. The Apostles preached, as we have seen, 'Jesus and the resurrection'. They did not just go round the world telling people their experiences. They preached that Jesus is Lord and they preached the great fact of the resurrection. These are the two elements in the content of saving faith.

The Christian position is that Jesus is the Lord. We have started to consider that and seen that it is not just a form of words. It is one of the most comprehensive statements that you can ever find, and I am just trying to draw out some of its implications.

What, then, do we find further? Having looked at this in terms of the eternal deity and universal sovereignty of Jesus, we must go on to show that this statement necessarily involves the doctrines of the incarnation and the virgin birth. The word *Jesus* at once, as it were, brings before us a human – a baby in a manger in Bethlehem; a boy in a carpenter's shop in Nazareth and in the temple at Jerusalem; and a young man who, about thirty years of age, begins to preach – and what the Christian believes is that this Jesus is the Lord!

So you see the implications of this? Everybody today is amazed at the power that is held in a little atom. We used to be taught that there was nothing smaller than the atom, that it was the ultimate division of matter. Of course, we know now that that is not true, but that the atom holds within it the proton, the neutron and the electron and so on. They are there in a tremendous tension, held together by all this nuclear force – in an atom!

Now it is exactly the same, only infinitely more so, with regard to this statement that Jesus is the Lord, the Lord of glory, the eternal Son of God. That baby in His smallness and helplessness contains all the fulness of the Godhead bodily. That is what is involved in this statement. But we are interested now particularly in the fact that if I say that Jesus is Lord, I am of necessity committing myself to the whole doctrine of the incarnation. The first summary of this is in Philippians 2:5–8, which says, 'Christ Jesus: who, being in the form of God, thought it not robbery to be equal with God: but made himself of no reputation, and took upon him the form of a servant, and was made in the likeness of men: and being found in fashion as a man, he humbled himself, and became obedient unto death, even the death of the cross.'

In the Gospels we have the facts recorded about His birth. Remember that angels informed Mary and Joseph in advance of it and the shepherds after it had taken place. The essence of what they said and sang was 'Jesus is Lord'. That was their proclamation. Then wise men came from the east and in effect did exactly the same thing. You see, these things in the Gospels are not merely for the children, they are tremendous historical and theological statements written for our faith and to establish us in the truth. That is why these things are all written, as Luke tells us at the beginning of his Gospel.

But this not only commits us to a doctrine of incarnation, it also includes the doctrine of the virgin birth, which is so scoffed at in these days. But how can you explain the passage in Luke 1:26–38, except in terms of the virgin birth? Why did Luke ever take the trouble to write that? Why did the angel speak of 'that holy thing which shall be born of thee', and say, 'The Holy Ghost shall come upon thee' [*Luke* 2:35]? 'Conceived of the Holy Ghost, born of the Virgin Mary,' says that old creed. Rightly so! That is the scriptural position.

Then people say, 'Ah, but there is no reference to the virgin birth in the Epistles'. Of course there is not! It is not mentioned because they all believed it. The Epistles were generally written to deal with problems and difficulties – and the virginal conception was not one of them. Even so in Romans 8:3 the Apostle Paul says Jesus was born 'in the likeness of sinful flesh'. And earlier, when we dealt with that,[1] we spent time in elaborating that point. That is no accidental statement. The Apostle is there saying that our Lord was not born like everybody else. Since the fall of Adam human nature has been polluted. But Jesus was merely *in the likeness* of sinful flesh. There was no sin in Him: 'that holy thing that shall be born of thee', said the angel Gabriel.

So to say that 'Jesus is Lord' is to say that we believe in the incarnation and in the virgin birth. It is all involved here. Paul's words are a summary and are meant to be expanded; we are meant to see the fulness of the content. So when we say, 'Jesus is Lord', we mean that Jesus Christ of Nazareth is God and man! We say with the Apostle Paul, 'Great is the mystery of godliness: God was manifest in the flesh' [*1 Tim.* 3:16]; and with John 'The Word was made flesh, and dwelt among us' [*John* 1:14]. We must not just utter these words without realising what we are confessing.

We now move on to proofs of His Lordship that were given while He was here in this world in order to fill this out and show how important this is. We can classify the evidence as follows. First, Jesus Himself claimed to be the Lord and did so many times. It is almost impossible to select examples of this because there are so many of them. Here are a few. He said to the Jews, 'You are from beneath; I am from above' and 'Before Abraham was, I am' [*John* 8:53, 58]. In speaking like this, He was saying: I am the Lord. I am Jesus but I am also the Lord of glory. You and I are essentially different.

But take a further statement of His. At the end of Matthew 11 we read, 'No man knoweth the Son, but the Father; neither knoweth any man the Father, save the Son, and he to whomsoever the Son will reveal him' [*Matt.* 11:25–27].

Now Christians believe all this, they accept it. They come to the

[1] See *An Exposition of Chapters 7:1 – 8:4: The Law, Its Functions and Limits*, 1973.

gospel and submit themselves to it. You cannot be a Christian without doing that. What do you know about Jesus Christ apart from what you read in the Gospels? So how can we sit in judgment upon them and say, 'I believe this but not that'? Doing that is no longer to believe that Jesus is Lord! You have made yourself the Lord. You look down upon Him, correct Him, say that He was a child of his age, and so on, and that He made mistakes. He is no longer Lord to you. But those who say, 'Jesus is Lord' are those who have entirely submitted to this evidence that is given us – His own claim.

The second line of evidence is His whole manner of teaching. Though He was not a Pharisee and never had any training in their schools, He did not hesitate to say, 'Ye have heard that it was said by them of old time . . . but I say unto you' [*Matt.* 5:21–22]. He was saying: I am Lord. I know what I am talking about. I am the authority. And of course the people realised that. They acknowledged that they were being spoken to with an authority which the scribes and Pharisees did not possess [*Matt.* 7:28–29]. His whole manner of teaching proclaimed His lordship.

Thirdly, his miracles confirm that He is Lord. John, in his Gospel, always refers to them as 'signs', for that reason. But there are many people today who misunderstand the whole purpose of the miracles and think they were merely expressions of His goodwill. They were that, but that was not really their purpose. Our Lord performed His miracles primarily in order to say that He was the Lord. We have absolute proof of this in John 14: 'Believe me,' said our Lord, 'that I am in the Father, and the Father in me: or else believe me for the very works' sake' [*John* 14:11]. He said: If you do not believe my words, look at the works.

He used that argument when He sent an answer to John the Baptist's inquiry. He pointed to His works to prove that He was the 'coming one' [*Matt.* 11:3–5]. It had been prophesied that when the Messiah came, He would attest the fact that He was the Son of God and the Messiah by doing such mighty signs – 'Then shall the lame man leap as an hart' [*Isa.* 35:6] and so on. 'That time has come,' said our Lord in effect. 'Go and tell John what you have seen.' He had not come primarily to heal people's sicknesses. He did do that, but He performed healing miracles mainly that they should be proofs that He is the Son of God, who has control over all things.

We must also of course mention His power over evil spirits in this connection. He was able to cast out demons and so showed His mastery over the powers of Satan, hell and evil. And He was also able to control the natural elements. All this is indicative of the fact that He is, in truth, the Lord of glory. We cannot play fast and loose with the four Gospels. There is your evidence to prove that Jesus is indeed Lord. That is the first element in the content of saving faith.

We must now consider the second element, which is this: '. . . and shalt believe in thine heart that God hath raised him from the dead.' What are we to make of this? What is the content here? First, of course, there is the fact of the resurrection. This is absolutely vital at this present time, as it is being denied on all sides in the Christian church. The Apostle means the literal physical resurrection. He does not mean that you just believe that the spirit of Jesus continues, that He can still influence and help us and that there is great value in His memory and His teaching. No, what the New Testament teaches is that our Lord came out of the grave literally, in the body, and that the tomb was empty.

The New Testament takes great trouble to tell us this. That is why we have those Gospel accounts of people going to the tomb and finding it empty, and two of the disciples even going into it. We are told also that the grave clothes were in one place and the napkin around His head in another. The body *had been* there but was not any longer. The Gospels go out of their way to emphasise the physical aspect, the literal account, the historical fact of the resurrection.

And of course this is not confined to the Gospels. You find exactly the same thing stated in the Acts of the Apostles. The Apostles claimed to be witnesses of these things; they saw Him dying on the cross; they saw His body taken down; they saw it laid in the tomb; and then they saw the empty tomb. They were witnesses of the fact of the physical resurrection; of the fact that the Lord came up out of the tomb in the body, the same body, though changed, in which He went into it. Matthew's Gospel even takes the trouble to tell us that the Jewish authorities were so annoyed that they bribed the Roman soldiers to say that the body had been stolen – they even went as far as that. Yet we are confronted today by people who claim to be Christians, and some who speak in the name of Christ, who deny the physical resurrection. But here the Apostle says that a Christian is someone who believes in his heart that this is an actual absolute fact.

Now we must recognise the relevance of all this. There were people in the early church also who denied these things; there is nothing new about the so-called 'Southbank theology'. It is so old that one is weary of having to go on correcting it. It is so old and yet these theologians think that they are so new and up to date when they say, 'Modern man has come of age. Post-war man, the atomic man, this new man with all his wonderful scientific knowledge, does not believe in the literal, physical resurrection!' But Paul writing to Timothy says, 'Remember that Jesus Christ of the seed of David was raised from the dead according to my gospel' [2 Tim. 2:8]. Then he goes on to say that there are people such as Hymenaeus and Philetus who have erred concerning the truth: 'saying that the resurrection is past already; and overthrow the faith of some' [2 Tim. 2:17–18].

The Apostles were primarily witnesses to the resurrection. It was pivotal, absolutely crucial. There would never have been a Christian church but for the resurrection. The Gospels tell us that the Apostles were disappointed and saddened. They felt utterly hopeless and they would never have been Christian preachers were it not that He had risen and appeared to them and given them absolute proof. And so the Apostle Paul declares it in the opening verses of 1 Corinthians 15 and goes on working it out throughout the length of that great and glorious chapter, dealing even with the way in which the body is raised. He asserts: 'If Christ be not raised, your faith is vain; ye are yet in your sins'. So the first thing that Christians proclaim when they say they believe that God raised Jesus from the dead is a fact of history – that there was an empty tomb because the Son of God, who had died on the cross, had risen.

But, of course, you do not stop at that. For if that is a fact, what is its significance? Why should you believe in your heart that God has raised Him from the dead? And here is the answer. First, it proves who He is. The Apostle has already told us at the beginning of the Epistle that his preaching was concerning God's Son, Jesus Christ our Lord, 'which was made of the seed of David according to the flesh; and declared to be the Son of God with power' – the Lord, in other words – 'according to the spirit of holiness, by the resurrection from the dead' [Rom. 1:3–4]. The resurrection of Christ is a proclamation of the fact that He is the Lord, the eternal Son of God.

Now the New Testament gives us further evidence to prove the same thing. Take the Apostle Peter preaching on the day of Pentecost in Jerusalem. He says that God in raising Jesus from the dead had 'loosed the pains of death: because it was not possible that he should be holden of it' [Acts 2:23–24]. Why not? Because He is the Lord! Peter then went on to quote from the sixteenth Psalm, indicating that it was fulfilled in Christ [vv 25–28]. He then expounded all this further in verses 29 to 37.

There it all is, as plain as can be. Remember that the first Christian sermon was a declaration of the resurrection. It pointed out that the resurrection was a proclamation that the same Jesus, who had died on the cross and had been buried, was 'the Lord'! His Lordship was proved by the fact that His soul and His body were not allowed to see corruption in the grave. But Peter, like every good preacher, was not content with saying a thing once, he went on saying it. And, you know, no one should ever enter a Christian pulpit without saying these things.

Furthermore, if we ever get tired of hearing these things we can be quite sure that we have either never been Christians or we are in a state of serious backsliding. Is there somebody who has been thinking, 'But I know all this; I was taught it in Sunday School when I was a child'? Were you? Did you realise what you were taught? Did you realise the significance of the facts that you claim to believe? There is something wrong with us – we are very poor Christians – if we can sit and listen to these glorious truths without being moved to the depth of our beings. When we get to heaven we shall spend our time there in praising Him, and doing so for these very things that we are now considering.

So pay attention to Peter. He goes over it again some time later, putting it in glorious paradoxes and saying, 'ye denied the Holy One and the Just, and desired a murderer to be granted unto you; and killed the Prince of life, whom God hath raised from the dead; whereof we are witnesses' [*Acts* 3:12–15]. Are you interested in paradoxes? There it is: You 'killed the Prince of life', the Lord of life, the originator of life, 'whom God hath raised from the dead'.

And of course all the other Apostles preached the same message. When the Apostle Paul preached the gospel in Athens, the people said, 'What will this babbler say? He seemeth to be a setter forth of strange gods: because he preached unto them Jesus, and the resurrection' [*Acts* 17:18]. This was the content of apostolic preaching. It started with this in order to establish once and for ever that Jesus is the Lord. The ultimate proof is the resurrection. Here is this unique event, here is the first who has risen from the dead, and this proclaims Jesus to be the Lord of glory!

Ten

> *That if thou shalt confess with thy mouth the Lord Jesus, and shalt believe in thine heart that God hath raised him from the dead, thou shalt be saved. For with the heart man believeth unto righteousness; and with the mouth confession is made unto salvation.* Romans 10:9–10

We continue with our consideration of the content of saving faith and let me emphasise again how important it is that we should realise its richness. We have seen that it has two divisions: the first is 'the Lord Jesus', which means that 'Jesus is Lord' and we have considered that. We have begun to look at its second part, which is: 'that God hath raised him from the dead'. We have seen that we must believe and confess the fact of the resurrection, that our Lord rose in the body from the tomb and that He was seen by chosen witnesses. Paul says, in 1 Corinthians 15, that there is no gospel apart from this, and it is quite clear that there never would have been.

Having looked at the fact of the resurrection, we are beginning to draw out its implications. The one we have just dealt with is that the resurrection proves who Jesus is. It is the final proof that He is the Lord.

The second point about the resurrection is that it explains to us why Jesus died. Now this, you see, is how His death comes in. The fact that His death is not explicitly mentioned in this confession of faith is therefore not significant. By asserting that Jesus is the Lord and that He has been raised from the dead, Paul is including everything that happened from the incarnation to the ascension. But it is interesting that he sets it out in this particular way.

There is an obvious problem here. If we are told that Jesus of Nazareth is the second Person in the blessed Holy Trinity, that He is Jehovah, the eternal Son, and that this is proved by the resurrection, then the obvious question that immediately arises is this: Why did He ever die? That is the right question to ask at this particular point, and it is, of course, the best way of all of approaching the doctrine of the death of the Lord Jesus Christ.

One of the greatest classics ever written on this doctrine was by a man called Anselm who lived in England in the eleventh century. He wrote in Latin and gave a very interesting title to his book. It was *Cur Deus Homo?* which means 'Why [did] God [become] man?' Although his book was about the atoning death of the Lord, that was its title. I am simply putting the question in a different form by asking 'Why did He die if He is the Lord of glory?'

Now we have evidence in the Gospels themselves that this was a stumbling block to His disciples, the men who ultimately became the Apostles. The classic passage on this is in Matthew 16 in the famous incident at Caesarea Philippi when our Lord asked the question: 'Whom do men say that I the Son of man am?' [v. 13]. Peter made his great confession, 'Thou art the Christ, the Son of the living God,' and our Lord declared him to have been blessed with revelation from God.

But then the record informs us that our Lord proceeded to tell them something about His approaching death, and immediately Peter and the rest got into trouble. Having made the confession that Jesus was the Christ, the Son of the living God, Peter found the idea of His dying an utter contradiction and therefore impossible to entertain. So Peter stumbled at this and our Lord had to rebuke him. But it was not only Peter who stumbled, all the disciples did.

The same sort of thing was said by the people at the foot of the cross, you remember. They said: 'Save thyself, and come down from the cross . . . He saved others; himself he cannot save' [*Mark* 15:29–31]. What they meant was: If you are who you claim to be, why are you dying like that in weakness?

It was a right question to ask, although in asking it, they exposed their ignorance, as had the disciples. Still, it is always the right way to approach this whole doctrine of the death of our Lord. Here He is, proved to be the Son of God by the resurrection from the dead, but that raises, inevitably and acutely, the question: Why then did He ever die? So this confession that God has raised Him from the dead implicitly involves the whole matter of the death of our Lord.

The answer to this question is, of course, given to us quite plainly in the Gospels and the remainder of the New Testament. In a very real sense, you see, what we are looking at in these two verses is a complete synopsis of the first Christian preaching. This is what the Apostles themselves preached and it is the only gospel today. All the philosophical talk given in the name of Christianity which is so rampant today has nothing to do with the faith at all. These verses are Christianity according to the New Testament and we have no other standard, no other authority whatsoever.

Why then did He die if He is the Lord of glory? Our Lord Himself answered this question. He said quite deliberately and plainly that if He had wanted to, He could have avoided death, commanding more than twelve legions of angels to deliver Him [*Matt.* 26:53]. Nevertheless, we are told that 'he set his face stedfastly to go to Jerusalem' [*Luke* 9:51]. He knew exactly what was going to happen. Those followers of His, and others, tried to dissuade Him on more than one occasion. He said once 'it cannot be that a prophet perish out of Jerusalem' [*Luke* 13:31–33].

So, going deliberately to the death of the cross, which He could have avoided, why did He do so? Why did He deliberately go to Jerusalem? Why did He tell His followers, when they pulled out a sword to defend Him, to put it back in the scabbard? Again, there is no difficulty about the answer. You see, people get into trouble because they will not believe the Scriptures. If you believe the Scriptures, there is no difficulty; but if you begin to say that you do not accept them, that they are just symbols, that they were written by people with primitive notions and that we now know so much more and have our great philosophies etc., then you are going to be in great trouble. You will have a Christianity of your own making: one which has nothing at all to do with the New Testament and so is not Christianity at all.

But if you come with simplicity and a childlike faith, realising that you know nothing and regarding the Scriptures as the revelation of God, there is no problem. Our Lord gave His own answer. Why did He set His face steadfastly? In His own words, it was because: 'The Son of man came not to be ministered unto, but to minister, and to give his life a ransom for many.' He said that quite explicitly, and it is recorded very carefully for us in Matthew 20:28 and in Mark 10:45 – his own specific statement.

Not only that, he made other statements, for instance, in John 12:23–33 and 17:12. But above and beyond everything else, and as He was dying on the cross, He said, 'It is finished' [*John* 19:30]. There on the cross 'the hour had come' when He finished 'the work the

Father had given him to do'. It is all so plainly expressed and so I warn you against these false teachings that deny all this glorious doctrine and leave you with nothing but philosophy and human suppositions and theories.

After His resurrection, our Lord Himself gave an exposition of His death and it is most interesting and important from the standpoint of Paul's statement in Romans 10:9. The disciples, as we have seen, could accept His teaching about His being the Lord and the Christ, but they could not see that it was compatible with His dying, apparently defeated by His enemies. So after the resurrection, when they realised afresh who He was, our Lord explained it to them.

Indeed, He even did so to two of them before they realised who was with them, as they walked on the road to Emmaus [*Luke* 24]. They were crestfallen, disappointed and dejected. They referred to the death of our Lord like this: 'But we trusted that it had been he which should have redeemed Israel.' They were saying, in effect, 'That is what we believed when we listened to Him and saw His miracles. But we realise now that we were wrong because if He had really been the Messiah, He would not have been killed. He would have conquered all His enemies and we would be the greatest people on the face of the earth. We trusted, we hoped, we were quite sure – but we have been all wrong. He died and they have buried Him in a grave.'

Then our Lord began to reprove their unbelief and to correct their thinking. He connected His messiahship and death with His being glorified and explained it all by means of the Old Testament Scriptures. He then did the same in Jerusalem to the assembled disciples. He showed them all that He had come into the world in order to die.

It is not surprising, therefore, to find that, in their preaching, recorded in the book of Acts, the Apostles did the same as Jesus had taught them in the days between His resurrection and ascension. We see the pattern in Peter's sermon in Jerusalem on the day of Pentecost [*Acts* 2] and in Paul's teaching in Thessalonica [*Acts* 17:2–4]. Of course, what we have there (and elsewhere) is but a synopsis of his teaching on each occasion. People often fail to realise that Paul took a long time to preach that message (see also Acts 20). Christians today should expand these summaries in order to discover the riches in their content.

The same is found in the rest of the New Testament. Paul reviews his ministry in Corinth in terms of his determination, in accord with the Lord's appearing to him on the road to Damascus and the Old

Testament Scriptures, to give priority to 'Jesus Christ and him crucified' [*1 Cor.* 2:2] – who 'died for our sins . . . was buried and on the third day rose again . . . and appeared' to many [*1 Cor.* 15:3–8]. The Apostle Peter stressed the same truths [*1 Pet.* 1:18–23]. They are also emphasised in 1 John 1:7–9; Hebrews 2:9 and Revelation 1:5.

The essence of the gospel therefore is those two things: that Christ died for our sins and that He rose again from the dead. All this is a fulfilment of all the prophecies of the Old Testament. In other words, if we do not believe that Jesus is the Lord, if we do not believe that He had to die before we could be saved, we are not Christians. If we do not believe in the resurrection we cannot be Christians. These are the first principles without which there is no such thing as Christianity at all.

To me it is nothing short of tragic that one has to go on saying these things, but scarcely a day passes without my either reading a book or a review of a book in which I find all this completely denied, and that in the name of the Christian church. We should thank God for these verses in Romans 10, because we are reminded here of the things without which we cannot be saved. You have got to keep these things in memory, says the Apostle in 1 Corinthians 15:2. If you have gone back on this, he says, there was no value in your belief, so-called; this is the thing that is absolutely essential. And notice that phrase: 'according to the scriptures' [*1 Cor.* 15:3]. It is most important. The Bible is one. The whole of the Old Testament predicts the events of the New Testament. Here is a unity, and you cannot shed your Old Testament; you need it all.

So then, when the Apostle tells us here that the second great element in the content of saving faith is the belief that God has raised Jesus from the dead, he is bringing us face to face with the doctrine of the atonement. It is important for us to realise that 'Jesus is Lord' does not mean that His influence is still persisting. No! The moment you begin to examine what, on the surface, looks such a simple statement, you see that it contains the essence of all Christian doctrine, and at the very centre is this tremendous, crucial doctrine of the death of Christ and the atonement, the doctrine that He is our substitute, that He is 'the lamb of God that taketh away the sin of the world'.

We have, in our own way, been putting Anselm's question, 'Cur Deus Homo?' This is why God became man, and this is why the God-Man died. It is the fulfilment of everything that God had promised throughout the whole of the Old Testament period. So, you see, you are subscribing here to the doctrine of the atonement. You say that you believe that? Well, that in turn will involve you in other doctrines, the doctrine of sin, the doctrine of the Fall, the doctrine of the wrath of God upon sin and of the truthfulness of the Scriptures.

I say this so often, and I am constrained to say it again – I cannot understand the type of Christian who dislikes doctrine. How do you live? What do you do with your mind? Do you never ask any questions? You say, 'But I am a simple person. I am told that if I believe on the Lord Jesus Christ, I am saved. I have said I believe that, therefore I am saved. Is anything more necessary?' But, my dear friend, do you not want to ask questions? Do you not want to ask who is this Lord Jesus Christ? What does it mean that I need to be saved? How does He save me?

And the moment you ask those questions, you are asking for doctrine, for an explanation, because doctrine is nothing but the biblical answer to our questions. Here we have the explanations given to us by the Spirit of God through His servants. So you are given an explanation of these truths, and you are meant to have it. You have no right to say, 'I am just a simple person, I am not interested in doctrine.' You are thereby saying that you are not interested in the Bible, for the Bible is full of doctrine; the Bible answers our questions. God is so gracious that He even asks them for us and then answers them.

And if you are not interested in these mighty questions, I do not know what sort of Christian you are. Christians long to know everything that they possibly can about this blessed Person and what He has done for them. You will never love Him truly unless you do. And it is only as you have an understanding of these things that you realise what He has done for you and why He did it. So you cannot come face to face with this doctrine of His death upon the cross as a substitution for our sins, without saying, 'What does that tell me about myself?' The moment you say, 'Jesus is the Lord,' and, 'God raised him from the dead,' you are asking, 'But why was He ever in this world and why did all this happen to Him?' And the answer is: It is all because of what is true about you.

Then that brings you to this question, 'What, then, is true about me?' The Bible answers that too, and it is the Bible alone that answers it. What is true about us? The answer is that we are all fallen creatures. That in turn raises further questions: How are we fallen? Have we always been like that? That sends you back to the beginning of

Genesis, because you have then got to ask: What is man? Are we struggling, wearily, to go upwards? Is that it? Are we living as we are, in the moral muddle and mess that the world is in, because we are just at one particular stage in the process of evolution and we have not gone on as far as we should – is that it? Or is there another explanation?

And, you see, there is another explanation: man has fallen, everybody has fallen; it is true of the whole human race. So you come to the biblical doctrine of man: men and women in a state of sin, alienated from God, under the condemnation of God's holy law, and under the wrath of God.

The Apostle states this at the very commencement of his teaching. In Romans 1:16, when he comes to grips with his subject, after his preliminary salutations, Paul says, 'I am not ashamed of the gospel of Christ' – indeed, he says, he glories in it, he exults in it. Why? Because 'It is the power of God unto salvation to every one that believeth.' This is what I am preaching, Paul says. God has intervened, and God has the power to save. Nobody else has, but He has, and my message is, 'The power of God unto salvation to every one that believeth; to the Jew first, and also to the Greek. For,' he continues, 'therein is the righteousness of God revealed from faith to faith: as it is written, The just shall live by faith. For' – now here is the explanation, the Apostle exults in this – 'For the wrath of God is revealed from heaven against [on] all ungodliness and unrighteousness of men, who hold the truth in unrighteousness.'

You cannot believe truly in the resurrection without believing in the doctrine of the wrath of God upon all sin. It is therefore not surprising that many modern writers do not believe in either judgment or resurrection. What they think is impossible for God determines what they will accept. What they do not understand, they regard as impossible. You see, if you deny one of these doctrines, fairly soon you will be denying them all. If you are logical and consistent you will have to. All these doctrines belong together – every single one of them. It is a complete body of doctrine. Omit any one of them and you are bound to be in trouble with all the rest.

All these things, then, are implicit in the statement 'God hath raised him from the dead.' Believing it, you are committed to all those biblical doctrines with regard to man and his condition, how he ever got into it, and what his most desperate need is. And that leads, in turn, to the other doctrines which the Apostle has already put before us. He had to spend the remainder of chapter 1, the whole of chapter 2 and chapter 3 up to verse 20,[1] in proving that this fallen state is universally true, and that it is as true of the Jew as it is of the Gentile. We are committed to that.

And then, of course, in chapter 5:12–21, Paul has that tremendous paragraph about our relationship to Adam. There was the cause of all the trouble; everybody has gone down with Adam: '. . . death passed upon all men, for that all have sinned' [*Rom.* 5:12]. So in this confession – that we believe that God has raised Him from the dead – we are asserting all that.

There is a further detail to note in the statement we are considering. The Apostle does not say, 'Christ rose from the dead,' although it is often put like that in the Scriptures. Here he says, 'God hath raised him from the dead.' That is very significant.

There is no contradiction here because the Father and the Son act in co-operation. But here Paul puts the emphasis on the work of the Father, and he does so for a definite reason. The resurrection asserts that Christ's death was sufficient. He had said on the cross, 'It is finished.' But is it finished? How can we know? He died. They took down His body. They laid it in a tomb. Has He triumphed? Has He done what He had come to do? If He had remained in the tomb, the answer would have been 'No', but the resurrection turns the 'No' into 'Yes'.

So, you see, at the end of chapter 4, Paul states that Christ 'was raised again for our justification'. The resurrection, as we emphasised when we were dealing with that great statement,[2] is God's public proclamation to the whole universe that He is satisfied with the work of His Son, that He has honoured the law absolutely and that He has borne the ultimate penalty of the law and its demands. In raising Christ from the dead, God was proclaiming that He and His law are absolutely satisfied, and that the work of salvation is complete.

So Paul tells us again in chapter 8:3–4, 'For what the law could not do, in that it was weak through the flesh, God sending his own Son in the likeness of sinful flesh, and for sin, condemned [has dealt with] sin in the flesh: that the righteousness of the law might be fulfilled in us . . .' And this is emphasised in two words in the wonderful and

---

[1] For expositions of the earlier chapters of Romans, see the first volumes in the series, published by the Banner of Truth Trust.

[2] See *An Exposition of Chapters 3:20 – 4:25: Atonement and Justification*, 1970.

beautiful statement in Romans 8:34, where, in answer to the rhetorical question 'Who is he that condemneth?' we read, 'It is Christ that died, yea rather, that is risen again, who is even at the right hand of God, who also maketh intercession for us.'

And the truth is in the little words *'yea rather'*! This is my certainty. If he had stopped before those words I would have no certainty. But I have a certainty, says Paul: 'It is Christ that died' – Ah yes, that is where the work was done, but how can I be sure of it? – 'Yea rather!' Risen from the dead! And it is there that I have my absolute certainty that the work was complete, that it was utterly finished, that He has paid my debt in full, that there is no condemnation, and never can be.

Eleven

*

That if thou shalt confess with thy mouth the Lord Jesus, and shalt believe in thine heart that God hath raised him from the dead, thou shalt be saved. For with the heart man believeth unto righteousness; and with the mouth confession is made unto salvation. Romans 10:9–10

We continue with our consideration of the fact that to believe that God has raised Jesus Christ from the dead involves a belief of a number of other things. We have said that the first of these is that the resurrection proves that Jesus is the Son of God and that He is the Lord of glory. Secondly, we found that it shows us the meaning of His death, and thirdly, it tells us that His death is sufficient, that by dying He completed the work that He had come to do here on earth.

We now go on to the fourth significance of the resurrection which is that it announced that all our enemies have been conquered. Salvation or deliverance means that there are a number of enemies from which we have to be released. The resurrection is the final proclamation that our Lord has conquered them all. We need not stay with this, because we looked at it when dealing with the proposition that Jesus is Lord. One of the proofs of the fact that He is Lord is that He rose from the dead and so He conquered death and the grave. Look at the resurrection from the standpoint of our salvation. He has conquered all our enemies, and the last enemy is death. As He conquered the devil and his underlings while He was here in this world, as He conquered evil and sin and temptation, so He has conquered death and the grave and has risen triumphant.

Now all this is summed up in a wonderful sentence which is used by the Apostle John in his first Epistle: 'For this purpose the Son of God was manifested, that he might destroy the works of the devil' [*1 John* 3:8] – all of them! And one of the works of the devil is that, as the result of his enticing man and leading him into sin, death has

[117]

entered in, and as the Epistle to the Hebrews reminds us in the second chapter, it is the devil that controls 'the power of death' [*Heb.* 2:14]. So, in the resurrection, our Lord is proclaiming that He has conquered all that.

All that we suffer from as a human race is the result of the works of the devil, and salvation means that these works are undone and rendered inoperative. So from that standpoint, the resurrection is extremely important. Further, to believe that God has raised Him from the dead is to have great assurance that everything that is necessary for my final, complete salvation and deliverance has been accomplished by the Son of God, this 'Jesus' whom we confess as Lord.

The next point which I would make is this: to believe in the resurrection is to understand why it was that the Holy Spirit was poured forth upon the early church on the day of Pentecost in Jerusalem. In the second chapter of Acts these followers of Jesus, filled with the Spirit, speaking in strange tongues, were all declaring 'the wonderful works of God', and the coming of the Holy Spirit was itself one of them.

This was something that was intimately connected with the resurrection of our blessed Lord and Saviour. If He had not risen from the dead, the Spirit could never have been poured forth and the many promises about His coming would not have been fulfilled. References in the New Testament to the Holy Spirit are often put in this form – 'the promise of the Father' [*Acts* 1:4] or the 'holy Spirit of promise' as the Apostle Paul writes in Ephesians 1:13–14. This means 'the Holy Spirit that had been promised'. All through the Old Testament there is that promise that God is going to 'pour forth his Spirit upon all flesh'. Peter quotes it in his sermon on the day of Pentecost in Jerusalem, and what he is saying is, 'What has been promised has come.' Yes, but the significant thing is that it could only happen after the resurrection.

There is a specific and most important statement about this in John 7:37–39: 'In the last day, that great day of the feast, Jesus stood and cried, saying, If any man thirst, let him come unto me, and drink. He that believeth on me, as the scripture hath said, out of his belly shall flow rivers of living water.' This John explains by saying, 'But this spake he of the Spirit, which they that believe on him should receive: for the Holy Ghost was not yet given; because that Jesus was not yet glorified.' Now there, you see, is the connection. If our Lord had not risen from the dead and been glorified, He would never have been able to send the Spirit as He did on the day of Pentecost.

This was a very important doctrine in the early church, and it should be in the church today. Often it is not; but it should be. It has been a vital doctrine in every great period of revival, and it is something that is intimately connected with the resurrection. That is why you have that extraordinary statement in John 16, which people often do not understand. You see, when our Lord announced His forthcoming death, all the disciples were cast down, so He said, 'Let not your heart be troubled: ye believe in God, believe also in me' [*John* 14:1]. Then He continued that theme in chapter 16, verse 7, where He told them that not only should they not grieve, but there was a sense in which they should be rejoicing. It is a good thing for you, He said, 'that I go away, for if I go not away, the Comforter will not come unto you; but if I depart, I will send him unto you.' That is this same argument, put from a slightly different aspect.

But we must also go on beyond this and look again at our Lord in His present position in the glory, because if we believe that God has raised Him from the dead, we must inevitably ask the question: Where is He now? What is He doing now? What significance has that for me? And this, too, is a part of the significance of His resurrection. We cannot just say that we believe that God has raised Him from the dead and stop at that, because the early preaching did not stop there. What else did it say? Well, it dealt with His present position, and taught that, having risen again from the dead, He ascended. We are given an account of His ascension in the first chapter of Acts. It is a vital part of Christian preaching. Again, we have a tendency to neglect this, but it is there for us. It was preached by the Apostles, who stood on Mount Olivet and saw Him ascending up into the heavens.

Then the teaching went beyond that to say that He not only passed, as it were, through these heavens that are visible to the naked eye, but also through the heavens that we cannot see and took His place at the right hand of God in the glory everlasting.

Now the best thing I can do, perhaps, is to give you a summary of that as it is put in the Epistle to the Hebrews. In chapter 1:3 we read, 'when he had by himself purged our sins, [he] sat down on the right hand of the Majesty on high' [*Heb.* 1:3]. There is another statement of it in chapter 4:14: 'Seeing then that we have a great high priest, that is passed into the heavens, Jesus the Son of God . . .' And you find it again in chapter 9:24, where we are told that our Lord has, as it were, sanctified the holy place – not the one on earth, not the earthly temple and tabernacle, but the holy place in the heavens itself. He has gone into the holiest of all in the glory everlasting.

The teaching about the resurrection includes that and, of course, it is of tremendous significance. The Apostle puts it like this in that great passage in Philippians 2. In verses 6–8, he deals first with the incarnation and with our Lord's humbling of Himself, becoming 'obedient unto death, even the death of the cross'. Then in verse 9 he continues, 'Wherefore' – because of this – 'God also hath highly exalted him, and given him a name which is above every name: that at the name of Jesus every knee should bow, of things in heaven, and things on earth, and things under the earth; and that every tongue should confess that Jesus Christ is Lord, to the glory of God the Father.' This is an essential part of the Christian message. It was a vital part of early Christian preaching that God, in the light of the work that the Son had done, exalted Him in this great way.

The Apostle says it again in writing to the Ephesians. He wants these people to know 'what is the exceeding greatness of his [God's] power to us-ward who believe, according to the working of his mighty power, which he wrought in Christ, when he raised him from the dead, and set him at his own right hand in the heavenly places, far above all principality, and power, and might, and dominion, and every name that is named, not only in this world, but also in that which is to come' [*Eph.* 1:19–21].

And He is there now! That is what the resurrection has led to and this is a part of our Christian belief. We do not just believe that our sins are forgiven because our Lord died on the cross and rose again. The ascension is also a vital part of our faith. He is there, seated at the right hand of God, exalted and given this name, which is above every name, 'that at the name of Jesus every knee should bow'. He is in this position of glory. All power in heaven and earth is His.

So these things are not only a part of Christian belief, they are a glorious part of it. And they result from the resurrection. If we say we believe that God raised Him from the dead, then we believe this also. We do not stop at resurrection. Ascension! Glory! Seated on the throne of the universe! All power given unto Him! Everything in His hands! That is a vital part of this teaching.

It was because they believed these things that the early Christians refused to listen to the Roman authorities who came to them and said,

'You must stop saying that Jesus is Lord; you must say that Caesar is Lord.' But they would not listen. They defied them. Then they were told that if they did not say this, they would be thrown to the lions in the arena. It did not make the slightest difference. Why not? It was their certain, assured confidence in this glorious truth. To them 'to die [was] gain' [*Phil.* 1:21], because it meant going to be with Jesus. And they could not deny the One who was the Lord of the universe. The Roman emperor was a great man but put him by the side of Christ and he was nothing, a nobody, here today and gone tomorrow. His empire would vanish – and it did, fairly soon. But here was One whose kingdom is without end, who shall reign for ever and ever. He is seated, waiting until His enemies shall be made His footstool [*Heb.* 1:13]. That is a part of this belief.

But then we must go even beyond that. 'Waiting until . . .' Until when? Or until what? And of course it is here everywhere in the New Testament, as it is prophesied in the Old Testament. 'Of his kingdom there shall be no end' [*Luke* 1:33]. At the Lord's table we declare His death 'until . . .' And here it is. The resurrection leads to the ascension, the heavenly session, the rule, the reign, yes, and to His coming again. You do not stop at the resurrection. It leads on to this whole great New Testament doctrine concerning the second coming – the coming again into this world of our Lord and Saviour Jesus Christ.

So here again is a vital part of Christian belief. These are the things which go into the content of this saving faith of ours. What does it mean? Well, it is the plain statement made by the two angels to those disciples standing there on the top of mount Olivet, looking up into the heavens, astonished at seeing our Lord ascending. They said: 'Ye men of Galilee, why stand ye gazing up into heaven? this same Jesus, which is taken up from you into heaven, shall so come in like manner as ye have seen him go into heaven' [*Acts* 1:10–11]. So that, too, was a part of their preaching.

The author of the Epistle to the Hebrews puts that in this interesting way at the end of the ninth chapter of his Epistle: 'And as it is appointed unto men once to die, and after this the judgment: so Christ was once offered to bear the sins of many; and unto them that look for him shall he appear the second time without sin' [vv. 27–28] – this time His coming has nothing to do with bearing sin – 'unto salvation'. He will come this time for judgment. The work of accomplishing salvation has been completed; the work of judgment remains to be done.

Obviously, this was a very important part of the saving faith of the early Christians. And it is not surprising that our Lord Himself devoted considerable attention to it. We have that great teaching in Matthew 24 and 25 (with the parallels in Mark 13 and Luke 21), and in other places, where our Lord, in parables and in direct speech, taught plainly and clearly about His coming back again into the world for the purpose of judgment. Indeed, early in His ministry He had taught, as you will find in John 5:27, that the Father had committed judgment unto Him because He was the Son of Man.

But I want to show you, in a very specific statement, the close connection between the resurrection and this coming again for judgment. It is in the sermon which was preached by the Apostle Paul in Athens to the Stoics and the Epicureans. In it Paul referred to the fact that God had 'appointed a day, in the which he will judge the world in righteousness by that man whom he hath ordained; whereof he hath given assurance unto all men, in that he hath raised him from the dead' [*Acts* 17:31]. The resurrection is the assurance, the certain knowledge, given to the whole of humanity by God Himself, that there is to be a final judgment of the world and of everybody who has ever lived in it.

This theme runs right through the whole Bible. Men and women are responsible beings, who are here, as it were, on a period of probation and have got to face judgment. Everybody has to die – and after death, that judgment. Everything here points forward to it. Now the resurrection is an absolute proof of the judgment which is to come, when our Lord will come back in a visible, bodily manner and will judge the world in righteousness.

But when He comes again it will not only be for judgment. That is the primary object: He will exercise this judgment, and the sentence will be pronounced, but that, in turn, will lead to the destruction of His enemies. I know of nothing more thrilling than this, particularly in this modern world in which we live, in which men and women have become so clever and so self-confident. The world does not realise what is awaiting it, but it is all laid out plainly here in the New Testament. It was an essential part of that first preaching. Here were this handful of people, these first Christians, and the great Roman Empire round and about them with its paganism and emperor worship, and the Jews opposed to them. Everybody was against them, and they were being ill-treated and martyred. And yet they stood out with their great courage and their spirit of rejoicing, and even when they were thrown to the lions in the arena they were found thanking God that, at last, they had been accounted worthy to suffer for His name's sake.

The opening chapter of 2 Thessalonians provides an excellent example of this spirit of fortitude amid persecution and faith that the Lord would recompense adversaries and more than reward His own when He would appear in glory and power. All this is connected with the resurrection. It leads to that which is to come, when He will judge, when He will destroy His enemies with the breath of His mouth. All that is opposed to God will be banished from the presence of the Lord with an everlasting destruction and He will be glorified in his saints.

That was a vital part of New Testament preaching, and must be believed by anybody who believes in salvation. God cannot pretend that there is no such thing as sin. Sin is the opposite of God and it must be destroyed; there must be an 'everlasting destruction'; there must be a judgment. God made a perfect universe, and, I say it with reverence, God will not be satisfied until it is restored to perfection. And all this is implicit in this doctrine of the resurrection. The resurrection makes a proclamation, gives assurance, concerning the judgment of the world by the Son of God 'at that day'.

And then the other thing that the resurrection will lead to is that He will set up His eternal kingdom. The Apostles began to preach this at the very beginning. Take, for instance, the third chapter of the Acts of the Apostles. Peter and John were going up to the temple to pray when they were accosted by a poor, lame man sitting at the Beautiful Gate and they healed him. A crowd gathered, so Peter began to address them, and, having given an exposition of what had happened, he began to apply the message, calling upon them to repent and believe, assuring them of pardon and new life in the Lord and predicting 'the times of restitution of all things, which God hath spoken by the mouth of all his holy prophets since the world began' [*Acts* 3:19–24].

Now our Lord Himself taught all this. He said, 'Verily I say unto you, That ye which have followed me, in the regeneration when the Son of man shall sit in the throne of his glory, ye also shall sit upon twelve thrones, judging the twelve tribes of Israel' [*Matt.* 19:28]. That is it. God is uniting, reuniting everything again in His Son, says Paul in Ephesians 1:10. The great teaching throughout the New Testament is that He is going to come, and He will set up this eternal kingdom, and 'Jesus shall reign where'er the sun doth his successive journeys run'. All this is implicit in this teaching that God has raised Him from the dead.

But now I want to take this further. So far we have been looking at the meaning of the resurrection and its significance in terms of these great and glorious truths about our Lord Himself. But it was also a vital part of the Apostles' preaching to apply all that to the believers, and to show its relevance and significance to them. So what does this include?

We already enjoy certain consequences and effects of the resurrection. Paul works them out in considerable detail, especially in the first part of Romans 6. The teaching in its essence is this. The resurrection is not only a fact, it is also a kind of picture of what happens to all of us who believe in the Lord Jesus Christ. The Apostle says that we are united to Him. As we were once in Adam, we are now in Christ. That means that we really are dead to the 'dominion' of sin.[1] Christians do not have to try to die with Christ. If they are Christians they *have* done so. You must not believe any teaching that tells you to crucify your old nature. For the Christian, the old nature has been crucified with Christ, it has died, and been buried. Christians have risen, in newness of life, and Paul tells them to realise this – that is the meaning of *'reckoning'* in 6:11.

Another thing that we realise and benefit from as the result of Christ's resurrection is that He has been made the Head of the church. There are many pictures of this in the New Testament. The church is described as the body of Christ. For example, Paul says, 'And hath put all things under his feet, and gave him to be the head over all things to the church, which is his body, the fulness of him that filleth all in all' [*Eph.* 1:22–23]. The church is the body and He is the Head. Then the Apostle repeats that thought in Ephesians 4:16.

And because of that, all that we receive, we receive from Him. We read in John's Gospel, 'Of his fulness have all we received, and grace for grace' [*John* 1:16]. We are united to Him, we are in Him. Having risen, not only is He above all principality, power, might, dominion, and every name that is named, He has also been made the Head of the church. That is a vital doctrine for us as Christian people.

And that in turn makes us realise that, risen and seated there at the right hand of God in the heavens, 'He ever liveth to make intercession' for us [*Heb.* 7:25]. He is there also as my great High Priest.

[1] See *An Exposition of Chapter 6: The New Man*, 1972.

How does that help me? Well, it helps me in prayer. Prayer is a very difficult matter. How can we pray? Who are we to go into the presence of God? Here is the answer: 'Seeing then that we have a great high priest. . . . Let us therefore come boldly unto the throne of grace, that we may obtain mercy, and find grace to help in time of need' [*Heb.* 4:14–16].

Here I am: I need mercy; I need grace to help in time of need. Who am I to venture into the presence of God? Here is my answer: there is One seated there at God's right hand. He is my great High Priest and He knows all about my need. He has been in this world and having become a man, He can be sympathetic towards our weakness and our ignorance – even He 'learned obedience by the things which he suffered' [*Heb.* 5:8]. Therefore, He is able to understand us when we come with our prayers. We are not left to ourselves. Our prayers are taken by our great High Priest and they are sent on to God. Our confidence in prayer is largely due to the fact that, having risen, He is ready to present our petitions before the eternal throne.

And then the last thing is that which the author of the Epistle to the Hebrews tells us in chapter 2 verse 18: 'For in that he himself hath suffered being tempted, he is able to succour them that are tempted.' It is wonderful that, having been in this world, and having been tried and tempted in all points as we are, yet without sin, He understands our human nature. He knows exactly what is happening to us. He can be touched by our infirmities so He is able to help us when we are tempted. Therefore we can turn to Him and pray, knowing that He is near.

These things are true in the present, but look at the future! What does our Lord's resurrection tell us about ourselves in the future? It tells us that our resurrection is guaranteed. The Apostle Paul, preaching before Agrippa and Festus, put it in this way: 'That Christ should suffer, and that he should be *the first* that should rise from the dead' [*Acts* 26:23]. The first! First means that there are others to follow: and you and I are to follow. All His people are to follow, but the Christian looks at it like this: 'Because He has risen, I shall rise!'

That is the great argument of 1 Corinthians 15. False teachers were going round saying that the resurrection was past already, and that there was no hope for the Christian, but the Apostle's answer is: 'If in this life only we have hope in Christ, we are of all men most miserable. But now is Christ risen from the dead, and become the firstfruits of them that slept. For since by man came death, by man came also the resurrection of the dead. As in Adam all die, even so in Christ shall all be made alive.' He is referring there to believers. 'But every man in his own order: Christ the firstfruits; afterward they that are Christ's at his coming. Then cometh the end, when he shall have delivered up the kingdom to God, even the Father, when he shall have put down all rule and all authority and power' [*1 Cor.* 15:19–24]. That is a tremendous statement. Let the world kill us, let it destroy us, let it do what it likes to us – nothing can prevent this happening. His resurrection is a guarantee of ours.

And not only our resurrection but our glorification also. In the first two verses of chapter 5, Paul says that 'we have peace with God' and 'access by faith into this grace wherein we stand, and rejoice in hope of the glory of God.' The resurrection alone enables you to do that. We are 'heirs of God and joint heirs with Christ' and await the redemption of our bodies – that is, our glorification so that we shall be like Him in body and spirit.

Because I believe that God has raised Him from the dead, I know that He will raise me from the dead, and will glorify me until I am completely and finally delivered from every vestige of sin in every shape and form. 'We shall be like him; for we shall see him as he is.'

That is the content of saving faith.

Is there somebody who feels that I have been reading a tremendous lot into that? Somebody might comment: 'All your text says is this: "That if thou shalt confess with thy mouth the Lord Jesus, and shalt believe in thine heart that God hath raised him from the dead, thou shalt be saved." Surely all that means is that a person says, "I believe Jesus is Lord. I believe that God raised Him from the dead." No more; you have been pressing the rest into it. You are a typical theologian, importing things from everywhere into it!'

If you feel that, let me read you two little verses at the end of the first chapter of Paul's First Epistle to the Thessalonians. Paul is reminding his readers of what he had preached to them. This letter is believed by some to be Paul's first Epistle, and if so, there is nothing more primitive than this – this was early apostolic preaching: 'They themselves shew of us what manner of entering in we had unto you, and how ye turned to God from idols to serve the living and true God; and to wait for his Son from heaven, whom he raised from the dead, even Jesus, which delivered us from the wrath to come' [*1 Thess.* 1:9–10].

It is all there, is it not? You see, I have not pressed anything into Paul's words in Romans 10:9. These two statements include all the rest. You cannot believe that Jesus is Lord, and that God has raised Him from the dead, without believing all these other things about which the Apostle reminds the Thessalonians. That is apostolic preaching in its simplest form, and people who are saved are people who believe that. That is the content of their belief – nothing less.

Twelve

*

That if thou shalt confess with thy mouth the Lord Jesus, and shalt believe in thine heart that God hath raised him from the dead, thou shalt be saved. For with the heart man believeth unto righteousness; and with the mouth confession is made unto salvation.   Romans 10:9–10

At the end of the last lecture, I quoted from 1 Thessalonians 1:9–10. I did that to show how much content there was to Paul's message when he preached the gospel. But there are those who cite the case of the Philippian jailor and point out that when he asked what he must do to be saved, Paul and Silas only said to him, 'Believe on the Lord Jesus Christ, and thou shalt be saved' [*Acts* 16:31]. Now my reply to that is taken from the verse which immediately follows the one quoted. It reads: 'And they spake unto him the word of the Lord, and to all that were in his house.' In other words, they told him what was meant by 'believe on the Lord Jesus Christ'. They preached the gospel to him. They told him all that they habitually preached, as we see in 1 Thessalonians. They gave him this doctrine that I have been putting before you as we have been drawing out the implications of these two summaries of the Christian faith.

But often people have not noted this, and because I believe that there is a great deal of misunderstanding with regard to this very matter, I feel constrained to come back again to this subject. Indeed, I believe that this misunderstanding is responsible for many of our troubles in the Christian church. I am sure it is responsible for most of the problems among evangelical people, who seem to me at the present time to be tending to listen far too readily to ecumenical talk, and to other types of teaching.

Let me put it like this. There are two main dangers, it seems to me, that arise over this question of the content of saving faith, and I want to talk about both of them. Incidentally, let me say that this illustrates my idea of biblical teaching, namely that it includes application. You do not rush through the Scriptures, giving out headings and saying, 'I have done the Epistle to the Romans, I know all about it.' No, you do not know it until you really have explored its meaning and have applied it. And it is because of the importance of application that I am coming back to this subject.

The two dangers are, as is invariably the case with any study of the Scriptures, two extremes. The commoner danger today, I think, is that of putting too little into the content. It is what I have been trying to counteract in the last four lectures. The second danger is that of putting too much into it. And I want to try to show that both extremes are wrong.

So let us take them in order and deal first with the danger of having too little content. Let me give you another illustration of what I mean. Take that thirteenth verse of Acts 16 – the famous scene of Paul at Philippi. We are told that Paul went out on the Sabbath to the river outside the walls of the city where he knew that a prayer meeting was held and spoke to the women who attended it.

Now a well-known contemporary evangelical scholarly commentator makes a comment on that which is a perfect illustration, I think, of putting in too little content. He says, 'They sat down among the women and told them the story of Jesus.' To which the answer is, 'Of course they did, but they did not stop at that; they did not stop at telling the story of Jesus.'

On what grounds do I say that? I say it on the grounds of the teaching of the book of Acts itself. Apostolic preaching did give the facts, but it never stopped at the mere recital of those facts; it always went on to give their meaning and significance. Take Peter in his first sermon on the day of Pentecost. He was, of course, primarily concerned with the great fact of the resurrection, but note how he drew out its significance. He quoted from Psalm 16:8–11, where David says, 'Thou wilt not leave my soul in hell, neither wilt thou suffer thine Holy One to see corruption' [*Acts* 2:25–28]. Peter pointed out that this was not true of David; he had died and was buried, but it was true of Christ and proves therefore it was in Him that salvation was to be found.

They did tell the story of Jesus, but they never stopped at that. The whole point was to show its significance. The story of Jesus shows that God 'hath visited and redeemed his people' [*Luke* 1:68], that He was the Messiah who fulfils all the prophecies. And the apostolic preaching tells how He had done this. So it is no use saying to people, 'Believe on the Lord Jesus Christ,' because their answer is: 'Who is Jesus Christ? What does believing in Jesus Christ mean?'

Now as you go through the Acts of the Apostles you always see that you have fact plus meaning. The Apostles always interpreted the message and pressed it home, and then they made their great call to repentance. But you find the same approach in other parts of the New Testament also. We have already seen it in that little summary at the end of 1 Thessalonians 1 and you also have it in that wonderful summary at the beginning of 1 Corinthians 15.

You see, Paul did not merely tell the story of Jesus and say that He had died, had been buried and had risen again. No, it was '*for our sins*' and 'according to the scriptures' [*1 Cor.* 15:1–5]. And then Paul worked out this great argument about the resurrection and showed why it is absolutely essential that we should believe in it. But that is what Paul says he preached at the beginning: 'Christ died for our sins'. The same is true in 2 Corinthians 5:20.

That was apostolic preaching; there is no question about it. The meaning was always given, in addition to the fact. And that is what we have been trying to do. So that once more I would remind you of this all-important point, and it is something which we must never forget as we read the Scriptures, and particularly a book like the book of Acts. What you have there is not a full report; it is not a complete and exhaustive account; it is not a shorthand note of every word uttered by the preacher; it is not a tape-recording! These are just summaries, synopses, given in the briefest possible form, and our business, therefore, is to realise that and to understand something of the fulness of their content.

Now all this is important, especially today, for many reasons. We are living in a time when there is a great emphasis on evangelism, and when pressure is brought upon preachers to get 'decisions'. And it is just at that point that all this becomes important. Men and women must know what they are deciding about, and why they should decide. Now the danger is that, in the anxiety to bring people to salvation, too little content may be given, so that if people merely say 'Yes' to something that is said to them, then all is thought to be well. I am just trying to show that that is not how the Apostles evangelised. There was a much bigger content to their preaching.

Very often you will find today that preaching may be too general. I myself have been in meetings when I would have said that the gospel was not preached at all. Nevertheless, appeals have been made at the end and people have come forward: but did they know what they were doing? This is a danger that confronts us at a time like this. Men and women may think that a mere subscription to a formula saves them; indeed, according to some, merely going forward saves them. Many people think that, having gone forward, they are automatically saved, though they do not know what they believe and exactly what they have done.

We are living in a time of trouble; many people are unhappy and face great problems. Some people cannot sleep; some are worried about money; others are anxious about their health and are afraid that they cannot get any help – the world is full of problems. And such people go to a Christian service and are told, 'Come to Jesus and you will get all that you require.' And they require so much, so they come, hoping that they will get what they want. Now if you merely say to those people, 'Confess with your mouth the Lord Jesus, and believe in your heart that God hath raised him from the dead,' I say you are misleading them. If you merely say to them, 'Believe on the Lord Jesus Christ and you will be saved,' and then ask, 'Do you believe on the Lord Jesus Christ?' and they say 'Yes!', if you then reply, 'You are saved,' you are misleading them. It is our business to make quite certain that they know what they are believing. We must 'speak the word of the Lord' to them, 'the word of God,' as Paul and Silas did to that Philippian jailor and to his household. We must draw this thing out, we must expound it. They must not merely believe the story of Jesus, but must know its significance.

In other words – and this is so often where the danger comes in – it is our business to show such people that their need is not what they think it is. People say, 'I want happiness,' but really what they need is to be reconciled to God. Our business is to show them the cause of their unhappiness. We do not medicate symptoms lightly. We do not say, 'Come to Christ and you will be happy.' No, we must show them that they have never realised their fundamental need – namely, that they are estranged from God and are under His wrath. Whether they are happy or miserable does not matter at that point. We must direct them to their real need and show them that it can only be met by what God has done in the Lord Jesus Christ.

We live in an age in which everything is subjective: we start with ourselves and we end with ourselves. So when people want help, they are told, 'Very well, here it is, it is in Christ for you.' But if we do not explain the way of salvation and show them their condition under the law, we are not doing what the Apostles did, we are not putting sufficient content into our presentation of the gospel.

Now let me give you some further reasons why I have been emphasising the content of faith.

One reason why it is essential to know the content is that this is the way in which the New Testament itself describes salvation. Salvation is coming to a knowledge of the truth. Paul wrote to Timothy: 'For this is good and acceptable in the sight of God our Saviour; who will have all men to be saved, and to come unto the knowledge of the truth. For there is one God, and one mediator between God and men, the man Christ Jesus; who gave himself a ransom for all, to be testified in due time. Whereunto I am ordained a preacher, and an apostle . . . a teacher of the Gentiles in faith and verity' [*1 Tim.* 2:3–7]. Salvation is by knowledge of the truth, so we must be clear about its content.

Furthermore, if we do not take trouble to put the right content into this belief and declaration, then we will have no standard by which to measure our experience. This is another very important point. Experience is essential. You cannot be a Christian, as I hope to show you later, without having experience. You experience the truth. You have got to believe 'in your heart': 'For with the heart man believeth unto righteousness'. Very well. But now the danger is that people say that any sort of experience is all right, and they say, 'What does it matter whether I understand or not? What does it matter what I believe? All I know is that I have got an experience. I used to be miserable, now I am happy. I have got what I wanted.'

But of course the answer to that is quite simple. The Bible tells us that there are many counterfeits of the truth. There is an enemy, the devil, who is most subtle, and he can simulate the Christian experience almost exactly. He has the power to give people experiences. So if you are going to base your whole position solely upon some experience, how do you know that you have the true experience? If the experience is not the result of biblical truth, then it is a counterfeit, false experience, and is very dangerous.

There are books in which you can read how men and women have undergone profound changes. I remember reading a most fascinating book in which a number of people were writing on turning-points in their lives. Indeed, it was an astounding book, because some had undergone a very profound change. I remember one man who had been a hopeless drunkard, poor fellow. He was a very able professional man, but he had become a helpless dipsomaniac. And one morning after a terrible night, that man got up and happened to look at himself in the mirror. He was so shocked at the sight that he never drank another drop and he became an entirely different man. Now that was a wonderful experience, and the other writers were saying similar things.

But what we are concerned about is this: What leads to the experience? The power of Satan to counterfeit and camouflage is well-nigh endless, so much so that he can almost deceive the elect. He can perform 'lying wonders'; he can produce 'miracles'; he can give 'signs'. That is New Testament teaching. So we must have objective truth by which to test all experiences.

There is another important reason why we should be so concerned about the content of saving faith. How do you test the various teachings that are put before you? You hear a knock on your door. You open it, and there is a man selling books. He says that he believes the Bible and its message and he adds, 'And here are books which will help you to understand it.' He is a pleasant man to look at; he talks in a very polite way. He has taken the trouble to call and see you. He is so concerned about you that he has given up his Saturday afternoon, and here he is, out in the rain, in order to help you. How do you test his teaching?

Now if all you have is 'the story of Jesus', or if all you know is this: 'Well, I went to a meeting and I felt something and I was told, "Believe on the Lord Jesus Christ and you will be saved." Then I was asked, "Do you believe?" and I said, "Yes," so I was told, "You are saved!"' – if that is all you have, then certain things may happen.

The man at the door may say, 'What do you mean by that; how does He save . . . ?'

'Well, I don't know,' you reply. 'All I was told was that I must believe, so I did, and I have felt very happy ever since, and I go to meetings and I am enjoying them.'

'But,' says this man, 'you know you really have not understood it properly; there is so much that they have not told you' – and out he brings all this wonderful teaching. How do you answer him?

You see, if there is not a full content to our faith, if we do not know why and what we believe, then we have nothing against which to test these false teachings that are round and about us at the present time. I know of nothing more dangerous than the attitude that says, 'It doesn't matter what you believe, as long as you somehow believe in the Lord Jesus Christ. You need not bother about the doctrine or the theology or the understanding of it all. As long as you feel something and want to be a Christian and to live a good life and to help others, then all is well.'

That is dangerous because, as we have seen, you have no answer to give to these other people. And how do you reply to the suggestion that is made so often today that all the religions of the world should come together? There is a World Congress of Religions, and we are assured that they all have their insights. We are told: 'There are many ways to get to the top of the mountain of God.' Christianity is one of them and is very valuable, but Buddhism, Confucianism, Islam and Hinduism all have insights and something to teach. What does it matter as long as we all believe in the same God and are out to serve Him?

And how do you answer that unless you know the content of your faith? It is not enough just to believe that Jesus is the Son of God and that He rose from the dead. You must believe much more than that before you can answer these people; you have to work it out, you must have an understanding of the doctrine.

The Apostle Peter tells us in his Second Epistle something that I think this present generation of Christians needs to take very seriously to heart. He is referring to how some 'wrest' the Epistles of the Apostle Paul and 'the other scriptures unto their own destruction'. This is because they are 'unlearned and unstable' – what makes them unstable is that they are unlearned. Content is so important. In the same way the Apostle Paul urges the Ephesians to 'henceforth be no more children, tossed to and fro, and carried about with every wind of doctrine, by the sleight of men, and cunning craftiness, whereby they lie in wait to deceive' [*Eph.* 4:14]. Children are ignorant, they do not know the content; and that is why they can be misled and carried away. The answer is to know the content of what you believe.

So then, without this understanding of the fulness of the content, we shall find ourselves unable to assess those other teachings that are round and about us at the present time, some of which are produced even in the name of the Christian church. How do you evaluate them? Do you just say, 'This man is a bishop, therefore it must be right'? Is that your position? But how do you turn him down if he is not right? It is not enough to say, 'I do not agree with him.' You must prove that he is wrong if you want to help people who hear these things and perhaps are attracted by them because they sound daring, and seem as if they are new. We cannot help such people unless we know the content of our faith.

But then there is another very important reason for doing what we have been doing. It is the only way to enjoy full assurance of salvation. Now if you have been satisfied with just believing the story of Jesus, or just saying mechanically, 'Yes, I believe on the Lord Jesus Christ and believe that because I say that, I am saved' – what happens when you suddenly pass through a very dry period of the soul? What happens when you are attacked by the devil and he makes you feel wretched and hopeless and damned? How do you answer him? You cannot.

No, there is only one way to answer the devil and that is to know the truth as it is in Christ Jesus. 'Whom resist stedfast in the faith,' says Peter [*1 Pet.* 5:9]. Without the faith you cannot do it, but with the faith you can. You know that you believe in One who conquered the devil and who is still living and able to help you and all who are attacked, as He Himself was, when He was on earth.

But without an understanding of the content, you will find that your assurance will soon go. It is all right, perhaps, for a while, when you are able to go to meetings, but what happens when you lose your health? What happens if death visits the family? What happens if you get trouble in your work? One is constantly having to deal with such people. They seem to be so happy, then suddenly they lose everything. Why? 'Well,' they say, 'it has not turned out as we thought it would.' They thought, 'Believe in the Lord Jesus Christ and all will be well,' but it is not all well. They are tempted; they are tried; they have troubles and tribulations and their whole foundation seems to have gone. They do not know the content of what they believe.

And, lastly, this is the only way in which you will ever be able to help anybody else. The Apostle Peter again puts it wonderfully: 'Sanctify the Lord God in your hearts: and be ready always to give an answer to every man that asketh you a reason of the hope that is in you' [*1 Pet.* 3:15]. You see, it is not enough for you to say to somebody, 'You know, I used to be miserable. Then I went to a meeting and I felt something, so I went forward and they said, "Do you believe in the Lord Jesus Christ?" I said, "Yes," and they replied, "Right, you are saved."' But that does not help the other person. He may ask you questions and if you cannot answer those questions, you cannot help him.

No, you have got to be able to give *a reason* for the hope that is in you. You must not only know the story of Jesus, you must also know its significance, and you must be able to apply it. You must show people why they are what they are. You must give them the biblical teaching of the fall and sin, and explain that they can never put themselves right, but that Christ came for that reason. You must expound the way of salvation. You cannot help others if you do not know the way of salvation in detail yourself. It is a sheer impossibility.

Therefore it is vital that, in addition to repeating the slogans, as it were, we should be able to expound them, to draw out their meaning and to show their full significance. There, then, is the one side – the danger of too little content.

But now let us turn to the second danger, that of putting too much into the content of faith. You see, it is very interesting to me, as I read Romans 10:9 and 10, to notice what the Apostle does *not* say. It is quite as important to observe that as to observe what he does say, because you will find that several of these Epistles had to be written because certain people were trying to put too much content into what Christians should believe. Why, for example, did Paul ever write the Epistle to the Galatians? He wrote it because false teachers had gone round saying: 'Now, you have believed what Paul taught you, but, you know, that is not enough; in addition, you must be circumcised.' It was not a question of choice. If you were not circumcised you were not saved. They were adding the law and circumcision to believing in Christ, and the Apostle had to write his letter in order to counteract that.

Then Paul had to write his First Epistle to Timothy very largely in order to do the same thing. At the very beginning of that Epistle, he reminds Timothy of why he had left him at Ephesus. It was to deal with people who were taken up with 'fables' and 'genealogies' because of their wrong interpretation of the law and its purpose. They were tending to make 'shipwreck' of the faith, because of this 'knowledge' which he describes later as 'falsely so called', translated in the Authorised Version as 'science falsely so called' [*1 Tim.* 6:20].

And why did he write the Epistle to the Colossians? The answer is the same. The Colossian heresy, the precursor of Gnosticism, was that some said, 'Ah, yes, Paul was all right as far as he went, but if you want the real thing, you have got to go further' – and they brought in the idea of angelic intermediaries, teaching that Christ was but one of them. They added a bit of philosophy also, and some asceticism, and so on – it was a jumble of teachings – and then they added some strange experiences into which you could be initiated. They said that you were not truly a Christian unless you went through all this, in addition to what Paul taught. So the Apostle had to write his Epistles in order to deal with these various matters.

Now the trouble in all those cases was that the false teachers were putting too much content into the teaching. How difficult it seems to be for Christian people to maintain a balance and to avoid both extremes! However, there it is in the New Testament.

'But what has all this got to do with us?' asks somebody. Well, I do not know that there is any more urgent problem for Christians at the present time when so many people are talking about 'going back to Rome'. But what is Roman Catholicism? Well, it is just this very thing about which I am speaking. According to the teaching of the Roman Catholic Church, it is not enough for you to believe what I have been expounding to you in our consideration of these verses. No, they say, you have got to believe other things as well.

Now this is not my opinion; look at their own books. You have to believe in the Pope as the vicar of Christ, the head of the church, and that he is infallible when he defines matters of faith. You must believe this because it is vital to salvation. Then you must believe in certain things about the Virgin Mary. It is not a matter of choice; you have to believe in the immaculate conception as it was defined in 1854. This doctrine declares that not only was our Lord born free from sin, but Mary was also.

Also now, since 1950, you have to believe in the assumption of Mary – namely, that she never died and was never buried, but went up bodily into heaven. It is a part of defined and essential doctrine. Likewise with the Mass and transubstantiation and the doctrine of Mary as co-redemptrix; and there is more with which I will not trouble you at this point. All I am trying to show is that the Roman Catholic Church insists upon your believing all these things. Now that is what I call putting too much into the content of saving faith. All that is not in Romans 10:9 and 10, is it? You cannot draw that out of those verses. But I have proved to you that everything that I have drawn out can be done so legitimately.

However, I want to be absolutely fair, so let me go on. The Roman Catholics are not the only people who are guilty of this. Some of us are guilty of very much the same thing. Let me put it bluntly. Is it essential to believe in the doctrine of election in order to be saved? Is the doctrine of election in Romans 10:9 and 10? I do not hesitate to answer that it is not there, and if you put it in, you are putting in too much content. There is all the difference in the world between believing in the way of salvation in Christ Jesus, and understanding how it is worked out, and to me, that is where the doctrine of election belongs.

We must be very careful at this point. Arminians can be true Christians. I say that they are very muddle-headed, and intellectually confused, but God forbid that I should ever say that they are not Christians. It is not belief in the doctrine of election that saves men and women. They should believe it. If they are students of the Bible, they should believe it. But you can be a Christian without believing it. Thank God, you can be saved, though you may be muddled in your head! I am not excusing your muddle, but I am thanking God that you can be saved in spite of it. Indeed, if this were not true, nobody would be saved. Who are we and what do we know? Thank God we are not saved by our understanding; we are saved by what God has done for us in and through the Lord Jesus Christ. We are 'commanded' to repent and to believe the gospel as it is presented to us.

So all that you must read into Romans 10:9 and 10 is that which is essential to salvation: no more. This is the primitive evangelistic message which we must give to men and women in order that they may be saved. We must give it in all its fulness, but we must not add to it, otherwise we are going beyond our text. Paul summarised this essential message when he said farewell to the elders of the church at Ephesus. He reminded them that they could bear him record that day and night he went from house to house and spoke in public, preaching – what? – 'repentance toward God, and faith toward our Lord Jesus Christ' [*Acts* 20:20–21]. What did he preach in Athens? God 'commandeth all men every where to repent' [*Acts* 17:30]. I defy anybody to give me a single example in the book of Acts where the doctrine of election was preached in evangelistic sermons. It is not there.

The principle, therefore, is this: a full and deep understanding of the whole of doctrine, thank God, is not essential to salvation. We ought to have it, and that is why we study these things, that we may grow in grace, and in the knowledge of the Lord, but at the moment of belief and of salvation we do not need to know it all. To include it in the evangelistic message is to do violence to that message. We are not saved by our understanding; we are saved by God in Christ and the understanding follows. What evangelistic preaching does is *call*: it calls us to repent; it commands us to do so. That is the message of salvation. 'Repent, and believe the gospel.' 'Repent, and believe in the Lord Jesus Christ.' It calls us to what the Apostle has already described in Romans 1:5 as 'obedience to the faith'.

Now this is such an important point that we must be fair on all sides. Have you ever noticed in Acts the difference between what was preached and the comment of Luke, the author of the book? Let me give two examples of what I mean. In chapter 2 we are given an account of Peter's sermon, and you remember that it was very convicting. Peter proved who our Lord is and how He fulfils the prophecies, and so on. And we read, 'Now when they heard this, they were pricked in their heart, and said unto Peter and to the rest of the apostles, Men and brethren, what shall we do? Then Peter said unto them, Repent . . .' He did not say to them, 'You can do nothing. You must wait until the Holy Spirit moves you. You must make sure whether you are elect or not.' He preached, 'Repent, and be baptized every one of you in the name of Jesus Christ for the remission of sins' [*Acts* 2:37–38].

But then notice the comment of Luke at the end – and this is where you see the difference – 'Praising God, and having favour with all the people. And the Lord added to the church daily such as should be saved [such as were being saved]' [*Acts* 2:47]. The Lord did it, of course. That is Luke's comment. But they never preached the doctrine of election. The preaching was, 'God commandeth all men everywhere to repent.' That is a command. That is preaching. That is the evangelistic message that leads to faith unto salvation.

Then there is another very good illustration of the same thing in Acts 13. The content of the preaching is found in verses 38 and 39. 'Be it known unto you therefore, men and brethren, that through this man is preached unto you the forgiveness of sins.' Here is preaching; you see the content? 'Through this man' – Paul has told them who He is – 'is preached unto you the forgiveness of sins.' There is the content I have been arguing for. 'And by him all that believe are justified from all things, from which ye could not be justified by the law of Moses.'

Now that is the preaching; but listen to Luke's comment in verse 48: 'And when the Gentiles heard this, they were glad, and glorified the word of the Lord: and as many as were ordained to eternal life believed.' But Paul, preaching in Antioch in Pisidia, did not preach that only those who are ordained, believe. That is true, but it comes later. You do not have to believe that to be saved. There is a difference between the content of the message and the comment that is made upon it.

Again, have you ever noticed the difference between the preaching recorded in Acts and the teaching of the Epistles? The difference is that the doctrine which is given in embryo in Acts is elaborated and worked out in the Epistles. The Apostles did not preach the whole content of the Epistles. No, they preached this message which was essential and did not go beyond it.

In other words, I would put it like this – and I am saying this to myself and to every other preacher. There is all the difference in the world between having your preaching controlled by theology, and preaching theology. Our preaching should always be controlled by theology, we must always be scriptural in our presentation of the truth, but that is a very different thing from preaching theology.

And what is this essential message? Somebody may say, 'Well now, here you are; you have told us that some put too little into it and others too much. So how do I know how much to put into it?' Well, I could answer that by saying I have been showing you that in all our consideration of these verses! The content must be a legitimate and a direct deduction from the text, and you must not add to it. Here is what I would call the great watershed and we may have to live through days when we will have to decide about this. There is a division between those who believe the evangelical message of the Bible and those who do not. And this is the thing that divides: revelation on the one hand, human understanding and reason on the other. That is the first great distinction. Do I submit myself entirely and exclusively to the Bible, or do I add what *I* think – *my* reason, *my* understanding, *my* conception of God, *my* conception of salvation? It is an absolute division. The true preaching submits itself utterly to the revelation.

The second division is between justification by faith only and reliance upon works. The content of justification by faith only is what we have been considering. It is 'faith in the Lord Jesus Christ'. It is this confession that 'Jesus is the Lord' and all that that means. It is this confession from the heart that 'God has raised him from the dead' and all that that means. And that is justification by faith and by faith alone. We must not subtract from that and we must not add to it. We must keep this message plain and clear. If we once begin to say, with the Roman Catholics, that people are not true Christians unless they believe this, that and the other, or if we say with others that people are not Christians unless they believe the doctrine of election, we are wrong. And the second group are as wrong as the Roman Catholics.

So do not be guilty of over-simplifying and not putting enough in. But also do not be guilty of putting too much in and adding your postulates which go beyond the teaching of the Bible about salvation. May God give us this wisdom that will keep us sane and balanced and, above everything else, true to the Word of God itself.

Thirteen

That if thou shalt confess with thy mouth the Lord Jesus, and shalt believe in thine heart that God hath raised him from the dead, thou shalt be saved. For with the heart man believeth unto righteousness; and with the mouth confession is made unto salvation.

Romans 10:9–10

Perhaps it would be good to remind ourselves at this point that we have described these two verses as the Apostle's summary of saving faith, and we are examining what is meant by that. I have suggested a threefold division: first, of course, you must consider the content of saving faith; then you consider its character, or its nature; and finally its proof. Those three things are suggested here by this statement which the Apostle makes.

We have already dealt with the content of saving faith: that we believe that 'Jesus is Lord,' and that 'God hath raised him from the dead.' We have considered those two statements and their full implications. So now we are in a position to move forward to the second division of this statement of saving faith, and that is its nature or character.

Now you notice that the Apostle deals with this in both verses, and there can be no doubt that the fact that the Apostle repeats in verse 10 what he has said in verse 9 means that he attaches very great significance to it. The purpose of repetition in the Scriptures is always to underline something. Evidently, therefore, there are certain dangers with respect to this whole matter of saving faith, and it is in order to safeguard us from those dangers that the Apostle puts the emphasis upon it by stating it twice over. In other words, he puts his emphasis upon the heart and upon the mouth.

When I introduced this statement, I called attention to the way in which Paul reverses the order. In verse 9 he puts 'confession with the mouth' before 'believing in the heart'; but in verse 10 he reverses that

[142]

and says, 'With the heart man believeth unto righteousness; and with the mouth confession is made unto salvation.' And the reason, of course, for that change in order is simply that in the ninth verse, which follows on from what he has been saying before, Paul is concerned with the statement of the fact of belief. He has been talking about 'the word of faith which we preach' and he is concerned now to show how you can tell whether people are Christians or not, and you do that by what they *say*. Therefore he puts the confession with the mouth first.

But then when Paul gives an account of the way in which someone comes to make this confession, he obviously has to reverse the order. You meet someone and you are concerned to know whether he is a Christian or not. Well, you will discover that by what he says. But then you know perfectly well that what he says is the result of something else that has gone before – the believing. So the believing in the heart comes first, and that is then given expression by what comes out of the mouth.

If you want a perfect exposition of this order you get it in our Lord's statement about the seat of sin in human nature. He was dealing with the Pharisees, who were always concerned about externals, but our Lord told them that what really matters is what is inside. He said, 'Do not ye yet understand, that whatsoever entereth in at the mouth goeth into the belly, and is cast out into the draught? But those things which proceed out of the mouth come forth from the heart; and they defile the man.' He then went on to list various sins which come from the heart of man [*Matt.* 15:17–20]. He says elsewhere: 'Out of the abundance of the heart the mouth speaketh' [*Matt.* 12:34]. So this need not cause any difficulty. If your emphasis is upon the Christian's confession, you put the mouth first, but if you are trying to discover how it is that someone really does believe, you put the heart first.

It is important, therefore, for us to discover why the Apostle goes out of his way like this to amplify his definition of saving faith. In doing that, perhaps we had better start with a negative in order to be quite clear as to what he is not saying. There have been those who have misunderstood both these verses by interpreting them in this way: that the Apostle is saying that it is our belief and confession that saves us. On the surface, of course, it looks like that. 'If thou shalt confess with thy mouth the Lord Jesus, and shalt believe in thine heart that God hath raised him from the dead, thou shalt be saved.' So it is argued that those who make this confession with their mouths and who believe that God has raised Him from the dead, thereby save themselves.

But of course that is impossible, because if that were the case, it would mean that we had turned belief into a work, and were saving ourselves in that way – it would be another form of salvation by works. Many people have fallen into that very error. They say, 'We agree that we do not save ourselves by doing particular deeds, but here we are told quite plainly that if we say with our mouths, "I believe Jesus is Lord, and I believe that God has raised Him from the dead," we thereby save ourselves.'

Now I say that that is impossible for this reason: the whole context in this tenth chapter – and particularly in the ninth, of which chapter 10 is an elaboration – is entirely against such an idea. That is the very thing the Apostle is concerned to disprove. His whole case is that we are all saved by grace, by what he has called in the ninth chapter 'the election of grace'. That is the whole context. But the moment we begin to say that our mere confession or statement of belief is the thing that saves us, we are denying this essential teaching that salvation is entirely of grace, that it is all of God and that we have nothing whereof we can boast. We must not say that we have saved ourselves by believing, because the answer is, 'For by grace are ye saved through faith; and that not of yourselves: it is the gift of God' [*Eph.* 2:8]. So we must clear that preliminary point.

Why, then, does the Apostle put it like this? Well, you remember that he has been dramatising this matter in verses 5–8 by, as it were, putting up two preachers with their different messages. He finishes by saying, 'That is, the word of faith, which we preach.' And it is a word which 'says', which makes the confession of faith that Jesus is Lord and God has raised Him from the dead. In other words, the Christian's confession is that we are not saved by the works of the law, but by the Lord Jesus Christ. So the emphasis is not upon our confession, it is upon what we are confessing, and all that that involves – which is, as we have seen, the way of salvation. That is what the Apostle is really saying. The statement which is made by saving faith is not that we justify ourselves in any way, but that we are justified by the Lord Jesus Christ and what He has done on our behalf.

We get rid, then, of what is nothing but a superficial and mechanical interpretation of the Bible. That is not the way to approach Scripture.

The whole emphasis of the Apostle is upon 'the thing confessed' and not upon our actual confession.

Now we shall see this as we go on with our exposition. Indeed, we have already made this point, but in passing let me emphasise again that faith is not the basis of our salvation; it is only the instrument. The foundation, the basis, of our salvation is the Lord Jesus Christ and His work on our behalf. Faith, then, is nothing but the channel by means of which the work of the Lord Jesus Christ becomes efficacious in the children of God.

So having dealt with that, we can now approach this subject positively and directly. Why does the Apostle put this emphasis upon the heart and the confession? Why is he not content with saying that all that is necessary is this belief in Jesus as Lord and in the fact that God has raised Him from the dead?

The answer is that Paul is anxious to safeguard us from certain dangers, and you get this same safeguarding in many other places in the New Testament teaching. This statement saves us from two great dangers in particular. The first, as we have already seen, is the danger of going to extremes. We are all aware of that; we are creatures of extremes. If we are corrected on one side, we go right over to the other side and lose our balance again.

Now the extremes here are these: having been shown – and shown so clearly – by the Apostle that we can never save ourselves by our works, our danger is to swing right over to the other side and say, 'Quite! They do not matter at all. All that matters is that we give assent to these propositions of saving faith.' So many have swung from a reliance upon works to a reliance upon nothing but a purely intellectual assent to certain propositions, and it is to safeguard us from that, that the Apostle amplifies his definition.

Or take the second danger which tends to assail us. It is the danger of superficiality, and this is, perhaps, the main one at the present time. It is the danger of failing to see the profound nature of the problem of sin, and correspondingly, therefore, the profound nature of the salvation whereby we are saved. We are always given to something glib, quick and superficial, whereas the whole of the New Testament teaching – indeed the whole of the biblical teaching – is to show us that the problem of sin is the profoundest problem in the whole universe, and necessitated everything that has happened in and through our Lord Jesus Christ. Because the problem is so profound, salvation is correspondingly great – 'So great salvation,' wrote the writer of

Hebrews. So it is in particular to safeguard us against those two dangers that the Apostle amplifies his definition in this way.

And now, returning to our text, the word we must concentrate on is, of course, the word *heart*. 'If thou shalt . . . believe in thine *heart* that God hath raised him from the dead, thou shalt be saved. For with the *heart* man believeth unto righteousness.' This is a most important word in the Scriptures and it is necessary for us to realise that it does not only mean the feelings. The *heart* in Scripture very rarely means only the feelings. It includes that, and sometimes it only means that – the context will generally make it plain – but in the vast majority of instances, the word *heart* in Scripture means the centre, the very innermost citadel, of the personality. Or, if you like, it means the whole personality. So when the Scripture says that with the heart we believe that God has raised Him from the dead, it means that with the whole of our being we believe that. 'With the heart man believeth unto righteousness': with the whole of his personality, not merely his feelings, not merely his intellect, but the totality of everything that he is.

We must, then, work this out, and in doing so, we shall see what I have just been referring to – namely, the depth of the problem, and also the corresponding height and greatness of the salvation.

So let me put it like this as a first proposition, and here I am going to show you the danger of superficiality. We are reminded by this statement of the Apostle that unbelief is not merely a matter of the intellect or understanding. It is primarily and essentially a matter of the heart, the centre of the personality.

Now, as I understand it, it is the failure to realise this that is the root cause of what we may call 'the modern fallacy' of the unbelieving world outside the church. That world, of course, regards the question of whether someone believes in the Christian faith or not, as being purely a matter of the intellect. Men and women think that they do not believe the gospel because of their brain and understanding, because of their logic, their reason and their knowledge, and because of all that they are able to deduce from this wonderful knowledge, especially scientific knowledge, which we have at the present time. The 'man in the street', the non-Christian, dismisses us as fools. Either we have no brains, or if we have, we do not use them. People say that we are either stupid, or else that we are deliberately burying our heads in the sand and refusing to face facts. Or else they may say that we are living in compartments, that we think scientifically during the week, then on Sundays we enter into another realm where we throw our brains overboard and allow ourselves to be carried away by our feelings.

That is what the world says. To the unbelieving world, the problem of Christianity, belief or unbelief, is nothing but a problem of intellect. That is why they often say that of course primitive races are religious. They are ignorant, they are not educated, and they have not been taught how to think. People in past ages used to be religious for the same reason. So belief is purely an intellectual problem, they think, and therefore on intellectual grounds they reject it and have nothing at all to do with it.

Now that is one aspect of what I call the modern problem, and of course you see the profound implications of all this. Men and women will not turn to the Christian faith, which is the only thing that can deal with their moral and all their other problems, they will not even look at it, because, they say, their intellects prohibit it. And unfortunately this error is not confined to those who are outside the church. It is also one of the most fashionable points of view within the Christian church itself.

I am referring, of course, to this popular modern school of thinking, this so-called 'South Bank theology'. It should not be called that because it is not theology, but speculation that masquerades as theology. It will undermine the Christian faith. Nor is it confined to the South Bank in London. You will find it in other places as well.

So what is the fallacy here? Well, it is exactly the same as that held by those who are out in the world. The whole motive behind this new movement in Christian teaching – it is not Christian but it is called that so I have to use the term – the rationale behind it is this: its proponents say, 'It is no use addressing modern man in the old way because he is different. Now,' they say, 'there was a time when man was not scientific, and then he was ready to believe in the supernatural and in the miraculous, in the unseen, and so on, and he also thought in a different manner. But he does not do that any longer. Science has advanced and has taught us a new way of thinking and of looking at the world.'

So they say that if you are going to evangelise modern men and women, you must stop talking to them in that old way; you must stop talking to them about a God 'up there' or 'out there'. That is wrong, they say, that is the old way of thinking. Neither must you talk in terms of the supernatural. No, people today are interested in instruments and in measurements and in things which can be seen and touched. So you must address them in that way, otherwise you will never make Christians of them.

Their desire, these people maintain, is to make men and women Christians, and the only way in which you can do that, they believe, is to talk to them in a manner that is 'intellectual'. You must not talk about miracles; you must not talk about a virgin birth, nor about a literal, physical resurrection. You must not talk about this 'substitutionary atonement' and things like that. Modern people cannot take it. You must not even talk about God as personal.

But, you see, quite apart from the errors in detail, that teaching is fundamentally wrong. Its presupposition is that the Christian faith is purely a matter of intellect. The proponents of this teaching offer a new creed and a new way of teaching, simply because they are guilty of exactly the same fallacy as the unbeliever. They do not see that. They do not know it. Yet that is the root criticism. Their problem is not only that they go wrong in details but, much more seriously, that their fundamental presupposition is wrong. So even if they should happen to say something now and again which is right, it is of no value. They think the trouble with men and women is entirely in their understanding. And this is the very thing that the Apostle is countering at this point.

To help us to be clear about this, I want to take it a step further. Not only is this modern school of teaching wrong at this point, it may interest you to know that the real argument behind the production of what is called the *New English Bible* was over exactly the same issue. What was the argument for that and for this spate of new translations that we are getting? It is that modern men and women no longer know anything about justification or sanctification and other things like that. There was a time when those categories did mean something, but not any longer. So you must have a new translation and get rid of all those terms that are meaningless to the people of today. Tom, Dick and Harry, they say, can make nothing of them. But if you get a translation to them that they can understand and follow, then they will probably become Christians.

But that is exactly this same old fallacy. It assumes that people are not Christians because they do not understand terms like justification and the others – and of course that is not the reason at all! Men and women of the world have never understood those terms. They have always had to have them explained. Preaching has always been essential. The people of two hundred years ago in London, when Whitefield used to preach on Kennington Common and in Moorgate, knew no more about justification and sanctification than Tom, Dick or Harry do today, and yet those are the very terms that Whitefield preached to them, explaining what they meant. People's failure to believe has nothing to do with intellectual difficulty about understanding terminology; that is not the trouble.

Now we have to grant, of course, and it would be foolish not to, that the gospel must be preached and presented – if I may use the term that was used by the Protestant Reformers – in a language 'understanded of the people'. What they meant was that it is no use speaking to people in Latin if they do not understand Latin! But that is a very different thing from imagining that the great terms of Christian salvation will ever be understood by the natural man or woman. Of course, we should be as plain and as simple as we can in our preaching, in our presentation of the Word: that is common sense. But that is not the argument of this other school. Their argument is that if only we use language that people can understand, then they will immediately believe the message.

And that is exactly where the fallacy comes in, because, as the Apostle shows us here, the trouble with men and women is not in the head but in the heart. The problem is not an intellectual one; it is much deeper than that. It is down in the very depths of the personality. They are not only partly wrong, they are entirely and completely wrong; they are utterly fallen.

This is a very important point, so I must establish it. Notice how the Apostle does it. Did you see, I wonder, in verse 6 of this chapter, how he has already thrown out a hint of what he is going to do? Paul says, 'The righteousness which is of faith speaketh on this wise.' Here is the preacher of 'righteousness by faith' – what does he say? Does he say, 'Do not say in your mind, or do not think with your intellect'? Not a bit of it! 'Say not *in thine heart*' – there is the trouble – 'Who shall ascend into heaven?'

In other words, as we expounded it, this is the fundamental unbelief of the natural person. People are always raising their objections. They express them intellectually but they do not arise in the intellect. All intellectual arguments simply substantiate what is really believed in the heart.

I do trust that I am making this plain. What people say is only the defence and the excuse for what they really are in their hearts. So the thing to pay attention to is not what they say, but what they are.

But the sixth verse is not the only example of this. Go right back to the first chapter of Romans and you will find that the Apostle has already said the same thing: 'For the wrath of God is revealed from heaven against all ungodliness and unrighteousness of men, who hold the truth in unrighteousness' [*Rom.* 1:18]. Now the right translation there is, as we saw,[1] 'who hold down the truth in unrighteousness'. What is the trouble with these men? Ah, the trouble with them is not in their minds, nor in their intellects, their trouble is that they 'hold down the truth in unrighteousness'. They will not have it; they are resisting it; they are stamping on it; they are keeping their foot upon it. They *hold down* the truth in their state of unrighteousness.

Now that is a tremendous statement of this very principle and it was made away back at the beginning of the Epistle. Look also at chapter 1:21. Here is the trouble with the human race: 'Because that, when they knew God, they glorified him not as God, neither were thankful; but became vain in their imaginations, and their foolish heart was darkened.' That was the trouble. It was not intellect. It was something much deeper – a fundamental attitude towards God. It was not just a question of terminology, nor of knowledge and intellectual apprehension. There was something down in the very depths of the human personality that would not glorify God. As the devil had raised himself up in his pride and had rebelled against God and had attacked Him, man has done the same thing. It is in his heart – 'his foolish heart was darkened'.

But still more clearly, perhaps, you have it in Romans 1:28: 'And even as they did not like to retain God in their knowledge.' They did not want to; they wanted to be doing something else. This was not because of their intellectual understanding, nor because of their great education. No, it was because they were governed by something much deeper than the intellect – their whole personality, their whole desire: they did not 'like' to retain God in their knowledge. That was why they turned their backs upon Him.

And again, of course, we have had a great statement of this in the eighth chapter: 'The carnal mind is enmity against God: for it is not subject to the law of God, neither indeed can be' [*Rom.* 8:7]. The trouble with Tom, Dick and Harry is not that they do not understand

[1] See *An Exposition of Chapter 1: The Gospel of God*, 1985.

the meaning of justification and sanctification; it is that they love sin and hate God.

So there is the essential cause of the trouble, and the Bible is full of this. 'The fool hath said in his heart, There is no God' [*Ps.* 14:1]. You notice where the psalmist says it is – 'in his heart'. That is why this modern movement is so completely fatuous and ridiculous. To me, if these things were not tragic they would certainly be laughable. These people pride themselves on saying something new when all they are saying is that 'The fool hath said in his heart, There is no God'! Away back a thousand years before the birth of the Lord Jesus Christ, that is what people were saying. The clever 'fools' were saying in their hearts, 'There is no God'! That is always the cause of the trouble.

There are many repetitions of that in the Old Testament. Indeed, we could have gone further back than the Psalms to Genesis 6:5. Here was the condition before the Flood: 'God saw that every imagination of the thoughts of his [man's] heart was only evil continually.' There is the seat of unbelief: in the heart. So you see why Paul emphasises that the heart is also the seat of belief.

Furthermore, look at how our Lord Himself puts this point: 'At that time Jesus answered and said, I thank thee, O Father, Lord of heaven and earth, because thou hast hid these things from the wise and prudent, and hast revealed them unto babes. Even so, Father: for so it seemed good in thy sight' [*Matt.* 11:25–26]. Now there it is, once and for ever. 'The wise and prudent' – those who believe in their brains and are so proud of their intellect – they are the people who never get this understanding of God. But the 'babes' get it; the babes, the unintelligent as it were, those who do not trust to their intellect, they are the ones to whom it is revealed.

You also find the same thing in John 3:19, one of the most amazing statements of all, which you would have thought would have been sufficient in and of itself to put this matter right once and for ever. 'And this is the condemnation, that light is come [or has come] into the world, and men loved darkness rather than light.' The light has come – why do people not believe it? 'Ah,' comes the answer, 'because they lack intellect.' No, it is because 'men loved darkness rather than light'.

The problem, then, is in our whole nature. That is why you and I need to be regenerate. If it were merely a matter of the intellect, that could be put right by instruction. But it is much deeper; it is a profound problem. The human race is totally fallen, entirely wrong. 'This is the condemnation . . .'

'How can ye believe,' says our Lord in another passage, 'which receive honour one of another, and seek not the honour that cometh from God only?' [*John* 5:44]. 'Your trouble,' He says in effect, 'is your pride, you receive honour one from another. You write your books to one another and you praise one another in your reviews; and there you are going round and round in your circles, and you are outside the knowledge of God.' And that is precisely what is happening today.

But let me give you another illustration to show the same thing. Look at this man, the Apostle Paul, before he became a Christian. He was a great intellect, a great brain, a most erudite man, but he was not a Christian. Why was that? It could not have been lack of intelligence. It could not have been lack of information, because like every other Pharisee he had heard all about Jesus. He tells us later on in addressing Agrippa and Festus, 'I verily thought with myself, that I ought to do many things contrary to the name of Jesus of Nazareth' [*Acts* 26:9]. He knew all about Him, but he regarded Him as a blasphemer. So what was the matter with Paul? Was his problem that he could not understand the terminology?

And you get the answer in the story of his conversion: 'And Saul, yet breathing out threatenings and slaughter. . .' [*Acts* 9:1]. That is not cold intellectual detachment, is it? That is not a scientific view of the situation! He was not rejecting Christianity because of his great brain and a detached, purely objective point of view! No, he was governed by something else – 'breathing out threatenings and slaughter'. Passion! Hatred! Venom! Spleen! He wanted to massacre these innocent Christian people!

And what was true of Saul of Tarsus before his conversion is the simple truth about all non-Christians today. It is this antagonism, this bitterness, this hatred. They cannot deal with Christian truth without making fun of it. Read their books, and you will see how they say that we ignorant Christians, like the people before us, have always thought of God as some glorified Father Christmas . . . How clever! And you can hear the little laughter and the titters as these things are said – how clever it all is! And they think they are intellectuals. The trouble is not only in their brains – it is there, but it is also much deeper; it is down in the very basis and depths of their personality.

[152]

Or take it again as this Apostle Paul puts it so plainly in the first two chapters of 1 Corinthians. He preaches 'Christ crucified'. He says he knows perfectly well that 'unto the Jews it is a stumblingblock, and unto the Greeks foolishness'. The point is not that they examine the Christian faith rationally, and then in a purely intellectual and objective manner reject it. No, they show this scorn, this derision – 'foolishness!' Why the heat and the passion? Because the trouble is not intellectual but altogether deeper.

And so you find Paul saying explicitly in 1 Corinthians 2, 'The natural man receiveth not the things of the Spirit of God: for they are foolishness unto him: neither can he know them, because they are spiritually discerned' [*1 Cor.* 2:14]. He does not merely reject them, he ridicules them. They are foolishness and unworthy of consideration.

Finally, let me give you a quotation concerning the state of the unregenerate from Ephesians 4. 'This I say therefore, and testify in the Lord, that ye henceforth walk not as other Gentiles walk, in the vanity of their mind, having the understanding darkened, being alienated from the life of God through the ignorance that is in them, because of the blindness of their heart' – that is why they are ignorant – 'who being past feeling have given themselves over unto lasciviousness, to work all uncleanness with greediness' [*Eph.* 4:17–19]. Is that not a perfect description of men and women of this modern generation: boasting of great intellectuality and yet living as if they were animals in the farmyard? No, it is the heart that is the key in unbelief, and in belief also, the belief which constitutes saving faith. And we shall go on to consider that next.

Fourteen

*

> *That if thou shalt confess with thy mouth the Lord Jesus, and shalt believe in thine heart that God hath raised him from the dead, thou shalt be saved. For with the heart man believeth unto righteousness; and with the mouth confession is made unto salvation.*
>
> Romans 10:9–10

We have seen that in Scripture the heart stands for the very centre and seat of personality. And the point that the Apostle is making is that our belief must be with our whole being and not merely with the intellect. We have shown, too, that unbelief is not merely intellectual, though the modern intellectuals would have us believe that. But on the negative side, Scripture teaches very clearly that unbelief is always primarily a matter of the heart, not of the intellect.

It is very interesting to me to observe how this is constantly being confirmed. I was recently reading a review of a book in an evangelical weekly journal and the evangelical reviewer, obviously not grasping this point, was chiding evangelicals because of what he called our failure to meet the modern intellectual sceptics and unbelievers on their own ground. He was not really defending the author, the Bishop of Woolwich, but he came very near to doing so, because, he said, we cannot persuade the modern intellectuals of the truth of the gospel.

The answer to that kind of argument is, of course, that the intellectuals have always found it hard to believe. 'Not many wise men after the flesh, not many mighty, not many noble, are called' [1 Cor. 1:26], says the Apostle Paul, the supreme evangelist. Even he could not persuade such people, because it is not an intellectual matter, and the last thing we must ever do is in any way try to change our message in order to accommodate these intellectual infidels. The trouble is in their *hearts*; and nothing but a new heart will ever enable them to believe.

Of course, we must do all we can to put the truth clearly to them;

[154]

indeed, I suggest that we are doing that, and that this criticism of evangelicals is not true. And, thank God, there are intelligent intellectual people who are being converted – not because they are intelligent, but because the Holy Spirit has dealt with them, because God has chosen them. Now I trust that that negative aspect, at any rate, is clear.

Let us move on, then, to the positive aspect, which is this. Belief, obviously, is primarily a matter of the heart and not of the intellect. In a sense, there is nothing more dangerous to the soul than to think that belief of the truth is purely something for the mind. It includes that; indeed, I go further, it starts there. But what is wrong is that it should stop there. This is something which is of great importance. As some people can delude themselves that they are Christians because they live only on their feelings, others can be equally guilty of the same misapprehension because of their purely intellectual attitude.

Now I want to try to show you, even from history, the importance of emphasising a matter like this. I believe it can be shown very clearly from church history that some of the greatest troubles which confront the church today, and which have always confronted the church, have been the result of failing to understand this point. I am one of those who hold the view that one of the greatest calamities that has ever happened to the Christian church occurred when the Emperor Constantine, at the beginning of the fourth century, decided to become a Christian and brought in most of the Roman Empire with him. The Christian church has never been quite the same since.

How did that happen? Well, it was because of a failure to understand this point. It is not for us to express judgments on Constantine himself, but I think a great deal can be said for the view that his attitude towards the truth was entirely intellectual. That is why he compromised, and led the leaders of the church to compromise so much, in order to accommodate him and the people of the Roman Empire. It was more or less a political and an intellectual decision on his part. And the Emperor having become a Christian, the Roman Empire became Christian, and the vast majority of the people in that empire became Christians also. It was merely a changing over from one point of view to another. It was a decision that they took. And in many ways the Christian church is still reaping the consequences of that. That is where the whole notion of a state church came in. That is where the idea of a Christian country, or a Christian empire, came in, an idea which has led to such grievous confusion throughout the centuries. So that is one very important reason for considering it.

But then here is another reason. The teaching of the Roman Catholic Church throughout the centuries, and still today, is in direct violation of this point made here by the Apostle. How does one become a Christian according to Roman Catholic teaching? Their answer is that you become a Christian merely by giving your intellectual assent to the doctrine of the Church. Now that is not my opinion, that is their official teaching. If you say, 'I am prepared to accept the teaching of the Church', you are immediately and of necessity a Christian.

Indeed, they go further, they even say that believing the teaching of the Church, without actually knowing what it is, is enough. In other words, if you say, 'Well now, I do not understand, I have not read much, I cannot think very clearly, but I am prepared to trust my soul to the Church' – that is enough to save you.

Now that is Roman Catholic teaching. There is no demand for experience at all. Becoming a Christian is primarily an intellectual matter, indeed, it is almost exclusively so. But that is the opposite of the teaching which says, 'With the heart man believeth unto right-eousness,' or of Peter's statement: 'Be ready always to give an answer to every man that asketh you a reason of the hope that is in you with meekness and fear' [*1 Pet.* 3:15]. Yet that is the Roman Catholic position, so, you see, it is not surprising that they divide up Christ-ians into the ordinary and the extraordinary. They divide up the Church into the lay Christian and the clergy, who are the separated, the spiritual Christians. All their teaching really emanates from this, and though you may be a worldly and an ignorant Christian, it does not matter; as long as you say that you trust the Church, all is well and you are saved. Now that is the complete antithesis of what we have here.

But unfortunately this is not confined to Roman Catholicism. This false notion of the character of saving faith has often afflicted the Protestant churches. One very notable example took place in the eighteenth century. This was a teaching that began in Scotland, first taught by a very able man called John Glas. Then a daughter of his married a man called Robert Sandeman, and Sandeman came to England and propagated this teaching; so it is commonly known as *Sandemanianism.*

What was this teaching? Well, its proponents put their great emphasis upon the words 'confess with thy mouth the Lord Jesus'. They said that though you felt nothing, though you were not aware of any change at all in yourself, if you accepted the teaching intellectually and were prepared to say so, then that saved you.

Now this became quite an important movement and it led to terrible results. It led in the Church of Scotland to a condition known as *Moderatism*. Not that they were all followers of Glas, but they more or less accepted his teaching without saying so. And the result was that the Church became entirely lifeless, and it really was not delivered from that condition until those great revivals took place under William Chalmers Burns and Robert Murray M'Cheyne, and people like them, in the 1830s and the early 1840s. For almost a hundred years, the Church of Scotland was in a parlous and lifeless condition, very largely owing to this kind of barren intellectualism.

And there is another notable illustration of this very point which has always impressed me. There was a great Baptist preacher in Wales, in the first forty years of the nineteenth century, called Christmas Evans, one of the great preachers of all time. That man for fifteen years in his ministry passed through a most barren, arid period, and it was entirely due to the fact that he had adopted this Sandemanian teaching, and he gives an account of how he was delivered from it.

So you see it is a truly important matter. To be wrong on this point may rob people of the gracious influences of the Holy Spirit. They can be correct in an intellectual manner, but they lose the life, the power, the joy and the real thrill of the Christian life. It has been very devastating in it effects.

But we do not even stop at that; there are certain tendencies in this direction even in our own day. I regret to say that this was also more or less the teaching of Professor C. S. Lewis. He believed that you could reason yourself into the Christian faith. The first book he ever published was called *The Pilgrim's Regress*, and its whole point is to say that by clear thinking you can move from a rationalist or an atheistical position into the Christian position. At one time he founded in Oxford what was called 'The Socratic Club' which met on Monday nights, in which he used to try to show people how to 'reason' themselves into Christianity. But 'with the heart man believeth unto righteousness'. You cannot do it merely by a process of intellectual reasoning.

There is what may be called 'believism', or, if you prefer it, 'decisionism' – the tendency to force people to a decision and to say,

'Now here it is, do you believe it?' And if they say, 'Yes', you say, 'You are right, you are saved.' Now I am not here to say that that is of necessity always wrong, but what is wrong is that men and women believe that merely 'coming forward' at the end of a meeting puts them right, or that merely *saying* that they believe the truth proves that they are true believers and that they have saving faith.

The greater the pressure to make people take a decision or to use a formula, the greater the danger. This is especially true when the formula is accompanied by some such remark as: 'Do not worry about your feelings, do not worry if you don't feel anything at all. Are you prepared to say this? If you are, you are a Christian.' That seems to me to be a complete denial of the teaching of the Apostle at this point. 'If thou shalt confess with thy mouth the Lord Jesus, and shalt believe in thine heart . . . For with the heart man believeth unto righteousness.' The mere repetition of a formula does not save men and women: they must believe in their hearts. So 'believism' or 'fideism' is again based upon the failure to understand this teaching.

But let me complete my list by adding a final reason for considering the danger of stopping at intellectual assent – and perhaps this is the reason that ought to be emphasised most of all amongst people who are engaged, as we are, in this study of Romans. There is such a thing as mistaking a theological intellectualism for saving faith. It is the danger of believing the doctrines of salvation instead of believing in the Person of Christ and having a living faith in Him. It is one thing to accept a body of doctrine with your mind, it is another to have a saving faith in the Lord Jesus Christ. You can be a perfectly orthodox theologian and yet have no spiritual life at all. That is not an exaggeration, it is the simple truth. I have known such people.

This is a terrible danger. Theological intellectualism is as bad as Sandemanianism, it is as bad as the Roman Catholic position, it is as bad as believism or decisionism. A man who thinks that mere acceptance of a body of doctrine is saving faith, is a man who is deluding himself. We are not saved by believing in doctrine, we are saved by believing in a Person. You must know the truth about Him, but you must not believe the truth about Him without believing in Him. You must not allow the doctrines to conceal the blessed Person. *He* is the Saviour. It is He who does the saving.

Now there are some of the reasons why it is so important for us to be clear on a matter like this and not to misunderstand the Apostle's teaching here. He is not saying that the opposite of justification by works is simply an intellectual acceptance of a proposition. That is why he is putting this emphasis upon the heart.

What Paul does here is what is done everywhere else in the Scriptures. Now there is nothing more important than this; our eternal salvation depends upon it. There is this terrible danger that some of us, having being brought up in Christian homes and having always gone to the Christian church, are saying, 'But I have always believed this.' But you may mean by that, 'I have always repeated the statements.' Are you sure that you have got saving faith?

I cannot expound the Scriptures without preaching. It is a terrible thing to feed people's intellects at the expense of their souls: this is a most searching statement. So let me work it out for you in terms of the Scriptures as a whole. The fundamental proposition therefore must be that a change of heart and regeneration are absolutely essential to salvation. There is no such thing as a saving faith without them.

Let me demonstrate this. The Apostle has already told us this. Take verses 28 and 29 of chapter 2: 'For he is not a Jew, which is one outwardly; neither is that circumcision, which is outward in the flesh: but he is a Jew, which is one inwardly; and circumcision is that of the heart, in the spirit, and not in the letter; whose praise is not of men, but of God.' Paul says that the whole trouble with the old nation of Israel was that they had never understood that circumcision is inward, a matter of the heart, and not merely external, of the flesh. And it is exactly the same now in the New Testament in the realm of faith.

And then there is Romans 6:17: 'But God be thanked,' says the Apostle, 'that ye were the servants of sin, but ye have obeyed from the heart that form of doctrine which was delivered you.' Now there he puts the same emphasis. How careful he is! He does not say, 'Whereas once ye were the servants of sin, ye are now believers in the Lord Jesus Christ.' That is all right, but he wants to make this point so certain that instead of saying that, he says, 'Ye have obeyed from the heart that form of doctrine which was delivered you' – or, 'that mould of doctrine into which you have been poured', which is what this phrase really means, as we saw when we were dealing with it.[1]

But let me give you some supporting evidence from Ezekiel 36:25–27: 'Then will I sprinkle clean water upon you, and ye shall be clean: from all your filthiness, and from all your idols, will I cleanse you. A new heart also will I give you, and a new spirit will I put within you:

[1] See *An Exposition of Chapter 6: The New Man*, 1972.

and I will take away the stony heart out of your flesh, and I will give you an heart of flesh. And I will put my spirit within you, and cause you to walk in my statutes, and ye shall keep my judgments, and do them.'

In the Parable of the Sower, our Lord quotes Isaiah: 'for this people's heart is waxed gross': John Wycliff translated that, 'this people's heart has become enfattened'. I rather like that. 'Waxed gross': too much fat about it! It is 'enfattened' so that it cannot function properly. That is their trouble. 'This people's heart is waxed gross, and their ears are dull of hearing' – as the result of that. If your heart is not working, none of your faculties will be able to work, you cannot hear properly – 'and their eyes they have closed; lest at any time they should see with their eyes, and hear with their ears, and should understand with their heart, and should be converted, and I should heal them' [*Matt.* 13:13–15]. Notice our Lord's tremendous emphasis upon the condition of the heart.

Our Lord expounds this Parable of the Sower in Luke 8. Its theme is 'saving faith'. Some people seem to be saved, but they are not, they only last for a while. The seed springs up, you think it is wonderful – but there is nothing there, there is no root. But there is one type, the fourth, which is right: 'But that on the good ground are they, which in an honest and good heart, having heard the word, keep it, and bring forth fruit with patience' [*Luke* 8:15]. You see, when He talks about having a 'root', He refers to the heart, and if there is not this root in the heart, the faith is ultimately of no value. It is a temporary, not a saving faith.

Another very interesting sidelight on all this concerns Nicodemus, who thought that all he needed was further understanding. Our Lord insisted that he had to be born again, born of the Spirit [*John* 3:1–8]. Regeneration is essential.

Now nothing so illustrates and confirms the teaching of Romans 10:9 and 10 as just that very teaching on the absolute necessity of regeneration. You do not merely accept the truth with your mind, you must be born again. That is New Testament teaching, and I am convinced that the main explanation of the state of the Christian church today is the neglect of the doctrine of regeneration. That is the fundamental need. There is too much 'believism' without regeneration. There is intellectualism without life. But the whole emphasis of the Lord's teaching is on the absolute necessity of regeneration.

All this is put very explicitly in Acts 2:37: 'Now when they heard this [Peter's sermon], they were pricked in their heart.' Not stimulated in their intellects! They ended by 'Praising God' [v. 47]. That is the proof that what had happened to them had happened in the realm of their hearts.

In Acts 7, we have Stephen preaching to those gainsaying Jewish authorities who were antagonistic to Christianity: 'Ye stiffnecked and uncircumcised in heart and ears, ye do always resist the Holy Ghost: as your fathers did, so do ye' [v. 51]. The trouble was not in their minds; they were 'uncircumcised in their hearts'. It is always the source of the trouble.

The famous story of Philip and the Ethiopian eunuch further illustrates this. Philip expounded the Scriptures to him and baptised him on his confession that 'Jesus Christ is the Son of God' [*Acts* 8:27–39].

Now you notice that Philip was not so anxious to report a convert that he said, 'Now if you are prepared to say this after me, yes, I will baptise you.' No. Philip said in effect, 'You say you believe and you want to be baptised, but only, "If thou believest with all thine heart." ' That is apostolic Christianity, that is apostolic evangelism. The mere fact that the man asked to be baptised was not enough. Because he made the affirmation from the heart, the Ethiopian eunuch was baptised.

Acts 15 reports a dispute about how one becomes a Christian – the very point that Paul is dealing with in Romans 10. The Judaisers, those Pharisees among the believers, were saying, 'These people must be circumcised and be put under the law.' Peter answered: 'God made choice among us, that the Gentiles by my mouth should hear the word of the gospel, and believe. *And God*' – observe! – '*which knoweth the hearts,* bare them witness, giving them the Holy Ghost even as he did unto us; and put no difference between us and them, purifying their hearts by faith. . . We believe that through the grace of the Lord Jesus Christ we shall be saved, even as they' [vv. 7–11].

Now you notice the emphasis: 'God which knoweth the hearts'. This was a reference to what happened when Peter preached to Cornelius and his household, and the Holy Spirit descended upon them [Acts 10]. Peter was convinced by this that these people were truly Christians, and therefore he baptised them. When Peter said, 'God which knoweth the hearts . . .', he meant that God would never have sent the Holy Spirit upon them if He had not known that they had believed in their hearts. God does not merely go by what a person says, by intellectual belief and apprehension. God knows the state of a person's heart.

Then comes the ninth verse of Acts 15: 'And put no difference between us and them, purifying their hearts by faith.' Here is a most interesting statement which, it seems to me, is almost invariably misunderstood. People say, 'Ah, that is teaching about sanctification. It says that sanctification is by faith. You do not strive, you do not do anything at all about it, you receive it by faith. As you took your justification by faith, you take your sanctification by faith.'

But it has nothing whatsoever to do with sanctification, because the Apostle was dealing with salvation – justification. So that is why he summed it up by saying, 'We believe that through the grace of the Lord Jesus Christ we shall be saved, even as they' [v. 11]. There is only one way of salvation. Jew and Gentile are saved in exactly the same way. Why, then, did Peter use this expression, 'purifying their hearts by faith'? It is because the whole trouble with the Gentiles was that 'their foolish heart was darkened' [*Rom.* 1:21]. It is the trouble with all unbelievers and they therefore need to be cleansed. Cleansing comes in only one way, and that is by faith – not in the sense of sanctification, but by becoming believers, by having believing hearts.

If you like, you can call this 'regeneration', but you must not call it sanctification. The Apostle Peter was not concerned about sanctification here. The issue here is: How are people saved? Can those who have not been circumcised be saved? Those who do not live under the law and do not try to keep the law, can they be saved? That was the bone of contention. And Peter said: Here is my proof. I was preaching in the household of Cornelius and there they were, Gentiles. I preached the gospel and God sent the Holy Spirit upon them, proving that they had believed from the heart.

How were they able to believe in that way? God had worked in their hearts, purifying them, taking away the stony heart of unbelief, giving them the new heart of flesh and the possibility of believing with the heart. That is what is meant by 'purifying their hearts by faith'. And it is still more important to notice that the tense in the Greek is the aorist: it is a single act. Peter said that God had dealt with them there and then and proved that he had done it by sending the Holy Spirit down upon them. The heart of man has to be changed, it has to be cleansed. It ceases to be profane and unbelieving and is made a heart of flesh, a believing heart. That is exactly what Peter was saying and no more.

The case of Lydia, the first convert to Paul's preaching in Europe, confirms all this. And how was she converted? She was a worshipper of the true God and as she listened to Paul, her 'heart was opened by the Lord' and she 'attended unto the things which were spoken by Paul' [*Acts* 16:13–14]. That is saving faith. The heart was opened by the Lord. Her heart was purified by faith, and so she was enabled to believe. She ceased to be a Jewish proselyte, which she probably was, and became a believer; but it was as the result of her heart being opened by God. It was not an intellectual acceptance of the teaching, but her heart was opened, and therefore she believed.

The Apostle is always saying the same thing: 'God, who commanded the light to shine out of darkness, hath shined in our hearts, to give the light of the knowledge of the glory of God in the face of Jesus Christ' [*1 Cor.* 4:6]. But you notice where He 'shined'? Not in the mind, but in the heart. It includes the mind, but it is deeper.

Then to continue this evidence, read Hebrews 3:12–15: 'Take heed, brethren, lest there be in any of you an evil heart of unbelief, in departing from the living God. But exhort one another daily, while it is called To day; lest any of you be hardened through the deceitfulness of sin' – not a hard brain but a hard heart is the trouble – 'For we are made partakers of Christ, if we hold the beginning of our confidence stedfast unto the end; while it is said, To day if ye will hear his voice, harden not your hearts, as in the provocation.' Perfectly plain and clear, is it not?

My final quotation is 1 Peter 1:21–22: 'Who by him do believe in God, that raised him up from the dead, and gave him glory; that your faith and hope might be in God. Seeing ye have purified your souls in obeying the truth through the Spirit unto unfeigned love of the brethren . . .'

I am proving to you that my exposition of Acts 15:9 is correct. The same person, Peter, who is speaking in Acts 15:9, is now writing in 1 Peter 1:22. So those who believe that Peter is teaching in Acts 15:9 that sanctification is by faith only – because it says that '*God* purified their hearts by faith' – must see that here the same Peter, dealing with exactly the same point of how someone believes, says, '[You] believe in God, that raised him up from the dead, and gave him glory; that your faith and hope might be in God. Seeing *ye* have purified your souls' – 'souls' here means 'heart'. Now if you are literalists you may say, 'But after all, Peter says in Acts 15, "*God* purified their hearts."' Right, I reply that he says here, '*You* have purified your hearts.' Which is it?

You see the mistake? Neither verse is dealing with sanctification. Peter, looking at this from the human standpoint, is in effect saying here: 'You have purified your souls, your hearts, in obeying the truth through the Spirit.' The context is, 'You believe in God through him', and in doing so you have purified your hearts, you have become believers. It is another way of describing a believer. In other words, the belief is not merely in the mind, it is in the heart. And in both places Peter is saying that only a faith that comes out of a new heart is a saving faith.

Very well, our Lord had really said it all, had He not, in giving the great commandment. One of the scribes had asked, 'Which is the first commandment of all?' And His answer was, 'Thou shalt love the Lord thy God' – not merely believe in Him – 'with all thy heart, and with all thy soul, and with all thy mind, and with all thy strength' – the whole being [*Mark* 12:28–30]. Belief is not enough. The demons believe and tremble [*Jas.* 2:19]. There is a hatred and an antagonism. The proof of saving faith is that it comes out of the heart. So you *love* the Lord your God, and if there is not an element of love in it, as I hope to show you in our next study, it is not truly saving faith.

We have, therefore, considered all this scriptural evidence in order to establish beyond any doubt at all that saving faith is not merely a matter of the intellect, but must of necessity be essentially a matter of the heart. So thank God for His Word. We thank Him for its instruction and for the way in which it searches us. We are conscious that we need to be searched. We are aware of a subtle antagonist who would persuade us that all is well, and lull us into a carnal, false security. So we thank God that His Word comes to us and exhorts us to examine ourselves to see whether we are in the faith or not.

We thank Him, too, for the character of saving faith. We thank Him that the truth is so great that it takes up the whole person, that His salvation is perfect, that He is not content with saving us partly, but gives us a complete salvation. 'O the depth of the riches both of the wisdom and knowledge of God!' [*Rom.* 11:33].

Fifteen

*

That if thou shalt confess with thy mouth the Lord Jesus, and shalt believe in thine heart that God hath raised him from the dead, thou shalt be saved. For with the heart man believeth unto righteousness; and with the mouth confession is made unto salvation.   Romans 10:9–10

We have spent some considerable time studying this statement, because it is such a crucially important one. As we have already seen, it affects evangelism; it affects our understanding of salvation; it probably affects the whole course of our Christian life. And we have been adducing a large number of statements from the Scripture in which we see so clearly that the heart is central in this whole matter.

So we are now in a position to ask a question: What does a saving faith, a true belief, really include? We have pointed out, negatively, that saving faith is not merely a matter of the intellect, and that the Apostle takes up this word *heart* in order to bring out and emphasise that point. We have been showing the difference between a mere intellectual assent to a number of propositions, and what the Bible really means by believing on the Lord Jesus Christ. It has always been a great snare, that we substitute mere assent, or intellectual acceptance, for what the Bible means by faith. So we must now go on to ask our question. What does true belief include?

In answer, of course, we must start by saying that faith obviously begins with the mind. It begins there because what we are dealing with, after all, is truth; and truth is something that comes to the mind and to the understanding and should be addressed to that. You remember Romans 6:17, which puts the whole thing perfectly: 'God be thanked,' says the Apostle, 'that ye were the servants of sin, but ye have obeyed from the heart that form of doctrine which was delivered you.' The Apostle says, in effect, 'Your position, you Roman Christians, once upon a time, was that you were the servants of sin, but you

[165]

are no longer that. What, then, are you? Well, you have become quite different,' he says, 'and for this reason. The truth was delivered to you. You heard the preaching of the gospel.' The facts concerning our Lord, and their meaning, were put before them.

And obviously that is something to which one listens with one's mind. We are told constantly in the book of Acts that the Apostle would go into a synagogue on the Sabbath and there he would 'reason' out of the Scriptures. 'Reason'! Proving and alleging – demonstrating, arguing it out. He would take Old Testament prophecies and show their meaning, proving that they had been fulfilled in the Lord Jesus Christ. Now all that is a process that is addressed to a person's mind.

That, I hope, is now quite clear to all of us. It is certainly not clear to everybody, of course. There are people who go to meetings just to get a feeling, and they really do not bother to listen; they are always looking for sensations. But that is not the Christian way. The first thing always is the mind, the intellect, the understanding. It is God's greatest gift, and therefore is the first thing which is addressed by the truth, by the preaching of the gospel. But having been clear about that, we go on to say that it does not stop there, that it does not end with the intellect and that, as we have seen, faith is not only a matter of the understanding.

What else? Well, our very term *heart* tells us all we need to know. It means that the whole person is included. The entire person! When people become Christians every part of them is involved. What does this mean? Well, there is an element of 'conviction', and conviction means that the truth has come to us with power. We have not merely been aware of it; we have not merely seen what it is. We do not remain in that position, we do not remain as we were. There is this disturbing element of conviction, which means that the truth has come to us very powerfully.

Now truth does not always come powerfully. Take an obvious illustration from the realm of politics. You can listen to people speaking on behalf of a party to which you do not belong and with which you do not agree. Well, you can apprehend intellectually what they are saying, but it does not touch you; it does not convince you or move you; you do nothing about it. You find it quite interesting, even enjoyable. You are able to follow the speakers quite intelligently and you can tell what they said, but it is nothing more than that; you have not been made to change your position from one party to another;

they have left you exactly where you were. And there are many people who listen to the gospel like that. But when the heart is involved there is always an element of conviction.

In other words, the truth comes to us and we are not only aware of it, but it challenges us, it disturbs us. It does not allow us to think in a passive and a detached manner only. We become engaged in it. We have the feeling that it is speaking to us directly, and speaking to us as persons. Now all this is involved in what is called 'conviction'. We are no longer merely spectators, taking our seats and looking on. No, we are involved in it and it is doing something to us; it is speaking directly to us, making us examine ourselves. It causes us to question everything that we have hitherto believed.

If we have been militantly opposed to the gospel, we begin to query whether we have been right, we begin to feel uncomfortable. Or if we have been quite passive and unaffected, it now begins to make us think. We say, 'Well, how can I have been guilty of neglecting this for so long? How is it that I have never realised before that this is something that has got to do with me?' We begin to realise that this is something that is of vital concern to us, to which we must pay attention because it is speaking to our whole condition as human beings. That is what is meant by conviction. The reality of the thing suddenly takes hold of us.

Now I do not know your background, but there are probably many who have been brought up from childhood to go to a place of worship and to listen to the gospel. At a certain age you did not even listen, but you spent your time amusing yourself in various ways. You got over that, you got a bit older, and then you began to listen – in a very general sense. And you may have gone on like that for years until, one day, you suddenly had a feeling: 'But this is tremendously important to me!' And at last you began to listen for yourself and you found that the truth was challenging you and making you think and reconsider all your ideas and your whole position. That is conviction.

Then, of course, there comes the next step in the 'engagement of the heart', and that is what is called *repentance*. Now conviction is not repentance; conviction leads to repentance. But you can be convicted without repentance. While you are convicted you may be annoyed by the truth. You may resent it because it is disturbing you, because it suggests that you are wrong, and that you ought to change and you do not want to. You are under conviction, but you may be intensely miserable, even antagonistic to the truth. Yet you cannot leave it alone. And it will not leave you alone until you go on to repentance.

Now repentance means at least two main things. The first is that you change your mind. Re-pent! That is a Latin word which means 'think again'. So it is obvious that men and women whose hearts are involved in the gospel are people who, under this conviction, are not only made to think again and to think more seriously and in a more personal manner and on a deeper level, but are made to think until they see that they are wrong, and they change their minds.

Now there is a classic illustration of this in one of our Lord's own parables. 'What think ye? A certain man had two sons; and he came to the first, and said, Son, go work to day in my vineyard. He answered and said, I will not: but afterward he repented and went. And he came to the second, and said likewise. And he answered and said, I go, sir: and went not. Whether of them twain did the will of his father? They say unto him, The first. Jesus saith unto them, Verily I say unto you, That the publicans and the harlots go into the kingdom of God before you. For John came unto you in the way of righteousness, and ye believed him not: but the publicans and the harlots believed him: and ye, when ye had seen it, repented not afterward, that ye might believe him' [*Matt.* 21:28–32].

Notice the first son in this story. When the father asked him to go and work in his vineyard, he did not want to go. He had arranged to do something else and he resented his father's interfering with his plans. So he refused. He said, 'I will not: but afterward he repented.' What happened? Well, instead of going away with his friends to spend the day, he stopped and began to ask himself questions. He 'thought again'! He *repented*! He said, 'Was I right in speaking to my father like that? Was I right to say, "I will not" to him?' You see, he re-examined the whole thing, and not only that, he came to the conclusion that he was wrong: 'Afterward he repented, and went' to the vineyard. He did the thing he said he would not do. So he not only thought again, he changed his mind.

So the first element in this process of repentance is 'a change of mind', and that is the meaning of the Greek word for repentance, *metanoia*. Like that son, you not only think again, but you think in such a way that you change your mind and come to a different conclusion. And that is a very vital part of believing with the heart. Unless there is a change in the opinion, a change in the outlook, a change in the point of view, there is no repentance and no true belief. But that is not enough. You cannot change your opinion with regard to God's whole plan of salvation and your relationship to him, without feeling sorrow for ever having held the wrong view. When that first son saw that he was wrong, he was sorry, and he felt it so much that he went to the vineyard. Sorrow! There is always the element of sorrow in repentance. The heart, as we saw in our definition, includes the mind, the feelings, and also, as we shall see, the will; but the heart and the feelings are of necessity involved.

Now the best statement, I think, in the whole of the New Testament on the aspect of sorrow is in 2 Corinthians 7. Paul says, 'For though I made you sorry with a letter, I do not repent, though I did repent: for I perceive that the same epistle hath made you sorry, though it were but for a season. Now I rejoice, not that ye were made sorry, but that ye sorrowed to repentance: for ye were made sorry after a godly manner, that ye might receive damage by us in nothing. For godly sorrow worketh repentance to salvation not to be repented of: but the sorrow of the world worketh death. For behold this selfsame thing, that ye sorrowed after a godly sort, what carefulness it wrought in you, yea, what clearing of yourselves, yea, what indignation, yea, what fear, yea, what vehement desire, yea, what zeal, yea, what revenge! In all things ye have approved yourselves to be clear in this matter' [*2 Cor.* 7:8–11].

This is very important. We cannot come to see that our whole relationship to God has been wrong, that our attitude to God has been wrong, that we have been rebellious, that we have been defiant, that we have thrust aside as nothing God's greatest act in giving His only begotten Son to the death of the cross – we cannot suddenly realise that we have been guilty of all that, without feeling intense sorrow: godly sorrow! If we have listened to these great truths all our lives and have never had any sorrow in our hearts because of our failure to see them, and to be moved by them, we have no right to think of ourselves as saved people.

You cannot have saving faith without knowing something about this sorrow – sorrow that you have grieved a holy, loving God, sorrow that you have treated God, who has been so kind and gracious, in the way that you have. Indeed, you can scarcely forgive yourself! 'What indignation,' says Paul. Indignation with yourself! And if you have never felt that you are unworthy, if you have never hated yourself, then I think you had better examine the foundations again. Christians are people who hate themselves because they see that they are miserable sinners who have rebelled against their Maker and Creator. Godly sorrow! It is essential.

But then we go even beyond that. The Apostle uses the word *fear*, and fear does come into it. We again have a classic example of this in the preaching of the Apostle Peter at Jerusalem on the day of Pentecost. In a sense it was the first sermon ever delivered under the auspices of the Christian church. Peter had preached to the people and then, we read, 'Now when they heard this, they were pricked in their heart, and said unto Peter and to the rest of the apostles, Men and brethren, what shall we do?' [*Acts* 2:37]. Fear! They were convinced, they were convicted, they saw how wrong they had been. Peter put it to them quite plainly: 'Him, being delivered by the determinate counsel and foreknowledge of God, ye have taken, and by wicked hands have crucified and slain' [v. 23]. He brought it home to them and they saw that he was right. They suddenly realised what they had done and in their agony and fear they cried out, 'Men and brethren, what shall we do?'

And exactly the same thing happened with the Philippian jailor. The earthquake and all that had happened contributed to his fear, and he was on the point of committing suicide. But, 'Paul cried with a loud voice, saying, Do thyself no harm: for we are all here. Then he called for a light, and sprang in, and came trembling, and fell down before Paul and Silas, and brought them out, and said, Sirs, what must I do to be saved?' [*Acts* 16:28–30]. That is how he said it. He was filled with terror.

Now let us be clear about this. I am not saying that there must be the same amount of terror in all cases. But I cannot possibly regard men and women as Christians unless they have known an element of fear: fear because they have sinned against God; fear because they realise that they are in the hands of God, and that He is a holy, just and righteous God, and they have got to stand before Him in the Judgment. If people know nothing about the fear of death and of the judgment, I cannot see how they can be Christians at all. Fear! It is a vital part of saving faith. Men and women begin to realise, as they have never done before, the holiness of the law, and the absolute character of its demands. They realise that they and all others are unrighteous and unworthy and unclean. In some way or another, and to some intensity or another, they cry out with the Apostle Paul, 'Who shall deliver me from the body of this death?' [*Rom.* 7:24]. They are afraid of the destruction that comes upon the ungodly.

The Bible is a terrifying book! It is meant to be, because we all of us are sinners and we need to be awakened. The Puritans of three hundred years ago used to emphasise this a great deal – as, for example, in Joseph Alleine's book, *An Alarm to the Unconverted*. 'Sinners in the hands of an angry God,' preached Jonathan Edwards. Why? Because, 'It is a fearful thing to fall into the hands of the living God', as Hebrews 10:31 tells us. And I have a feeling that what is the matter with so much of Christian life today is that men and women have never known anything about this element of fear. Everything is made so easy, so quick, so glib. You just repeat a formula and then, 'You are all right,' they say.

But where is the fear, my friends? Where is the godly sorrow? You cannot have any glimmering of an understanding of the holy character of God without this. Isaiah was a very godly man, but when he had a glimpse of God, he said, 'Woe is me! for I am undone; because I am a man of unclean lips' [*Isa.* 6:5]. John 'fell at his [Christ's] feet as one dead' [*Rev.* 1:17] when he had his vision. The sight of holiness must be alarming to sinful creatures. If we know nothing about fear and alarm, it is the measure of our ignorance of the being and the character of God. John Bunyan knew fear for eighteen months. I am not saying we all need to be eighteen months in that state; all I am saying is that the element of fear must come in, it must be there.

But we go on beyond that: the next thing, obviously, is a desire for deliverance: 'Who shall deliver me?' [*Rom.* 7:24]; 'Men and brethren, what shall we do?' [*Acts* 2:37]; 'Sirs, what must I do to be saved?' [*Acts* 16:30].

You see, people who just sit and listen intellectually never feel any desire to be delivered. They have not been convicted; there is nothing to be delivered from. People say, 'What is that preacher getting so excited about?', which just means that their hearts have not been engaged. They can give an account of what has been said, but it has not penetrated, they have not felt it. The Spirit has not applied the gospel to them, so they do not see any need of deliverance.

You see how important all this is? This is one of the factors that control whether you call for immediate decisions or not. If you have the true view of saving faith and belief, you will know that when people are convicted by the Spirit of God, they will seek help. You need not force them to, they will have to, they will be so miserable, frightened and alarmed. You often find in a time of revival that not only do you not have to ask people to come forward, you often have to restrain the crowd. And the difficulty is to deal with all these people who, in their agony of conviction, are demanding help and release.

On the great occasion at Kirk O'Shotts in Scotland when John Livingstone preached one sermon which led to the conviction of so many, that was the thing that could be heard all over the countryside – people groaning in agony, asking for release, knocking at the door of the minister, keeping him up all night because they were frantic. Desire for deliverance! Again, do not put too much emphasis upon the degree or the amount of feeling, but upon its reality. 'Who shall deliver me? I cannot, I have tried, I have taken my resolutions and my vows, I cannot keep them, I am a failure, I cannot save myself . . . "Who shall deliver me from the body of this death?" [*Rom.* 7:20].' A longing for deliverance is an inevitable part of 'believing with the heart'.

And this leads to the next thing – trust and confidence in our blessed Lord and Saviour. You see, I started with the mind, but I am now dealing with the heart, this other element. Trust! Confidence! Reliance! This is a vital part of what the New Testament means by belief, by faith. The meaning of the Greek word translated 'faith' is 'to adhere to', 'to cleave to', 'to trust', 'to rely on'. You see, in your fear and alarm, in your desire to be relieved – you know you cannot do it yourself and you cannot find anybody else who can – suddenly you see this One and you believe the truth about Him. You believe that He is the Lord, that God has raised Him from the dead, and you come to this conclusion: He is able to do it for me! 'Who shall deliver me? . . . I thank God through Jesus Christ my Lord' [*Rom.* 7:24–25]. You trust Him, you cleave to Him, you adhere to Him, you rely upon Him, you have faith in Him – all that is involved.

Or take the same kind of definition which is given by Professor Louis Berkhof in his *Systematic Theology*. 'Faith,' he says, 'saving faith, is a certain conviction, wrought in the heart by the Holy Spirit, as to the truth of the gospel, and a hearty reliance (trust) on the promises of God in Christ.' That is it! It is more than being aware of the truth, it is a reliance upon it, it is a committal of yourself to it and a casting of yourself utterly and entirely upon it.

A statement in Hebrews says all that: 'He that cometh to God must believe that he is' – yes, but also – 'and that he is a rewarder of them that diligently seek him' [*Heb.* 11:6]. That is it; it is included in that. You have this reliance, this confidence, and therefore you trust and commit yourself to it. So this, too, is an essential part of saving faith. You can believe with your mind that Jesus is the Son of God, you can have your head packed with theology, but unless you have felt your need of a Saviour, and unless you have committed yourself utterly to Him and rely only upon Him and give yourself to Him that He may save you, you have not got saving faith.

And that in turn leads to this: you are conscious of a sense of rest and a sense of peace. This again is quite inevitable. You cannot have had this conviction, this fear, and then have seen that the Lord Jesus Christ is the One appointed by God, and sent by God, in order to do for you everything you need – you cannot believe that without immediately feeling rest and peace. 'Being justified by faith,' as Paul has already told us in Romans 5:1, 'we have peace with God through our Lord Jesus Christ.' There is an element of rest in faith. The seeking has come to an end – you have found Him!

> *O happy day, that fixed my choice*
> *On Thee, my Saviour and my God! . . .*
> *'Tis done! the great transaction's done!*
> *I am my Lord's and He is mine.*
> Philip Doddridge

The rest of faith! It is always there, it must be there.

And added to it, of course, is the inevitable element of thankfulness and praise. How can anybody believe that the Son of God left the Courts of Heaven, came to earth, endured all He did, even to the extent of dying in agony upon the cross, being laid in a tomb, and rising again – how can I believe that He has done all that for me and not feel thankfulness and praise?

Now once more the Epistle to the Hebrews gives us a good exposition at this point, where the writer is talking about these great giants and heroes of the faith. 'These all,' he says, 'died in faith, not having received the promises, but having seen them afar off, and were persuaded of them, and' – here is the word I want – '*embraced* them, and confessed that they were strangers and pilgrims on the earth' [*Heb.* 11:13]. And the word 'embraced' really means 'greeted them', 'welcomed them'. That is the ultimate greeting, that you 'embrace' the person you are welcoming. That is what these men and women did with the promises, and that is what made them the people they were, that is what 'believing with the heart' really amounts to.

So you do not become a Christian in cold blood, unmoved, undisturbed. You do not sit down in a detached manner and say, 'Well, I have agreed with that doctrine, and therefore I am a Christian.' Not at all! You have been through these stages – conviction, repentance, fear, desire for deliverance, recognition of Him, casting yourself upon Him, thankfulness and praise, glorying in Him, greeting His truth, desiring to know more and more about it!

That, then, is what the Apostle means when he tells us, 'That if thou shalt confess with thy mouth the Lord Jesus, and shalt believe in thine heart that God hath raised him from the dead, thou shalt be saved. For with the heart man believeth unto righteousness.' John Calvin summed it up perfectly when he said, 'The seat of faith, it deserves to be observed, is not in the brain, but in the heart; not that I wish to enter into any dispute concerning the part of the body which is the seat of faith. But since the word "heart" generally means a serious, sincere, ardent affection, I am desirous to show the confidence of faith to be a firm, efficacious and operative principle in all the emotions and feelings of the soul, not a mere naked notion of the head.' And that is the simple truth. That is exactly what the Apostle Paul is telling us here.

So, the final conclusion is this: saving faith is not a natural quality which everybody possesses. I have heard people teaching the truth about faith like this. They say, 'Everybody has faith, everybody is born with it.' I remember a preacher using this illustration: 'I will tell you what faith is. When I finish here next Thursday night I shall travel back on the train to London. I have already booked my sleeping berth. But how do I put myself down to rest on that bed in the sleeping berth? Well,' he said, 'I have faith in the engine-driver. So,' he continued, 'what you need to do is to take that faith which you have, and everybody else has, and apply it. You turn it in the direction of the Lord Jesus Christ. There is nothing to stop you doing it,' he said. 'If you only accept this testimony and turn your faith to it; that is saving faith.'

But it is not! Saving faith is a matter of the heart, and the human heart is by nature 'desperately wicked' and deceitful. Paul says, 'The carnal mind' – which means heart – 'is enmity against God: for it is not subject to the law of God, neither indeed can be' [*Rom.* 8:7]. When we realise this, when we understand that we are all 'dead in trespasses and sins' [*Eph.* 2:1], that we 'must be born again' [*John* 3:7], that 'the natural man receiveth not the things of the Spirit of God: for they are foolishness unto him: neither can he know them, because they are spiritually discerned' [*1 Cor.* 2:14], then we see that it is no use saying we have all got the faith we need. We have not; not one of us has it. 'By grace are ye saved through faith; and that not of yourselves: it is the gift of God' [*Eph.* 2:8].

Saving faith is something that is wrought in the heart by the Holy Spirit of God. This natural man who is supposed to have the gift of faith, how can he believe in the Son of God? He does not believe that he is a sinner. He knows nothing about God. He is utterly antagonistic to the truth. Before he can believe it, he needs to be changed. Faith is the first active, positive demonstration the soul gives that it is born again. Before men and women can believe, their hearts must be changed. The natural heart is dead and rebellious, and regards all this as foolishness. It is only those who have become 'spiritual' who can believe these things. Nobody else.

'Eye hath not seen,' says Paul, 'nor ear heard, neither have entered into the heart of man, the things which God hath prepared for them that love him' [*1 Cor.* 2:9]. He has already said in verse 8, 'Which none of the princes of this world knew . . .' And in verse 10 he adds, 'But God hath revealed them unto us by his Spirit: for the Spirit searcheth all things, yea, the deep things of God.' Then in 1 Corinthians 2:12 he says again: 'We have received, not the spirit of the world, but the spirit which is of God; that [in order that] we might know the things that are freely given to us of God.'

Romans 10 verses 9 and 10 are inevitable in the light of the argument of Romans 9. 'It is with the *heart* that man believeth', and, before that can happen, 'the stony heart' has to be taken out, and we must have 'a heart of flesh'. It is not merely an intellectual matter. It is not taking this natural faith which we all have and switching it to Christ. We have not got *this* faith! It is the gift of the Spirit of God. It is the work that He does in the soul, in the heart, and without that, saving faith is a sheer impossibility. 'With the heart man believeth unto righteousness.' He is a new man, and he has not only been aware of the truth, he has felt its power. It has changed him!

Sixteen

*

That if thou shalt confess with thy mouth the Lord Jesus, and shalt believe in thine heart that God hath raised him from the dead, thou shalt be saved. For with the heart man believeth unto righteousness; and with the mouth confession is made unto salvation. Romans 10:9–10

We have described the statement in these two verses as Paul's definition of saving faith and have suggested a threefold division – the content of saving faith, the character of saving faith, and the proof of saving faith. Now we are still engaged with the second division, and the emphasis, as we have seen, is upon the 'heart'. Faith is not merely a matter of the intellect, but it includes the whole personality, and especially the element of conviction, repentance and fear leading to trust and committal, gratitude and praise. The heart is the centre of the personality and Christian salvation is so great and so glorious that it does indeed take up the whole person; there is no part of us that is not involved. So faith is not merely an intellectual assent to truth or a purely objective awareness of truth. There is conviction; there is repentance; there is emotion; and it leads to this reliance on, and abandonment of ourselves to, our Lord and Saviour.

Finally, we have seen that, clearly, faith is not some natural endowment which we all have. As the Scripture teaches everywhere, it is the gift of God. 'For by grace are ye saved through faith; and that not of yourselves: it is the gift of God' [*Eph.* 2:8]. Nobody has faith except the believer. It is the special possession of those who are the called by God and are the children of God.

But in the light of this, it is quite clear that another question arises with regard to the element of *certainty* or *assurance* in this saving faith. Now the more we emphasise that the heart, the whole personality, is involved, the more it seems to be the case, on the very surface, that an essential part of faith is an element of knowledge or of assurance. If faith were merely an intellectual apprehension, assurance would not be involved; but we have emphasised – and have had to do so because of the way the Apostle puts it – the fact that the heart is engaged and that it is 'with the heart that man believeth unto righteousness'. Therefore, of necessity, this whole question of assurance arises. So we must examine that before we can regard our treatment of this great statement as complete.

Now this is obviously a very important subject from the practical or the experimental standpoint. To what extent should we *know* that we are saved? To what extent should we have assurance of salvation? Nobody who is at all familiar with the New Testament can fail to see what an important subject this is, because it is something that is dealt with very frequently there. But also as regards the practical daily living of the Christian life, it is obviously a most important subject because when we become Christians we are not transported out of this world, and it remains the same. The world, the flesh, the devil, and the things that happen in a fallen world of sin – illness, accident, disappointment, wars, calamities – we have to face all these things. And for this reason it is important for Christians to know exactly where they stand, to be able to explain what is happening to them and to be able to relate the faith that they have to those things.

But it is an important subject also from the standpoint of history. It has played a very prominent part in the history of Protestantism in particular, and I must tell you something about that in order that I may show you its importance.

The Roman Catholic Church – as I indicated when we were dealing with the last portion of the eighth chapter of Romans[1] – the Roman Catholic Church does not teach a doctrine of assurance, indeed, she teaches the exact opposite. Her teaching is that no individual can be certain of his or her salvation in this world, apart from some miraculous happening which God in His grace grants in a very few cases in order to give this assurance. But the teaching is that, apart from such miraculous interventions, individual believers do not and cannot have assurance of salvation, and it is presumption to claim that they can. Believers have to hand themselves over to the Church and the Church takes care of them, and she has her great apparatus, as you know, in order to do that. Even when people are dead, she cannot be sure about their ultimate destiny. They go to purgatory, and therefore

[1] See *Exposition of Chapter 8:5–17. The Sons of God*, 1974.

you have to pray for them, light candles, say masses, and so on. You trust 'Mother Church' and hope that eventually you will arrive in a state of ultimate salvation.

But the Protestant Reformation burst forth, first and foremost, of course, in Martin Luther, and from the beginning the Reformers began to teach a doctrine of assurance. Of course, disagreements inevitably arose over the whole question of authority, because what the Roman Church was saying – as she still says, only much more politely now! – is that once you leave the church, you are risking your soul, and you can be sure of nothing. So it was vital to be able to assert and to prove that one was not only saved but that one could be quite sure that one was saved; it was a question of authority. And, over against the church and the Pope, Protestantism pointed to the Scripture, the Word of God, and said, 'Here is the authority.'

'Ah yes,' said the Roman Church, 'that is all right but how do you interpret the Word of God? How can you be sure of what it teaches you – if you say it is the final authority? How do you know that you are not misinterpreting it? How do you know that you are not leading yourselves astray? After all, who are you? You are setting yourselves up against these centuries of tradition, study, scholarship and teaching. You may very well be deluding yourselves.'

Now the Protestant Reformers had to answer that, and they did so in this way. They said that the Holy Spirit gives a double testimony which leads to assurance. He testifies to the Word and He testifies in the believer. These two agree together. And so by an internal operation of the Holy Spirit, men and women know that this is the Word of God and they are given an understanding of it. The Reformers taught quite plainly – and, of course, quite rightly – that no one can believe that the Bible is the Word of God without the Holy Spirit. It is the testimony of the Spirit that finally gives us the certain knowledge that the Bible is the Word of God. And in the same way, the Spirit applies the Word to us, and lets us know exactly where we ourselves stand in the light of it.

So the result was that both Martin Luther and John Calvin, and all their followers, not only taught that a believer can have assurance of salvation; they went further and said that this certainty is an essential part of saving faith. They said that anyone who did not have assurance did not have saving faith.

Now this is a very important point. Calvin puts it like this: 'We shall have a complete definition of faith if we say that it is a steady and certain knowledge of the Divine benevolence towards us, which, being founded on the truth of the gratuitous promise in Christ, is both revealed to our minds and confirmed to our hearts by the Holy Spirit.'

Now that includes, of course, assurance – an absolute certainty. Calvin taught it in many places, and Luther taught it still more strongly, almost violently, as was characteristic of him. So if a believer said, 'Well, I cannot say that I know that I am saved', the Reformers would say that he had not got saving faith.

But very soon people began to see that as too extreme a position. It was wounding tender young souls. It was setting up a standard higher than that which is indicated by Scripture itself. Scripture does not teach that unless you have an absolute assurance of your salvation you are not saved. What the Scripture says is, 'Believe on the Lord Jesus Christ', or, as it is here, 'If thou shalt confess with thy mouth the Lord Jesus, and shalt believe in thine heart that God hath raised him from the dead, thou shalt be saved.'

Now one of the first people to put this fairly clearly was William Perkins, a very great Puritan theologian and teacher in the Church of England. He put it like this: 'This doctrine' – that is to say, saving faith – 'is to be learned for two causes. First of all it serves to rectify the consciences of weak ones that they be not decayed touching their estate; for if we think that no faith can save but a full persuasion, such as the faith of Abraham was, many truly bearing the Name of Christ must be put out of the roll of the children of God. We are therefore to know that there is a growth in grace as in Nature, and there be differences and degrees of true faith, and the least of them all is infolded faith' – by which he means saving faith. 'Secondly, this point of doctrine serves to rectify and in part to expound sundry catechisms.'

Some of the first Protestant catechisms asserted, you see, that full assurance of salvation was essential to saving faith, so William Perkins continued, 'It serves in part to expound sundry catechisms in that they seem to propound faith unto men at so high a reach as few can attain unto, defining it to be a certain and full persuasion of God's love and favour in Christ. Whereas though every faith be from its nature a certain persuasion, yet only the strong faith is the full persuasion. Therefore faith is not only in general terms to be defined but also the degrees and measures thereof are to be expounded, that weak ones to their comfort may be truly informed of their estate.'[1]

[1] *Reformed Catholic.*

So at the end of the sixteenth century, Perkins had come to see that Luther and Calvin, in fighting off the attack of Roman Catholicism, had allowed themselves to be drawn into an extreme position. They had so defined saving faith as to make it something which belongs to people who have the highest form of assurance. And they were, therefore, hindering the faith of many of the weaker brethren and causing great heart-searching and much unhappiness.

But in 1643, some forty years or so after Perkins, the famous Assembly met in Westminster Abbey that drew up the *Westminster Confession of Faith*. The members of this Assembly dealt with saving faith in a conclusive manner, and what they taught has generally been accepted as the true teaching ever since. The *Westminster Confession* deals with this in chapters 14 and 18. Chapter 14 deals with saving faith – the heading is, 'Of Saving Faith' – and this is the second section:

> By this faith, a Christian believeth to be true whatsoever is revealed in the Word, for the authority of God Himself speaking therein; and acteth differently upon that which each particular passage thereof containeth; yielding obedience to the commands, trembling at the threatenings, and embracing the promises of God for this life and for that which is to come. But the principal acts of saving faith are, accepting, receiving, and resting upon Christ alone for justification, sanctification, and eternal life, by virtue of the covenant of grace.

Then the third section reads like this:

> This faith [the one it has just been defining] is different in degrees, weak or strong; may be often and many ways assailed and weakened, but gets the victory; growing up in many to the attainment of a full assurance through Christ, Who is both the author and finisher of our faith.

You see, the *Westminster Confession* takes up the point made by William Perkins, elaborates it and makes it even clearer. But the section which deals still more specifically with 'Assurance of Grace and Salvation' is chapter 18, where we read:

> Although hypocrites, and other unregenerate men, may vainly deceive themselves with false hopes and carnal presumptions of

being in the favour of God and estate of salvation; which hope of theirs shall perish; yet such as truly believe in the Lord Jesus Christ, and love Him in sincerity, endeavouring to walk in all good conscience before Him, may in this life be certainly assured that they are in the state of grace, and may rejoice in the hope of the glory of God; which hope shall never make them ashamed.

This certainty is not a bare conjectural and probable persuasion, grounded upon a fallible hope; but an infallible assurance of faith, founded upon the divine truth of the promises of salvation, the inward evidence of those graces unto which these promises are made, the testimony of the Spirit of adoption witnessing with our spirits that we are the children of God: which Spirit is the earnest of our inheritance, whereby we are sealed to the day of redemption.

That is a mass of scriptural quotations, and now, here is the point:

This infallible assurance doth not so belong to the essence of faith, but that a true believer may wait long, and conflict with many difficulties, before he be a partaker of it: yet, being enabled by the Spirit to know the things which are freely given him of God, he may without extraordinary revelation, in the right use of ordinary means, attain thereunto.

That is a most important statement. In other words, you can be a true believer without having this full assurance of salvation. But they go on to say:

And therefore it is the duty of every one to give all diligence to make his calling and election sure; that thereby his heart may be enlarged in peace and joy in the Holy Ghost, in love and thankfulness to God, and in strength and cheerfulness in the duties of obedience, the proper fruits of this assurance: so far is it from inclining men to looseness.

True believers may have the assurance of their salvation divers ways shaken, diminished, and intermitted; as, by negligence in preserving of it; by falling into some special sin, which woundeth the conscience, and grieveth the Spirit; by some sudden or vehement temptation; by God's withdrawing the light of His countenance, and suffering even such as fear Him to walk in darkness, and to have no light: yet are they never utterly destitute of that seed of

God, and life of faith, that love of Christ and the brethren, that sincerity of heart and conscience of duty, out of which, by the operation of the Spirit, this assurance may in due time be revived, and by the which in the meantime, they are supported from utter despair.

That, too, is a most important and a most valuable statement.

We can sum it up like this: in view of the fact that 'with the heart man believeth unto righteousness' there is always, and of necessity, a certain degree of knowledge, but the degree may vary. It is not a bare intellectual belief; there is more than that. When men and women are convicted, they know and feel it, something has happened in the realm of their emotions. So there is always that element of knowledge in true saving faith. Those who have never felt anything at all have not got saving faith; they give an intellectual assent. It is a part of saving faith to know that something has happened, but that is a very different thing from saying that we must always have the full degree of assurance of faith before we are saved. Or, as the *Confession* puts it so rightly, the degree of assurance that we have may vary tremendously from time to time.

Saving faith is always satisfied about the promises of God. It knows the way of salvation, it knows that it is the only way, and it knows that it is God's way. It sees that quite clearly, and it has no doubt about it. Those who are doubtful about the way of salvation have no faith at all in a saving sense. Men and women who have saving faith see it; they understand it; they are quite clear about it; they can say that it is this and it is not that. They are quite clear about the objective aspect. But what they may not be always clear and certain about is their own relationship to that. They say, 'That is it, I have no hope apart from that, I am trusting only to that.' Now that, to me, is saving faith, because they are certain about the thing that saves them, about the Person who saves them, and the way in which He saves them; but they may lack the inward assurance that they themselves are saved.

Now we must not exclude people like this from having saving faith. Any man who can tell me that he realises that he is a sinner, that he cannot save himself, that nobody else can save him, that he richly deserves the wrath of God, and richly deserves hell, and that, furthermore, he has no hope at all apart from the Lord Jesus Christ and what He has done – I say that such a man has saving faith, even though he is unhappy. Someone may say, 'I wish I knew that I was saved. I wish I had the certainty that I read of in the Scriptures and that I have heard others testify to in their experience, and that I have read about. I have not got that.' But I say that that person has got saving faith.

Indeed, I would even go so far as to put it like this. The fact that such people are concerned about this is a proof to me that they have got saving faith, because they would not be troubled or grieved about it otherwise. They want it. The unregenerate do not want it. But here is someone who is tremendously concerned, who says everything that is right about being in a state of sin, about the Saviour and the way of salvation. Such a person has saving faith though not assurance of salvation at that point.

That is what William Perkins was saying, and what the *Westminster Confession of Faith* says. It was not what Calvin and Luther said; they went too far. Assurance of salvation is not an essential part of saving faith, but as we are offered full assurance in the Scriptures, and as the *Westminster Confession* ends, we should all 'give diligence to make your calling and election sure' [2 Pet. 1:10]. And the ways to do that, of course, are indicated to us quite plainly in the Scriptures themselves.

Finally, I will put it to you like this. I remember an old minister, a man who had preached the gospel in all its purity, not only faithfully but with great power, and indeed a man who had passed through experiences of revival – I remember that man on his deathbed. He had a lingering, painful illness which weakened him very much, and he was in trouble. He was not happy about his soul's salvation, and on one occasion he put it to a friend of mine like this, 'About the way itself, I have no difficulty. I have no doubts about the Saviour and His all-sufficiency and His fulness, and that He has done everything that is necessary; there is no trouble about that.' Then, with his hand on his heart, he said, 'I am troubled about this, about its registration here.'

Now that is the kind of distinction that I think is so important. That man had saving faith, but at that point – partly, perhaps, owing to his illness – he lacked the assurance. I think that in his case some of the reasons were exactly as the *Confession* put it. He was a man who did not discipline himself in certain respects, and I think that he lacked his assurance partly because of that. But I am happy to end the story by saying that I saw him two days before he died and he looked into my eyes and said, 'I know that I am going to Jesus Christ.' He had now got his full assurance. But he had saving faith even when he lacked that assurance.

That, then, completes our second division of Paul's definition of saving faith – the *character* of that faith – and now we must move on to the third, which I have called the *proof* of saving faith and which is 'confession with the mouth'. In the light of what we have already been considering, it is inevitable. It needs no demonstration. The moment you put the emphasis that the Apostle puts upon the heart, confession must follow. The moment you see that the whole person is engaged, the moment you emphasise each person's understanding of the human position, and of God and of the way of salvation, then this is what must of necessity happen. The heart cannot be engaged without its leading on to this.

Now of course in Romans 6:17 the Apostle has already prepared us for this very thing. This is how he defines what has happened to these Romans to whom he is writing: 'God be thanked,' he says, 'that ye were [once] the servants of sin . . .' but no longer. Why not? Because '. . . ye have obeyed from the heart that form of doctrine which was delivered you.' We have been emphasising the heart, now we emphasise the *obedience*. That is faith. The form of doctrine is delivered. The mind, enlightened by the Spirit, understands it and receives it. But it does not stop at that. The heart is moved and because the heart is moved, action is taken. Obedience!

This, again, is something that is taught everywhere in the New Testament but it has very often been forgotten. Faith is a whole. These three elements are always involved and are always there together and, further, if any one of them is absent, there is something wrong; it is not true saving faith.

Now that becomes important for this reason. There is a form of teaching that draws a sharp, almost an absolute, distinction between an evangelistic service and a teaching service. According to this view, in an evangelistic service you are aiming to get people to accept the Lord Jesus Christ as their *Saviour* and you do not go beyond that. But then, having got them saved, you take them to a different type of meeting. This is no longer evangelism; there is a deeper message now. In this second meeting they are encouraged to take the Lord Jesus Christ as their *Lord* in exactly the same way as they took Him in the first meeting as their Saviour. So if you are a Christian, you do not listen during an evangelistic service but you pray for the unconverted. You do not listen because there is nothing for you in that service; you are already saved!

Now that to me is nothing but a complete denial of Paul's definition of saving faith in Romans 10:9 and 10. It is a grievous error. It is dividing the Lord Jesus Christ in a way that He cannot be divided. Saving faith is indivisible. You cannot take Him only as your Saviour. Whom are you taking? Well, you take the One who is Lord. 'If thou shalt confess with thy mouth' – what? – 'the Lord Jesus'! And He is the Lord of the whole of the universe. He is the Lord of the whole of your life. You cannot take Him in bits and parts.

If you believe in the 'Lord Jesus Christ', if you really believe in Him, if you have been convinced and convicted of your sin, and if you see that all your troubles are due to the fact that you have been a rebel and that you have sinned and that the wrath of God is upon sin – then you do not stop at desiring deliverance from punishment and hell. You want to get out of sin; you want to get out of the clutches of the devil; you want to start serving God; you want to be absolutely different. It is impossible to believe in a saving sense in the Lord Jesus Christ only as Saviour. You cannot believe in Him as Saviour without all the rest being involved.

Of course, once again there are degrees in this. You can grow in your understanding. But if a man tells me that he has believed in Christ and tells me at the same time that he feels exactly as he did before, that he has no desire which is different from what he had before, that he is not anxious not to sin, that he has no sense of anxiety to serve God and the Lord Jesus Christ – then I say that that man is not saved. He was looking for happiness, for a bit of release and relief, for deliverance from hell. But that is not salvation.

You remember what the angel said to Joseph even before our Lord was born: 'Thou shalt call his name Jesus, for he shall save his people from their sins' [*Matt.* 1:21] – not merely from their punishment, but from their sins. He came to deliver us from sin, from the dominion of Satan, the devil. He came to separate and 'to purify unto himself a peculiar people, zealous of good works' [*Tit.* 2:14].

This distinction between accepting Christ as Saviour and taking Him as Lord is utterly unscriptural. He 'of God is made unto us wisdom, and righteousness, and sanctification, and redemption' [*1 Cor.* 1:30]. You cannot divide Him, He is one. And looking at it from the experimental, or the subjective side, those who have believed in Him from the heart are those who will confess Him with the mouth. It is quite inevitable. This, you see, is how you draw the distinction between the true believer and the false. This is how you draw the distinction between saving faith and intellectual assent.

But if you hold to that other division between Saviour and Lord, that wrong division, you have no test at all; you have got to grant that someone who says, 'I believe in Jesus,' is truly saved. But the Apostle takes the trouble to bring in the heart and the confession. Why? Because it is a vital part of saving faith. 'God be thanked,' says the Apostle, that you are no longer what you were: 'Ye were the servants of sin' – but you are no longer that. What are you? What is a Christian? 'Ye have obeyed from the heart that form of doctrine which was delivered you' [*Rom.* 6:17].

Paul, you remember, began saying this in verse 5 of the very first chapter: 'By whom,' he says, 'we have received grace and apostleship, for obedience to the faith among all nations, for his name.' 'Obedience to the faith'! And as Paul begins the Epistle in that way, so also he ends it. 'But now', he says, '[Christ] is made manifest, and by the scriptures of the prophets, according to the commandment of the everlasting God, made known to all nations for *the obedience of faith*' [*Rom.* 16:26].

'With the heart man believeth unto righteousness; and with the mouth confession is made unto salvation.'

Seventeen

*

That if thou shalt confess with thy mouth the Lord Jesus, and shalt believe in thine heart that God hath raised him from the dead, thou shalt be saved. For with the heart man believeth unto righteousness; and with the mouth confession is made unto salvation.   Romans 10:9–10

Before we continue with our consideration of saving faith, let me remind you of the context. The Apostle is concerned about the failure of the Jews to believe the gospel. They were 'going about to establish their own righteousness' and had rejected the 'righteousness which is of faith' [10:3, 6]. And Paul says that this was a great tragedy. They were exerting all their energy travelling backwards and forwards to 'compass sea and land to make one proselyte' [*Matt.* 23:15], when the whole time the gospel was, as it were, there before them. 'It is this word of faith,' he says, 'which we preach.' Then come the words of our text and we have been considering saving faith under our three headings.

We have now arrived at the third and last of these, which is the *proof* of saving faith, and the Apostle puts that before us, of course, by his emphasis upon 'confession with the mouth', and it is important for us to realise this emphasis. You will notice that Paul repeats this in both verses, and his object in doing so is to show us what a vital part this is of a true saving faith.

Now I have had occasion to point out with regard to the first two sections that we must never divide these things, that the three aspects must always be present together or there is no true saving faith. There must be the true content; there must be the experiential aspect, the heart; and equally 'confession with the mouth' must also be involved. And, as we have seen, the Apostle is saying that the confession with the mouth is the inevitable outcome of believing with the heart the true content of the Christian faith. It is confession that ultimately

[187]

gives proof of the fact that our heart is engaged in this matter, and that what we have is not merely some kind of theoretical or intellectual belief.

This, let me emphasise again, is a very important matter and it is interesting to notice the attention that is paid to it in the teaching of the New Testament as a whole. Our Lord frequently made this self-same point. Take again, for instance, His parable on the question of repentance in Matthew 21. I have quoted this already in connection with the believing from the heart, but I want now to quote it to show you where the element of confession comes in: 'What think ye? A certain man had two sons; and he came to the first, and said, Son, go work to day in my vineyard. He answered and said, I will not: but afterward he repented, and went. And he came to the second, and said likewise. And he answered and said, I go, sir: and went not' [*Matt.* 21:28–30].

Now that is a perfect commentary on this very thing. You see, when his father came and asked him to go to the vineyard, the second son said, 'I go, sir.' But he did not go, so there was no point in his saying that he would. But the first son, who at first had said, 'I will not', 'afterward repented', which we interpreted as meaning that he thought again and was sorry that he had spoken like that to his father. *Metanoia.* He thought again. He changed his mind. Yes, but the really important point about it is that he went.

Now that is a vital part of repentance. That is, in essence, the difference between remorse and repentance. A man suffering from remorse is sorry that he has done that thing and he is annoyed with himself. He is suffering the consequences and he sees that he was a fool. But then he gets up and goes and does it again! Now that is just a useless remorse. Repentance means that you not only change your attitude towards something but you give proof of it by doing the exact opposite.

Now in that parable our Lord was putting the emphasis upon the *expression* of what one feels. You do not merely get the right view and feel it, you prove it by doing the thing that you had formerly said you would not do.

In Luke 12 there is another statement of our Lord's with respect to this whole matter. Here, our Lord is sending out His disciples to preach and to cast out devils, and He warns them that they must not expect to be received with open arms by everybody. They must expect persecution, and indeed it may even be the case, he says, that they will have to choose between saving their lives and loyalty to Him and to the truth. He tells them not to be afraid of men, but only of God, and says: 'Also I say unto you, Whosoever shall confess me before men, him shall the Son of man also confess before the angels of God: but he that denieth me before men shall be denied before the angels of God' [*Luke* 12:8–9].

Then there are also the verses in Acts 2 which bring out this self-same point. The moment those people on the day of Pentecost were 'pricked in their hearts', repented, believed the gospel and were baptised, they gave expression to it by joining the church, and by adhering to believers – 'And they continued stedfastly in the apostles' doctrine and fellowship, and in breaking of bread, and in prayers . . . And all that believed were together' – you see, these are the terms – 'And they, continuing daily with one accord in the temple, and breaking bread from house to house, did eat their meat with gladness and singleness of heart' [*Acts* 2:42–46].

You will find these points constantly emphasised in the New Testament. The moment these people were truly convicted, repented and were converted, they showed it. And, of course, you find it still more explicitly in the Epistles. Now people have sometimes foolishly tried to say that there is a division of opinion here between the Apostle Paul and the Apostle James. There is not, of course. When James says that 'faith without works is dead' [*Jas.* 2:20] he is concerned only to show that a mere intellectual assent is of no value. So he argues – and on the surface it seems as if he is arguing for justification by works – that Abraham was justified by what he did. 'Was not Abraham our father justified by works, when he had offered Isaac his son upon the altar?' [v. 21]. What James means is this: if Abraham had merely said to God, when God told him to sacrifice his son, 'All right, I will do it,' but had done nothing about it, then his faith would have been of no value. Abraham, James says, gave proof of his faith by proceeding to do the thing which God had told him to do. 'Seest thou how faith wrought with his works, and by works was faith made perfect?' [v. 22].

Now that is the point – the works 'make faith perfect', which means that it is the works which ultimately prove the reality of the faith. So James says, 'Ye see then how that by works a man is justified, and not by faith only' [v. 24]. He means by that 'not by saying that you have faith only'. It is the works that prove the faith, hence the last verse: 'For as the body without the spirit is dead, so faith without works is dead also' [v. 26]. In other words, if there are no works present, then it is not faith; it is nothing but an intellectual assent, a kind of academic or theoretical belief. So the Apostle is not saying that a man saves himself by repeating a formula. No, what he is saying is that a man shows that he is saved by making the confession. This is the way in which he establishes the thing beyond any doubt whatsoever. 'With the mouth' he confirms and makes known the fact of his salvation. And this, therefore, is the ultimate proof of whether someone really has saving faith or not.

This is the way that you test the difference between a mere theoretical interest in truth, an acceptance of it with the mind, and a saving faith that really does mean salvation. Now there is a very good paraphrase of these verses in the *Amplified New Testament,* which puts it like this: 'With the heart a person believes, and so is justified; and with the mouth he confesses – declares openly and speaks out freely his faith – and confirms his salvation.' Now that is the thing – he 'confirms' his salvation. He does not *procure* it, he does not produce it, that would be justification by works. No, what a man does by the 'confession with the mouth' is to confirm the fact that he is saved.

Now there is a similar statement to this in 1 Corinthians 12:3. Paul is dealing with the spiritual gifts and says, 'Wherefore I give you to understand, that no man speaking by the Spirit of God calleth Jesus accursed: and that no man can say that Jesus is the Lord, but by the Holy Ghost.' Obviously that cannot mean that it is impossible for anyone to use the actual expression, 'Jesus is Lord', without the Holy Spirit, because anyone, even the greatest unbeliever, can say it.

No, what the Apostle is talking about is this: it is impossible for someone really to say (knowing what he says and giving proof in the whole of his life that he does mean it), that Jesus is the Lord, but by the Holy Spirit. So it is not just a question of the words as such, but of the way in which they are said. And therefore the statement means that the 'confession with the mouth' is the last bit of evidence that we have of the fact that someone has a true and a saving faith and not merely a temporary faith or an intellectual belief.

We see this still more clearly when we come now to the next question, which is: What does this 'confession with the mouth' mean exactly? How is it done, and what does it include? Again, we have a comprehensive statement. I feel the best way to consider it is to look at what they did in the early days of the Christian church and what we do at the present time.

In the early days, becoming a Christian was a momentous happening, and it was a very difficult matter, both for the Jew and for the Gentile. One of the most difficult things a Jew could ever be asked to say was, 'Jesus is Lord.' The Jew had been brought up to say that Jehovah was the Lord and there was but one God. The Jews were monotheists in a world that was given to polytheism. They confessed, 'There is one God.' That was the great emphasis of the law of Moses and the teaching of all their prophets through the centuries, and the idea that a man who had lived on this earth, whose name was Jesus and who was crucified, should be 'the Lord! Jehovah!' was to a Jew something that was incredible.

That is why they accused our Lord of blasphemy, and that is why the early Christians were accused of the same thing. That is why the Apostle Paul, as Saul of Tarsus, persecuted them. So for a Jew to say that 'Jesus is Jehovah' was a tremendous thing, and that is why the Apostle says there in 1 Corinthians 12:3 that nothing but the Holy Spirit could make a man say such a thing. No Jew, by nature, would ever say it, it was blasphemy! So when you get a Jew saying, 'Jesus is the Lord,' 'Jesus is Jehovah', you can be absolutely certain that the Holy Spirit has dealt with him, that he has been regenerated, that he has a new heart and a new mind and a new outlook, that he is altogether changed.

This was also difficult for the Gentiles, but for a different reason. At this particular time the Roman emperors had been claiming deity for themselves, and the people had been granting it to them. They were offering up a kind of worship to them, and the Roman authorities were insistent that people should say, 'Caesar is Lord.' So Gentiles, when they became Christians and were asked to make the confession that Jesus – and only Jesus – is Lord, began to be in difficulties. They were asked to say something that was contradictory of that which was demanded by the Roman Empire with all her authority and power. So we must bear that in mind as we consider exactly what saying 'Jesus is Lord' meant to these early Christian believers. It was not a simple matter at all, but extremely difficult.

What then did it involve? Well, first of all it involved a statement of their belief. The question was: could they or could they not say that they had come to see and to believe that Jesus is the Lord?

Then the second step, as you will find everywhere in the book of

Acts, was baptism. Peter included it on the day of Pentecost; it happened again with the Ethiopian eunuch, as it had already happened in the case of the people who had believed in Samaria. Philip had been down there preaching and we are told: 'But when they believed Philip preaching the things concerning the kingdom of God, and the name of Jesus Christ, they were baptized, both men and women' [*Acts* 8:12]. And again I ask you to bear in mind what it meant that these Samaritans, these half-Jews, were making this astonishing, public statement with regard to this Person, Jesus of Nazareth.

And in Acts 10 you find exactly the same thing in the case of Cornelius and his household. Here was a Roman citizen, a Gentile. He believed the message, he made this statement, and on the strength of that he was baptised. The same happened to the believers in Ephesus, in Acts 19. Paul preached to them and, 'When they heard this, they were baptized in the name of the Lord Jesus' [v. 5].

So the second point in this 'confession' is submission to baptism. Now the purpose of baptism is not merely that the candidates for baptism may make their confession. It is a part but not the most important part. Those who ask for baptism, or submit to it, are 'making a confession', and their confession is that 'Jesus is the Lord'. They believe the content of saving faith – 'Jesus is the Lord. God raised him from the dead'; giving them an assurance that Christ's work on the cross was sufficient to atone for the sins of His people.

The third step then is, of course, belonging to the Christian church, to the company of believers. Now I take you back again to that second chapter of Acts. The moment these people believed, they were 'added to the church'. We are told, 'and the same day there were added unto them [the church] about three thousand souls' [v. 41]. And they continued, they all kept together. It was quite inevitable that these people who had suddenly seen this tremendous truth should all be together, because they had become alike, they were believing the same things, and they wanted fellowship with one another.

There is a very wonderful statement of this, I always feel, in 1 Thessalonians 1:6, where Paul puts it like this: 'And ye became followers of us, and of the Lord, having received the word in much affliction, with joy of the Holy Ghost.' Now that is a statement that you can slip over without observing it, but it is crucially important: 'You became followers of us, and of the Lord'. They were like those first believers in Jerusalem who 'continued stedfastly in the apostles' doctrine and fellowship, and in breaking of bread, and in prayers' [*Acts* 2:42]. These people had 'turned to God from idols to serve the living and true God' [*1 Thess.* 1:9]. How do we know that? We know it because they became followers of the Apostles; they joined the company and they continued to do so. So that was the third way in which they made this 'confession with the mouth'.

Then, of course, they did it also in their lives. They stopped going to the idol temples, and they began going to the meeting-place of the Christians. They met in one another's homes; they had stopped offering their sacrifices to idols, and had aligned themselves with God's people.

And then the final test of confession was their behaviour under persecution, in time of trial, and their readiness for martyrdom. You find that in many places in the New Testament. You see the martyrdom of Stephen; you see the Apostles. When the Apostles were thrown into prison and forbidden to preach or to teach any more 'in the name of this Jesus', they stood and answered, 'Whether it be right in the sight of God to hearken unto you more than unto God, judge ye. For we cannot but speak the things which we have seen and heard' [*Acts* 4:19–20]. They went on preaching, and they were ready to lay down their lives.

So the Apostle Paul reminds the Philippians, 'Unto you it is given in the behalf of Christ, not only to believe on him, but also to suffer for his sake' [*Phil.* 1:29]. They were ready to do so, and they were massacred by the thousand. They were thrown to the lions in the arena and became the sport of the emperor and the great people. It did not matter. Whatever people did to them, they still went on saying, 'Jesus is Lord', and refused to say, 'Caesar is Lord.' That was how the confession was made with the mouth in the early times.

Well, how is it done today? This is an important question, and in my pastoral work I have often had to deal with people who have been in distress because they have had a feeling that somehow or other they are not doing this, and therefore are not saved. You see, they are a little wrong in their doctrine and in the outworking of the teaching. They have got hold of the idea that it is 'saying it with the mouth' that saves, and because they are not doing that, they are not saved. So it is very important that we should be clear about exactly what this means.

So I start once more with a negative. It is not merely making the statement in a mechanical way – still less in some showy manner.

What do I mean? I have known – and you, too, have probably known – men and women who are always making this sort of statement. They repeat it almost like parrots, almost like a gramophone record which just has one thing to say. So these people are always muttering the words, and they think that in doing so they are fulfilling this statement about confessing with the mouth the Lord Jesus. You know, people who in ordinary conversation say, 'Praise the Lord!' in almost every other sentence! That is their way of saying that they are letting people know that they are Christians.

But I do not think Paul means that for a moment, because that very often brings the Lord and His gospel into ridicule and contempt. It is unintelligent, and a Christian should never do anything unintelligent. The world does not understand the Christian, but Christians should not make themselves unintelligent and aggravate that! Christians should not be foolish. They should never do anything parrot-fashion, or mechanically. Confessing the Lord Jesus, as I have tried to show in the case of the early church, is a much bigger and deeper thing than this.

Now I am not going to be dogmatic about my next statement but I put it before you in order that you may think about it. Where does the wearing of badges come in this matter? What exactly is the place of wearing a badge to show that you are a Christian? It is not a simple question. It is difficult, and there are many sides to it. Or let me put it in a much more extreme form. The Quakers of the seventeenth century were very concerned about this and George Fox taught that everything about the Christian should be distinctive – Christians should dress and speak differently from people of the world. That is why he taught his people to say 'thee' and 'thou' instead of 'you'. And they dressed in a manner that made it abundantly clear that they were Christian people who did not belong to the world.

This is not true of Quakers today but it did persist for a very long time. The difficulty about this matter, it seems to me, is that, looked at from one side, there is something excellent about this. It does show that these people are prepared to suffer for what they believe. At this point, I often quote quite a striking illustration that I remember stumbling across when I was a student. There is a disease which is known as Hodgkin's disease, because it was first described by a man called Thomas Hodgkin, who belonged to Guy's Hospital, London. Now although Hodgkin was a great doctor, he never became a surgeon at Guy's, he never had any office or any post higher than that of curator of the museum. Why not? Because he was a Quaker. And as a Quaker he dressed in a peculiar manner. For example, he wore a long coat that was unlike the coats that were worn by the average medical men. This was regarded as an eccentricity by the authorities of Guy's and therefore this man, who richly deserved to be made a full surgeon, was never made one. But it did not trouble or worry him; he was perfectly happy. He made this notable contribution to knowledge with regard to that particular disease, and others, but was never anything beyond the curator of the museum.

Now there is an aspect of that which is very noble. Here was a man who was not going to sacrifice what he believed to be right in order to get earthly human advancement. That is one side of it. But there is another side: Ultimately, is this 'confession with the mouth' something mechanical? This is a subject that can extend itself in many ways. For instance, why does anybody wear a clerical collar? How did that ever arise? To what extent should we, by external appearance, either clothing or the wearing of badges or anything like that, make it known that we are Christians or ministers of the gospel?

Now there are certain things which obviously need no discussion; the unbelieving world does some things which a Christian should not do. There are sinful attitudes in dress as well as in everything else; there a Christian must certainly be different. But that does not seem to me to justify, of necessity, the wearing of badges or going to the point at which we become a little eccentric in our clothes.

In other words, while in one sense it is true to say that 'the apparel proclaims the man', there is another sense in which it is equally necessary to emphasise that the man is much more important than his apparel, and that the important thing is the man himself, what he really is. And I would be prepared to argue that it should not be necessary for us to wear badges in order to show that we are Christians. *We* should show that we are Christians. It should be obvious to anybody who meets us, by the totality of the impression we make upon them, that we are Christians.

The difficult point, of course, is the point at which you decide where you cross the line from *proclaiming* that you are a Christian to *parading* the fact. It is right to praise the Lord, but if you keep on saying it after almost every sentence, it becomes meaningless repetition and almost gibberish. Indeed, you become exposed to the charge that was brought against the Pharisees who 'made broad their phylacteries' [*Matt.* 23:5] and stood at the street corners proclaiming that they were very godly men.

You see, there is the other side to this matter. We are told, 'Let not thy left hand know what thy right hand doeth' [*Matt.* 6:3]. It is one thing to proclaim, it is another and a very different thing to parade. And it often happens that people who are nervous about this matter, or who are mechanically minded or simple in their understanding, tend to do things in an utterly mechanical and almost showy manner. And in the end it has the exact opposite effect from that which they intended to produce.

I think I can best put it like this: it is the child who is apt to be demonstrative; it is the child who dresses up and who wears badges and so on. But as you grow up, you grow out of that kind of thing, and you realise that it is you yourself, what you are, that does the proclaiming, rather than these external advertisements. But that is only the negative aspect. We must now look positively, and go on to consider how we can confess 'with the mouth' the total content of the belief that 'Jesus is the Lord' and that God has raised Him from the dead.

Eighteen

*

That if thou shalt confess with thy mouth the Lord Jesus, and shalt believe in thine heart that God hath raised him from the dead, thou shalt be saved. For with the heart man believeth unto righteousness; and with the mouth confession is made unto salvation.   Romans 10:9–10

Our analysis of the great definition of saving faith which the Apostle gives us here is nearing completion. We have considered its content, and its character, and now we are considering the *proof* of saving faith. The Apostle, you notice, is very concerned about this. He is dealing here, as he has dealt, indeed, from the very beginning of his Epistle, with the great question of salvation. In these verses in particular he is focusing on the refusal of the Jews to believe the gospel. So Paul is anxious to make the whole character of saving faith perfectly clear and definite. It is the last time he really does so in this Epistle, so he is, as it were, summing up his great doctrine of salvation. That is why he troubles to put it in the way that we have been considering. Now we are concerned here with this last test, which is the proof, and here the emphasis is upon the 'confession with the mouth'. 'If thou shalt confess with thy mouth the Lord Jesus'; 'with the mouth confession is made unto salvation'.

Now having defined what Paul means by that, we have spent some time in showing how this worked itself out in the first age of the Christian church, in the New Testament itself. And then at the close of our last study we began to consider how we do this at this present time. We began with a negative, and to me the negative is very important. We saw that this is not something that we do mechanically, or in some kind of demonstrative manner. And we raised the question of wearing badges, dressing in a particular manner, and so on.

We must now go on from that point. It seems to me that if we are worried about this text, we have entirely misunderstood it. I have

[197]

often had people come to me and express their distress about the way in which they – to use their language – are not 'witnessing' to the Lord as they should be doing. There are many people who are almost in acute anxiety about this. At times people have given me the impression that they feel they are guilty if they have not deliberately spoken to every member of their office, for instance, about these matters or, perhaps, even asked them directly whether they were saved or not. They have somehow got hold of the feeling that this 'confession with the mouth' means that you tell every person you know or meet that you are a Christian, that you believe that Jesus is the Lord, and that God has raised Him from the dead. And so they seem to spend much of their time making sure that they have always done this, and that they have never failed at any time or with any individual.

But that, to me, is to come to this statement in an entirely wrong manner. It is, again, to approach it mechanically, an approach which is far removed from this particular statement and from the whole spirit of the Scripture. What, then, does it mean? Well, I suggest that the Apostle is saying that it is inevitable that any true and clear conviction with regard to the content of saving faith will of necessity give expression to itself: 'For out of the abundance of the heart the mouth speaks' [*Matt.* 12:34]. So, having put his emphasis upon 'believing with the *heart*', having brought in that holy affection, it is inevitable that Paul should show how this expresses itself.

What I am trying to say was put in a pithy phrase by one of the great Puritans who went out from this country to New England in the 1630s, a man called Thomas Hooker, who lived and preached in Cambridge, Massachusetts. He put it like this: 'If a man hath faith within, it will break forth at the mouth.' And that, I believe, is exactly what the Apostle is saying here: that this true, heartfelt, sincere belief in the content of saving faith will inevitably give expression to itself.

Which leads us to ask a question: Why is this inevitable? Why is Thomas Hooker right in what he says? And it seems to me that there are a number of answers to that question. The first is that the very nature of the truth of necessity leads to this. If we really do believe the gospel, if we have really understood something of what it means, and have felt something of its power in our hearts, if we believe that 'God so loved the world, that he gave his only begotten Son, that whosoever believeth in him should not perish, but have everlasting life' [*John* 3:16] – if we really believe that, we are bound to give expression to it.

If we really believe in the glorious and wonderful love of God; if we believe that, in spite of the fact that we have rebelled and sinned against Him and have no claims upon Him at all and deserve nothing but His wrath and eternal punishment, yet God in His great and eternal love has sent forth His own Son; that, as the Apostle has put it so eloquently and wonderfully, He 'spared not his own Son, but delivered him up for us all' [*Rom.* 8:32] – if we really believe all that, then it is inevitable that we should give expression to it.

Or look at it in terms of the Lord Jesus Christ Himself. If we really do believe that 'Jesus is Lord'; if we believe that the eternal Son of God laid aside the signs of that glory which He had shared with the Father from all eternity, and humbled Himself and was born as a babe and lived in this world such as it is, endured the contradiction of sinners against Himself and was buffeted and tempted and finally nailed on a tree, and did it all willingly, for us and for our salvation – then because of the very character of what we believe, we must give some expression to it. We cannot believe that and be utterly silent about it.

Or let me put it like this to you: this truth is such that it changes everything. Paul says, 'If any man be in Christ, he is a new creature [a new creation]: old things are passed away; behold, all things are become new' [*2 Cor.* 5:17]. And that, of course, is a fact about anyone who really becomes a Christian and is regenerate. The Apostle here, in Romans 10, is talking only about the regenerate, we have seen that quite clearly. He is not merely talking about a man or woman who has a theoretical or academic interest in truth but is talking about someone whose 'heart', and whose whole personality, is involved.

Now my argument is that to such people everything has become different, and because everything is different they are bound to give expression to that. They are so amazed at it, and so taken up by it, that they cannot refrain from confessing it and making it known. Take again, for instance, that fifth chapter of 2 Corinthians. Notice there how the Apostle points out that men and women who believe the truth do indeed find that everything is different. They have a new view of themselves. They used to think of themselves 'after the flesh', but not any longer; they think of themselves now 'after the Spirit'. They have a new view of other people. 'Henceforth,' Paul says, 'know we no man after the flesh.' He used to know everybody after the flesh, but he does so no longer. Christians have a new view of Christ. 'Yea,' writes Paul, 'though we have known Christ after the

flesh, yet now henceforth know we him [so] no more' [*2 Cor.* 5:16].
Paul knows now that Christ is the Lord of glory.

And you notice that in addition to that, Paul says he has a new view
of life and of death. Before conversion, this life, this world, was
everything to him and he lived for it, and death to him was the most
terrible thing conceivable – an awful spectre always advancing
toward him – and he was horrified. No longer! 'If our earthly house
of this tabernacle were dissolved, we have a building of God, an house
not made with hands, eternal in the heavens' [*2 Cor.* 5:1]. 'For we that
are in this tabernacle do groan, being burdened' [v. 4]; 'earnestly
desiring to be clothed upon with our house which is from heaven'
[v. 2]. You see, the Apostle is right; once you believe this truth with
your heart, nothing is the same.

Now my argument is that you cannot undergo a revolution like
that with regard to your ideas about everything in life without saying
so, without making it known; the thing is inevitable. Thomas Hooker
is perfectly right: 'If a man has faith within, it will break forth at the
mouth.' The man is astounded, he does not see anything as he saw it
before, and therefore he must inevitably make this fact known. He
cannot talk to other people about life and about what is happening in
it, he cannot talk about death, he cannot talk about racial divisions
and distinctions, and all these things that are defacing the life of the
world today, without showing that he has an entirely new
standpoint. So that is what Paul means by 'confess with thy mouth
the Lord Jesus' and 'with the mouth confession is made unto salvation'. The very nature of the truth itself makes this quite inevitable.

But there is more. The Apostle says that this truth has a *constraining power* with it. All that we have seen so far is a part of this constraining power, but there is something still more – the people who
really believe this truth cannot help themselves. Now this is a point
that is made very frequently in the New Testament. For example, in
Acts 4 we read that the Apostles Peter and John were arrested and
thrown into prison for preaching and working miracles in the name
of the Lord Jesus Christ. Commanded by the Jewish leaders not to
speak 'in this name', they declared, 'we cannot but speak the things
which we have seen and heard' [vv. 17–20]. They had witnessed
Christ's life, death, burial and resurrection. And, especially, they had
received the outpouring of the Holy Spirit on the day of Pentecost at
Jerusalem. 'We cannot but speak!'

Arrested once more, Peter and the other apostles said, 'We ought to obey God rather than men. The God of our fathers raised up Jesus, whom ye slew and hanged on a tree. Him hath God exalted with his right hand to be a Prince and a Saviour, for to give repentance to Israel, and forgiveness of sins. And we are witnesses of these things; and so is also the Holy Ghost, whom God hath given to them that obey him' [Acts 5:29–32]. It is the same idea. There is this constraining power that makes it impossible for men and women who really believe these things not to give expression to them in some shape or form.

2 Corinthians 5 deals with this subject in a very extensive manner. Paul describes the position of the Christian: 'For we must all appear before the judgment seat of Christ; that every one may receive the things done in his body . . . whether it be good or bad. Knowing therefore the terror of the Lord, we persuade men; but we are made manifest unto God; and I trust also are made manifest in your consciences . . . For whether we be beside ourselves, it is to God: or whether we be sober, it is for your cause. For the love of Christ *constraineth* us . . .' Now the picture there is of a man, as it were, in a vice, and the vice is being tightened up: 'For the love of Christ constraineth us; because we thus judge, that if one died for all, then were all dead: And that he died for all, that they which live should not henceforth live unto themselves, but unto him which died for them, and rose again' [vv. 10–15].

The Apostle has already said the same thing in 1 Corinthians 9:16, 'necessity is laid upon me'. Why does he preach? He says in verse 17, 'A dispensation of the gospel is committed unto me.' Yes, but there is more than that. It is not that he has a message, there is something above the message – '. . . necessity is laid upon me; yea, woe is unto me, if I preach not the gospel!' That is what I mean by the constraining power of this truth. A man or woman who really sees it cannot remain silent.

Now this is a very important matter for all of us, and I can illustrate it from biography. Take, for example, the early years in the Christian life of Howell Harris. Now that man received assurance of his salvation and he just went on enjoying it for himself. But then he received a great experience of the love of God, and from that moment he could not keep silent. He began visiting the sick and reading to them; then he began to talk to them and so on, and eventually became a great and famous preacher and evangelist. There is this constraining power about the truth, so that when we really believe from the heart, we are bound to give expression to it.

[201]

The third argument I can put like this. When men and women believe in the fact of the Lordship of Jesus and the resurrection, it affects their daily lives, and these consequences in their lives make it inevitable that they will speak of it. Is it conceivable that a man like the Apostle Paul, who had been a blaspheming, injurious person as a Pharisee, but who then was given to know that the Son of God had loved him, and given Himself for him – is it conceivable that such a man could be silent? The change in his life, the joy that had come, the liberty, the abandon – this inevitably leads to the dictum of Thomas Hooker, which we have quoted. Our expression of our faith is a measure, therefore, of the extent to which we really have believed these things from the heart.

Now let us be still more practical. How, then, do we give expression to this? And it seems to me that the answer can be put like this: If we believe that Jesus is the Lord, we do not just *say*, 'Jesus is Lord!' but work out this great argument that is found so constantly in the New Testament Epistles. The great New Testament argument for sanctification is that it is not an experience to be received but is the outworking of the fact that we believe that Jesus is the Lord, and that God has raised Him from the dead.

So how does this work? Well, first of all, it leads to submission to Him. If we believe that Jesus is the Lord, then He is inevitably the Lord of the whole of our life. He is the Lord of our thinking.

Now all this is of tremendous relevance and importance just at this present time in the history of the church in general and of evangelicals, perhaps, in particular. What do I mean by that? Well, Paul says in 1 Corinthians 3 that if a man is a Christian, he has to become a fool for Christ's sake. 'If any man among you seemeth to be wise in this world,' he says, 'let him become a fool, that he may be wise' [v. 18]. He says that he himself has become a fool in this way. In the eyes of the Greeks, the philosophers, the clever people, that is what he was. Any man, according to the Greeks, who believed that this carpenter of Nazareth was the Son of God, and that He saved by dying in utter weakness upon a cross – 'Anybody who can believe a thing like that,' said the wise Greek philosopher, 'is nothing but a fool.' You cannot, says the Apostle, be a Christian without becoming a fool.

And if that was true in the first century, it is quite as true today. But it is a fallacy to think that it is *more* true today. It is not. The Christian, in the eyes of the wise man of the world, has always been a fool. We cannot believe that Jesus is the Lord, and that God has raised Him from the dead, without the world regarding us as fools. That is just another way of saying that all our thinking must be governed by the Scriptures, by the Word of God.

If you read the Gospels, you will find that our Lord's thinking was governed entirely by the Old Testament. He believed the whole of it. He quoted it repeatedly and He obviously believed that all of it was the Word of God. And my argument is that, as Christians, we are bound to be like Him. My thinking, if I believe that Jesus is the Lord, must be governed entirely by the Bible. In other words, I am not governed by modern thought. If I am governed by that, then Jesus is not the Lord of my intellect.

So I cannot be governed by modern thought or by recent knowledge or by the latest discoveries of science. The moment I begin to be governed by those things, then Jesus is no longer Lord to me. I am putting myself in a superior position. I am making myself the lord. I am looking back at Him and saying, 'Well, of course, He lived, after all, in the first century and look what has happened since. Look at the growth of knowledge. He could not and He did not know. He had not got our scientific knowledge. Therefore He was wrong in certain things and we are right.' But if we say that 'Jesus is Lord', then our thinking is governed entirely by what He believed, and by this revelation which He Himself gave in His teaching and which we find in the writings of the Apostles.

Let me give you one illustration to show you what I mean. There are some of us who do not believe in the theory of evolution. We believe that man is a separate and a special creation of God, that he was made in the image of God, that he was perfect, and that he fell. Why do I believe that? Because that is what is taught in the Bible and that is what our Lord believed. 'But,' you say, 'what about science?' All I say is that science cannot prove anything in this matter at all. It has its theories, but it has no facts. And I am certain of this, that the teaching of this Book cannot be finally wrong.

Now I must be careful not to import my ideas into the Bible. I am governed by it. I have no understanding of the way of salvation unless I believe that an individual man fell – that is the argument of Romans 5:12–21.[1] The whole case depends upon this: that 'as in Adam . . . so in Christ'. The one man fell and brought down calamity; the other man gave obedience and thereby saves. That is Christian salvation.

[1] See *An Exposition of Chapter 5: Assurance*, 1971.

The moment I begin to deny the fall of man or believe that man is gradually evolving upwards, there is no need for an atonement, no need for miracles and so on.

Now that is just one illustration in passing of how I shall be called a fool by this so-called scientific age. They regard as a fool anyone who does not believe in evolution as a fact. Incidentally, they are not scientific in doing that, but I am not concerned about that at this moment! Even if I had no scientific reasons or arguments at all, I must still be completely governed by this Book. Anything that contradicts this teaching I must reject, whatever the world may say about me. That is being 'a fool for Christ's sake'. We are called upon to do that. That is confessing with the mouth Jesus as Lord.

The second way of confessing Christ is that He governs my behaviour. There is no need to argue about this. Here is the argument in 2 Corinthians 6: 'Be ye not unequally yoked together with unbe-lievers: for what fellowship hath righteousness with unrighteous-ness? and what communion hath light with darkness? And what concord hath Christ with Belial? or what part hath he that believeth with an infidel? And what agreement hath the temple of God with idols? for ye are the temple of the living God; as God hath said, I will dwell in them, and walk in them; and I will be their God, and they shall be my people' [vv. 14–16].

Now, negatively, that means that because I believe that Jesus is the Lord, because I believe that He died for my sins and rose again, there are certain things that should be unthinkable for me. The Apostle Paul describes them at length in Ephesians 4:17–24. You see, it is no use saying that you believe that Jesus is Lord, and that you believe in this great salvation, if you go on living as you used to live or as people live who do not believe that.

You see the argument? Christ is the Lord of your mind and He is the Lord of your will, so He governs your actions. And, negatively, you cannot go on doing the evil, foul things that you used to do, and when you hear certain modern scholars talking about 'a new morality' you just know that it is the lie of the devil. There is no need to argue about these things, the one follows the other as the night the day.

But let me put it all positively. Philippians 1 has a wonderful state-ment of this: 'Only let your conversation' – your life and conduct in this world – 'be as it becometh the gospel of Christ' [v. 27]. You see the familiar image that the Apostle uses? He says: There is only one rule for Christian living – let it fit in with the gospel of Christ which you claim to believe, let it be becoming to it, let your dress, as it were, conform to your character. What is more pathetic than to see an old woman trying to dress as if she were in her twenties? It is not becoming! It is foolish! You should always be becoming in your dress. That is one of the scandals of this modern age, is it not? Apart from anything else, the thing is not becoming.

'Only let your conversation be as *becometh* . . .' You are a person who claims to believe that Jesus is the Lord of glory. The carpenter of Nazareth – the Lord of glory! Creator of the universe! You believe that He died that you might be forgiven, that He has conquered death and the grave, and has risen and is seated at the right hand of God – let your conversation be as 'becometh' that, let it be fitting, let there be no clash, no contradiction. There is the positive teaching.

Now that means that Christ is the Lord of your life, and if He is the Lord of your life you proclaim it, you confess it. You confess it with your mouth, you confess it in everything that you do – the whole of your conversation. 'Conversation' there does not simply mean speech, it means the whole of your conduct in the world. In other words, if I really believe that Christ is Lord and that He has done all this for my salvation, I shall not have a 'form of godliness, but denying the power thereof' [*2 Tim.* 3:5]. My life will be a life of godliness.

The third way of confessing Christ is by belonging to His people. If we all belong to the same Lord, then we also belong to one another. 'Know ye not that . . . ye are not your own?' wrote the Apostle. 'For ye are bought with a price' [*1 Cor.* 6:19–20]. He is the Lord; He is the owner; He is the master. We do not belong to ourselves and we have no right to ourselves. 'For ye are dead, and your life is hid with Christ in God' [*Col.* 3:3]. And so we realise that all who are in that position belong together. You cannot believe that Jesus is Lord and live a private life. I mean by that: 'None of us liveth to himself, and no man dieth to himself' [*Rom.* 14:7]. You cannot be an isolated Christian. Christians belong to all other Christians. They belong to the church and they feel that the church is a necessity. Not only that, they prefer the company of Christian people to anybody else in the whole universe. These are very thorough tests. The place which the Christian community or the church has in our lives is a very good index of the reality of our belief. We belong to His people, our delight is to be with them, and we will forgo any other company, however highly the world may regard it, in order to have the company of these people.

That is a tremendous way of confessing that Jesus is Lord.

The fourth way is a concern for His glory. Obviously! We confess Jesus as Lord by our concern about His kingdom, by our concern about the church. I do not mean merely church attendance, because that can be done for many reasons. It can, for instance, be a purely social act. But when we have a real concern it is a very different matter. Does it grieve you to find His name blasphemed? Does the state of the church grieve and concern you? Do you pray about it? Are you praying for revival? If you are, you are confessing the Lord Jesus. All these are ways in which we make this great confession actively and positively.

And then, fifthly, Peter says, 'Be ready always to give an answer to every man that asketh you a reason of the hope that is in you' [*1 Pet.* 3:15]. In other words, I know what I mean when I say, 'Jesus is Lord', and 'God raised him from the dead.' And I can help someone who comes to me and says, 'I am muddled about this. I don't understand it. What does it mean? Why do you call yourself a Christian? How is a person saved?' I am able to give a reason for the hope that is in me. That is a way of confessing that Jesus is Lord.

But finally, I would add as my sixth way of confessing His Lordship a kind of negative statement. We confess that Jesus is Lord by not being ashamed of Him. This is a very practical matter. It was obviously a part of the problem for a man like Timothy, so Paul has a good deal to say about this in the Epistles to Timothy, especially in the second. He says, 'Be not thou therefore ashamed of the testimony of our Lord, nor of me his prisoner: but be thou partaker of the afflictions of the gospel according to the power of God' [*2 Tim.* 1:8]. If you are ashamed of suffering for Christ, or of associating your name with someone who is suffering for Him, you are not confessing Jesus as Lord. So the Apostle says, 'Do not be ashamed.'

The Apostle Peter, before Pentecost, was ashamed of our Lord and denied that he knew Him. But Paul says to Timothy, 'Don't be ashamed!' He says about himself, 'For the which cause I also suffer these things: nevertheless I am not ashamed: for I know whom I have believed, and am persuaded that he is able to keep that which I have committed unto him against that day' [*2 Tim.* 1:12].

Paul says in 2 Timothy 1:16, 'The Lord give mercy unto the house of Onesiphorus; for he oft refreshed me, and was not ashamed of my chain.' To confess the Lord Jesus does not only mean that you go buttonholing people and saying, 'Are you saved? Do you believe in

Jesus?' It means that when a person is in prison for his faith, you go and visit him, whatever the risk may be, and you are not ashamed of him or his position; you identify yourself with him. 'He oft refreshed me, and was not ashamed of my chain.' That is the way to confess the Lord Jesus.

What does it mean? Well, let me try to put it very practically like this. If you find that in certain circles you try to conceal the fact that you are a Christian, then you are not confessing that Jesus is Lord. If you have two kinds of behaviour, if you are ready, of course, to confess Him when you are in church on a Sunday but in other places you try to hide the fact and are a little bit nervous that it may be known, then that is denying Him. If you try to explain away your faith, it is still worse. Or if in this modern sophisticated age you are so anxious to be intellectually respectable that you soft-pedal some aspects of what you believe, that is not confessing the Lord Jesus.

No. When He is Lord, He comes first whatever the consequences may be. There were certain people, we are told, even in our Lord's time here on earth who really did believe in Him but hid it! John wrote, 'Nevertheless among the chief rulers also many believed on him; but because of the Pharisees they did not confess him, lest they should be put out of the synagogue' [*John* 12:42]. If you are more concerned about your place in the synagogue than in acknowledging Him, you are not confessing Him. It is very difficult at times, but this is the test. To those first Christians, it might mean death; still they said, 'Jesus is Lord,' and they would not say that Caesar is Lord.

Another Puritan – George Swinnock – says, 'He is a base servant that is ashamed of his Lord's livery.' That is very good. Never be ashamed of your Lord's livery. He has given you that uniform. Be proud of it. What a base thing it is to be ashamed of the livery of such a glorious, such a wonderful Lord and Master!

So finally, we must say of ourselves that we, like the first Christians and the martyrs down the running centuries, are ready, if need be, to lay down our lives for Him. If you are not ready to die rather than renounce Him or deny Him in any way, you are not really confessing Him. There is no need to argue about this. If you really believe that Jesus of Nazareth was the Son of God, that that babe in Bethlehem is the eternal Son of God, and that He came deliberately into this world to die that you might be eternally saved – if you really believe that, then it has so changed your view about yourself and everything in this world, that death has no terrors for you. You would infinitely prefer to die rather than to deny Him or in any way be ashamed of Him.

Look at 'the noble army of martyrs' – the aged and the young. Read about those glorious people who laid down their lives so readily and gladly for Him, those who accounted it the highest honour to be put to death for His name's sake. Are we ready to follow? It is not a light matter to say that you believe that Jesus is Lord, and that God has raised Him from the dead. If these things are true, then nothing else matters. This is everything. Everything is subordinated to this and has to be fitted in to it. This is the thing that controls my life – mind, and heart, and will, the whole personality, everything I am.

'If thou shalt confess with thy mouth the Lord Jesus, and shalt believe in thine heart that God hath raised him from the dead, thou shalt be saved. For with the heart man believeth unto righteousness; and with the mouth confession is made unto salvation.' The men and women who really believe this cannot refrain. It is impossible. That which is in the heart must of necessity express itself. And it does so not only from the mouth but in the whole personality, in every realm and department of our lives. Speech is in many ways the easiest of all, but the rest must be included, and the rest becomes the speech and there is no contradiction. Our whole person proclaims that Jesus is the Lord, that He is our own personal Saviour and Redeemer, and that we have no hope in life, in death, or in eternity, save in this same Jesus, who is Son of God and Lord of glory.

Nineteen

*

For the scripture saith, Whosoever believeth on him shall not be ashamed. For there is no difference between the Jew and the Greek: for the same Lord over all is rich unto all that call upon him. For whosoever shall call upon the name of the Lord shall be saved. Romans 10:11–13

When we were making our general survey of this tenth chapter of Romans, we indicated that these three verses form a kind of sub-section on their own. This is a division which is made for convenience as we study the argument of the great Apostle, who always moves from step to step. Now everybody is not in agreement about making such a division at this point. There are those who would include verse 11 with what we have already been considering, especially in verses 9 and 10. However, it does seem to me that the logical connection is actually between verses 11, 12 and 13 which, I want to try to show you, go together.

In this chapter, the Apostle is putting his great case against the Jews, who were criticising him and other Christian preachers on two main grounds. First, they criticised him with regard to the character of the gospel, which seemed to them to be doing away with the law. Secondly, they criticised him because he was offering salvation to the Gentiles and did not seem to be drawing what they regarded as a vital distinction between them and the Jews. That is the great theme of this whole chapter and we have seen how the Apostle has been working out his argument and has brought it to verses 9 and 10, which give the character of saving faith. Under that heading we have been considering the content, the characteristics and the proof of saving faith.

But now Paul wants to establish that still further and he does so, as we shall see, in the way that is so characteristic of him and so instructive for us. It is a model of Christian apologetic. He makes his basic statement and then supports it. Verses 9 and 10 are that statement and verses 11–13 are the proof – made up of quotations from Scripture. In proceeding from step to step, it may seem that Paul is repeating himself, but he is not doing so exactly. He always adds something more. Something else strikes him and grips him and so he lifts the argument to a still higher level.

As we approach these verses, it seems to me to be very important that we should once more refer to Paul's use of the Scripture. I have commented on this before, but Paul does this so repeatedly that we must mention it again. This is his invariable method of establishing a point, particularly, of course, when dealing with the Jews. He reminds us in 1 Corinthians 9:20–21 that he has been made 'all things to all men'. He used the Old Testament law to those who knew it but not to others. He has a great message, yes, but it was his business as a preacher and a teacher to present it in the way that made it most acceptable to the people whom he was addressing.

The Apostle Paul, unlike some preachers, always preached *to* his congregation. Now I suppose it is the danger of young preachers in particular to forget their congregations. They have been sitting in a study reading books, and have been living in that realm. Their great danger when they go into a pulpit is to preach the thing that interests them and they do not preach to the people who are actually sitting in the pews and listening to them. That is not good. It may show a great knowledge of theology and of the Bible but it is thoroughly bad preaching. A man who does not preach to his congregation should never enter a pulpit. The task of preaching is to convey the truth to the people who come to listen. And the Apostle is a wonderful preacher. So here, as he has his eye primarily on the Jews, he knows that there is no argument that will be so convincing to them as a quotation from the Scripture. So Paul brings out his scriptural quotation.

What Paul says here, in effect, is that the Jews were entirely without excuse because the Scriptures, of which they boasted so much, had already said the very thing that he and others were now preaching as the Christian gospel. In this way he established that their real trouble was that they were blinded to their own Scriptures. Now he makes that point in 2 Corinthians 3, where he says that the whole trouble with the Jews was that there was a 'vail upon their heart' [v. 15]. He says that the Scriptures were read to them every Sabbath but they did not understand them. 'Even unto this day, when Moses is read, the vail is upon their heart.'

Paul is saying exactly the same thing here. He is not putting it as explicitly, but that is the effect of his argument. He says, in effect, 'I have been saying to you that it is with the heart that man believes unto righteousness, unto salvation, and so it is a question of faith, not of works.' He goes on, 'I am therefore regarded as an innovator, as if I had propounded some strange new doctrine of my own, but,' he says, 'this is the Scripture. It is the Scripture that says, "Whosoever believeth in him shall not be ashamed."' So that here he undermines the whole position of the Jews. He shows that they were not only without excuse, but in their minds and in their hearts – and particularly in their hearts – they were blinded to the truth of the Scriptures which they revered so much.

Therefore, secondly, and incidentally, the Apostle is able to prove the truth of his own message and that of the other Apostles and preachers of the Christian gospel. He shows that it is not some new doctrine, but is the fulfilment of all that had been prophesied in their own Scriptures.

We have already found the Apostle writing like this in many places. There is a very notable example of it in chapter 3, where he brings in his first grand statement of the gospel.[1] Having said that 'by the deeds of the law there shall no flesh be justified in his sight: for by the law is the knowledge of sin,' he adds, 'But now' – here is this new thing – 'But now the righteousness of God without the law [apart from the law] is manifested' – but notice – 'being witnessed by the law and the prophets' [vv. 20–21]. How careful he is to say that! And he was constantly making that point, and it is so important that we should remember this. It was, of course, the essence of his method of evangelising the Jews. Furthermore, he did the same thing exactly, as we saw,[2] right through chapter 9.

Now let me make one final comment about the way in which the Apostle does this. You notice that he always has exactly the right quotation. That is the wonderful thing. We have two here in this little subsection and, to use the modern phrase, they are 'dead on'! I have often heard people quoting the Scriptures but their quotations often seem to me to be almost irrelevant to the particular matter at hand. You do not help the friend you are talking to by quoting verses which are not relevant to the matter that is being discussed. So let us make sure that our quotations are always apposite.

[1] See *An Exposition of Chapters 3:20–4:25: Atonement and Justification*, 1970.
[2] See *An Exposition of Chapter 9: God's Sovereign Purpose*, 1991.

This, then, is what we see as we look at the Apostle's method. But let us pause for a moment to make sure that we really are learning the lesson which we should be learning from him. Our methods are very important. The message is the first thing, but the methods are also important. We are to be apostolic and New Testamental in our methods, as well as with regard to our message, and therefore we must always learn to pay attention to the exact position of the people to whom we are speaking. We must handle them and present our message to them according to their condition. Here was a man who could speak on Mars Hill in Athens, but he was equally able to evangelise the Jews in Galatia and the servants and soldiers in Caesar's household.

So we must learn this and at the same time, we must know our Scriptures. Now this is valuable and important for us, and not only if we are speaking to Jews who still follow Judaism, but also when we are dealing with nominal Christians, with people who are members of churches but who do not seem to understand very much about the gospel and who do not give much evidence in their lives that they are truly Christian. But if they do claim to be Christians, they are making a claim that the Bible is their book. So there is nothing more effective in dealing with them than to know our Scriptures in such a way that we can give a relevant quotation. Otherwise, what they are likely to say, and what they do say, as we all know, is: 'Ah, but that is only your opinion.' 'But,' you say, 'it is not my opinion: listen' – and you have your apt quotation.

So if they claim to believe, in any sense, in the authority of the Scriptures, they will have to pay attention. And we will often find that such people are in trouble because they do not know their own Scriptures. So if we can answer them by giving the precise quotation that is needed, it will be of great help to them and it will aid us in doing our work. Let us know our Scriptures, therefore, and let us always be sure that we select the quotation that is most appropriate.

But another lesson that we learn here – and this is a general one – is not so much about our method, but is the fact that it opens our eyes again to the glory of the Scriptures. You see, the Scriptures are one. This gospel is presented by the law and the prophets. It was the Holy Spirit who led the early church to keep the Old Testament. The temptation obviously was to say, 'Now that belonged to the Jews; that was the old religion. But we have something absolutely new; we do not need the Old Testament.' There are many foolish people who say that today. I have even heard ignorant Christian people say, 'I am not interested in the Old Testament.' What a tragedy! There is a grand unity in the whole of Scripture. That is why the Apostle is able to establish the point that he is making as a New Testament preacher by an Old Testament quotation.

Not only that, it shows us that since what is preached in the gospel was predicted under the Old Testament dispensation, it is proof positive that God has a great plan of salvation and that nothing recorded in the New Testament happened by accident. It is all a part of the outworking of God's great purpose and plan of redemption which He foreordained before the foundation of the world. Paul says this and Peter, too, who writes exactly the same thing: 'Who verily was foreordained before the foundation of the world, but was manifest in these last times for you' [*1 Pet.* 1:20–21].

I do not know about you, but I find this very thrilling. There are many books in the Bible, but there is this absolute unity among them. Why? Because they are nothing but the unfolding of God's great eternal plan. He foretold it in the Old Testament. He showed what He was going to do, and He kept on indicating it in parts and portions. Then the great event happened and you get the glorious fulfilment of the prophecies in the New Testament Scriptures. 'For all the promises of God in him are yea, and in him Amen, unto the glory of God by us' [*2 Cor.* 1:20].

That now leads me to a further point which is implicit in this quotation. It is that here we have an absolute proof of the inspiration of Scripture. There is no other explanation. Here is the Apostle quoting the prophet Isaiah, who lived eight centuries before Christ was born. How could Isaiah possibly have foretold this? This element of foretelling in prophecy is one of the greatest proofs of the divine inspiration and inerrancy of the Scripture and therefore of the authority of the Bible as a whole. All these details were prophesied, and here they are all fulfilled.

Again, the Apostle Peter uses that argument in the first chapter of his Second Epistle. He says in effect, 'Listen to what I am saying. I was with James and John on the Mount of Transfiguration. We saw Him transfigured. We heard the voice from the excellent glory speaking and we are eyewitnesses of His glory.' But, he says, '*We have also a more sure word of prophecy*' [*2 Pet.* 1:19]. That is even more important, he says. More important than my testimony is the fact that in this Person the word of prophecy has been verified; it has been made more sure; it has been substantiated; it has been proved to be the Word of God.

So, you see, the very quotation which the Apostle uses here to substantiate what he has been saying leads us immediately into this whole matter of the character of the Scripture. It shows us how our faith is not dependent either upon our feelings, or upon what we may be doing or not doing, but upon the infallible Word of God. So we have an answer to all the changes of fashions in theology and all that is happening round and about us at the present time. We look back at this great unity, this great unfolding purpose determined, indicated, inaugurated, and yet to be fulfilled. And whatever may be happening around us, we plant our feet firmly, securely, steadfastly upon the unshakeable Word of God.

So that is the kind of thing that a quotation of Scripture sometimes says to me. Let us thank God for it, and for the fact that God in His infinite grace and kindness has stooped to our weakness, and for coming to us and helping us in this particular way.

We now come to the actual verse – verse 11: 'For the Scripture saith, Whosoever believeth on him shall not be ashamed.' Here is a quotation from Isaiah 28:16, and it is, and has always been recognised as, one of the great messianic prophecies in the book of Isaiah. Some people call Isaiah 'The Evangelical Prophet'. That is quite a justifiable way of describing him, because in various parts of his long book, he certainly has the gospel in some of its most glorious expressions. In this twenty-eighth chapter there is this remarkable statement of the salvation that was to come.

Now we must remember that the way to approach the teaching of the prophets is always to understand that the prophets had two objects in view when they wrote. First and foremost, they were responding to the immediate conditions which they were facing. Let us remember that the prophets were wonderful teachers and they preached to the people of their own day and generation. They dealt with the circumstances and conditions of the time and always had a direct message with regard to them. But that was not the only thing. In and through that, the prophet, by the Spirit of God who guided him, was led to see something greater and in a yet higher realm.

Let me explain: the prophets dealt with the religious and moral decline of the people, and showed how God was going to raise up an enemy to conquer the nation and to chastise them. There they were in trouble – yes, but they were going to be delivered. Now that was true and Isaiah had a message about that, but, he said, there was something bigger here: this was a picture also of the great spiritual salvation which God was going to send for His own people. There is a perfect example of all that in Isaiah 28:14–16, which speaks of the Lord laying a cornerstone in Zion and 'he that believeth shall not make haste'.

Now that is what the Apostle is quoting. He quotes it from the Septuagint translation of the Old Testament, so we have it translated here, 'Whosoever believeth on him shall not be ashamed.' Sometimes it is translated: 'Whosoever believeth on him shall not be confounded'; but in principle, the essence of the message is exactly the same. This is one of the great foreshadowings in the prophet Isaiah of the coming of the Son of God and the glorious salvation in and through Him. The Apostle Peter quotes it, too, in 1 Peter 2:6. And that is why, you see, the Apostle has already quoted it in Romans 9:33. We just glanced at it there,[1] because what was being particularly stressed was that Jesus was a 'stumblingstone and rock of offence' to the Jew. Here, however, Paul takes up the other positive side.

What does this quotation prove? Well, once more, it just gives us the whole essence of the gospel. That is what Paul is out to prove. Having said that faith in the Lord Jesus Christ is the way of salvation, he is out to show by this quotation that Isaiah has already foretold that. So the first thing he wants to establish is that it is *believing* that matters: 'Whosoever believeth on him shall not be ashamed.' In other words, Paul says that the evangelical prophet reminds us that the character of this great salvation, when it comes, will be that it is not a matter of works, of observation of the minutiae of the law, but of believing on this stone that God Himself was going to lay in Zion.

At once you see that the Apostle has returned again to what is, of course, the central theme of the whole of this Epistle to the Romans, the theme which he has already announced in verse 16 of the first chapter. As many great musical composers, in their overtures, give the leading themes which they intend to take up and expand, here Paul has given a theme at the very beginning of his Epistle. This is the characteristic, this is the thing of which he is proud. The righteousness God provides for Jew and Gentile is given in response to faith in Christ. It is the essence of the gospel. That is what the Jews were stumbling at. So, again, as he deals with this matter for the last time, intending to prove it to the hilt, Paul brings out this quotation –

---

[1] See *An Exposition of Chapter 9: God's Sovereign Purpose*, 1991.

'Whosoever believeth on him shall not be ashamed.' In other words, it is believing on Him or not believing on Him that determines one's salvation, and not 'going about to establish one's own righteousness' by means of works.

So, believing is the thing that was prophesied and emphasised by the prophet. And, Paul says, that is exactly what I have been saying; that is my argument; that is my preaching; that is the very essence of my gospel. My gospel is that God has done something. Isaiah said He would: 'Thus saith the Lord God, Behold, *I* lay in Zion.' Very well, says Paul, He has done that and therefore it is obvious that salvation is not something that man does, it is something that God provides. God says, 'You scoffers in Jerusalem were saying, "Let the floods come, it is all right, we have taken our refuge in lies, we have made a covenant with that. We are all right, let anything come that may come." Listen,' says God, '*I* am going to show and lay down the only way of escape from my judgment.'

So escape is something that comes to us simply by availing ourselves of what God has done. These words take away from us any confidence in ourselves, or in anything that we may or may not have. All that is immediately removed and abolished. Deliverance comes by 'believing on' the salvation that God has provided.

So Paul uses this quotation to remind us of what it is that God has provided. What is the essence of the message? It is, 'Whosoever believeth on him shall not be ashamed.' But who is He? The 'him' on whom we believe is this stone, 'a tried stone, a precious stone' which, God says, 'I lay in Zion.' He is Jesus, the Lord who was raised from the dead by God. He is a 'tried stone', a stone that is capable of bearing the weight that will be put upon it; the whole edifice can rest upon this cornerstone. It has been tried; it has been tested. Yes, the stresses and strains of the whole building are known to this architect, and He knows that this stone is able to bear them. And that is the One on whom we believe, none other than the Son of God!

He is a *precious* stone. Precious because He is the Son of God! He is the Lord! 'If thou shalt confess with thy mouth the Lord Jesus . . .' Yes, He is not a man only, this Person is unique! This is God's only-begotten, dearly beloved Son! He is the One who is precious in the eyes of God! He is God the Son who is eternally in the bosom of the Father – this precious Son of God!

This is the One on whom we must 'believe', the stone that God Himself will lay. 'God so loved the world, that he gave his only begotten Son' [*John* 3:16] – that is God laying this stone in Zion. 'When the fulness of the time was come, God sent forth his Son, made of a woman, made under the law' [*Gal.* 4:4] – that is God setting the stone in Zion. It is all the action of God. God has laid it, not man. It is all from His side. It is His salvation. He gave His only begotten Son, the most precious of all His possessions. He put Him there as the means of salvation, the way of escape.

As a *tried* stone He was perfectly adapted to all that He had to do. We need the strength of the eternal Godhead to save us, but He must also be a man. So He was born of a woman: the incarnation took place. We believe in the virgin birth; we believe that He really had a true human body and a true human soul. Truly man! He had to be. This salvation set there by God must be perfectly adapted to the needs of fallen humanity. And He is; He was tried in every respect as human.

What is more, He was able to render a perfect obedience to God's law in this world, so that He could say, 'The prince of this world cometh, and hath nothing in me' [*John* 14:30]. Nobody was able to bring any charge against him that could be substantiated. He rendered a perfect obedience to God's law. But He was also tried to the uttermost. He was led by the Spirit up into the wilderness to be tempted by the devil. He 'was in all points tempted like as we are, yet without sin' [*Heb.* 4:15]. And so He experienced life as we experience it, with all its adversities and its disappointments and everything else.

But then there came the greatest moment of trial. 'The wages of sin is death' [*Rom.* 6:23]. Could He bear the weight of this test? Could He take the punishment decreed by the law? Could He bear this punishment and still come out victorious? He has indeed been 'tried'! He was tried in the Garden of Gethsemane, and that trial caused Him to sweat great drops of blood, but He went through. 'O my Father, if it be possible . . . nevertheless not as I will, but as thou wilt' [*Matt.* 26:39]. And on the cross He bore the wrath of God against sin; His heart was broken and He died. But He rose 'triumphant o'er the grave'! A tried stone! Yes, He has met every single need of man and woman in sin. There is nothing but that He has accomplished it. He has borne it all. He is a 'precious stone'; He is a 'tried stone'; and He has succeeded in bearing this weight of our salvation.

So, you see, the way of salvation is to believe on Him, the tried, precious, conquering, infallible stone; the Son of God, who bears the weight of salvation Himself and is thereby able to give it to those who believe on Him. We can do nothing; we are all condemned; we are all sinners; we are all 'without strength'. 'When we were yet without strength, in due time Christ died for the ungodly' [*Rom.* 5:6]. Can you not see this? asks the Apostle. The Scripture saw it all coming. If God had not laid this tried, precious stone in Zion there would have been no salvation. We cannot do it, nobody can. God has done it, and all we do is believe on Him.

And we must believe on Him, because it is God who laid Him there, and because He is who and what He is, because 'Jesus is the Lord', and because He bore the punishment of our sins, died and was buried – but was raised by God from the dead! This is what we must believe in our hearts, and it is all summarised here. 'Believing on him' – yes, but in terms of what the prophet Isaiah had stated in greater fulness. The Apostle puts it like this, knowing that his readers would have the full context in mind. Do we? What matters supremely is this: Do we believe on Him? If we do, we shall never be ashamed. If we do not, we shall be eternally lost.

Twenty

*

For the Scripture saith, Whosoever believeth on him shall not be ashamed. For there is no difference between the Jew and the Greek: for the same Lord over all is rich unto all that call upon him. For whosoever shall call upon the name of the Lord shall be saved.   Romans 10:11–13

These verses are a good example of Christian preaching. The Apostle supports what he has been laying down about God's way of salvation by means of quotations from the Scripture. He always does this and it is so important that we should do the same. We do not preach our own ideas and experiences. We must be able to show that our whole position depends upon the Scriptures, the revelation of God and of God's gracious purpose in this world of time.

We have been examining the first of the two quotations which Paul uses in this section and have seen that salvation is by 'believing on him', that is, the Lord Jesus Christ, God's tried and precious stone. But Paul also emphasises the words which conclude the quotation, namely 'Whosoever believeth on him *shall not be ashamed.*'

Now what is the meaning of this? Well, it is something which is vital to the Apostle's argument, and is very important and wonderful from the standpoint of our faith and our assurance. He is establishing the certainty of this way of salvation. That is the force of the expression here. The original Hebrew of Isaiah 28:16 is, 'Whosoever believeth on him shall not make haste.' The Septuagint rendered this as 'not be ashamed' and that is reproduced in the New Testament.

So what does it mean? Well, there are several things that the Apostle has in mind as he quotes this statement. The first is: 'He that believeth on him shall never be refused'. Never be refused! Here Paul is thinking in particular of the Jews who had been wrongly brought up to believe that salvation was to be obtained by the observance of the law, by their good deeds, and their own worked-up righteousness

[219]

which they were 'going about to establish' as Paul puts it. But, suddenly, they are told that they must not think that, but must turn to this Person and believe on Him.

But their question is: What if that is wrong? What if there is something false here? Can we be sure that we will be received if we do this? Now this quotation is a part of the answer to that. 'Whosoever believeth on him shall not be put to shame.' You will not, as it were, leave everything else and go to Him and then be refused by Him. This is a most important point. You will never turn to Him in vain and find that He is not there when you need Him most of all.

Now this is just another way of saying what our Lord Himself said in one of the most glorious statements to be found anywhere in the Gospels. 'I said unto you, That ye also have seen me, and believe not. All that the Father giveth me shall come to me; and him that cometh to me I will in no wise cast out' [*John* 6:36–37]. Our Lord is saying: Anybody whom the Father calls and sends to Me, I will never, at any time, or in any way, refuse. It would be a terrible thing for us to forsake everything and go to Christ, appeal to Him and cast ourselves upon Him, and for Him to throw us out and to refuse us. But such a thing, Paul says, is quite impossible. The prophet Isaiah had prophesied that a long time before Jesus came.

But I think that this has a second meaning also. When we considered verses 9 and 10, we said that 'to confess with thy mouth the Lord Jesus' means, among other things, never to be ashamed of him.[1] Verse 11 links up with this. If we are never ashamed of Him, then He will never be ashamed of us. 'Whosoever believeth on him shall not be put to shame.' Put your trust and confidence in Him at all costs and never be ashamed of Him, and He will not be ashamed of you. He said that Himself, when He was sending out a number of His disciples to preach and to teach. He said, 'Also I say unto you, Whosoever shall confess me before men, him shall the Son of man also confess before the angels of God: but he that denieth me before men shall be denied before the angels of God' [*Luke* 12:8–9]. He will never deny us. If we are truly his people, He will never say of us that He never knew us and that we have no connection with Him.

But we know what He will say to certain people who come before Him on the last day saying, 'Lord, Lord, have we not prophesied in thy name? and in thy name have cast out devils? and in thy name done

---

[1] See pages 206ff.

many wonderful works?' To those people He will profess, 'I never knew you' [*Matt*. 7:22–23]. He will not acknowledge them. They are definitely put to shame. Why? Because they were false believers. But what He says here is that true believers, men and women who really believe in Him from the heart, shall never be put to shame in that final sense – never!

And these words have a third meaning and this also is a great comfort. 'Whosoever believeth on him' – to put it very simply in modern terms – 'will never be let down by Him. He will never fail them.' He has promised, 'I will never leave thee, nor forsake thee' [*Heb*. 13:5]. There will never be an occasion in these people's lives when they will feel that Christ has in any way let them down. He will do everything that He has promised to do. He will never fail in any single respect.

Now there are various enemies confronting us in this world, opposing our salvation and we must recognise that. We are creatures who have to face so many foes who are standing between us and our salvation, and what we are told here is that our Lord has defeated every one of them. There is nothing that is opposed to our interests and salvation but that He has either dealt with it, or will deal with it.

We have seen quite a number of these enemies as we have worked through this great Epistle. First and foremost, perhaps, is the law. The law of God has become an enemy to us, though it is the law of God. It is an enemy because of our weakness. It makes a demand of us that, in and of ourselves, we can never fulfil. So Christ, in order to save us, has to deal with the law. And He has. Believe on Him and there will never be an occasion when the law can bring anything whatsoever against you which will condemn you. Paul has already told us, 'There is therefore now no condemnation to them which are in Christ Jesus' [*Rom*. 8:1]. He says that, in the context of his treatment of the law which led to nothing but 'sin and death', but I am free from its 'condemnation' because Christ has kept it.

And it is the same with the devil. The devil is our enemy, the 'adversary', the 'accuser of the brethren'. But our Lord has defeated him completely. Whoever believes on Him will never be defeated by the devil; and it is only as we forget Him and His strength that we are vulnerable. 'Resist the devil and he will flee from you' [*Jas*. 4:7]. That is the position. Resist him 'stedfast in the faith' [*1 Pet*. 5:8–9]. 'They overcame him by the blood of the Lamb, and by the word of their testimony' [*Rev*. 12:11]. Thus, you see, He has conquered the devil, and the devil has no hold upon the child of God. 'The whole world lieth in wickedness' but 'that wicked one toucheth him not' [*1 John* 5:18–19].

As with the devil, the same is true with regard to death itself. Christ has conquered 'the last enemy'. The Christian is, therefore, in this happy position.

All these things are included in the words of our text. Those who believe in Christ will never be ashamed (that is, never be put to shame), or make haste (that is, be in a frenzy, frantically wondering what they are going to do). Nothing in the whole cosmos can ever put a believer in Christ into the position of being let down, or ashamed. He will never find that Christ has failed, or allowed some detail to go wrong. No, it is a perfect salvation as can be seen from the glorious climax at the end of the eighth chapter of this letter.

This is another way of saying that whoever believes on Him is absolutely safe and has eternal security. The final perseverance of the saints is due to the fact that they believe on Him, who has conquered all the enemies. Salvation is in Him, and not at all in us. If our salvation depended in any single detail upon us, we would all be lost. Not a single person would ever have been saved, or ever would be saved.

But, thank God, from beginning to end salvation does not depend on us. It is the purpose of God, and it is certain because it all depends upon this tried, precious stone, Jesus! He is the 'Conqueror renowned' who has conquered every enemy and from whom nothing and no one can ever separate us. No one shall be able to pluck us out of His hand [see *John* 11:28]. That is exactly what Paul is saying, and that is the third thing that is emphasised in this quotation from Isaiah 28:16.

Then, because of all that, it follows as a logical necessity that this is a salvation for '*whosoever*' believes on Him. Here is the argument: as it is 'believing on him', on His strength and perfection which matters, then our salvation does not depend on anything in us but entirely upon Him. Consequently, it is a salvation which is possible for anybody.

Now I know that immediately this great word 'whosoever' is used, there will be an immediate reaction from some people. 'Ah,' they say, 'there you are, free will after all – "Whosoever"! "Whosoever believeth".'

Yes, but that is not the point, of either the prophet or of the Apostle Paul here. They are not considering what it is that makes anyone a believer. Paul has done that in chapter 9. All he is showing here is that

anyone – whosoever he may be, whether Jew or Gentile – who
believes on Jesus Christ the Lord will not be put to shame. In chapter
9 Paul has told us very clearly what determines whether a person
believes or not, as he does in many other places. But having already
dealt with that, he is not concerned about it here.

I have always felt that this is one of the most futile and time-
wasting arguments that human ignorance and sin has ever invented.
People say, 'It is the "whosoever". "God so loved the world . . . that
whosoever believeth . . ." You see,' they say, '*if someone only decides
to believe . . .*'. But the verse does not say that. All it says is that
whosoever does believe on Him shall not perish. The point at issue is
this: as salvation is a matter of believing, as it is altogether His activity, as it is a matter of His being who He is, and stems from nothing
in me, then we are all in the same position. '*Whosoever*' believes on
Him shall not perish, and shall never be put to shame.

Now to prove that I am simply expounding the Scriptures at this
point, let us go on to verse 12. The importance of the 'whosoever' is
this: 'For' – this is Paul now expounding what he has just been saying,
as he always does. He makes his statement, proves it by a quotation,
then elaborates upon the quotation – 'For there is no difference
between the Jew and the Greek.' In other words, the 'whosoever'
may be a Jew or a Greek. That is all the Apostle is concerned to say.
'There is no difference between the Jew and the Greek: for the same
Lord over all is rich unto all that call upon him.'

Now this is a great and such a glorious statement that again we
must pause, as it were, in the porch of it. I have often commended the
importance of staying a little time in the porch, as it were, before you
come into the building. Paul's vestibules are always very wonderful,
and here is one. As I said earlier, the Apostle never exactly repeats
what he has said; he always adds to it. And here is a perfect illustration of that very thing. He expounds – so always watch his additions.

What makes him do this? Well, I think there is only one adequate
explanation of it. The Apostle was not just a logician. He was that,
and there was never a greater. His is the great orderly mind of the
whole of the New Testament. But there was something even greater
about him. His head was great but his heart was much greater. We
instinctively think of Paul as a man of giant intellect, but he is one of
the most moving characters in the New Testament. His emotional
nature was as profound as, if not more profound than, his intellectual
capacity and, as a result, he could never contemplate some massive

truth without being moved by it. Indeed, he was so moved by it that he had to turn aside, as it were, and put in some new feature, add another thought, and throw in some word – and that is the very thing that he does here.

You see, all he is concerned to demonstrate when he begins his exposition here is that 'there is no difference between the Jew and the Greek'. But in saying that, he is fired, his imagination is stirred, his heart is moved – 'For the same Lord over all,' he says, 'is rich . . .' *Rich* – there it is in one word. He has thrown in, I am almost tempted to say, the whole cosmos of love – 'rich unto all that call upon him'. There is the new thought.

So, having paused in that way as we are entering from the vestibule into the building, let us consider exactly what Paul is saying. Now he takes up this point 'whosoever'. It is believing that matters. It is believing on the Lord Jesus Christ that matters, because that guarantees that those who believe can never be failures, they can never finally be lost. And of necessity that implies this 'whosoever'! The word comes first in the quotation but you arrive at it last in your process of thinking. So Paul takes it up and says, 'For there is no difference between the Jew and the Greek.'

Now we can put the steps in the argument like this. As 'believing' is the way of salvation, it is obviously the way for all. This is a most material point, therefore, in his argument with the Jews. If it is believing, utterly, absolutely, with nothing in ourselves, on this divine Saviour – if that is what saves us and gives us security – then obviously it is rather ridiculous to be drawing distinctions between one person and another. If everybody who is to be saved has to believe on Him, then that is the only thing that matters. Therefore, there is no difference between the Jew and the Greek.

But the whole trouble with the Jews was that they were arguing, and had been brought up to argue, that salvation was something special to the Jew. They said that the Jews alone were God's people and that salvation was therefore only for them. They maintained that the Gentiles were 'dogs', outsiders, and that preaching the gospel to Jew and Gentile alike and saying that they were equally saved was blasphemy. That was the very argument that was brought against the Apostle. He was regarded as, and charged with being, a blasphemer on the grounds that he was preaching salvation to the Gentile as well as to the Jew.

Now you notice that we have here the word *Greek*. The ancient world was often divided like that – 'Jew and Gentile', or 'Jew and Greek'. And 'Greek' here stands for men and women apart from God's saving revelation, relying on natural understanding, knowledge and wisdom. That was the Greek mentality. So 'Jew and Greek' means 'Jew and Gentile'. In other words, the Apostle is saying that in the light of this way of salvation, it is obvious that nothing in human nature can bring salvation and that therefore all human divisions are ultimately completely irrelevant. Why? Because all people are in Adam to start with, and – as Paul has proved to us in chapter 5 – all sinned in Adam, all have fallen in Adam, and all die because of the original sin of Adam. Therefore we are all equally sinners; we are all equally failures; we are all equally under the condemnation and wrath of God.

The Apostle had come to see this, and that was why his conversion was such a climactic and dramatic matter. Here was 'a Hebrew of the Hebrews' and yet he suddenly came to see, as he puts it in Ephesians 2:3, that 'We all . . .' – Jew as well as Greek – '. . . were by nature the children of wrath' – the wrath of God was upon us – 'even as others'. That is the most amazing thing a Jew could ever say, that he as a Jew was as much under the wrath of God as those Gentile 'dogs', those outsiders. And he works it all out in that second chapter of Ephesians.[1]

So, then, this is the second point that the Apostle wants to establish here. Let me remind you that he has two big points which he must establish, and that is the whole purpose of the tenth chapter. One is that salvation is by faith alone. Justification is by faith, not by works. The other is that, consequently, it was equally open to the Gentiles as to the Jews, and in verses 30–33 of the ninth chapter, Paul makes that assertion. Now chapter 10 is nothing but a sermon on those verses. The two big themes are summed up in the words 'By faith', and 'Gentile as well as Jew'. Paul is now winding it all up and presses home this point upon the Jews. He says three things. First, that the Jew is, inherently, in no special position face to face with God in spite of what they thought. Paul has said the contrary to them many times in this Epistle, proving that 'all had sinned' and all 'are guilty'.

Secondly, it must follow that if all are in the same position of condemnation, then the gospel is also universal in the sense that it is for the Gentile as much as as it is for the Jew, which is again the point

[1] See *God's Way of Reconciliation: An Exposition of Ephesians 2:1 to 22*, 1972.

he is making. It is therefore to be offered to all people because 'there is no difference'.

And then, thirdly, he shows that the Jew was doubly wrong. The Jew was wrong in not believing the gospel and he was also wrong in objecting to the fact that it was offered to Gentiles. He was wrong in objecting to the fact that the Gentiles, on believing it, were received into the Christian church with the assurance that they were now citizens of the kingdom of God, and fellow-heirs and fellow-citizens with all the great and glorious saints of the Old Testament who were exclusively Jewish. Those are the things of which Paul convicts them. Firstly, they should have believed this gospel and gloried in it because all their prophets had been pointing to it. But they had not. Secondly, they should not have been annoyed or upset or even surprised that the Gentiles were believing it and were coming into the kingdom. They were doubly wrong.

Now how does the Apostle prove this? Here is his proposition: 'There is no difference between the Jew and the Greek.' It is as possible for a Greek, a Gentile, to be saved as it is for a Jew. But on what grounds? What right has he to say this? What right has anybody to say it? And the first answer that he gives is this: 'the same Lord over all'. They were all – Greek and Jew, Jew and Gentile – under the same Lord. This is a great proposition. What Paul means is that the Lord Jesus Christ, as we saw in working out the meaning of the statement that 'Jesus is Lord', is 'Jehovah'; and Jehovah – God – is the Lord of the whole universe.

This is a very important point. Because the Gentiles were pagans and did not believe in the only true and living God, the Jews had falsely concluded that God was not the God of the Gentiles, but only the God of the Jews. And many people in the history of the church have dropped into that particular fallacy and have put the Jews in an entirely different and separate position. But the answer to that, as the Apostle points out here, is that God is God and Lord of the whole world, of the entire universe. God is the God of all people, and the fact that, in the Old Testament, God dealt directly and primarily with the Jews does not mean that He is not concerned about others, or that He has nothing at all to do with them.

You see the importance of this? Let me allow the Apostle to expound himself. This was in many ways the theme on which he preached in Athens on Mars Hill. You remember that he was addressing there a company of Stoics and Epicureans. He had noticed that they were too superstitious – too religious, if you like. They had temples to the various gods everywhere in their city, and among them was this altar with its extraordinary inscription 'To the Unknown God'. 'Right,' said Paul, 'here is my text – "Whom therefore ye ignorantly worship, him declare I unto you"' [*Acts* 17:23].

And how did he do it? 'God that made the world and all things therein, seeing that he is Lord of heaven and earth, dwelleth not in temples made with hands.' You cannot localise Him. The Greeks were foolishly localising their gods and thought that they could even localise this 'unknown God' at a particular altar. Yes, but the Jews were doing exactly the same thing; they were confining Him to Judaism; they were equally in error. '[He] dwelleth not in temples made with hands; neither is worshipped with men's hands, as though he needed any thing, seeing he giveth to all life, and breath, and all things; and hath made of one blood all nations of men for to dwell on all the face of the earth' – fancy a Jew saying things like that! – 'and hath determined the times before appointed, and the bounds of their habitation; that they should seek the Lord, if haply they might feel after him, and find him, though he be not far from every one of us: for in him we live, and move, and have our being; as certain also of your own poets have said, For we are also his offspring' – He has made everybody. Now then – 'Forasmuch then as we are the offspring of God' – he is speaking to Greeks, remember – 'we ought not to think that the Godhead is like unto gold, or silver, or stone, graven by art and man's device.' Then here is the crucial statement – 'And the times of this ignorance God winked at; but now commandeth all men every where to repent' [*Acts* 17:24–30].

In other words, you have to go back to the beginning of Genesis. You must not start your Bible-reading even with Abraham. Do not start reading the Bible at Genesis chapter 12; go back to the beginning. Many have started, and still start, in their thinking, in Genesis 12. Salvation, they say, begins here with the Jews. Oh no! It goes further back. The promise that was given to Adam and Eve in the Garden of Eden was given to the whole of mankind. The distinction between Jew and Gentile did not exist at that time. God is the Lord of the whole universe. He is the Lord of all and we must be extremely careful to maintain this truth.

At this point there is perhaps a danger, particularly for those of us who are evangelical Christians, that in our right and natural emphasis upon God as the Saviour we sometimes forget God the Creator! God is the Creator before He is the Saviour. The whole world is still God's world. He is Lord of all. He is as much the Lord of the Gentile as he is of the Jew.

Now, of course, in saying that here, the Apostle is once more repeating what he has put very clearly for us before. The whole purpose of the second chapter of the Epistle to the Romans was to establish this very point. You see, he has demonstrated in chapter 1, from verse 18 to the end, that the Gentiles are in terrible need of salvation. In chapter 2 he shows that the Jew is equally in need of it and leads up to the all-embracing statements at the end of chapter 3. 'There is no difference', he says. All have sinned and salvation is available to all who believe in the Lord Jesus Christ. This is because God is the Lord of all. He is not 'the God of the Jews only'. He is also 'of the Gentiles'. He is the Lord of all people. That is why in His sovereign grace He saves men and women out of every tribe and nation, of every colour and every continent. He is the Lord of the whole universe; not only of the Jews.

There is Paul's first proof, then, of this contention that there is no difference between the Jew and the Greek. It was only a temporary distinction, and was for the purpose of giving the revelation of Himself. He made this nation in order to do a particular task, but not to give the idea that only Jews are saved. No! Salvation is for Greek as well as Jew. All are in Adam and come from Adam, and God was the God of Adam. So God is the God of all men in this sense. All are equally sinners, all are equally failures, all are equally helpless and hopeless. All can be saved by this one and only Lord, and by Him alone, this 'precious', 'tried' stone which God Himself has laid for the salvation of men and women.

Twenty-one

For the Scripture saith, Whosoever believeth on him shall not be ashamed. For there is no difference between the Jew and the Greek: for the same Lord over all is rich unto all that call upon him. For whosoever shall call upon the name of the Lord shall be saved.   Romans 10:11–13

We are still considering this little subsection. I say 'little' because it only contains a few verses, but it is certainly not little in content. According to his custom, the Apostle here is proving the proposition that salvation is a matter of faith and that it is for all – 'For there is no difference between the Jew and the Greek.' There is only one Lord, and He is 'Lord of all'. So all are confronted by the same situation: their relationship to this one and only Lord.

But now we move to Paul's next argument. In this twelfth verse he is not merely putting in his own language what he has been quoting from the Scripture in verse 11, but he brings out another aspect which is found in the one word *rich*: 'The same Lord over all is rich unto all that call upon him.'

Here, then, is the second great argument, which is based upon the riches of God's grace. That is why Paul introduces the word here. It is a most powerful argument. God is the God and the Lord of the whole world. That is the first argument. But this is equally forceful: that all stand in need of grace and He has such riches of grace that He is able to give to all, to Gentiles as well as Jews.

The argument, you see, is roughly like this. Salvation depends entirely upon God and His power, His ability to give. It does not depend upon anything in us at all. That was Paul's way of bringing down the Jew and raising the Gentile. There is no difference between the Jew and the Gentile, because 'all have sinned, and come short of the glory of God' [*Rom.* 3:23]; all are equally helpless, lying on the ground. There is no point in having any comparisons when you are

[229]

all licking the dust, and that is the position of the whole of mankind. Therefore all these comparisons and contrasts are a sheer waste of time.

Yes, but look at it from the other angle. It is God's power that saves anyone and, therefore, as it is entirely His power and what is in Him, and what He has put into the Lord Jesus Christ, there is obviously hope for anyone. So, again, the distinction between the Jew and the Gentile is entirely demolished.

Now this is the great theme, of course, of the New Testament and particularly of the Epistles. Above all, it is the theme of this great man who was known as the Apostle to the Gentiles, and who gloried in that office which had been given him. It is seen supremely in this very Epistle to the Romans; he announces it at the very beginning. Watch Paul's 'architecture', watch his structure. He announces it in chapter 1:16: 'I am not ashamed of the gospel of Christ' – why not? Well – 'for it is the power of God unto salvation to every one that believeth; to the Jew first, and also to the Greek'.

He had already said that he was a debtor to all people: 'to the Greeks, and to the Barbarians; both to the wise and to the unwise' [*Rom.* 1:14]. Why? Because the gospel 'is the power of God unto salvation to every one that believeth; to the Jew first, and also to the Greek' [v. 16].

In these verses Paul comes back again to this great theme. 'The same Lord over all is rich unto all that call upon him.' This is what staggered the Apostle and the thing in which he gloried – 'the riches of his grace'. It is enough for the whole world. So, because salvation is in the Lord Jesus Christ, and because He is who and what He is, it is a salvation for the Jew *and* the Gentile. There is no limit.

Now I want to take this up with you because it is such a glorious theme. It is germane to the Apostle's argument here, and it is a very powerful point; but over and above that, the thing itself is so glorious that we must pause and look at it. It is all in this one word *rich*, and we are meant to examine it and to work out its content.

What is the New Testament evidence for this term? What is the basis upon which the Apostle is able to say this? Well, we find it, of course, even in the four Gospels, where our Lord's earthly ministry was, almost exclusively, given to the Jews. But there are some very interesting statements with regard to this, in which our Lord threw out hints about what was going to happen later, and one of them is a very beautiful story.

It is the story of the so-called Syrophoenician woman [*Mark* 7:25–30]. This woman came and told our Lord about her demon-possessed daughter and asked for His help. Not only did our Lord not provide it immediately, but He seemed to rebuff her. He told her that such 'bread' as she was asking for belonged to the 'children' of the family and not to 'dogs' – the Jewish description for Gentiles. Her reply was that she knew she was 'a dog' but reminded the Lord that there were crumbs from the children's table which reached them.

In effect, our Lord was saying, 'Primarily, while I am here, I am preaching and ministering to the Jews.' But this woman had a real insight and He blessed her. He granted her request and the daughter was healed in order to show that ultimately He had come, not for the Jews only but also for the Gentiles. The same truth is seen in our Lord's dealings with the woman of Samaria [*John* 4] and in his massive statement, when viewed in its context, 'if I be lifted up from the earth, I will draw all men unto me' [*John* 12:32].

Now that was His real answer to the search by the Greeks. 'All men' does not mean every single individual in the whole world, it means Gentiles as well as Jews; people from any nation whatsoever. He did not show Himself to the Greeks then, but said, 'If I be lifted up' – after I have been crucified, after my work is finished, then – 'I will draw all men unto me.' And John adds, 'This he said, signifying what death he should die' [v. 33]. It is a most important and crucial statement. He was really saying that as long as He was but a human teacher here in this world, His ministry was to the Jews; but as the Saviour, He is the Saviour of Greeks as well as of Jews.

Then when you come to the book of Acts, of course, you find all this being worked out. You see the initial difficulty through which Peter, especially, had to pass. He was not clear about this. It was difficult for any Jew to be clear about it. And yet, from the very beginning, he seemed to have had some inkling of it, because he made the tremendous statement: 'Neither is there salvation in any other: For there is *none other name under heaven given among men, whereby we must be saved*' [4:12]. That is a universal statement. He is the only Saviour, and He is the Saviour of the world.

Of course, when you come to the Epistles, all this is worked out still more fully. You find this teaching, as we have seen, in this Epistle to the Romans. But it is equally clear in the First Epistle to the Corinthians. There, you see, Paul is writing particularly to Greeks, and he says, 'We preach Christ crucified . . .' Why? Because Christ crucified is 'the power of God, and the wisdom of God' [*1 Cor.* 1:23–24]. This is God's way of dealing with mankind, Greeks as well as Jews, and Paul brings out this element of Christ's sufficiency and fulness. It comes again in the third chapter of 1 Corinthians where Paul says, 'all things are yours; whether Paul, or Apollos, or Cephas, or the world, or life, or death, or things present, or things to come; all are yours; and ye are Christ's; and Christ is God's' [*1 Cor.* 3:21–23]. He is speaking of Gentiles, and shows again that salvation is all in this one great and glorious Person.

Paul brings out this universal aspect of the truth still more strikingly in his letter to the Ephesians, where he speaks on such a grand scale. He says that God has exalted Christ over every single authority, present or future [1:20–23], and that God will gather everything and everyone together in Him [1:10]. The whole cosmos is included: Jews [vv. 11–12] and Gentiles [v. 13]. The inclusion of the Gentiles alongside the Jews is described in chapter 2 and, in the following chapter, Paul shows what a tremendous thing this was. It was not known to many before it happened. Paul does not mean that the inclusion of the Gentiles was not known at all – because he quotes many passages from the prophets in which they had had a glimpse of it – only that the Jews had not understood it. It was not clear to them. As we have seen, it was not clear even to Peter after Pentecost, and it took a vision to convince him that he must go to the house of Cornelius and open the door to the Gentiles to come in. It needed a vision! It was there, but they could not see it – 'That the Gentiles should be fellowheirs and of the same body, and partakers of his promise in Christ by the gospel' [*Eph.* 3:6]. So you see, it is a very crucial part of the argument of the first three chapters of the Epistle to the Ephesians.

But then, if it is possible, Paul takes this theme of the exclusiveness and fulness of Christ to an even greater height in the first two chapters of the Epistle to the Colossians. It is the great point that he makes there. For Paul, salvation was all in this one Person, the Lord Jesus Christ – but He is the cosmic Christ! All things will be reconciled in Him by God – 'whether they be thrones, or dominions, or principalities, or powers: all things were created by him, and for him: and he is before all things, and by him all things consist. And he is the head of the body, the church: who is the beginning, the firstborn from the dead; that in all things he might have the pre-eminence. For it pleased the Father that in him should all fulness dwell' [*Col.* 1:16–19].

Then you find the same thing worked out in the second chapter, which also speaks of Christ's fulness and is just meant to prove that salvation is entirely in Him. So he puts it like this: 'In whom are hid all the treasures of wisdom and knowledge. And this I say, lest any man should beguile you with enticing words' [*Col.* 2:3,4]. You must realise, he says, that it is all there, and it is all in Him, and it is all absolutely perfect; and so the one thing that matters is your relationship to Him.

There is the essence of the argument. Now what are the conclusions to be drawn from this? Well, this is what Paul is saying: 'The same Lord over all' – the One who is the Lord of the whole cosmos – 'is rich unto all that call upon him'. He is all-sufficient and He is, indeed, everything that we need.

Let me put it like this. He needs no help; He does not need to be supplemented. That is the meaning of Peter's words in Acts 4:12: 'There is none other name under heaven given among men, whereby we must be saved.' Someone has rendered that like this: 'There is no second name!' You do not say, 'Jesus Christ and Company Limited'. You say, 'Jesus Christ!' There is no 'and'; there is no 'company'. Add anything to Him and you have destroyed it all. He is everything! 'There is no second name under heaven given among men, whereby we must be saved.'

And that, in particular, is the great argument of those first two chapters of Paul's Epistle to the Colossians. The Colossian heresy was a mixture. False teachers had come and were preaching another gospel. Paul refers, in verse 5 of chapter 1, to 'the word of the true gospel'. This is translated in the Authorised Version, 'The word of the truth of the gospel', but it really means, 'The word of the "true" gospel' in contradistinction to the false gospel. The false gospel was a queer mixture, as most cults and heresies are, a jumble of many false teachings. There was a bit of Judaism – that you had to go back under the law – and then there was the observation of days and times and seasons, which Paul deals with at the end of the second chapter – 'Touch not; taste not; handle not.' This was that false kind of asceticism which says that such things are essential to your salvation, and which was to appear later in Roman Catholicism, and so on. Then there was a good deal of astrology mixed up with it, and a lot of philosophical speculation. There is a great deal of that in the modern world, but it had all started in the days of the Apostle himself, nineteen hundred years ago.

So the Apostle wrote back and in effect said: 'This is all wrong, because you are making the Lord Jesus Christ but one of a number of intermediaries between man and God.' These people said that there were all sorts of intermediaries; there were various angels, for instance. So Paul talks about 'worshipping of angels' [*Col.* 2:18]. What they said was this: Here is man and there is God in that great glory, and you need a series of intermediaries between man and God. So there are various angels and Jesus Christ is just the head of this hierarchy of intermediaries and you have to go through all those steps and stages before you can arrive at God.

Now Paul is refuting all that. He says that salvation is all in this one Person. That is why he keeps on repeating this. 'It pleased the Father that in him should all fulness dwell' [*Col.* 1:19]. And if all fulness is in Him, you do not need to add to Him. You cannot add to God, can you? Well, you do not add to Jesus Christ either. It is an insult to Him to do so. And then Paul says, in verse 10, 'And ye are complete in him, which is the head of all principality and power.' Everything is in Him. You do not need any other help.

That is why some of us cannot abide nor tolerate a doctrine which tells us that Mary is Co-redemptrix! That is why we cannot grant that we need to pray to any of the saints, or to anybody else, for help, or do penances and so on. It is simply a denial of this teaching in the Epistle to the Colossians, as of the whole of the Bible. Salvation is in Him, and in Him alone; there is no other intermediary; there is only one Name. 'There is one God, and one mediator' – and only one mediator – 'between God and men, the man Christ Jesus' [*1 Tim.* 2:5]. He is enough. He is the all-sufficient One. He is the all and in all. He is the Alpha, the Omega, the first, the last, the beginning, the end. He is everything; He is *rich*. Exactly the same point is being made at the very beginning of the Epistle to the Hebrews and for the same sort of purpose.

What, then, is the point of saying all this? It is the emphasis on the fact that salvation is all in Him. 'Whosoever shall call upon the name of the Lord shall be saved.' There is only one Lord. He is the Lord of all. Yes, and He is rich! And that is why it is all in Him, because of these riches. So I draw this deduction: because He is so rich, and because all the fulness of the Godhead is in Him, He is able to give this salvation to anybody, to *whosoever*. 'He is rich unto all that call upon him!'

'Yes,' says somebody, 'I can see that good, godly, religious people like the Jews should be saved by Him, but what about the Gentiles? What about the "dogs" who were outside? What about the people who were living the kind of life that the Gentiles then lived as described in the second half of Romans 1? What about people who lived as some of the Corinthians were living before they became Christians – 'adulterers, effeminate, abusers of themselves with mankind, thieves, covetous, drunkards, revilers, extortioners' [*1 Cor.* 6:9–10] – what about them? Can they be saved?

The answer is, 'Yes!' Why? Because He is 'rich'! He is so rich that He can take any pauper who may like to come. He can take them all. No ignorance is too profound. No sin is too great. No one has committed too great a number of sins. You do not talk about numbers or the greatness of sin when you are thinking of His riches. If you are talking about some moral standard, of course, the number of sins and the depth of sin is important. But when you are talking about the riches of God, you do not worry about that; one person can be saved as easily as another. There is no distinction. This is a way of salvation that postulates no merit in human beings, but which preaches 'the riches of his grace', the fulness that is in Him.

So the next deduction I draw is that He is sufficient to meet them all. Now it is wonderful to watch the great Apostle bringing out these points. You see, he could never think of them or mention them without being thrilled and moved to the very depth of his being. Read what he says in the second chapter of the Epistle to the Ephesians. In the first three verses he describes the appalling condition of man in sin – every person. And then! Verse 4: 'But God'! What about Him? Oh, 'who is rich in mercy'! It is the same word – *rich* in mercy.

And then Paul goes on – this is not enough – 'for his great love wherewith he loved us, even when we were dead in sins, hath quickened us together with Christ (by grace ye are saved); and hath raised us up together, and made us sit together in heavenly places in Christ Jesus: that in the ages to come he might shew' – what? – 'the *exceeding riches* of his grace.' What a treasure of words. Grace! Free! Unmerited favour! 'The riches of his grace'! And on top of that, 'the *exceeding* riches of his grace'! And another word comes in – 'in his *kindness* toward us through Christ Jesus' [*Eph.* 2:4–7].

On Paul goes; he cannot stop himself as he thinks of this. So you notice that in the third chapter he even adds to that, describing himself as 'the least of all saints' and his ministry as the result of God's grace to him and his message as 'the *unsearchable* riches of Christ'

[*Eph.* 3:8]. Not just 'exceeding' riches but 'unsearchable' riches! You never come to the end of them. You can go on searching, examining, collecting, putting down records; you will never finish.

And then towards the end of the chapter, Paul says, This is my great prayer for you: 'That he would grant you, according to the *riches* of his glory' – Paul cannot get away from this word, it is all so wonderful – 'to be strengthened with might by his Spirit in the inner man.' Why? 'That Christ may dwell in your hearts by faith; that ye, being rooted and grounded in love, may be able to comprehend' – get some glimmering understanding of – 'with all saints' – what? – 'what is the breadth, and length, and depth, and height; and to know the love of Christ, which passeth knowledge' [*Eph.* 3:16–19].

And then Paul goes even beyond that in Ephesians 3:19: 'That ye might be filled with all the fulness of God.' And you get filled with the fulness of God when Christ dwells in your heart by faith, because all the fulness of the Godhead is in Him and it is in Him bodily. You see, that is it. That is the content of this little word 'rich' that Paul slips into Romans 10:12.

Because of who He is, He has these riches to give to everybody. You, says Paul to the Ephesians, You were right outside, you were absolutely hopeless, 'having no hope, and without God in the world' [3:12]. What has brought you in? It is 'the exceeding riches of his grace'; 'the unsearchable riches of Christ'. 'He is rich unto all that call upon him.' He has enough for all.

So, because of these riches, there is hope for everybody – not only for Jew and Gentile, but for Barbarian or Scythian, bond or free, male or female. But not only can He give to anybody – He gives everything that we need: 'For by grace are ye saved through faith; and that not of yourselves: it is the gift of God' [*Eph.* 2:8]. And that means that the faith is a gift of God: He gives us the faith. Furthermore, the Apostle said in 1 Corinthians 1:30: 'But of him are ye in Christ Jesus, who of God is made unto us wisdom, and righteousness, and sanctification, and redemption.' What else do you need? Well, anything you may need is all in Christ, in His glorious all-sufficiency.

Had you noticed how this glorious way of salvation is always described in terms of superlatives and of profusion? 'The same Lord over all is *rich* unto all that call upon him.' Had you noticed the terms that are always used? You get it even in the books of the prophets who looked forward and saw the coming of our Lord. Listen to Isaiah in that great prophetic word: 'For unto us a child is born, unto us a son is given: and the government shall be upon his shoulder: and his name shall be called Wonderful, Counsellor, The mighty God, The everlasting Father, The Prince of Peace.' He is everything! 'Of the increase of his government and peace there shall be no end' [*Isa.* 9:6–7]. So later on this great evangelical prophet is able to issue a universal invitation: 'Ho, every one that thirsteth' – wherever you are – 'come ye to the waters, and he that hath no money: come ye, buy and eat; yea, come, buy wine and milk without money and without price' [*Isa.* 55:1]. Wherever you are or whatever your condition, 'Come!' It is all here in all its fulness.

In the synagogue at Nazareth, our Lord read from the book of the prophet Isaiah: 'the Spirit of the Lord is upon me' – what for? – 'because he hath anointed me to preach the gospel to the poor' [*Luke* 4:17–18]. Nobody else had ever been able to do that. Here is one who can preach to the 'poor'. Why? Because they have nothing, but He has everything. 'Rich!' 'He hath sent me to heal the brokenhearted, to preach deliverance to the captives, and recovering of sight to the blind, to set at liberty them that are bruised, to preach the acceptable year of the Lord' [vv. 18–19]. There, again, is a great summary of the riches.

But you have it still more wonderfully in John's Gospel. 'And of his fulness have all we received, and grace for grace' [*John* 1:16]. But look at our Lord putting it in detail to the woman of Samaria in the fourth chapter: 'Jesus answered and said unto her, Whosoever drinketh of this water' – that is to say, the water in the well – 'shall thirst again: but whosoever drinketh of the water that I shall give him shall never thirst; but the water that I shall give him shall be in him a well of water springing up into everlasting life' [*John* 4:13–14]. There is no end to it. Rich!

You find the same thing in John 6:35: 'Jesus said unto them, I am the bread of life: he that cometh to me shall never hunger; and he that believeth on me shall never thirst.' Rich! 'I am come,' He says in John 10:10, 'that they might have life, and that they might have it more abundantly.' Not just a little. Overwhelming! Showered, as it were, upon us! I have already quoted Colossians 2:10: 'Ye are complete in him.' Absolutely complete! There is no conceivable blessing but that we have it in Him, and we have it in all its fulness.

So it is not surprising that the writers of our hymns, once they have truly known this, once they have had the fulness of the Holy Spirit, see nothing but this – 'the riches of Christ'. Listen to Charles Wesley:

> *Thou, O Christ, art all I want!*
> *More than all in Thee I find.*

Or again:

> *Plenteous grace with Thee is found,*
> *Grace to cover all my sin.*

You need never worry about it. The same Lord over all is rich unto all.

> *Let the healing streams abound,*
> *Make and keep me pure within.*

> *Thou of life the fountain art,*
> *Freely let me take of Thee:*
> *Spring Thou up within my heart,*
> *Rise to all eternity.*

Or take it in what is, perhaps, the greatest of all Charles Wesley's hymns:

> *Thou hidden source of calm repose:*
> *Thou all-sufficient Love divine.*

'All-sufficient'! 'Rich unto all that call upon him'! And then Wesley gives his list of blessings:

> *My Help and Refuge from my foes,*
> *Secure I am if Thou art mine;*

> *Thy mighty Name salvation is,*
> *And keeps my happy soul above;*
> *Comfort it brings, and power, and peace,*
> *And joy and everlasting love:*
> *To me, with Thy dear Name, are given*
> *Pardon, and holiness, and heaven.*

> *Jesus, my All in All Thou art,*
> *My Rest in toil, my Ease in pain,*

The Medicine of my broken heart;
In war my Peace; in loss, my Gain;
My Smile beneath the tyrant's frown;
In shame, my Glory and my Crown.

In want, my plentiful Supply
In weakness, my Almighty Power;
In bonds, my perfect Liberty;
My Light in Satan's darkest hour;
My Help and Stay whene'er I call;
My Life in death, my Heaven, my All.

He is everything.

Christian people, are you enjoying the riches? Do you know about it? Are you able to say -

Just as I am, of that free love
The breadth, length, depth, and height to prove,
Here for a season, then above,
O Lamb of God, I come.

Charlotte Elliott

You see the argument? Do not draw these foolish distinctions between religious and irreligious, between Jews and Gentiles, do not talk about a great sinner and a little sinner. When you come to Christ, forget everybody, everything. Nothing matters but – what? Oh, that He is *rich*! 'Grace to cover all my sin.' Or, as old John Bunyan put it: 'Grace Abounding to the Chief of Sinners'.

So do not talk about human divisions and distinctions. What matters is that He is the Lord of the whole universe and He has such riches that He can deal with the whole problem of sin in general or in particular. 'It pleased the Father that in him should all fulness dwell' [*Col.* 1:19]. 'The same Lord over all is rich unto all that call upon him.' That is God's way of salvation. Nothing matters but the riches of His grace.

Twenty-two

For the Scripture saith, Whosoever believeth on him shall not be ashamed. For there is no difference between the Jew and the Greek: for the same Lord over all is rich unto all that call upon him. For whosoever shall call upon the name of the Lord shall be saved. Romans 10:11–13

We come now to consider Paul's third point in his argument that salvation is by faith and not by works. He has shown that *all* people need salvation – there is no difference between Jew and Gentile. Secondly, he says that God is able and so rich in grace that He can give to whosoever calls upon Him. There is no need for us to bring any-. thing at all. To start with, we have nothing to bring; but it is also unnecessary because of the riches of His grace.

And now, thirdly, Paul points out that the only thing that is demanded of us is that we should *call upon him*. He has been looking at salvation from the Godward side and he says that there is no trouble there. God can save a Gentile as easily as a Jew; He is so rich in grace that there is no difficulty for Him in that. You can describe the Gentile and his degradation and his foulness in sin, as the Apostle himself has described it in the second half of Romans 1, yet it does not matter, for God's riches are so great that all sin is covered.

But now we are looking at this from our side. Nothing is asked of us except that we should 'call upon him', and this, Paul reminds his readers, was something that had already been prophesied by the prophet Joel. Verse 13 is a quotation from Joel 2:32 and it is a very important quotation. It is important, first, because it shows the way of salvation, which is to 'call upon the Lord'. But secondly – and it is very germane to the Apostle's argument at this point – it shows that this way of salvation is not anything new. The particular charge that the Jews constantly brought against Paul, as the great Apostle to the Gentiles, was that he was an innovator, that he was doing something that was contradicting the whole of the Old Testament. He countered that objection by pointing out that he was preaching something which was long ago prophesied, and his quotation from Joel proves that to the very hilt, as did Isaiah 28:16, quoted in verse 11. The great point here is that this is the way of salvation which had been long since prophesied. All that anyone has to do is to 'cry out' to the Lord.

This ancient prophecy was used by the Apostle Peter to explain the extraordinary events at Pentecost. He was saying that the whole of the Old Testament pointed forward to this; now it has actually happened. So there is no contradiction between the New and the Old; the New is the fulfilment of the Old.

Now it is very interesting to notice that even Peter himself did not fully understand what he was saying on that occasion. Later, when he was called to go to the house of Cornelius, who was a Gentile, he was not ready, and it took a vision to open his eyes to the truth that he had himself been preaching on the day of Pentecost! That is something that often happens. We are told in 1 Peter 1:10–12 that the prophets did not always understand what they were writing under the inspiration of the Spirit. They looked into these things and wondered. That is the proof of their divine inspiration. And here was Peter in the same condition. Had he but realised it, the very text on which he was preaching was already proclaiming that the Gentiles were to come in, as the Apostle shows us here in Romans 10:13.

It is interesting also to notice how, in Peter's quotation from the prophet Joel, two things are brought together which are also brought together here by Paul. They are, first, the profusion of the outpoured Spirit, so that all kinds of people will be filled with the Spirit, not only exceptional men, as under the old dispensation, but now servants, handmaidens, young men, old men, sons and daughters – anybody. The profusion! And, secondly, in connection with that, 'Whosoever shall call upon the name of the Lord shall be saved.' It is the same sequence. 'The same Lord over all is rich unto all that call upon him. For whosoever shall call upon the name of the Lord shall be saved.' This is, in other words – and it is the whole point that the Apostle is setting out to prove here – the great characteristic of this gospel age, to which he belonged and to which we still belong.

Let us now examine the statement itself. What does it mean? Well, you notice, the emphasis is put upon this 'call'. 'Whosoever shall *call* upon the name of the Lord shall be saved.' We take that first. That is all that we are to do and all we can do. Nothing else comes into this question of salvation at all. Race does not come in – it does not matter whether you are Jew or Gentile, there is no difference. So do not bring that in, says the Apostle.

Now the Jews, as we have seen, thought that salvation was for the Jew only. And they were relying for salvation on who they were – on their birth as Jews. Some people still do that, and in doing so, proclaim that they do not understand even the first beginnings of Christianity. What we must realise is that when we come to salvation, we have literally nothing at all; nothing.

It does not matter who you are. It does not matter what race you belong to or what colour you are. Nothing matters at all, because there is nothing that is of any value. You do not bring your race, your family, your name, your circumcision, your good works or your morality. If you bring anything, you are not saved. So it is not the man who comes saying, 'I was baptised when I was an infant. I have always lived a good life. I have never done anybody any harm . . .' He is arguing his own case. It is 'whosoever shall *call* on the name of the Lord' – that is the man who is saved.

This, of course, is absolutely crucial, and it is not surprising that this Apostle, of all men, should emphasise this as he does, because this was the great crisis in his own life. In Philippians 3, he says, 'We are the circumcision' – not those Jews who are relying upon it – 'which worship God in the spirit, and rejoice in Christ Jesus, and have no confidence in the flesh' [*Phil.* 3:3]. None at all! If you have any confidence in the flesh you are not a Christian. Notice how he looks back upon his own upbringing and his own nationality [vv. 4–9]. 'The stock of Israel'? Dung. 'The tribe of Benjamin'? Dung. 'An Hebrew of the Hebrews'? Dung! All these things are refuse, and unworthy to be mentioned.

No, what leads to salvation is that a man or woman 'calls' upon the Lord. What does this calling mean? First of all, it means that they realise that they are in trouble. They are like people drowning; they cannot swim any further and they know that they are going to sink. They are in desperate need and they are aware of it.

Secondly, they realise that they are absolutely hopeless. As long as they feel they can still make the shore, they will not shout for help; they are too proud to do that. They say, 'People will laugh at me and say that I was afraid, that I thought I was going to drown.' So they go on trusting to themselves. But the moment they realise that they are finished, then they cry out.

And, thirdly, they realise their complete helplessness; they have no reserves, nothing on which they can rely. So what do they do? In their desperation they cry out for help. It is the only thing they can do. That is exactly the meaning of this word 'call'.

And, remember, we must give it its full content. There are people who seem to come to Christ relying on certain things in themselves. They have heard that they must believe on the Lord Jesus Christ but they add that on to everything else. That is no good. This 'call' means that you have got nothing, that you are a pauper, that you are desperate. That, according to the New Testament, is all that is demanded of us. All we do in this whole matter of salvation is 'cry out'.

Now our Lord Himself made that perfectly plain in His parable of the Publican and the Pharisee: 'Two men went up into the temple to pray.' The Pharisee went right to the front. 'God, I thank thee,' he said, 'that I am not as other men are . . . or even as this publican. I fast twice in the week, I give tithes of all that I possess.' The other man, away back by the entrance, could not so much as even look up to heaven, but smiting his breast, said, 'God be merciful to me a sinner.' He cried out! That is all he did. And our Lord said, 'That is the man who went down to his house justified' [*Luke* 18:9–10]. Realising his helplessness, his vileness, he simply cried out, smiting his breast in his utter hopelessness.

That is the person who is justified. Not the man who can boast of his fasting and of all the good he does. He is not only not justified, he is condemned. Why? Because he does not see any need of the Lord Jesus Christ; he is self-sufficient. That is the greatest insult you can ever offer to God. There is no greater sin than not to see your need of Christ. To be a Pharisee is infinitely worse than to be a murderer or an adulterer. There is nothing more abhorrent to God than that men and women should think that anything about them is sufficient to commend them to God. There is no greater sin than to refuse the Son of God and His sacrificial atoning death. That, then, is the meaning, the content of this great expression of crying out to the Lord, as shown by our Lord Himself.

And we see this happening in practice under the preaching of the Apostles. Look at Peter preaching in Jerusalem on the day of Pentecost. We are told that before he had finished his sermon, people were crying out, 'Men and brethren, what shall we do?' [*Acts* 3:37]. Crying out! Calling upon the Lord. That is all they did. There was no self-defence, no attempt at self-justification. 'They were pricked in their heart' – they were convicted by the Spirit, and they responded by crying out for help.

Perhaps the most striking instance of all this is in the conversion of the great Apostle Paul himself. There he was, a self-righteous, self-satisfied, self-sufficient Pharisee going down from Jerusalem to Damascus to exterminate the church, when suddenly about noonday he was apprehended on the road. 'And he fell to the earth, and heard a voice saying unto him, Saul, Saul, why persecutest thou me?' And this was the answer of this proud, religious, moral Pharisee: 'Who art thou, Lord? And the Lord said, I am Jesus whom thou persecutest: it is hard for thee to kick against the pricks. And he trembling and astonished, said, Lord, what wilt thou have me to do?' [*Acts* 9:4–6].

For the first time in his life, Paul did not know. It was the first occasion in the history of Saul of Tarsus when he did not know how to direct himself. The proud Pharisee was such an expert on the law and on religion, that he had never failed for a word. He had always known what to do; he could direct everybody else as well as himself. Now he wanted direction and help. He was like a little child, trembling in his helplessness, and he could do nothing but cry out and call out to the Lord.

And then there is another equally striking example in the book of Acts – the Philippian jailor. 'Sirs, what must I do to be saved?' said this man [*Acts* 16:30]. He was desperate. He did not talk; he did not argue or reason. He saw he was absolutely hopeless – 'Sirs, what must I do to be saved?' Now that is the position. And what the Apostle is saying here is that the only thing we do in salvation is to cry out and acknowledge our complete hopelessness and helplessness.

And, of course, the next thing is that we call on '*the name* of the Lord'. What does 'the name' stand for? It is a Hebrew expression which is often used in the Old Testament and means the person himself. 'The name of the Lord is a strong tower,' says Proverbs 18:10. This does not just mean the name, it is the Lord Himself in all that He is as Lord. He is the One who is over all, who reigns and rules, as we saw when we considered the ninth verse.

But let us look further at this question of 'calling on the name of the Lord'. It is not only a confession of our weakness and failure, it is our acknowledgment of who the Lord is and what He can do for us. Take, for instance, the way in which the Apostle Peter explained to the people at Jerusalem how it was that the man whom they used to see every day sitting by the Beautiful Gate of the temple asking for alms, was healed. The people came crowding together, and Peter said to them, 'Ye men of Israel, why marvel ye at this? or why look ye so earnestly on us, as though by our own power or holiness we had made this man to walk?' [*Acts* 3:12–16]. Denying that, he declared that it was through God's own Son, Jesus of Nazareth, the Prince of Life, that he had been healed. Note that it was by 'his name, through faith in his name' that the man had been made strong and perfectly well. Yes, the name represents the Person and His strength and ability.

So, when men and women call on the name of the Lord, they are doing all that. They are confessing their own utter weakness and hopelessness, and they are also confessing that they know that Jesus of Nazareth is the Son of God and the Lord of glory. The persecuting Saul of Tarsus, who had regarded Him as a blasphemer, when he saw Him on the road to Damascus, said: 'Lord, what wilt thou have me to do?' [*Acts* 9:6]. 'Jesus is Lord!' It was the theme of Paul's preaching ever afterwards. So one makes this confession of one's own utter nothingness. His Person! His deity! His lordship! This is what had been prophesied. It is 'whosoever shall call upon the name of the Lord' who is saved.

This is one of the Apostle's favourite definitions of what is meant by a Christian. There is no better definition than this: Christians are people who call on the name of the Lord. Listen to Paul: 'Paul, called to be an apostle of Jesus Christ through the will of God, and Sosthenes our brother, unto the church of God which is at Corinth, to them that are sanctified in Christ Jesus, called to be saints, with all that in every place call upon the name of Jesus Christ our Lord, both theirs and ours' [*1 Cor.* 1:1–2]. Paul says: I do not care who they are, whoever calls upon the name of the Lord is a Christian, just as we are Christians.

So the last word we must deal with is the word *whosoever*. There is no difficulty with that now, is there? If it is this 'calling' and 'calling on the name of the Lord' that brings us to salvation, then, obviously, that is open to anybody, open to all. As we have seen already, it is all in Him, nothing in us. If what saves us is living a good life, or morality, then, of course, one person may be better than another. But here, because nobody has anything, anyone can call and cry out. As the qualification is that you are a pauper and a complete bankrupt, then it is open to everybody, to 'whosoever'.

Now the Apostle is thinking of these Jews who could not see this. He says, in effect, 'You are going back on everything. You do not understand your own Scriptures. They are read to you every Sabbath but there is a veil over your understanding. You have got it all wrong; you have materialised everything; you are bringing something with you. And it is no good; you are keeping yourselves outside the kingdom. There is only one way of entering the kingdom, and that is to call upon the name of the Lord!'

So let us draw some conclusions from all this which, as I want to show you, are as vital today as they were in the first century. We have seen their relevance in the first century but are we all equally clear that all this is very relevant at the present time? A confusion has been created by a certain teaching – a teaching that has been popular amongst evangelicals in particular and which is to be found in certain famous 'Notes'.[1]

The first proposition I would lay down, or the first big deduction that we must draw from the teaching of the Apostle here is this: that there is only one way of salvation, and that is in and through 'Jesus Christ and him crucified'. As our Lord Himself put it: 'I am the way, the truth, and the life: no man cometh unto the Father, but by me' [*John* 14:6]. He also says, 'I am the door' [*John* 10:7]; and He is the only door. 'For there is none other name under heaven given among men, whereby we must be saved,' says the Apostle Peter in Acts 4:12.

Now that was as true in the Old Testament days as it is now. And that is where so many people go astray. No one has ever been saved, no one has ever been reconciled to God, no one has ever become a child of God, except in and through Jesus Christ and Him crucified. We must all be clear about that. Nobody was saved under the old dispensation except in and through Him. He is the only way. How do we prove that? Well, the Apostle has already proved it for us in the fourth chapter of this great Epistle, where he shows that Abraham was justified by faith and not by the deeds of the law. The law had not been given in the days of Abraham, who is the father of all believers. Our Lord Himself had said the same thing: 'Abraham rejoiced to see my day: and he saw it, and was glad' [*John* 8:56].

And what was true of Abraham was true of every saint under the old dispensation. They did not understand it clearly. As the author of the Epistle to the Hebrews puts it, they saw these things 'afar off' [*Heb.* 11:13], but they believed the promise given by God in the

[1] The reference is to notes in the *Scofield Reference Bible*.

Garden of Eden that the seed of the woman should bruise the serpent's head [*Gen.* 3:15]. All the Old Testament saints had relied upon that, they had believed it and had called upon the name of the Lord. They realised that they could not be saved in any other way. Of course, they did not have the understanding of it that we have, because we look back upon these things, while they were looking forward. But they saw them and they rejoiced in them.

There is no other way of salvation. If there were, the Son of God would never have come from heaven and He would never have died upon the cross. Because this happened in time, we must not be foolish enough to think that anyone living before He came, could be saved without Him. He is 'the Lamb slain from the foundation of the world' [*Rev.* 13:8]. This is how Peter puts it: We are redeemed 'with the precious blood of Christ . . . who verily was foreordained before the foundation of the world, but was manifest in these last times for you' [1 *Pet.* 1:19–20]. But He was *ordained*. This matter is quite crucial because of the artificial distinction that is drawn by what is known as *Dispensationalism*, which is a denial of, and does violence to, the Scriptures.

The second observation is this: there is only one gospel. Dispensational teaching will tell you, 'Oh no, there are several gospels.' These teachers actually say that when our Lord came and John the Baptist before Him, they preached the gospel of the kingdom. They say that our Lord offered the kingdom to the Jews, but they rejected it. Then, because the Jews rejected it, our Lord began to indicate that there would come in a gospel of the grace of God – a different gospel. If the Jews had accepted the offer of the kingdom, they would have had it, and they would have entered it and been saved in that way. But they rejected that, so then another gospel came in.

And this second gospel has been preached ever since the death of Christ. Furthermore, this will go on, they say, until a certain point and then, once more, when the church has been taken out of the world, the gospel of the kingdom will be preached again. And then the Jews will see the truth of it and will believe and accept it. They will not be saved by the gospel of the grace of God, they will be saved by believing and accepting the gospel of the kingdom.

Now this is actually being taught and believed. It causes great confusion, and it is a complete denial of the verses which we have been considering. My answer to this is that there is only one way of salvation, there has always been only one way and there will never be another. Salvation is always by the grace of God in and through our Lord and Saviour Jesus Christ.

But, you see, these people divide up the whole Scripture into dispensations, and some say that the only message applicable to us is that which is found at the beginning of Ephesians 3. A famous man, Dr Bullinger, who was a great scholar and a very godly, saintly man, was the chief exponent of this doctrine, but it seems to me to make havoc of the Scriptures. The Gospels, they say, do not speak to us because they are the gospel of the kingdom. So the Lord's Prayer has nothing to do with us, because it says, 'Forgive our debts as we forgive our debtors.' That, they maintain, is legalism, not grace. And the answer to all that is that there is only one gospel!

And here is the proof of that. In Acts 20:24, the Apostle Paul addresses the Ephesian elders and tells them, 'The Holy Ghost witnesseth in every city, saying that bonds and afflictions abide me. But none of these things move me, neither count I my life dear unto myself, so that I might finish my course with joy, and the ministry, which I have received of the Lord Jesus, to testify the gospel of the grace of God.'

'Ah,' they say, 'that's all right. Of course, Paul was an apostle after the death of Christ, and of course he preached nothing but the gospel of the grace of God. The Jews had now already rejected the gospel of the kingdom – it is now the gospel of the grace of God – but the gospel of the kingdom will come back again.'

But then, how do you explain what Paul says in Rome when he arrives there? Luke tells us: 'And when they had appointed him a day, there came many to him into his lodgings; to whom he expounded and testified the kingdom of God, persuading them concerning Jesus, both out of the law of Moses, and out of the prophets, from morning till evening' [*Acts* 28:23].

You see, preaching the gospel of the grace of God and preaching the kingdom of God are exactly the same thing, because it is the grace of God alone that admits anybody into the kingdom. Nobody has ever entered the kingdom, or will ever do so, except by the grace of God. There is only one gospel, it is the gospel of the grace of God which tells us the one and only way by which anyone at any time has ever been able to enter the kingdom of God. That, then, is my first deduction.

My second is that in the light of that, it is obviously the same for everyone, everywhere and at all times. In other words, as the Apostle puts it in Romans 10, 'There is no difference between the Jew and the Greek.' But this same dispensational teaching to which I have been referring says that there is a very great difference indeed between them. There was, when the gospel of the kingdom was preached, though there is not now, they say. But there will be again. So they maintain and preserve the difference.

But the teaching of the Apostle here, as it is indeed the teaching everywhere, is that all these differences have been abolished once and for ever. Paul, of course, is explicit about this: 'There is neither Jew nor Greek, there is neither bond nor free, there is neither male nor female: for ye are all one in Christ Jesus' [*Gal.* 3:28]. In writing to the Colossians, he adds to it and makes it still more specific: 'Where there is neither Greek nor Jew, circumcision nor uncircumcision, Barbarian, Scythian, bond nor free: but Christ is all, and in all' [*Col.* 3:11]. All become Christians in the same way; all become citizens of the kingdom of God in exactly the same way.

'Well, then,' you say, 'what about the Old Testament, where the Jews alone were the people of God?'

Certainly. But that was only temporary. The whole tragedy of the Jews in the time of our Lord and the Apostle Paul was that they thought that this was to be permanent. But it was only a temporary arrangement. God, for a special period and for a special purpose, confined His attention to this one people, but only for a certain time. The division is not to be perpetuated.

Now this can be proved quite simply out of Paul's Epistle to the Ephesians. 'Wherefore,' he says, writing to Gentiles, 'Wherefore remember, that ye being in time past Gentiles in the flesh, who are called Uncircumcision by that which is called the Circumcision in the flesh made by hands; that at that time ye were without Christ' – what does that mean? It means – 'being aliens from the commonwealth of Israel, and strangers from the covenants of promise, having no hope, and without God in the world. But now in Christ Jesus ye who sometimes were far off are made nigh by the blood of Christ' [*Eph.* 2:11–13]. So he goes on to say this: 'Now therefore ye are no more strangers and foreigners, but fellowcitizens with the saints' – that is to say, the saints of the Old Testament – 'and of the household of God; and are built upon the foundation of the apostles and prophets, Jesus Christ himself being the chief corner stone' [*Eph.* 2:19–20].

Then in the third chapter of Ephesians, Paul returns to this point, speaking of the 'mystery' – which was 'that the Gentiles should be

[249]

fellowheirs, and of the same body, and partakers of his promise in Christ by the gospel' [vv. 1–6].

So, you see, what has happened is this: Gentiles have been added to the Jews, who had alone up until that point been the people of God. It is 'the people of God' that matters. They start with Abraham, and everyone enters in the same way. The Gentiles are now in exactly the same position as the Jews, and therefore no difference between the Jew and the Gentile must be perpetuated. As we see in Galatians 3, all who are believers in the Lord Jesus Christ are children of Abraham, and all the promises of God to Abraham belong to them – not to the Jews only, but to all who are the children of faith. And this is where the Jews in our Lord's and Paul's time had gone wrong. They thought it was all a matter of physical descent. We saw that refuted in the ninth chapter of Romans. But these people, these Dispensationalists, are saying it now – that the Jews are still in a special position, that there are certain promises given only to them which do not belong to Gentile Christians. But this, I repeat, is a denial of the Scriptures. All the promises of God to Abraham are shared equally by all who are children of faith, by all who cry to the Lord for salvation, by all who look to and rely only upon, the Lord Jesus Christ.

So we must do away with this distinction between Jew and Gentile. It has finished once and for ever; it has been abolished. Our Lord Himself made this quite clear. For instance, we read in Matthew 21:43: 'Therefore I say unto you, The kingdom of God shall be taken from you, and given to a nation bringing forth the fruits thereof.' That is the church. How do I prove that? I do so by reminding you that the Apostle Peter applies to members of the Christian church exactly the same words used by God, through Moses, to the children of Israel just before the giving of the Mosaic law: 'Ye are a chosen generation, a royal priesthood, an holy nation, a peculiar people; that ye should shew forth the praises of him who hath called you out of darkness into his marvellous light' [*1 Pet.* 2:9, quoting *Exod.* 19:5–6].

So it is wrong and unscriptural to maintain any difference between the Jew and the Greek, either now or at any time in the future. There is only one church, and there has only ever been one church. Do you remember the words of the martyr Stephen? He says, 'This is he, that was in the church in the wilderness with the angel which spake to him in the mount Sinai, and with our fathers: who received the lively oracles to give unto us' [*Acts* 7:38]. The church in the Old Testament, 'the church in the wilderness', is the same church as the church in the New Testament.

But Dispensationalists do not believe that, and this is what they say. Israel in the Promised Land was never called a church, but Israel called out of Egypt and assembled in the wilderness is called the church. Israel in the wilderness was a true church but different from, and in striking contrast with, the New Testament *ecclesia*. So they draw a distinction. The only point of similarity, they say, is that both were 'called out' by the same God, all else is contrast. This teaching is all in the *Scofield Reference Bible* in a note on Acts 7:38. But to me it does violence to the Scriptures. The church is one.

Now the Apostle Paul, as we shall find when we come to the eleventh chapter of Romans, makes this thing perfectly plain. Talking about Jew and Gentiles, he says, 'If the firstfruit be holy, the lump is also holy: and if the root be holy, so are the branches. And if some of the branches be broken off, and thou, being a wild olive tree, wert graffed in among them, and with them partakest of the root and fatness of the olive tree; boast not against the branches. But if thou boast, thou bearest not the root, but the root thee. Thou wilt say then, The branches were broken off, that I might be graffed in. Well; because of unbelief they were broken off, and thou standest by faith. Be not highminded, but fear: for if God spared not the natural branches, take heed lest he also spare not thee' [*Rom.* 11:16–21]. Which just means this: there is only one trunk; it is the same in the Old and in the New. There is only one church. The Jews under the old dispensation were in this church; the Gentiles are in it now. There is no division.

There are not two ways of salvation. Salvation was by faith in Christ, in the Old exactly as in the New, and it always will be. There is no other way whereby anyone can be reconciled to God, and it is of vital importance that we should always be clear about this. The only difference is in administration, nothing else. It is merely the form that is different, but the thing itself is the same. Christian believers now, whether Gentiles or Jews, are children of Abraham. They are heirs of all the promises of God to Abraham. These promises are not confined to the Jews. They are to all who believe.

So, 'There is no difference between the Jew and the Greek: for the same Lord over all is rich unto all that call upon him. For whosoever shall call upon the name of the Lord shall be saved.' Nobody else will be saved, because there is no other way of salvation.

Twenty-three

✢

How then shall they call on him in whom they have not believed? and how shall they believe in him of whom they have not heard? and how shall they hear without a preacher? And how shall they preach, except they be sent? as it is written, How beautiful are the feet of them that preach the gospel of peace, and bring glad tidings of good things! But they have not all obeyed the gospel. For Esaias saith, Lord, who hath believed our report? So then faith cometh by hearing, and hearing by the word of God.   Romans 10:14–17

In these verses we are moving on to a new subsection of the entire argument of chapter 10. We must start, therefore, with the mechanics. The Apostle has a method; he proceeds from step to step and stage to stage, and it is important that we should see why and how he is doing so. It is not enough merely to understand the teaching. It is also interesting and important to follow the way in which his mind works. So we must do that now, and it is not an easy task.

Dr Benjamin Jowett, the famous Master of Balliol College, Oxford in the nineteenth century, who wrote a commentary on Romans, says of verse 14 to the end of the chapter: 'These verses as regards style are one of the most obscure portions of the Epistle', and there is no doubt at all but that he is right. Now he does not say, you notice, that the teaching is obscure, but the style. In other words, he is referring, very largely, to the connection of this subsection with the previous one and with what is to follow; and if Dr Jowett of Balliol found this to be difficult, then there is very good reason for assuming that it is so! Furthermore, all other commentators have found the same thing, and do not agree in their explanations of the connection. But it seems to me that though on the surface it does appear to be a bit obscure, if you take trouble with it, it should be possible to resolve the difficulty.

I would suggest that the connection is something like this – and with regard to this matter I certainly find myself agreeing with the majority! The connecting link is in the word *then* in verse 14: 'How then'. Or you might translate that word 'then' by 'therefore': 'How therefore shall they call on him in whom they have not believed?' Obviously the Apostle is continuing the argument. He takes up a different aspect of it, but it is connected, for when he says, 'How then' he is clearly referring to what he has just been saying. His previous statement has raised a question, or a difficulty, and Paul introduces his response by these words. So we are entitled to say that this is a part of the previous argument; it follows in logical sequence from what Paul has already been saying. In other words, it is a part of the whole argument of the entire chapter.

Now, in parenthesis, let me say here that when you come across a subsection such as this, or even a verse which seems to you on the surface to be difficult, and you say to yourself, 'Why does he say that here? What is the connection?' then a very good principle to follow is not to spend too much time with the immediate connection. Go further back! Look at the larger context, and very often that will give you the key to the solution of your immediate problem.

Let me use an illustration here. In athletics, if you come up against a particularly high hurdle that you have to jump, you take a longer run! If you want to vault over it, you go further back. You do not try to lift yourself up over this very high hurdle from where you are on the ground. The further back you go, the longer your run, and the momentum will carry you over. That is a very valuable principle in the exposition of Scripture and in the elucidation of some of these problems with which it presents us.

So, it seems to me that the way to look at this is to go back and remind ourselves of the object of the entire chapter, and then we see that there is really no difficulty at all. The Apostle, at the beginning of chapter 9, has taken up this whole question of the position of the Jews. Why is it that the Jews, of all people, were refusing the gospel and were outside the church? They should have been the first to come in. They had the prophets and the teaching of the Old Testament and it was all pointing to this. Yet the Gentiles, who had not got the Scriptures, who did not believe in 'the only true and living God', had been more ready to believe the gospel and had come crowding into the kingdom.

Now we have seen that the Apostle has dealt with the main answer to that question in the ninth chapter;[1] but here in the tenth chapter he deals with it not so much on a high theological level as in a more practical manner. He has been saying that the Jews were under a grievous misapprehension on two points. The first was about the way of salvation. They believed that they justified themselves before God by their works, and that was fatal. As Paul said at the end of chapter 9: 'But Israel, which followed after the law of righteousness, hath not attained to the law of righteousness. Wherefore? Because they sought it not by faith, but as it were by the works of the law' [9:31–32]. That was their whole trouble.

Now Paul takes that up and expands it in the first section of the tenth chapter, and establishes beyond any doubt at all that the way of salvation is by faith only. It is by calling upon the name of the Lord in your utter failure and desperation, without being able to do anything at all, that you are saved. So, that was the Jews' first big mistake: they were wrong about the way of salvation.

And that, in a way, produced their second difficulty, the next stumbling block, which was that Paul and others were preaching the gospel to the Gentiles. To the Jew that was sacrilege, it was almost blasphemy that these Gentile 'dogs' should have the gospel preached to them, and that people like the Apostle Paul, a Pharisee of the Pharisees, should now be mingling with them and saying that they were all one in Christ Jesus! That was the second great difficulty and, of course, the two are intimately connected.

Now when he answered the first difficulty, Paul established that *whosoever* calls upon the name of the Lord shall be saved. It does not matter who he or she is, whether Jew or Gentile. And, as Paul proved by his quotations from the Scripture, there is nothing new, nothing surprising about all this. It had been prophesied by prophets like Isaiah and Joel in the Old Testament. Then, having finished that first question, and having brought it to this 'whosoever', Paul introduces the second question: 'How then?' The second question is: How does anyone, whether Jew or Gentile, become this 'whosoever' who calls upon the name of the Lord? Here is the general proposition: anybody who calls upon the name of the Lord shall be saved. But what makes anybody do this? What brings people into this company of believers?

That is the problem which the Apostle is now taking up, and in this section, from verse 14 to verse 17, he has two answers. The first is: a

[1] See *An Exposition of Chapter 9: The Sovereignty of God*, 1991.

man or woman becomes 'whosoever' by the preaching of the gospel to Jews and Gentiles; it is by hearing the message. That is what Paul deals with in verses 14 and 15.

But that is not the only answer; there is a second part to it. Here is a gospel that is preached to everybody – 'whosoever', Jews and Gentiles – but it is quite obvious that everybody does not believe it. 'But they have not all obeyed the gospel,' says Paul. So you do not answer the question of what makes a person 'whosoever' simply by saying that it is the result of the proclamation of the gospel to all, there must be another factor. Some believe, some do not. So the second factor, he tells us, is that the Word is made effective to those who become 'whosoever'. That is what Paul deals with in verses 16 and 17.

Let me, then, just complete my analysis like this. Paul says, 'How then shall they call on him in whom they have not believed?' And he answers in this way. First, there must be the giving of the information. But then, 'They have not all obeyed the gospel. For Esaias saith, Lord, who hath believed our report?' So Paul comes to this conclusion: 'So then faith cometh by hearing, and hearing by the word of God', or 'the word of Christ', as we shall see. So there is a double answer to the question: How does a man become one of the company of people who are covered by the word 'whosoever'? And the answer is: by the proclamation of the message, but also by something on top of that, something that differentiates this particular kind of 'hearing' that is true of some and not of others, and leads them to call upon the name of the Lord.

Now if you like this in theological terms, in this subsection, verses 14 to 17, Paul is telling us that there is a general call to all but there is also an efficacious call to some. There is a general call to all people everywhere to repent and believe the gospel. But it is not efficacious in the case of all. A person belongs to the company of the 'whosoever' because of the 'efficacious' call, this special call, which goes beyond the general. So in verses 14 and 15 you have the general call, and in verses 16 and 17 you have the efficacious call.

Now that is my suggestion as to the connection between verses 14–17 and the preceding verses. You see, they follow by a logical necessity. Paul is carrying the argument a step further on. And it will help him also, ultimately, to show again why the Jews are outside and the Gentiles are in, which was the original point from which he had set out.

But, in order that we may have this clear in our minds, let me add this: from verse 18 to the end of the chapter Paul does nothing but produce a catena, a little chain of quotations, in order to prove from the Old Testament that this again, like everything else he is saying, is not something new. It had all been foretold, it is nothing but a fulfilment of the prophecies of the Old Testament dispensation.

So we see that the Apostle is true to his own method. He always is. And we will find it now even in this little subsection with its two subdivisions. He makes a statement and has a scripture quotation to prove it. He does this in both of them. He says here, to prove his first point, 'As it is written, How beautiful are the feet of them that preach the gospel of peace, and bring glad tidings of good things!' He then proves the second by saying, 'For Esaias saith, Lord, who hath believed our report?' Apart from anything else, this is the most brilliant argument, it is superb debating. He is dealing with Jews. He knows how to deal with them and he always has his scriptural quotation to clinch what he has already been saying. And so he leaves the Jews without anything to say at all; his argument is quite unanswerable.

So let us now proceed to work this out in detail, and we start with this first division in verses 14 and 15. Salvation is the result of calling upon the name of the Lord. Then, if that is so, he says, it follows of necessity that the knowledge concerning this Lord on whom they are going to call must be available. If it is for 'whosoever', then this knowledge must be given to all and sundry. So the conclusion he arrives at is that Christ must be preached to all.

Now the way Paul proves that is very interesting; you notice how his mind works. 'How then shall they call on him in whom they have not believed?' People will not call on the Lord unless they believe in him. The thing is impossible. You do not ask a person for help unless you are quite sure that that person is able to help you. You must have confidence in him.

But then that raises another question. What is it that brings them to believe in Him? So Paul says, 'How shall they believe in him of whom they have not heard?' You cannot believe in a person of whom you have not heard and about whom you know nothing.

Well, how did they ever get to know something about him? Paul again puts that in the form of a question: 'How shall they hear without a preacher?' How do they arrive at this knowledge? How would they ever have known anything at all about Him if someone had not told them about Him? In other words, they cannot know anything about Him without a preacher.

And then that raises still another question: But what ever makes a man a preacher? What makes anyone go out and announce all this? Where does the preacher come from? How do you explain the existence of preachers at all? 'And how shall they preach,' he says, 'except they be sent?'

So Paul has moved from step to step asking the inevitable question and has arrived back at this: that preachers have been sent out to give men and women the knowledge concerning this Lord, in order that they may call upon Him. And his argument is, of course, that the preachers have been sent out by the Lord Himself, and that is how this whole process of salvation takes place. And then, in his customary manner, he says in effect, 'It is all right, this is no new doctrine, all this has been prophesied long ago.' And so he proceeds to quote Isaiah 52:7, or Nahum 1:15 – 'As it is written, How beautiful are the feet of them that preach the gospel of peace, and bring glad tidings of good things!'

Eight hundred years or so earlier, those two prophets had been given a preview of the age of the Messiah, of this great day when 'The glory of the Lord shall be revealed, and all flesh shall see it together' – the great prophecy in Isaiah 40:5. Indeed, the whole of prophecy looks forward and here it is in particular in Isaiah 52:7. The news has come! This wonderful good news of His Son and His great salvation. It had all been prophesied. 'All flesh shall see it together.'

There, then, is a more or less mechanical consideration of this subsection. But, of course, this statement is tremendously important because it contains teaching concerning matters that are of vital concern in the life of the Christian church. The Apostle's immediate aim is to show these Jews why he and others preached to the Gentiles. He justifies it fully in the way we have just seen. But we never stop at his immediate concern because, of course, in doing that, he lays down certain great principles that are always valid and always true in the history of the church and in the outworking of the life of the church. So let us see some of these great principles which emerge from this particular section.

The first is that these verses are the great charter for foreign mission enterprises. They apply, of course, to any missionary enterprise, but they are in particular, and have always been regarded as, the great charter for foreign missionary work. They are the argument for the necessity and the urgency of taking the good news of salvation to all countries under the sun. They show that it is the business and duty of the church to see that all men and women have this knowledge without which they cannot possibly call upon the name of the Lord and be saved.

Now let us look into this for a moment because there is often a good deal of misunderstanding about it. The Apostle's argument is quite inevitable. He has established that there is only one way of salvation, there is only one gospel and there will never be another. It is the gospel of the grace of God. Salvation is only possible in and through our Lord and Saviour Jesus Christ. Therefore He must be preached to everybody! He must be preached to all nations, Jews and Gentiles. In order that this 'whosoever' may come into being, the knowledge must be disseminated, the news must be broadcast. As Paul puts it so perfectly: 'How shall they believe in him of whom they have not heard?' Here, then, is the great reason for sending this gospel right away through the whole world. Here is the great charter of the foreign mission movement.

Now there is no difficulty about that, but a difficulty does arise in connection with it, and it has often troubled many people. I have had to answer this question on innumerable occasions: 'What, then, is the position of those who have never heard the gospel?' It is an inevitable question. The Apostle himself raises the question by his statements: 'How shall they call on him in whom they have not believed? and how shall they believe in him of whom they have not heard? and how shall they hear without a preacher?' So if a poor man is living in a country where a preacher has never appeared and the message has never been given, how can he believe? What is the position of that man who has never heard the gospel?

Many people are troubled by this and these days they are not only troubled by this question with respect to people living in foreign countries. I have often been asked at the present time: 'What about people in parts of our own country where to our certain knowledge no evangelical gospel has been preached for many a long day? What about people who live and die there who have never heard the gospel at all? This is all too possible. We are living in a pagan land. There is a famine of hearing the Word of the Lord. What of such people?'

Now there is a false position, it seems to me, which is taken by many people with regard to this particular question. It arises in this way. Some people teach that men and women are condemned when they do not believe in the Lord Jesus Christ. Ever since Christ came and died and rose again, this is the one thing that matters: Do people believe in Him or not? Not believing in the gospel is, they say, the one cause of condemnation. At the same time, they say that the gospel is to be preached, and they are great supporters of the foreign missionary enterprise.

What, then, is their answer with regard to these heathen who have never heard the gospel? 'Ah well,' they say, 'obviously people will not be condemned for not believing a gospel which they have not heard; that would be unfair.'

'Well then,' you reply, 'what happens to them?'

They will then give you one of two answers: 'Ah,' they will say, 'those people who have never heard the gospel will be judged according to the way in which they have lived.' They either say that, or else they say, 'Of course, you cannot condemn them for not believing a gospel they have never heard, so obviously they are all saved.'

But, you see, those are impossible positions. Let me take both of them. If you say that these heathen who have never heard the gospel are therefore going to be judged by the light they had, and their loyalty and faithfulness to that light, then you are back again to justification by works. But that is a denial of the gospel. The Apostle has proved conclusively in chapters 1, 2, 3 and 4 that salvation has always been a matter of faith. Yet here we are saying that these people who have never heard the gospel are going to be judged according to whether they have lived a good or a bad life.

Or take the other argument. This says that because they have never heard the gospel they cannot be condemned for refusing it, and therefore they are all saved by the love of God. But if you say that, then you should never send out a single foreign missionary. If you send out a missionary to those people and give them the knowledge, and they do not now accept it, they will be damned, so it would have been better for them if they had never heard it. If they are all saved because they have never heard it, then do not send them the news! The result of your sending out your missionaries is that you are going to condemn some of them to eternal damnation. It would have been better not to send out a single missionary – which is absurd. It is not only a contradiction of the plain teaching of the Scriptures at this point but it does, indeed, reduce the whole situation to one which is simply ridiculous.

'Very well, then,' says somebody, 'what is the true teaching here?' Now this is most important. The first thing we must be clear about is this: What is the cause of anybody's condemnation? Think of somebody dying in unbelief and going to perdition, what is the cause of that? Now here is where these false arguments always go wrong. The primary cause of anybody's condemnation is the sin of Adam. You see, the Apostle took great trouble to make that perfectly plain in chapter 5, verses 12 to 21, which is in many ways the hinge on which the whole of this Epistle to the Romans turns. 'Wherefore, as by one man sin entered into the world, and death by sin; and so death passed upon all men, for that all have sinned.'[1]

There is the plain statement. Adam was the representative of the entire human race, and when Adam sinned we all sinned [*Rom.* 5:12–14]. That is the main cause of our condemnation. If we had done nothing at all, we are all already condemned in Adam. It is quite unscriptural and wrong to say that it is belief or rejection of the Lord Jesus Christ that now determines salvation. It is not. A man or woman is already condemned. 'He that believeth not,' says our Lord Himself in John 3:18 – 'He that believeth not is condemned already.' He is already condemned! Everyone is born in sin and in condemnation. We have all sinned and we are all dead in Adam.

There is a subsidiary cause, and that is our own subsequent actions. But the primary cause of condemnation for the whole world is still: 'We all . . . were by nature the children of wrath, even as others' [*Eph.* 2:3] – because we are the children of Adam. And we must not substitute anything for that.

Then the subsidiary cause is our own sinfulness, our own wilful disobedience, whether it is a wilful breaking of the law of Moses as given to the Jews, or whether it is, as Paul argues in Romans chapter 2, the law of God which is written on the heart of every person. The most ignorant heathens in the remotest parts of the earth have the law of God written upon their hearts; that is this moral sense that everybody has. And they show that it is there, Paul says, by 'their thoughts the mean while accusing or else excusing one another' [*Rom.* 2:15]. Very well, there is the first point – the cause of condemnation is that we are in Adam.

The second proposition is that Christ, and Christ alone, is the way of salvation. There is only one way whereby we can be reconciled to God and that is through Jesus Christ and Him crucified. If anything else could have saved men and women, Christ would never have come. It is because there was nothing else that the Son of God had to

[1] See the discussion of this passage in *An Exposition of Chapter 5: Assurance*, 1971.

come, and even had to go to the death of the cross. So we must never talk again about 'being faithful to the light we have' and so on. No; 'Other foundation can no man lay than that is laid, which is Jesus Christ' [*1 Cor.* 3:11]. These are absolutes. One cause of condemnation; one, and only one, way of salvation.

'But,' you ask, 'if you say that people can only be saved through Jesus Christ and Him crucified, then what about those who have never heard of Him; are they all of necessity condemned to everlasting perdition and destruction and punishment? How do you answer that?'

Very well, I accept the challenge, and I suggest that there is an answer. The position of the heathen who have never heard the gospel is, in essence and in principle, no different at all from the position of infants that die almost as soon as they are born. Here is an infant who is born and lives, but who dies, let us say, immediately or in a few days or months. What is the position of these infants who cannot think, who cannot understand, and to whom you cannot preach the gospel? They are in exactly the same position as the heathen.

Now, again, people also tend to go wrong about the infant. There is a teaching – and to me it is always a mystery how a man like Charles Hodge could ever have taught it – to the effect that all dying in infancy go to heaven, that they are all saved. All I can say with regard to that is that there is not a single Scripture to support that statement.

Furthermore, when we were considering the false teaching with regard to the heathen who had never heard the gospel, I pointed out that it would be a disservice to them to send foreign missionaries. If they are saved because of their ignorance, to give them knowledge is a cause of damnation for some. And it is the same, of course, with infants. If all infants are automatically saved and go to heaven, then it is a most unfortunate thing that we did not all die when we were infants! That is the inevitable implication according to that argument, and it is monstrous and ludicrous. God meant us to grow and develop.

No, such a teaching is pure speculation. I should like to say it, but I cannot. I have no right to say it. There is no Scripture whatsoever that says that. It is very comforting, I know, but, my dear friends, we are not here to say nice things nor comforting things; we are here to expound the Scripture.

So what is the answer? There is only one answer to me and it is that of the ninth chapter of the Epistle to the Romans – the sovereign election of God! I see no other answer. It is a great mystery. I cannot give you details but I can say this: it is God who saves. Chapter 9 has told us, 'Jacob have I loved, but Esau have I hated' [v. 13] – and that was true of them even before they were born, when they were still in their mother's womb and had not had an opportunity of doing either good or bad. That was the great argument of chapter 9: 'the purpose of God according to election' [v. 11]. Salvation is entirely God's work. It is all of him. And the moment you begin to look at it like that, I think that you can have a little light on this question of the infant and the heathen who have never heard the gospel. It is a part of the mystery of the working of God.

So what is the Apostle saying here in Romans 10:14–15? Is he saying that the only way whereby men and women can be saved is by hearing the preaching of the gospel and believing it? No, he is not. What he is saying is that it is the normal and customary method, but he does not say that it is the only method. If that were the only method, then what does happen to infants and to the heathen?

Fortunately, the Apostle does not say that. Let us look at the comment on these verses by John Calvin, of all men. He says, 'But if any man shall hereby contend to prove that God could not otherwise than by the means of preaching, infuse or pour His knowledge into men, we deny that to be the meaning of the Apostle, who had respect only to the ordinary dispensation of God, and would not prescribe any law or limitation to His grace.' What that means is this: all the Apostle is saying here is that normally God does save through the preaching of the Word, but he does not go on to say that that is the only way. He does not say that God cannot, if He chooses, do it in some mysterious manner, which Calvin calls here 'by infusing or pouring His knowledge into men'.

Then let me give you another quotation from the Second Helvetic Confession of Faith, drawn up in Switzerland by the Reformers in the sixteenth century. Having said that the normal way is by preaching, they go on, 'We at the same time admit that God can, even without an outward ministry, illuminate men whom and when He pleases, it lies in His power. But we are speaking of the means and manner which He ordinarily uses in teaching men, and of the commandment and example which is given us by God.' And that is what I profoundly believe, and have indeed always believed and taught.

I will put it to you like this. Salvation is of God and there is no limit to what God can do. Show me a man, if you like, who is dying and who has never believed the gospel. You say to me, 'That man is going to hell.'

I say, 'You cannot say so; he may not.'

'Well, how?' you say. 'He has never heard the preaching of the gospel.'

I agree with you. But what is there to stop the almighty God from illuminating the man's mind, and giving him a revelation of Christ and the gospel, even in the last agony of death? Do you tell me that God cannot do that? I believe He can. He can do that to a heathen who has never heard the gospel. In His own mysterious manner by the Holy Spirit God can give that man the knowledge of Christ which is adequate to save him.

He can do the same to an unconscious infant, and it is there I see the salvation of the unconscious infant or of men and women who may have died in a state of what we call insanity. It is no more difficult for God to save an unconscious infant than it is for him to save an adult by preaching. It is God who does it in both cases. It is not the preacher; it is not the man who listens; it is not my preaching; it is not your power of decision; it is not the exercise of your will-power; it is not your 'deciding for Christ'. God, in Christ, by the Spirit, saves everybody and because it is God who saves, He can save an infant; He can save a heathen who has never heard the gospel. He can give them the knowledge and the understanding and the ability without any difficulty; and I believe He does so.

And that is my answer concerning the heathen. All the heathen are not lost. All the heathen are not saved. But that is just to say exactly the same thing as I say about the people in this country. All the people who have not heard the gospel in this country are not lost, and they are not all saved. It is God who saves in all cases, and from God's standpoint there is no more difficulty in the one than in the other. You see, we do not know, do we? We are so ignorant and we are so ready to put forward our opinions and suppositions and imaginings and speculations. But the Scripture teaches that salvation is always the work of God and there is nothing here which confines it to one particular method. Preaching is the usual method. This is the habitual, this is the ordinary, but it is not the invariable method. As God dealt with Saul of Tarsus in a special way, distinct from the other Apostles, so He still does, and will continue to do.

'Great is the mystery of godliness' [*1 Tim.* 3:16]! Let us be humbled and give glory to God, and not try to intrude into matters that are beyond our understanding and beyond the revelation given.

Twenty-four

*

How then shall they call on him in whom they have not believed? and how shall they believe in him of whom they have not heard? and how shall they hear without a preacher? And how shall they preach, except they be sent? as it is written, How beautiful are the feet of them that preach the gospel of peace, and bring glad tidings of good things! But they have not all obeyed the gospel. For Esaias saith, Lord, who hath believed our report? So then faith cometh by hearing, and hearing by the word of God.   Romans 10:14–17

We have seen how the Apostle Paul is dealing here with the normal and customary manner whereby the news of salvation is spread. We have seen that verses 10–14 give the charter for missionary work. And we have looked at the problem of what happens to the heathen and babies who die without hearing the preaching of the gospel. But other questions also arise in people's minds with regard to this matter of the preaching of the gospel. Some often put this kind of question: 'If it is, as you say, a matter that is determined solely by the love and by the will of God, why is any preaching at all necessary?' – a question which is often asked, also, after reading Romans 9.

People do have that difficulty, so we must look at it, and the answer, again, is that this is God's customary way of working, of bringing His purposes to pass. It is not His only way, as I have shown you, but it is the way that He normally chooses to employ.

Let me illustrate what I mean. God is all-powerful and, if He so chose, He could cause food to rise from the ground immediately, at any moment. But God in His eternal wisdom has not chosen to do that. He has chosen that men should plough the earth; that they should harrow it and break it up; that they should sow the seed into it and then smooth it over. They do all that in the spring, or perhaps even earlier, but they do not get the harvest until the autumn. God has chosen to work through means indirectly, in that manner. He could have done it all immediately, but He chose not to.

And it is exactly the same with this matter of the gospel, of bringing men and women to a knowledge of salvation. We must always say, remember, that God is not tied to means. He can do things directly, and He undoubtedly does so in the case of infants, the heathen and others. But His usual manner is by preaching.

Or, if you prefer another illustration, there is the whole question of miracles. God has the power to work a miracle whenever He chooses. But He does not keep life going by an endless succession of miracles. A miracle is exceptional. God normally works through the laws of nature – cause and effect – but at times He acts independently of that. And that is what a miracle is. A miracle is not a breaking of the laws of nature, it is God choosing at a given point, and for a given purpose, to act apart from His own laws that He has placed in nature. So a miracle is an exceptional action; the normal is for God to use the means that He Himself has brought into existence.

Now it is exactly like that with this matter. God has chosen that the gospel should be known and that men and women should be brought to salvation by this method of preaching the gospel.

So, if people say, 'Well, if God determines who is to be saved, why do you need preaching?' our answer should be: 'God ordains the means as well as the end.' So there is no contradiction at all at this point.

Then another question arises. The Apostle here talks about preaching, so someone may say, 'Am I to assume, therefore, that the only method of salvation is by means of preaching this Word? What about reading the Word? Is it not possible for people to come to salvation as the result of reading the Word on their own?' Again, the answer is the same. Salvation is not confined to preaching only. There are instances of men and women who have been saved by reading the Word on their own.

What, then, do we conclude about this aspect of the matter? Well, I must say the same thing once more: that it seems perfectly clear from the teaching of the Scriptures that God's ordained, customary method is to save people by means of preaching, but it does not exclude this other possibility. The truth is in the Word, and some people have come to salvation, almost accidentally, it appears to the outside world, by casually picking up a Bible and opening at a given passage. Immediately their attention is focussed on a word which there and then is used by the Spirit to their salvation. This does happen and what the Apostle says here does not exclude that.

Now I must digress at this point because I feel compelled to look into that matter a little further. It is important that we should always apply the teaching of the Scriptures and here, I feel, is another point that has a great deal of relevance at this present time. We are living in days when preaching is not as popular as it once was and when people do not believe in it as they once did. We have got to face that. We are living in an age which talks a lot about 'reading'. I know that there are aspects of modern life which do not even include reading, because modern life is so muddled; but it is perfectly clear that preaching is at a discount.

At the present time there is undoubtedly a reaction against the historic preaching of the Christian church. People will only tolerate ten, fifteen or twenty minute 'addresses' or 'remarks' which are not even called 'sermons'. That is the modern attitude and I believe it is a very serious matter. It is a part of the whole general reaction of modern men and women, which affects even the people of God. There is this tendency to discount preaching, and we want to read quietly, at leisure, and so on.

So it seems to me to be important that we should realise that the Bible puts a great emphasis upon preaching. It is God's normal method, says the Apostle: 'How shall they hear without a preacher?' So I want to show why it is that the Bible undoubtedly puts preaching before reading, and I think the modern Christian needs to know something about this. Preaching, after all, is that which has been ordained by God. It is He who has ordained that 'by the foolishness of preaching' – the thing preached – 'to save them that believe' [*1 Cor.* 1:21]. So He calls apostles and prophets and evangelists and pastors and teachers to this work.

Now why do I say that it is important for us to realise the truth concerning preaching as against reading? Why do we come to listen to preaching on Sunday? Why do we not all stay at home reading the Bible or reading books about the Bible? Why is it important that we should come together and listen to a preacher? Well, quite a number of answers are suggested in the Bible with respect to this matter, and here is one of them. Though the Word is here before us and in a language that we can understand, and though as Christians we have all received the Holy Spirit and He is in us, it does not follow that we are therefore competent in and of ourselves, without any aid, to arrive at a true knowledge and understanding of the Word of God.

Let me give you two examples of what I mean. Take what our Lord said to the two disciples on the way to Emmaus: 'O fools, and slow of heart to believe all that the prophets have spoken: ought not Christ to have suffered these things, and to enter into his glory? And beginning at Moses and all the prophets, he expounded unto them in all the scriptures the things concerning himself' [*Luke* 24:25–27]. And it ended with their eyes being opened and they said one to another, 'Did not our heart burn within us, while he talked with us by the way, and while he opened to us the scriptures?' [v. 32].

The whole trouble with the Jews, in a sense, was that they they read their Scriptures every Sabbath, but they did not understand them, and their own teachers did not help them. There was a veil over their minds. That was their whole tragedy. They had the Scriptures but that was not enough on its own. 'But,' says somebody, 'what about the statements in 1 John 2:20 and 27, where it says that, "Ye have an unction from the Holy One, and ye know all things", and, "Ye need not that any man teach you"? What about that?'

The answer is that the Apostle cannot possibly mean that because someone is a Christian, no more instruction is needed, because by writing that very Epistle, John was giving instruction. He was doing that very thing, as were the other Apostles who wrote their Epistles. No, what John means there is that there is an ability in all Christians to receive spiritual instruction.

No, even our anxiety to know the truth is not enough. Let me give one other interesting and instructive example of this selfsame thing. It is the case of the Ethiopian eunuch on his way back from Jerusalem, sitting in his chariot and reading Isaiah the prophet. 'Then the Spirit said unto Philip, Go near, and join thyself to this chariot. And Philip ran thither to him, and heard him read the prophet Esaias, and said, Understandest thou what thou readest? And he said, How can I, except some man should guide me? And he desired Philip that he would come up and sit with him' [*Acts* 8:29–31].

Now there was the man with the truth in front of him, but he did not understand it. He needed help; he needed a teacher, an expositor; he needed someone to preach to him. And, of course, Philip did this very thing. 'Then Philip opened his mouth, and began at the same scripture, and preached unto him Jesus' [v. 35]. And as the result of this preaching, he came to a saving faith.

That, you see, is God's normal method, and that is why He has given these various gifts to the church. '. . . he gave some, apostles; and some, prophets; and some, evangelists; and some, pastors and teachers.' What for? 'For the perfecting of the saints, for the work of the ministry, for the edifying of the body of Christ: till we all come in the unity of the faith, and of the knowledge of the Son of God, unto a perfect man, unto the measure of the stature of the fulness of Christ' [*Eph.* 4:11–13]. Those instances, then, show us the need of preaching. It is not enough that you have the Word and that you have the Spirit in you, you still need this further help.

Why should this be so? Now that is a very difficult question to answer. Phillips Brooks, a nineteenth-century American, defined preaching as 'truth mediated through personality'. Truth – it must always be truth – but mediated through personality. This means that God can use everything about the preacher in order to bring the truth home. Notice, *God* can do so. When the preacher tries to do so, it is thoroughly bad. It is meretricious and even worse. But God can use everything pertaining to a man.

The classic example of this, of course, is a man like George Whitefield, whom God endowed with so many gifts in order to use him. His personality, the whole man, was involved in the act of preaching. God can use the man as He uses the Word in order to produce His desired end. And the history of the church shows that abundantly. It shows how God has given men gifts of mind and intellect, of understanding and insight into the truth, of voice and appearance and a thousand and one other things, as it were, all of them working together under the power of the Spirit to make a man an effective preacher – effective in the service of God and in the salvation of souls.

Now all this comes into this question. You say, 'But why can I not get all this quite as well by reading at home?' And my answer is that you cannot. And I will go further. You cannot even get it by watching television or listening to a radio. It will, no doubt, be reported now that I say that no one has ever been converted by listening to a sermon on the radio or television! I am not saying that, but I am saying that that is very exceptional. It does happen. But I am asserting that there is something about the gathering of the saints which is vital to preaching. That is why the church is so important. We are in danger of becoming individualists. But, you see, 'the church . . . is the pillar and ground of the truth' [*1 Tim.* 3:15], and it is when the church is assembled together that the preaching is generally most effective.

That is why I have often pleaded with people to realise the importance of attendance at the house of God.

Let me put it to you like this. Take the people – ninety per cent of this population, at the present time – who never darken the doors of a place of worship. Let us imagine a man who is in trouble, whether it be illness, or death in the family or something else. He is disturbed; he is at the end of his tether and nobody can help him. He begins to think of God. Can God help? Can the church help? Then let us assume that he comes off the street into a church. What if he comes in and finds just a handful of people? I maintain that immediately he will be discouraged; he will be somewhat depressed. He will say, 'Well evidently not many people believe in this. There was a time when they must have done or they would not have put up a big building like this. But evidently Christians have come to see now that there is nothing in it and they do not use their own building.' Already the devil is having a marvellous opportunity.

On the other hand, if the man comes in and finds the building packed with eager people, waiting on the preaching of the gospel, I maintain that he is carried a considerable distance by that in the direction of salvation. That alone is not going to save him, but who can say that that is not used by God? The church, the community of God's people. There is a spiritual atmosphere. People have come to me often and have told me that the first step in their salvation was entering this building and feeling something that they did not understand, feeling that there was some atmosphere, a 'something' that they had never known before, and it made them attentive to the gospel, though at first they did not understand it and did not know what I was talking about. But they had sensed something which had held them and had made them come back.

So this is where this whole question of preaching comes in. The congregation is used as well as the preacher; the whole testimony of the people gathered together, the whole atmosphere of people in whom the Holy Spirit resides is a witness to the truth.

But here is another argument for preaching over and against reading, and that is the vital necessity always of application. Now I know that I am saying things that sound dangerous! I often advise you to buy books and to read them. And yet, you know, reading can be extremely dangerous; it can almost become an addiction, in the sense that drugs may be addictive. And I believe there is a danger in this respect at the present time, and it is one of the greatest dangers of all.

If you are reading a book on your own, you can put it down whenever you like, and if it begins to disturb you, you put it down and you take up a newspaper or something else.

But there is this about being in a congregation, that it is not always easy to get out of that congregation! You have to stay there, and the power of the truth comes to you mediated through the person of the preacher. You feel you would like to get up and leave, but you do not want to create a disturbance, so you have to sit and listen, and the teaching is applied to you. And that may be the very thing, under the power of the Spirit, that leads to your conversion. Application! It is one thing to read; it is a very different thing to apply the message to yourself. We need application, we need exhortation to deliver us from a mere intellectual, theoretical, academic interest in the truth.

And that is one of the greatest functions of the preacher, and that is why people who read their sermons are denying the very essence of preaching. It is to be applied the whole time. That is the first task of the preacher. The truth is, as it were, available to people, but the preacher has to have a sermon with a shaft and a spear point. It has to penetrate, and that is the whole business of preaching. And that is why I believe that God has ordained this as the regular method; reading and other things are the exception in the economy of God.

And the facts confirm everything that I am saying. The Bible, we are told, is the best seller in the world today, but look at the state of the world! The Bible is the best seller in Great Britain, but look at Great Britain. What is the point of saying it is the best seller? There is something wrong somewhere. Yes, and what is wrong is that people do not listen to preaching. The possession of a Bible, good though it is, is not enough. It can be read as literature; people can pick out what they like and they can leave out what they do not understand. The message of the Bible needs to be presented in a manner that is calculated to lead to salvation.

It is an interesting thing that in an age which reads more, perhaps, than any previous age, the church has not flourished. If the reading of the Bible, books, tracts, journals and all the rest were really doing the work, our churches would be packed. But they are not. No, if you go back across the history of the church you will find that it is through preaching that God produces His revivals. He clothes a man, or a number of men, with power, and the truth is presented in this extraordinary manner.

And, finally, let me give you another important argument for preaching. The business of preaching, after all, is to explain the message of the Word, and I maintain that that can only be done by preaching. Now, today, because people do not believe in preaching, they believe in new translations of the Bible. Have you ever thought that that was the main reason for all this excitement about new translations? It is because people do not believe in preaching. I work that out like this. What is the argument for the new translations – any one of them? The argument is that people no longer understand the Authorised Version and the Revised, which is very similar. They say they do not understand these terms 'justification', 'sanctification', and so on. We need, they say, a new translation in which these terms will be put in a form that the modern man and woman can understand.

So they drop terms like 'propitiation', and they write of being 'delivered'. They drop any idea of 'ransoming' and they use some very general terms such as 'liberation' and 'freedom'; and they really believe that men and women now understand the truth. And that is one of the greatest dangers, as I see it, in the present religious situation. These great terms like justification and sanctification, glorification and many others, I would argue, cannot be presented simply by using alternative translations. They are terms that have to be expounded and illustrated.

Modern translations are evacuating these terms of their real meaning. It is only the preacher who can really show their profound content. That is why preaching is absolutely essential. You cannot get single terms to explain propitiation, or justification, or sanctification. These terms must be worked out; they must be explained and expounded by the preacher, and alternative translations cannot do it. Many translations are ultimately standing between the people and the real meaning of the terms.

I support this argument, of course, by again appealing to history. Men and women have never understood these terms. But two hundred years ago, before there was popular education, under the inspired preaching of people like Whitefield, the Wesleys and the rest, ordinary men and women were given an understanding of the meaning of these great and glorious terms, and thereby were led to a knowledge of the Lord Jesus Christ as their personal Saviour and Redeemer.

So I would sum it up like this: preaching first! Preaching is God's ordained method. Here it is: 'How shall they hear without a preacher?' This is the way still. Reading is supplementary – a good supplement, but never a substitute. It is when people substitute reading for preaching that disaster comes in. But reading as a supplement to the preaching is, of course, excellent. And so it is that I advocate your buying books that you may be well informed. That will supplement what I am trying feebly to say. And we thank God, therefore, for all literature that does supplement the preaching, but God forbid that it should ever become a substitute for it. We must adhere to God's method. Preaching is the usual method of God throughout the ages. It always will be. But He is not tied to it. For the infant, the heathen, the poor man who has lost his reason, anybody, God can exceptionally – and as it were miraculously – do the thing which He normally does by His chosen method.

There, then, is the first great section to which our attention is called in this important paragraph. It is by preaching that God has always done, still does and will do this great work. 'How shall they hear without a preacher?'

Then the second problem is the calling of the preacher, and that is also dealt with here by the Apostle. It is through the preacher that one hears the message about the Lord, but how does anyone ever become a preacher? Now the word that is used here for preaching is very interesting. You will find that a number of different Greek words used in the original are translated as 'preaching'. But there are two main words, the others are only used very occasionally. And I want to call your attention to these two words which are used with considerable regularity.

I can convey this matter to you very simply. In Acts 8:4–5 they are both used. Let me read them to you. We are told in verse 1 that 'at that time there was a great persecution against the church which was at Jerusalem', and that as a result 'they were all scattered abroad throughout the regions of Judaea and Samaria, except the apostles'. Then, in verse 4, 'Therefore they that were scattered abroad went everywhere preaching the word.' And in the next verse, 'Then Philip went down to the city of Samaria, and preached Christ unto them.' You have the word 'preached' in verses 4 and 5; but it is not the same word in the original Greek.

So what is the difference between the two words? Well, the word that is used in the fourth verse is a word from which our word 'evangelise' comes, and it means 'reporting the good news'. It is a word which puts its emphasis upon the character of the message, the gospel good news; whereas the word that is used in the fifth verse has a different emphasis. It means to 'herald'. The whole notion there is of a herald proclaiming a message. So that the main emphasis in verse 5 is not so much upon the content of what is proclaimed as upon the fact that the preacher stands up, as it were, in a public place and makes a proclamation or an announcement.

Now it is very interesting that in those verses next to each other, you have these two words, so close together and both translated as preaching, but actually there is a difference between them. The people scattered abroad went everywhere, as somebody once translated it, 'gossiping the good news'. But Philip, we are told, 'went down to the city of Samaria and heralded Christ unto them'.

Then, in the twelfth verse of that same eighth chapter we read, 'But when they believed Philip preaching the things concerning the kingdom of God, and the name of Jesus Christ, they were baptized, both men and women.' In verse 5 we are told that Philip was sent down to Samaria to 'herald' the message, but here, in verse 12, that other word is used which means 'reporting the good news'. In verse 12, you see, the author is anxious to show what it was that brought these people to believe, and why they were baptised, and the point was that they believed the good news. So the word 'preaching', there, is the word which conveys the notion of giving good news, the message, rather than the way in which the message is being delivered.

Now I do not want to make too much of this distinction but it does seem to me that it is rather important because the word that is used by the Apostle here in Romans 10 is the second word, the word used about Philip in Acts 8:5. How shall they hear without a 'herald', without a 'proclaimer', without 'someone who is sent to proclaim the message'?

I want to suggest to you, therefore, that we can draw this general conclusion: that every Christian should be able to give the good news, but that every Christian is not called upon to be a herald. Any man or woman who is a Christian should know the way of salvation and should be able to tell another, should be ready, as Peter puts it, 'to give an answer to every man that asketh you a reason of the hope that is in you' [*1 Pet.* 3:15]. When they were scattered abroad by the persecution, those ordinary members of the church were able to tell people the good news of 'Christ and him crucified', and of God's way of saving. But when you come to an evangelist like Philip, who was sent with a kind of official commission, you get the word 'herald' used, the word which is used by the Apostle here. There is, in connection with the preacher, then, this suggestion of an appointment, that he is called and appointed to make this great proclamation.

Furthermore, it is important to observe that there is not a single instance in the New Testament of this word being used about anybody except those who are in some kind of special appointment. It is used about John the Baptist, about the Lord Himself, about the Apostles Peter and Paul, and it is used about evangelists such as Philip, Timothy, Titus and so on. There is a suggestion, therefore, that immediately, even in New Testament times, a distinction was drawn between one Christian and another, and some were officially regarded as the proclaimers, the heralds, the preachers of the gospel.

So we all need to think about that distinction and to think of it in terms of what the Apostle says here: 'How shall they preach, except they be sent?' We must try to think out some of the applications of that distinction, especially in terms of the present state of the Christian church. This is a great paragraph. It throws great light, as I am trying to show you, upon our whole present situation – the confusion and the lack of discipline.

So here, then, is one of these important points – the sending of the preacher. It is something that we should all consider. It applies to us all. We are all meant to be preachers in the sense of Acts 8:4. But we must go on next to consider the meaning of Acts 8:5, and its application here and in other instances. God grant that we may be given wisdom, understanding, discretion and a sense of our high responsibility in these days in which we live.

Twenty-five

*

How then shall they call on him in whom they have not believed? and how shall they believe in him of whom they have not heard? and how shall they hear without a preacher? And how shall they preach, except they be sent? as it is written, How beautiful are the feet of them that preach the gospel of peace, and bring glad tidings of good things! But they have not all obeyed the gospel. For Esaias saith, Lord, who hath believed our report? So then faith cometh by hearing, and hearing by the word of God.   Romans 10:14–17

We have been considering the two New Testament words which are translated 'preaching' in the Authorised Version. There is one other thing about these two words which is of interest. It is that they do vary according to the matter which is being spoken about. An example of this can be seen with regard to our Lord Himself and His preaching in Nazareth, recorded in Luke 4:18–19. There, the Lord is described as preaching the gospel to the poor, preaching deliverance to the captives and preaching the acceptable year of the Lord.

Both Greek words are used in the two verses, so we might read it like this: 'The Spirit of the Lord is upon me, because he hath anointed me to *evangelise, to speak the good news of the Evangel* to the poor.' That is the same word which is used in Acts 8:4. That is what the scattered members of the church at Jerusalem did. Here Luke, the writer, is anxious to show that the good news is given 'to the poor' in this way.

But let us go on: 'He hath sent me to proclaim, to *herald*, deliverance to the captives, and *herald*, to proclaim, that is to announce, the acceptable year of the Lord.' So we see our Lord reading from Isaiah 61, and this distinction is made: when you are giving the good news of salvation, you use the first word, but when you are making a proclamation – a proclamation which announces 'deliverance to captives', or 'the coming of the acceptable year of the Lord' – you use the second word, which carries this connotation of heralding.

Now the vital point at this juncture is that here, in Romans 10, it is the second word that is used, the word which means *herald*. 'How shall they hear without a herald? And how shall they go out and herald, except they be sent?' And let me repeat again, although all Christians should be able to evangelise, in the sense of telling the good news, that word, 'herald', is never used except with respect to those who have some kind of official commission; those who are sent specifically and are set apart to do this work.

I want to develop this a little further because it seems to me that it is of great importance at the present time. The whole question, the whole doctrine of the nature of the Christian church is in the melting-pot once more. In the talk about reunion there will, in the coming years, be a fight over the question of episcopacy. Are there such things as bishops in the New Testament? To what extent is it right to talk about any offices in the church? These and similar questions will be discussed and written about at great length, and I think it is, therefore, important that we should know something about it. It may be that in the providence of God, all of us will have to arrive at certain decisions; some of us will never be able to go into a mammoth world church. So, then, what kind of church do we belong to? This is a time when it is good for us to re-examine these things once more, because in the minds of most people the whole notion of the church is some-what chaotic. We shall not now be going into the whole doctrine of the church, but will take up this one question about the preacher, because the verse which we are studying makes us consider it.

'How shall they hear without a preacher? And how shall they preach except they be sent?' Now what does that mean? Paul is talk-ing about preachers, about these 'heralds' of the gospel, so let us approach it in this way. This is a phrase that is used, as I have reminded you, with regard to all who are specially appointed. It is used about John the Baptist himself. We are told that '. . . the word of God came unto John the son of Zacharias in the wilderness.' And as a result of the Word of the Lord coming to him, John began to preach the 'baptism of repentance for the remission of sins' [*Luke* 3:1–3].

But, you remember, there was an ancient prophecy with regard to John: 'Behold, I send my messenger before thy face, which shall prepare thy way before thee' [*Matt.* 11:10]. 'Behold I *send* my messenger.' 'How shall they preach except they be *sent*?' And the prophecy was that John the Baptist should be sent as a herald of the coming of the Lord Jesus Christ, to call the people to prepare themselves for Him and for His message.

So there it is with respect to John, and the same thing is true of our Lord. I have already quoted from Luke 4:18–19: 'The Spirit of the Lord is upon me, because . . . he hath sent me'. Our Lord was a sent messenger. He was a preacher of the kingdom of God, and He had been sent to preach it.

The same, of course, was obviously true of the Apostles. Our Lord called them from their various occupations, and called them to follow Him. And then He 'sent them forth'. 'Behold, I send you forth,' He said, 'as sheep in the midst of wolves' [*Matt.* 10:16]. He sent them to preach and to cast out devils. *They* did not suddenly decide to do this. He called them, commissioned them and sent them. 'How shall they preach except they be sent?'

And, of course, in the case of the Apostle Paul himself, it is not a bit surprising that he writes as he does here. He started this Epistle by referring to himself as 'Paul . . . called to be an apostle'. He was a 'called' apostle; he was not self-appointed. There were such self-appointed apostles in the early church, and this Apostle who had been called and commissioned had a great deal to say about them. They 'wrote letters of commendation to one another, and for one another' [*2 Cor.* 3:1]. But Paul did not need such things, because he had been called by God.

And not only that, Paul was very concerned about this. No man was ever more concerned about his authority which was being constantly questioned, very largely because he had not been one of the disciples of the Lord when He lived on earth. Paul had been such an opponent of Christianity; he had been a leading Pharisee. And when he became a preacher, they were suspicious of him; he always had to defend his commission. So he says in Galatians 1:15–16: 'When it pleased God, who separated me from my mother's womb, and called me by his grace, to reveal his Son in me, that I might preach him among the heathen; immediately I conferred not with flesh and blood . . .' He says, you see, that he has been set apart for this from his mother's womb, and that he has been called in a very definite way. And then we read that great statement in Acts 26:15–17, where it is put so plainly. There the Lord says to him, 'I am Jesus whom thou persecutest. But rise, and stand upon thy feet: for I have appeared unto thee for this purpose, to make thee a minister and a witness both of these things which thou hast seen, and of those things in the which I will appear unto thee; delivering thee from the people, and from the Gentiles, *unto whom now I send thee.*'

'How shall they preach except they be sent?' The Apostle says: I have been sent by the risen Lord who appeared to me on the road to Damascus.

There it is, then, in the case of the Apostles, the first great preachers, and the same thing is made plain with respect to others whom we see and meet as preachers in the New Testament.

Now how does this happen? How is it that a man becomes 'sent' to preach the gospel? And the answer is that there are two elements in this. The first is, of course, a personal element: a man is dealt with individually and personally by the Lord Himself. He becomes aware of a call, an inner call. It happens in many different ways – we need not go into that. But it does happen and a man is aware of the fact that he is being called and is going to be sent. That is one side.

But there is another side, and that is the church. Now there is a great deal of evidence in the New Testament about this second element, and what is so interesting is that you find it quite early on in the history of the church. A most important chapter in this respect is the sixth chapter of Acts. At the beginning of the chapter we read of a dispute. Until that point, as far as one can tell, the early church had virtually no organisation at all, but now found it necessary to develop an element of organisation. The position had become difficult, so the wisdom that was given to the Apostles was that they should call upon the members of the church to choose out from among themselves men who should be set apart to do this work and who, therefore, should be afterwards confirmed by the Apostles. The choice was made by the church; the appointing was done by the Apostles. Seven suitable men were chosen to be deacons. The same thing emerges with regard to the choice of elders.

Now we must follow this through a little, so we go next to Acts 13 – I am trying to show you now how, in the early church, a distinction of function arose between believer and believer. They were all believers, they were all able to give a reason for the hope that was in them, but it became necessary that certain people should be set apart for specific functions. So in Acts 13:1 we read, 'Now there were in the church that was at Antioch certain *prophets* and *teachers*.' All the members of the church were not prophets, all were not teachers. This was a distinction which had come into being.

These prophets and teachers were 'elders', or 'presbyters', whichever you prefer to call them. They are named and were directed by the Holy Ghost to set apart Barnabas and Saul for the work of spreading the gospel. And that is how Paul and Barnabas set out upon their first missionary journey: they were 'sent' by the church. They did not suddenly decide to go, nor did they have a feeling that they ought to go; they were sent, and they were sent through the action of the church. It was the church that sent them out to 'herald' the gospel, to preach this good news, and to make known the way of salvation.

Then, go on to Acts 14:23. We are again dealing with Paul and Barnabas, who having finished this first journey, 'ordained elders in every church, prayed for them with fasting and commended them to the Lord', just as they had been. Once more it seems clear that the elders, the men who were actually chosen by the churches, were 'ordained', 'appointed' by these two 'sent' messengers who had gone out from the church at Antioch.

But then let us come to something which is perhaps still more specific. Take the case of Timothy. This is what we are told about him in 1 Timothy 1:18: 'This charge I commit unto thee, son Timothy, according to the prophecies which went before on thee, that thou by them mightest war a good warfare; holding faith, and a good conscience . . .' Notice the terms: 'according to', that is, in line with, as a continuation and a furtherance of, 'the prophecies which went before on thee' – which means, of course, the messages that were delivered to Timothy when he was being charged and sent out to do this work of an evangelist.

Then there is also another very interesting statement in 1 Timothy 4:14: 'Neglect not the gift that is in thee, which was given thee by prophecy, with the laying on of the hands of the presbytery' – a presbytery is a gathering of elders. The point that is being made is that the gift which he had, which he exercised as an evangelist, is one that had come to him by prophecy accompanied by the 'laying on of the hands'. The hands of the presbyters were laid upon Timothy, and thus he was sent forth as a preacher.

And there is one final statement about Timothy in 2 Timothy 1:6 and 11: 'Wherefore I put thee in remembrance that thou stir up the gift of God, which is in thee by the putting on of my hands.' It sounds there as if Paul alone had put his hands upon him, but he was one of the company. It is clear that they had done it together, but as Timothy was Paul's particular disciple whom he addresses as his 'son', he refers only to his own hands. And then in verse 11, where the Apostle is speaking about himself, he says, 'Whereunto *I am appointed* a preacher, and an apostle, and a teacher of the Gentiles.'

Timothy, then, was an evangelist, as was Titus. But you must not take it that that means what we mean today by an evangelist. Evangelists in New Testament times were a very definite order of people, who came next in position to the apostles and prophets. You will find that in Ephesians 4:11. The evangelist in New Testament times was a most important man; he was a sort of delegate for the Apostles. He was a man who was given authority and commission to preach as the Apostles preached, to establish churches, and to deal with difficulties in them.

So, to be strictly accurate in our thinking, we must say that as the apostles and the prophets ceased, so did the evangelists. That does not mean that we do not believe that a man can be an evangelist now, in our sense; but he is a teacher, a pastoral teacher, a preacher who happens to have, in an unusual degree perhaps, the gift that should belong to all preachers. But that is not the New Testament evangelist. It is good that we should keep these things clear and straight in our minds. The modern evangelist does not claim that he comes before the pastor and teacher, but the New Testament evangelist did claim that. He was indeed a kind of apostolic delegate and a man who had authority to settle the affairs of churches.

So I am trying to establish that in all these cases it is perfectly clear that there was a kind of commission, that the preacher who was sent was a man who was really sent by the church. I emphasised earlier that one of the most important distinctions between preaching and reading the Scriptures is that preaching is an act of the church, of the whole church. And this is one of the ways in which that comes out.

How, then, should we think about this matter? Let me try to summarise it under a number of headings and here is the first. It is obvious from those New Testament excerpts that all church members are not meant to be preachers in the sense of 'heralds' set apart to do this particular work. All church members should be able to give a reason for the hope that is in them and to do what was done by the members of the church at Jerusalem, scattered abroad by the persecution, but all Christians are not meant to preach in the sense of a public herald, set apart for this work. Preaching in the New Testament is confined, it seems to me, only to the apostles, prophets, evangelists and elders. Not even all the elders preached. There were some who were ruling elders, and the deacons looked after the material aspect of the life of the church, and so on. But there were elders who did preach and teach, and the members of the churches are told to pay especial honour to these elders who taught the Word.

So it is clear that we must not have this notion that any man who becomes a Christian should, therefore, become a preacher. I say that because there are certain sections of the church that more or less assume that every member, every man in particular, is to be a preacher. But that seems to me to be entirely contrary to what is so plainly taught in the New Testament and implied in this word 'sent', which always has a limiting connotation. That is my first rule, therefore. As the church at Antioch set aside Paul and Barnabas and 'sent' them, so preachers are set aside and are sent by the whole church.

Secondly, and this is very interesting, the usual method in the New Testament and in the subsequent history of the church has been for the two things to which I referred earlier to take place. In other words, a man has a personal call, and the church also is led to give a call to the same man. That is what I have illustrated to you from the Scriptures. That is what happened in Acts 6: the church chose men who were filled with the Holy Spirit, and then the officials laid hands on those men. And it is so with all these others – the personal call, and the action, or the confirmation, of the church.

And, of course, to that end instructions are given in what are called the Pastoral Epistles – the Epistles to Timothy and Titus – as to the qualifications that the church must look for in a man whom she is going to choose as an elder, that is, a man who would be preaching and teaching. For instance, an elder must be a man of a certain character: he must not be a brawler nor addicted to wine, he must be able to rule his own house, and so on.

And, obviously, in addition to that, the church must be able to exercise judgment as to whether the man has an ability to speak. You do not appoint a man as a preacher if he cannot speak. He may be an excellent man, he may be a great thinker, he may even be a good writer, but if he cannot speak, then you do not choose such a man as a preacher. The church is, therefore, given instructions about the qualities and qualifications she is to look for.

You see, according to the Apostle, the church is 'the pillar and ground of the truth' [*1 Tim.* 3:15]. He means that the church is like a great sign set up on a pillar. It is holding forth the truth. And the church does it by selecting these men to do the preaching on her behalf, as it were.

But, thirdly, it is very interesting to observe, in the subsequent history of the church in particular, that sometimes this calling takes place mainly through the church. There have been many instances of famous preachers who did not at first feel the personal call. In each case, the church felt the call and the elders of the church then approached the man and said, 'You know we feel that you should be preaching, you seem to be a man in every way eminently suited to this work.' They may have had great difficulty in persuading him, but eventually he felt the inner call for himself. In such a case the initiative started with the church.

These things are of great interest. Indeed, I want to say this, because we must be fair to history and we must be fair also to the New Testament itself. Take the case of a man like the Apostle Paul who had received this very individual and personal call. The church was at first suspicious of him, but then became persuaded. He was quite certain of his call, in spite of the hesitation of the church, and there have been similar men in the subsequent history of the church.

Again, there are times when the church is so apostate that she does not recognise her own prophets, her true preachers, and there have been times when men have preached in spite of the ban and the refusal of the church. You find this in the case of a man like Howell Harris of two hundred years ago, and there are others whom one could cite. Now all I am concerned to say is that that is most exceptional – it is not the rule. The customary thing is for the man himself to feel the call and the church to be led to call him or to confirm the call at the same time.

Why am I emphasising all this? Well, this is my fourth point. It is because of the danger of being guilty, either of what we read in Jeremiah 23:21, where God says of the false prophets, 'I have not sent these prophets, yet they ran: I have not spoken to them, yet they prophesied'; or of what we find our Lord saying at the end of the Sermon on the Mount, when he speaks of the people who come to Him and say, 'Lord, Lord, have we not prophesied in thy name? . . . and in thy name done many wonderful works? And then will I profess unto them, I never knew you: depart from me, ye that work iniquity' [*Matt.* 7:22–23]. They thought that they were pleasing him and preaching in his name and doing everything with his approval, but He said, 'I never knew you.' There is this terrible danger.

So my fifth point is that it is very interesting to notice that the greatest preachers have, like Paul, always approached this question of preaching 'in fear, and in much trembling' [*1 Cor.* 2:3]. They have said with the Apostle Paul – 'Who is sufficient for these things?' [*2 Cor.* 2:16]. I could tell you endless stories of saintly men of God upon whom great pressure has been brought to bear by the church. The church has told them to preach, and they have said, 'I am not fit; I am not worthy; who am *I* to preach?' They have been conscious of their unworthiness. And there is no greater confirmation of a man's call than his humility, his fearfulness to undertake such a tremendous, such a serious task. Indeed, the greatest preachers have always desired this unmistakable confirmation, and they have always shown themselves to be very humble men.

Take, again, that instance in Acts 13, where it was the church at Antioch that sent out Paul and Barnabas. Think of this mighty man, this Apostle Paul, this great personality and genius, this great brain, this mighty man who had had such experiences. He humbled himself to become the servant of the church. It was not an easy thing to do, but it is something that he did. And it is clear that all these men in the New Testament – even the Apostles – always submitted themselves to the church and did not act in and of themselves.

If you will pardon a personal reference, I think it may, perhaps, help some of you a little at this point. The most difficult question I personally had to deal with, when I felt called to leave my one-time profession to become a preacher of the gospel, was the question of submitting myself to the discipline of the machinery and the call of the church to which I belonged. Everything within me revolted against it. I felt I was being questioned and examined by men who really had never been called themselves, many of whom did not know the truth. But I was so fearful of acting on my own that I felt the need of this confirmation. It was very good for me and very good for my sanctification to be questioned, to be held back, and even to be in charge of a church as minister for nine months and not allowed to administer the sacrament of baptism nor the Lord's Supper because I had not yet been ordained. The members of my church chafed against it, and so did I, but we submitted to it and I thank God more and more that I did. Why?

Well, here is my last reason. Preaching is the most important thing under the sun. There is nothing more important than to be a 'herald' of this good news. How vital it is that the right doctrine should be preached. How easy it is to preach false doctrine and to lead people astray. It is therefore essential that great care should be exercised to ensure that a man is really competent, that he does understand, that he knows what he is to herald. And in the same way, you see the importance of discipline. What if a man starts with the right doctrine and begins to go wrong, what do you do about it? Well, if he is sent by the church, you can do something; if he is not, you cannot. So, you see, these are some of the reasons why this question of the preacher being 'sent' is such an important one. It is utterly unscriptural for a man to set himself up as a preacher. There is no such thing in the New Testament or the Old, apart from the false prophets and the false teachers.

Do we always remember that, I wonder? We are living in times of chaos, when people do not think scripturally. They say, 'The message is not being preached. I know what it is, I, therefore, am going to preach.' That is utterly unscriptural. Such a man has denied the Scriptures he claims to believe. A man does not send himself. There is no preaching in the New Testament apart from the action, the corporate action, of the church in 'sending'.

Now I am not going into the question, you see, as to whether it is one church only. One church is enough, in my opinion, to send a man, but he must have a church to send him; he does not appoint himself. It is equally wrong for men to appoint one another. There is a great deal of that going on at the present time. One man says to another, 'Why don't you preach? Of course you can, you could do it quite well.' And the second man begins to preach at once. They have appointed themselves. There has been no action by the church; there has been no commission; there has been no real 'sending' at all. There is a difference between a man 'going' and a man being 'sent'. 'How shall they preach,' asks the Apostle,' 'except they be sent?' And the preacher is a man who should have this consciousness of being 'sent', 'commissioned'. He is a man who is a 'herald', and there is no heralding in the New Testament in terms of self-appointment.

So look at it like that, and remember what I have been trying to emphasise. Remember the humility of this Apostle Paul – 'Who is sufficient for these things?' [2 Cor. 2:16]. Yet I know men who run up into pulpits with great self-confidence. They feel that they are very sufficient. Let us be careful, my dear friends. Let us be very careful about these matters. Read the New Testament. Read the history of the church on this question, and you will find that they have always exercised great care. We are living in days of confusion. It is like the time of the book of Judges: 'In those days there was no king in Israel: every man did that which was right in his own eyes' [*Judges* 21:25]. And it is the easiest thing in the world to start a movement, to set yourself up as an organisation, to open your own mission.

In other parts of the world it is even worse than it is here, with hundreds of different denominations. A man, if he has the money, can set up his own tabernacle. You do not find that in the New Testament; you do not find it even in the Old. There were men there who set up their own priests, but it was condemned and disaster came upon the people who did that. So let us learn, as we look at these things in the New Testament. The word of the Apostle here in Romans 10 encourages and warns us. 'How shall they hear without a preacher? and how shall they preach, except they be sent?' Ultimately, you are sent by God, and God will tell you if He wants to send you, and He will confirm it to you by telling the church also.

Twenty-six

*

> How then shall they call on him in whom they have not
> believed? and how shall they believe in him of whom they have
> not heard? and how shall they hear without a preacher? And
> how shall they preach, except they be sent? as it is written, How
> beautiful are the feet of them that preach the gospel of peace, and
> bring glad tidings of good things! But they have not all obeyed
> the gospel. For Esaias saith, Lord, who hath believed our report?
> So then faith cometh by hearing the word of God.
>
> Romans 10:14–17

We have seen that these four verses can be divided up into two equal pairs. Verses 14 and 15 show us how the general call of the gospel goes out, and verses 16 and 17 show us how the call becomes efficacious in those who believe. At the moment we are looking at the first section, which is the great charter of the missionary enterprise, and deals, incidentally, as we have seen, with some of the problems that arise as the result of that enterprise. We have also noticed how it strongly emphasises the primacy of preaching. Preaching is, after all, God's ordained method of making known the news of salvation. It is not the only one, but it is pre-eminently the chief one, and that which has been used of God throughout the running centuries.

That, in turn, has raised another question, which is the calling of the preacher. 'How shall they preach, except they be sent?' We have established that always in the New Testament the preacher is one who is *sent* and we have seen from the New Testament that church order began almost at once.

In considering the calling to be a preacher, I showed that in general there is a personal element in the call to preach, and also that confirmation is given by the church. Now, though it is not essential in the exposition of our passage, I would like to stay with this point, because the verses are very important in view of the chaos that obtains at the present time. Somebody may ask me, 'How does the man himself know? You have emphasised the church side of it, and you have given us reasons why it is essential that there should be confirmation from the church of what the man himself feels. But what does he feel? How may he know whether he is being called and sent by God as one of these preachers who herald this good news?'

Well, I shall only suggest some headings here. It is an important subject. In a sense, it raises the whole question of guidance. But with regard to the call to preach certain things are made very plain in the Scriptures and are confirmed abundantly in the biographies of preachers throughout the centuries. One thing which is invariable is a *pressure upon the spirit*. In other words, you do not seek the thing, but it is put upon you. And it does not just come as a passing idea – I do want to emphasise this element of pressure – you cannot get rid of the thing, it keeps on coming back.

It is a very good test, therefore, when you begin to feel this call, that you should, as it were, try to get rid of the feeling. And if it is a call of God, it will come back, it will persist until it becomes a very definite pressure upon you that you cannot evade. Try as you will, you cannot get rid of it. Anybody who has ever been through this will know what a very definite thing it is; it is one of the most real things that can ever happen to us.

You may decide, 'Well, this thing doesn't seem to me to be right, and I don't see how I can preach. So I shall not have anything to do with it, I am not even going to think about it!' But you cannot help yourself, it will come back again and again. Indeed, there are those who could tell a story along these lines and indicate how the pressure can be such that if you resist, you may even suffer physically. I know a man who lost over a stone in weight while going through this struggle.[1] That is one thing.

Another characteristic of a true call from God is that *a burden comes upon you*. Now by that I mean a burden in the sense in which the prophets talk about 'the burden of the Lord'. It is a message given and a sense that you have got to go and deliver it. The man called to be a preacher is a man who has *an unusual concern about the glory of God*. All Christians have this concern, but the man who is to be a preacher has it to an exceptional degree. He feels that this is a very

---

[1] On reading these pages in manuscript, Mrs Lloyd-Jones' comment was, 'He is describing his own experience of going into the ministry.'

special burden that is put upon him, to contend for the honour and the glory of God, and the truth of God. In other words, there is nothing casual about it. The man does not take it up as an aside as it were, though he may be a man of such ability that he could easily do it in that way, not understanding preachers who always seem to be in difficulties, while he takes it in his stride as he goes along.

But there is nothing like that about the true preacher. He feels a burden. This burden is also a *concern about the souls of men and women*. He does not preach because he likes speaking; he does not preach because he enjoys speaking or because he likes to be in a position of influence, but because he has a concern for people's souls. Again, he may try to get rid of this and say, 'Well, it is, after all, none of my business' – but he cannot get rid of that burden, it keeps on coming back to him. Every Christian should be concerned about the souls of others, but the preacher is, obviously, more so. This is his burden: the glory of God and the well-being of the souls of men and women.

And then – I give as a separate heading, though it is implicit in what I have already been saying – I feel that the *sense of constraint* that the Apostle speaks of in 1 Corinthians 9 and in 2 Corinthians 5 is a very definite part of this call. I will put it like this: a man who preaches is a man who feels that he can do no other, that he cannot help himself. There is no credit to me, says the Apostle Paul. 'Yea, woe is unto me, if I preach not the gospel!' [*1 Cor.* 9:16]. He cannot help himself. 'The love of Christ constraineth us' [*2 Cor.* 5:14]. Or you remember the case of Jeremiah who decided, because he was being persecuted and was in trouble, that he would not speak any more. But he could not remain like that. He said that the word of the Lord was in his heart 'as a burning fire' [*Jer.* 20:9], and he had to go on speaking, whatever the consequences.

This has been put very well in a saying that is attributed to Mr Spurgeon, who had some very wise things to say about this whole subject. He used to put it like this: 'If you can stay out of the ministry, stay out.' You should only be in the ministry when you cannot stay out of it; when you can no longer refuse; when you have to give in, as it were, and you stop resisting. That is the call; that is the 'sending'. It becomes inevitable. You cannot do anything else. So what I am now asking is this: Has any man a right to preach who does not feel some of these things?

Finally, then, I would put it in this way: this man is under such pressure that, at all costs, he has got to go and proclaim the gospel. It may cost him a good deal, but he is ready to do it, and he does not regard what he is doing as a sacrifice. He is so clear about his call that he has to venture out. In doing so, he definitely takes a risk, and this is particularly true nowadays with the increasing cost of living. It is no small matter for a man to enter the Christian ministry at this present time. He knows before he starts that financially he will suffer.

But that does not make any difference to him. He is a man who sees that this has got to be the work of his life. He turns away from everything else; he gives up every other calling because he is called to preach. Whether he was in a profession, or whether he worked with his hands, or had a business, it does not matter. He feels called to do this one thing, so he has to give up everything else. 'No man that warreth,' says the Apostle Paul to Timothy, 'entangleth himself with the affairs of this life; that he may please him who hath chosen him to be a soldier' [*2 Tim.* 2:4]. That is Paul's illustration, and that is true of the preacher.

Of course, you remember, it was true of the Levites in the Old Testament, and that is the analogy which the New Testament uses, as we see in 1 Corinthians 9. Because they were the people who handled the holy things, the Levites did not have any possessions, as the other tribes did, but they were supported. Now this principle is worked out in 1 Corinthians 9, especially in verses 7 to 14, a portion of Scripture which is grievously neglected. Here is the material statement: 'Do ye not know that they which minister about holy things live of the things of the temple? and they which wait at the altar are partakers with the altar? Even so hath the Lord ordained that they which preach the gospel should live of the gospel' [vv. 13,14].

Preachers are in the same position as the Levites. They depend on the goodwill and the faith of the members of the Christian church. They are not men who earn their living by doing something else and also preach. No; they 'live of the gospel'; they have been set apart; they have been called by God; they have been sent by God and they are utterly dependent.

As I have already hinted in passing, this is a very material and important point in my opinion. That is why I have always felt that it is most dangerous for a man to be a lay preacher. He is in a position of great responsibility without knowing this sense of insecurity. There is no greater discipline than to be a minister and to be dependent entirely upon other people. That is the position of the minister.

Somebody may say, however, 'But surely, your passage contradicts what you are saying? The Apostle Paul is there saying that he did not receive anything from the Corinthians. He was not paid anything by them.' Now this is most interesting. I have often heard that used as an argument against the ordained ministry, and against this whole notion that the minister is supported and kept by the members of the church. It is amazing how people can wrest the Scriptures!

No, what the Apostle is saying is this: 'This is the rule. The Lord has ordained this.' It is as strong as that. It is not Paul's opinion. 'Even so hath the Lord ordained that they which preach the gospel should live of the gospel.' 'Now then,' he says, 'in your case at Corinth, I have made an exception.' He more or less tells us why there were peculiar circumstances there. There were enemies and people who were misunderstanding him and bringing charges against him. So in the particular case of Corinth, he took nothing from them. Paul explains this very fully in 2 Corinthians 11:7–12.

The thing is as plain as anything could possibly be. Paul varied the rule, his custom, because of these circumstances in the church at Corinth and in the regions of Achaia. But he was kept by other churches, who made up for this. He shows that by saying, 'I received wages of them', in order that he might not receive anything from the people of Achaia. The principle, therefore, is that the Lord has ordained that the man who preaches the gospel should live by the gospel.

Now while showing you that this is the clear teaching, I want to point out also that this is not to argue, of course, for a distinction between clergy and laity. That is not involved at all. This is not to argue for a priesthood or to say that the minister or the preacher is a man who is essentially different from every other. Those of us who are nonconformists and who belong to the Free Churches dissent completely from that teaching, which is found in the Roman Catholic Church and in every episcopal church. We do not recognise this distinction between laity and a priesthood, and we do not agree that there is something special about the latter.

All I would say is that the New Testament teaches order. According to the New Testament, all Christians do not preach, it is only some who do, and we have been considering the terms and conditions on which they do so. In the New Testament, an order of preachers came into being, and we have seen something of the way in which that happens. All Christians are one. We are all saved in exactly the same way. We are in the same relationship to God. We all have the same access to God. We assert the universal priesthood of all believers. But, in addition, in terms of the Scriptures, there are offices amongst people who are equally Christians, so that everything may be done decently and in order, so that the truth may be safeguarded and that we may have discipline.

And so it is the case that the preacher is the man who lives by the gospel. He has been so conscious of this call, this pressure, that he has forsaken everything else. It has been confirmed by, and he has been set apart by, the church; and so he has cut himself off from every other means of subsistence and he is in the hands of, and at the mercy of, the members of the Christian church. But his faith is in God. He knows that God has called him and that whatever may happen to him, God will never leave him nor forsake him. That is his position, and that is the New Testament rule with regard to this matter. 'How shall they hear without a preacher? and how shall they preach, except they be sent?'

This is a most interesting matter. The preacher in Presbyterianism and in Congregationalism, among the Baptists and others, is an elder, like other elders. But he is an elder who has been set apart by the church because members of the church have noticed certain aptitudes in him, and because he is aware of a call, and because they are aware that he is called. He is a man who has been set apart, and thus he speaks on behalf of the whole church; he is a sent messenger, sent by God and the church, and he heralds forth the good news of salvation.

But now we must go on to the next great matter which is taught us in this passage, and that is, of course, the message of the preacher. The Apostle is moving in a definite order. People are going to hear from a preacher. What, then, is this preacher going to say? What is his message? And the Apostle makes this quite clear by giving us a quotation from Isaiah 52:7, which is also part of Nahum 1:15.

Now it is very interesting to notice the way in which the Apostle introduces and handles this quotation. He puts it like this: 'As it is written, How beautiful are the feet of them that preach the gospel of peace, and bring glad tidings of good things!' The first point to which we must pay attention is that in the oldest manuscripts the phrase 'them that preach the gospel of peace' is absent. It reads like this: 'How beautiful are the feet of them that bring glad tidings of good things!' The other words about 'preaching the gospel of peace' are found in later manuscripts.

'How do you explain this?' asks someone. Well, the probability is, of course, that somebody later felt that by adding these words the quotation would be closer to the original in Isaiah 52:7.

'But,' says the questioner, 'are you not suddenly becoming a higher critic?'

No, I am not! I am a textual critic, and there is all the difference in the world between those two things. It is right that you should know the different texts and their relative value, and I am simply saying that in the oldest and the most reliable texts this phrase is absent. It does not make any difference at all, but it is fairly clear that it was added, and for that reason, probably by some later editor.

What is much more important is that the Apostle, instead of quoting, or translating the original directly, or even using the Septuagint translation, which was available to him and which he normally used, does neither. He gives his own translation and summary of the statement of the prophet Isaiah. We have seen him doing that before, and here is another instance of the same thing.

Now this may be problematical to some people. 'What is the point,' they ask, of talking about the Scriptures and their infallibility, 'if the Apostle, instead of quoting the Scripture exactly as it is, summarises it, gives the essence of it, and even does that in his own language? How do you explain that? Does not this invalidate what you claim for the Scriptures?' Well, far from in any way detracting from the doctrine of the inspiration of the Scripture and its infallibility, it rather tends to prove it.

No man had greater respect for the Old Testament Scriptures than the Apostle Paul. All the Jews revered the Scriptures, they were the oracles of God, as Paul reminded us at the beginning of chapter 3, and the Jews were proud of the fact that it was to them only such oracles had been given. They were most careful in their handling of them, and in their copying of them, and it is indeed a miracle how they have been copied and preserved. It was because of the great respect the Jew felt for every letter. Every jot and tittle of the Scripture was something wonderful. Indeed, the danger for the Jew was to worship the Scriptures. And yet, you see, you have the Apostle doing what he does here.

And there is only one explanation. The same Holy Spirit who had inspired and led the prophet Isaiah was inspiring and leading the Apostle Paul. It is the same inspiration. The Apostle Paul would never have dared to do this thing himself. Of course not! The Spirit who gave the message to Isaiah was now taking His own message and putting it in summary form and doing so to serve the same purpose that He had in view at that previous time.

So Paul's way of using Isaiah 52:7 not only leaves the question of the inspiration and the infallibility of the word of Isaiah intact, it shows us that the word of the Apostle Paul is equally inspired and equally infallible. So that when the Apostle Peter in his Second Epistle, in chapter 3, says that people wrest the words of the Apostle Paul 'as they do also the other scriptures, unto their own destruction' (v. 16), he is being very accurate. The writings of Paul are inspired Scriptures in exactly the same way as the Old Testament documents are inspired Scriptures. That is what it proves.

The next point about the way Paul uses it is this: it gives us, once more, a very interesting sidelight on prophecy. We have already seen, in chapter 9, that when you are reading the Old Testament prophecy, you must always remember that there are generally two elements in it. One element is the immediate one, the one then current. Now in the case of this prophecy of Isaiah it is perfectly clear what it is. Isaiah was writing to the children of Israel before they ever went in captivity to Babylon, but in his message he was given a preview of their deliverance from that captivity. He warned them that it was coming, he saw it coming, but he also saw their return; it was all given to him by God. That is revelation. And then, by the Holy Spirit, he was inspired to write his revelation.

That was the immediate meaning. So Isaiah puts it like this: he gives a picture of a number of people in a hopeless state of captivity. They are quite helpless; they are in the hands of a very powerful enemy who is well armed, who has soldiers and great battalions, and they have nothing at all. What is their hope? Well, they have only one hope, and that is that some power right outside themselves will do something about their deliverance; and so they are always waiting.

There they are, as it were, in the plain, surrounded by mountains, and a rumour has reached them that someone is preparing for their deliverance. They are waiting for him, and they set people in watch-towers to watch for this. And one day they see a messenger coming over the top of a mountain; suddenly he is in sight and moving rapidly towards them, and they say, 'Here is the news we have been waiting for!' 'How beautiful upon the mountains are the feet of these messengers that bear us glad tidings of good things.' That was the immediate application. It was a foretelling of the liberation of the children of Israel from the bondage of Babylon.

But, you see, that is not its only meaning. The Apostle shows here that there was a larger meaning, and it was this: 'Ah yes, this is going to happen to you on the physical plane. You will be delivered from the captivity of Babylon, you will be brought back to Jerusalem, but on an infinitely higher level in the realm of your spirit you are going to be redeemed.' So Isaiah's words are a foreshadowing and a preview of the coming of our Lord and Saviour Jesus Christ and His glorious gospel of salvation. Now this is something that we must always be keeping our eye on as we read the prophecies of the Old Testament: the double meaning – the immediate and then the remote; the material and then the spiritual.

You get exactly the same thing, of course, in connection with the deliverance of the children of Israel from the captivity in Egypt. That was a fact, but it was more than a fact, it was a prefiguring of the coming of the Christian salvation. Egypt represents the world, the flesh and the devil. Moses is a type of Jesus Christ, as the New Testament makes so plain, especially in the Epistle to the Hebrews. And this deliverance – the Red Sea – the Jordan – these are figures of the great Christian salvation. The New Testament uses it like that, and we are entitled to do exactly the same thing.

And so, as we have seen, after the temptation in the wilderness, when our Lord returned to His home town of Nazareth, and went into the synagogue on the Sabbath day, they handed Him the scroll to read, and He read from Isaiah 61: 'The Spirit of the Lord is upon me, because he hath anointed me to preach', and so on. And he said, 'This day is this scripture fulfilled in your ears' [*Luke* 4:18–21]. It had an original meaning but this is the great meaning. And so you find the gospel in the prophets; and if you do not find the gospel there, then there is something wrong with your reading of them. The prophecies are full of gospel, and some of them especially so. Isaiah is a particularly evangelical prophet and he generally goes by that name for that reason.

The point, then, is that the Apostle takes up this old word from Isaiah 52:7, and says, 'This is it.' The preacher is like that messenger coming over the mountain tops bearing the good news. And so that leads us directly to a consideration of the message of the preacher. Here he is: 'How beautiful upon the mountains,' says the Old Testament prophet, 'are the feet . . .' – they are the feet of someone who bears this wonderful news. What is it?

Now that is a most important question. The Apostle has told us many times what it is, but he tells us again. And that is the business of the preacher, to go on repeating the message, the gospel, the evangel. It is the only thing he has to say, and he goes on saying it. Why? Because people are so ready to forget it, because they so often fail to understand it, because they are so ready to misinterpret it. So you have to go on repeating it; and here Paul does it once more.

What is the message? And the answer is quite plain to us. The message of the preacher is a message about *Him*. Here is the question: 'How then shall they call on him in whom they have not believed? and how shall they believe in him of whom they have not heard? and how shall they hear without a preacher?' So the message of the preacher is about the Lord Jesus Christ. 'Whosoever shall call upon the name of the Lord shall be saved.' How can they know about Him? The answer is that the preacher tells them. This is his message; he tells them about the Lord in whom they are to believe.

Which leads me to remind you again that Christianity is Christ. Christianity centres in Christ – it is in Him. Without Him there is no Christianity. It is the Person who matters; it is this Lord who counts. We have already been told, 'If thou shalt confess with thy mouth the Lord Jesus' – there is no salvation apart from Him. 'There is none other name under heaven given among men, whereby we must be saved' [*Acts* 4:12]. It is always this Person. And never was it more necessary to repeat that than at the present time. People are preaching Christianity. There is no such thing. Christianity is a message altogether in Him and about Him.

What is it? It is His Person, who He is. Jesus is Lord! That is exactly what the first preachers preached. Read the book of Acts, what did they preach? 'Jesus, and the resurrection' [*Acts* 17:18]! Philip preached it to the Ethiopian eunuch. They were all preaching Jesus. Of course! There is no message apart from Him. So the preaching of the preacher is to tell people about Him, this Person, that He is indeed the Lord of glory, that nearly two thousand years ago 'God sent forth his Son, made of a woman, made under the law, to redeem them that were under the law' [*Gal.* 4:4–5]. 'The beginning of the gospel of Jesus Christ' [*Mark* 1:1]. 'In the beginning was the Word, and the Word was with God, and the Word was God' [*John* 1:1]. That is preaching! It starts way back in eternity! And it proclaims this great event, the coming of the Son of God into this world! Then it tells people the facts about Him.

I want to underline that word *facts*. The facts are all-important. If you do away with them you have no message. I am putting it like that because the most popular theological movement in Europe today, taught mainly by a man named Bultmann, is a movement that says the exact opposite. It says that the facts do not matter at all, and you really cannot be sure of anything except that Jesus died on a cross. They do not believe in the resurrection, they do not believe in the virgin birth, and so on. But according to the New Testament, the facts are all-important. The New Testament asserts the miracle of the virgin birth. We are even told that Mary stumbled at this, in order that we might know that it was a fact. Jesus was born of a virgin, no human father, conceived of the Holy Spirit. 'That holy thing which shall be born of thee' [*Luke* 1:35]. Sinless!

And it was the facts concerning Jesus Christ that the Apostles preached – His birth, His life, His teaching, His miracles – He 'went about doing good', healing the sick, raising the dead. They preached the miracles. Why? Because these were proofs of the fact that He is the Son of God. So they told the people about that [*Acts* 10:34–40].

And then they told of His death upon the cross. This was a vital part of it: 'Jesus Christ, and him crucified' [*1 Cor.* 2:2]. But then they proclaimed the resurrection as a physical fact, that He literally rose in the body out of the grave and revealed Himself to certain chosen witnesses. They were witnesses of His resurrection, that He had risen in the body. Then His ascension from Mount Olivet! They told how they stood there and saw Him going into the heavens.

Yet it is the facts that are being attacked today, as you know. They are being dismissed, ridiculed, as though we do not need them. People are saying, 'It is the teaching we want.' But it is not! The message of the preacher is to tell about Him, and the facts concerning Him – His taking His place at the right hand of God in the glory; how on the day of Pentecost He poured forth His Holy Spirit upon those members of the early infant church, according to His own promise.

There, then, is the first element in the message of this 'sent' preacher. He is a preacher of the Lord Jesus Christ; he is a preacher of His deity, His eternity! He is a preacher of the facts in connection with His coming into this world, what He did in the world and how He went out of it, and what He is doing at the present time. But it does not stop at that, so, God willing, we must go on to consider how the preacher explains to the people the meaning of the facts. You start with facts, then you give their meaning. And it is all here in the words that are used by the great Apostle.

Twenty-seven

✳

> *How then shall they call on him in whom they have not believed? and how shall they believe in him of whom they have not heard? and how shall they hear without a preacher? And how shall they preach, except they be sent? as it is written, How beautiful are the feet of them that preach the gospel of peace, and bring glad tidings of good things! But they have not all obeyed the gospel. For Esaias saith, Lord, who hath believed our report? So then faith cometh by hearing, and hearing by the word of God.*
> Romans 10:14–17

Having considered together the calling and the sending of the preacher, we have now begun to consider his message and we have seen that, first of all, it is about the Person of the Lord Jesus Christ and the facts about Him. But now let us take a step further forward and ask: What are the general characteristics of this message about Him? And here the Apostle answers that question by his quotation from Isaiah 52:7: 'How beautiful are the feet of them that preach the gospel of peace, and bring glad tidings of good things.' We have seen that there probably is an interpolation there and that it should read: 'How beautiful are the feet of them that bring glad tidings of good things!' That gives us the key to the general characteristic of this gospel message.

What, then, is it? And the answer is that it is *glad tidings*. Paul quotes Isaiah because the prophet had been given this preview, and he had seen that this is what it was, and his very imagery suggests it. Here are people in bondage; they cannot do anything for themselves, but they are always looking to the hills, waiting for a deliverer to come. At last they see the messenger, and we feel the excitement as they hear the 'glad tidings'. The very feet of the man are a joy to them because they know that he is the bearer of 'good things'.

Now I want to show the importance of this aspect of the gospel.

The word used by the Apostle here in his translation of Isaiah 52:7 is the word that we found in Acts 8:4, which brings out the element of good news, of glad tidings. It is the announcing of good news. And what I am trying to emphasise is that once we have applied the main test about the Lord Jesus Christ and the facts concerning Him, then the one test which we must always apply to the preaching of the gospel is this: Is this good news? This is a most wonderful test, and you will find that it will never fail you. When you are listening to a sermon, or when you are reading one, this test will help you to discriminate between what is true and what is false. The gospel must always be glad tidings.

Now it has always been important that we should be aware of this particular test but perhaps never more so than just at this present time, and that is why I am going to stay with it for a while. The state of society, the moral condition of this country and of the whole world, and also the state of the church, all demand that we should be absolutely certain as to what the gospel message really is, because there is nothing that can deal with the present situation apart from the gospel. Everything else has been tried; everything else is failing before our eyes. We cannot go on repeating that too often. This is perhaps in many ways the most educated, cultured century that the world has ever known, and yet here we are with these problems staring us in the face in a most terrible form. The only hope is the gospel.

Why is the Christian church so ineffective? Why is it that only ten per cent of people go to a place of worship? Why is it that the Christian church counts for so little in this country? Now many answers are being given to those questions. For myself, I have only one answer to give. I believe that the state of the church is to be explained by one thing only, and that is that the message of the gospel is not being preached, and has not been preached for a number of years. I believe that the people have been more or less driven out of the churches by false gospels, by false preaching, and that is why it is so important that we must be clear concerning the true gospel.

Now let me say this: there is nothing that I dislike so much as having to be controversial. Nothing would give me greater pleasure than just to be able to give you a positive exposition all the time and nothing else. But I have no choice in this matter. The Apostle tells us that we are 'set for the defence' as well as the propagation of the gospel [*Phil.* 1:17], and if we see the moral state of the world and the state of the church, then it behoves us to discover the cause of the trouble and to correct it. I would to God that I had not got to do these things, but I would regard myself as a very poor teacher if I did not warn you against error, if I did not show you how to detect the error and how to differentiate between the true and the false. The gospel is to be applied, and the tragedy today is that Christian people do not any longer seem to have any sense of discrimination, but judge by appearances. They see a man like the late Pope [John XXIII] on the television and they say, 'He looks a nice man and he seems so pleasant, therefore he must be right!'

Well, there is only one thing to do with a condition like that, and that is to instruct. It is children who are carried away by 'every wind of doctrine' [*Eph*. 4:14]. It is children who can be taken in by a seemingly kind, nice, plausible man, and the only antidote is teaching. We cannot afford to be sentimental. We are living in a momentous age; the whole future of morals in this country depends upon these matters and, indeed, even beyond that, the whole state of the Christian church depends upon our understanding the nature of this message.

Now here the Apostle at once gives us a general test. Whatever else the gospel is, it is 'glad tidings'! Here is the comparison – 'How beautiful are the feet of them that bring glad tidings of great joy!' Sometimes people think that I have suddenly gone mad if I announce Christmas hymns at some other time of the year. But I have not! I do it deliberately in order to introduce this very theme – and why should we not sing these hymns all the year round? Why should we leave them only to that particular time of the year? The gospel in its fulness should be constantly in our minds. It is glad tidings, good news!

This is so important that I have got to give you some negatives. In the light of this definition which tells us that it is glad tidings, let us see what the gospel is not. It is very important that we should know this. The mere fact that a man gets up and preaches in a pulpit which is called Christian does not mean that he is preaching the gospel. This is really almost too pathetic for words. People today seem to think that you define an evangelist as a man who speaks in the open air! But it is not *where* a man preaches that decides whether he is an evangelist, it is *what* he preaches. And a man can preach a lie in the open air as easily as in a church building. But that is the kind of loose, sentimental way in which people think.

Let me say, then, negatively, first of all, that the message of the Christian gospel is not merely a message about morality and ethics. I start with that because that is the commonest misconception of all. It is a very old idea, of course, there is nothing new about it, but it is very popular at the present time. It was popularised in the last century by the famous Dr Thomas Arnold, the headmaster of Rugby School. He was the man who gave this particular emphasis its greatest currency. His idea of Christianity was that it produced good little gentlemen. So his message was one purely of morals. And there are large numbers of people who think today that the Christian message is a message to encourage us to live a good life. So we get little homilies or addresses just to urge us to be good, and to help one another, and so on.

Now that cannot be the gospel, for this reason: Where is the element of glad tidings in it? If preachers simply urge people not to drink and not to smoke and not to do this, that and the other, and stop at that, where do the glad tidings come in? You see, that is the way you test the preaching: there must be the element of good news, and if it is merely ethical teaching there is no glad tidings at all. So that cannot be the gospel. That is going back under the law, that is the very thing which Paul is denouncing in the whole of this Epistle, and particularly at this point in the tenth chapter. It is almost incredible that anybody could ever fall into this confusion, but that is where the devil comes in. He robs the gospel of its glory and turns it into nothing but a new kind of law, and so it is no longer the gospel.

Secondly – and I am being as practical as I can in order to help you to discriminate at this present time – other people seem to think that the main business of preaching is just to answer people's questions, to help them to live by giving them answers. Now I think you will find that this is becoming increasingly popular. People are saying that it is no use preaching because the days of preaching are gone. 'The thing you must do now,' they say, 'is to get your congregation to bring their questions and then you answer them.' And that is regarded as preaching.

Thirdly, the gospel is not a series of discourses on political and social matters. It is not the enunciation of a kind of political or social programme to improve the world. I need not stay with this, which, again, is very common. These people always talk about the kingdom of God. The teaching is entirely removed from the New Testament, but they are always saying that the business of Christianity is 'to bring in the kingdom of God'. And you do that by taking an active part in politics and in social matters; you urge people to improve and to reform and so on, and you enter into it with them.

In a broadcast sermon a few years ago, a very well-known preacher said quite deliberately: 'Missionaries must get rid of this notion that their business is to go and what they call "preach the gospel" to people. That,' he said, 'is not the thing to do' – he was talking in particular of Africa. He went on, 'This is what you must do, you missionaries. You must go and live among those people; you must enter into their politics; you must share their problems and live the Christian life among them in their political, social environment. And if you do that,' he said, 'there may be some hope that the grand-children of the people with whom you are living now may become Christians.' Now that was said by the Moderator of the General Assembly of the Church of Scotland a few years back, and that is regarded as the way of propagating the Christian message. And, of course, we are familiar with others in this country who teach a similar kind of thing – just political social action, and nothing else.

But all I would ask is: Where is the good news? It is not there. It is not there at all.

Fourthly, another misconception of the gospel is the idea that the message of Christian preaching is that people must 'imitate' the Lord Jesus Christ. In a recent interview on the subject, 'Can Christianity Survive?' a well-known retired minister said: 'Christianity, to me, is a way of life. A Christian is someone who believes that Christ's way is the supreme way of life; who tries to follow it and who tries to respond to the demands of life in a Christ-like spirit.' That is his idea of Christianity. Then he commented, 'It is utterly wrong to tell a man that he cannot be a Christian unless he declares unconditional assent to a set list of theological propositions.' This man, you see, in a public interview, published in a religious paper, is denying and attacking all that I am trying to tell you in these lectures on Romans. That is why I am driven to reply to it.

He continued, 'In the course of a recent television interview between Malcolm Muggeridge and a distinguished ecclesiastic, Muggeridge said that he was greatly attracted to much of Christ's teaching, although he had reservations about, among other things, the virgin birth. Muggeridge then asked this ecclesiastic where, in view of these reservations, he stood. To this came the reply that he was "out"! Jesus would never have said that,' declared the man being interviewed.

Then: 'I asked him,' wrote the interviewer, 'to elaborate on this line of thought.' And here is the result: 'Well, Jesus never demanded intellectual assent to a statement of doctrine. It is quite alien to the spirit of Jesus to tell anyone that such relatively unimportant matters as the virgin birth should stand between a person and his coming to Christ. There must be thousands of thoughtful men and women, I've met some myself, who are put off the church because they cannot subscribe to some of the so-called "fundamentals" of its theology. Take the doctrine of the Trinity. How can you believe that it expresses all the fulness of God, the infinite Creator of all things? How can you put a credal tape measure around His august being? Professor Lovell of Jodrell Bank says he thinks it likely that other planets are inhabited. How, then, can I honestly repeat the creed which speaks of "The only-begotten Son of God"? How do I know that, far from three Persons in one, there may not be three thousand or three million in one?'

And this, you see, is the thing that is so popular today.

Asked whether he thought that people outside the churches had a wrong mental picture of God, he answered: 'They can hardly fail to have, when so many churchgoers seem to have it. Can you blame people for not wanting to worship a God who is supposed to give people cancer, or who subjects to "eternal torture" those who, during their earthly lives, have rejected Him? God is mirrored in Jesus – indeed, the Master said so. Nothing can be true about God if it obviously conflicts with the spirit of Jesus – not even if it is in the Bible. We must judge the Bible by Jesus, not the reverse.'

Now I do not want to weary you, or waste your time, but I put all that before you to show you how essential it is that we should work out these statements of the great Apostle. You noticed the incredible muddle in that last statement. Here is a man who is not going to believe anything, even though the Bible says it, if it is in conflict with the spirit of Jesus. But what does he know about the spirit of Jesus apart from what he finds in the Bible? Nothing at all! And yet he is going to judge the Bible by the spirit of Jesus!

In other words, it comes to this: it is what *he* thinks that matters, neither the Bible nor Jesus. But, you see, this is the position at which we have arrived, and I do not hesitate to say that *that* is why the churches are as they are. It is very difficult, is it not? I have been criticised in the past for not belonging to the same [Congregational] Union as this man. But how can I? This teaching of his is a lie! This is antichrist! And though I were alone, I would never join with such a man, nor have anything to do with an association of churches that can tolerate such a man. This is a denial of the Christian message. Not only is there no good news in it, it goes out of its way to attack the good news, and to pour scorn upon it. Very well. All that talk about 'the imitation of Christ', about trying to put His teaching into practice and so on, is nothing but sentimentality.

Then, fifthly, neither is the message of the gospel – and we are going up the scale, intellectually at any rate – merely a philosophical view of life and of Christ. Now again, I have to put this before you. All misconceptions of the gospel are not as crude and as unintelligent as the one I have just been giving you. There are other people who, of course, are too intelligent and too intellectual to accept that kind of thing, but they can be equally wrong, and they so intellectualise the gospel that it is no longer the message.

Let me quote to you here a review of a book recently published under the title *The Secular Meaning of the Gospel*. This is what it said: 'The author then tackles the "Easter event" and concludes [here the review quotes from the author]: "Jesus of Nazareth was a free man in his own life, who attracted followers and created enemies according to the dynamics of personality, and in a manner comparable to the effect of other liberated persons in history upon people about them. He died as a result of the threat that such a free man poses for insecure and bound men. His disciples were left no less insecure and frightened. Two days later, Peter, and then other disciples, had an experience of which Jesus was the sense-content. They experienced a discernment situation in which Jesus, the free man whom they had known, themselves, and indeed the whole world, were seen in a quite new way. From that moment, the disciples began to possess something of the freedom of Jesus. His freedom began to be 'contagious'."' And that is the resurrection!

And so the reviewer concludes by saying that 'Mission' – the work, the mission of the church – 'is not the conversion of unbelievers, but the practice by Christians of Jesus' "contagious liberty".' You see the idea? Peter and the other disciples had some sort of experience, not the literal rising of the Lord Jesus Christ in the body from the tomb, but some sort of 'experience of which Jesus was the sense-content'. They had some feeling of exultation, and it came to them in terms of the Person of Jesus and so on. Well, all I can say is that if that is gospel, I have no idea what gospel is, and I should not be standing in this pulpit!

But let me come to the last of the misconceptions, the sixth

[303]

negative, showing what the content of the message is not. It is not the message of Roman Catholicism. Now I am not going into Roman Catholicism, but its essential message is this: believe in the church and her teaching. It includes teaching about the Lord Jesus Christ, I know, and many other things that are right, but the essential teaching is, 'Believe in the church and her teaching, and submit yourself to it.' So I put it down among these negatives.

But why am I putting these six negatives before you? Here is my first answer: because they are not true to the New Testament teaching. You do not find any of them there.

Secondly, none of them can be gospel, because they leave it all to the individual, to me. They are all telling *me* to do something, to live a good life; or they are helping me to live the good life, and telling me to ask my questions in order that they can help me. But nevertheless, I myself have got to put what they say into practice. When I offer my question to the great preacher and he answers, it is still I who have to do it, whatever it is. He does not believe in anything else. Everything is natural.

But this is my main reason for rejecting them all. Where are the glad tidings? Where is the notion of a preacher being sent to proclaim, running across the mountain tops, and the people rejoicing to see him – where is that element? It is absent. Take that last quotation. Did you understand it? I do not think you did and I do not blame you for it. What does this 'sense-content' of Jesus mean? So, you see, these things must be rejected.

However, let me now come to the positive. What is the essence of the message of the preacher of the gospel? I say once more, it is good news! After having digested those quotations that I have put before you, read now about the preaching of the Son of God himself: 'The common people heard him gladly' [*Mark* 12:37]! What do the common people know about this 'sense-content', this 'freedom of Jesus becoming contagious', and this strange experience which these disciples had?

No, the whole genius of Christianity is: 'The common people heard him gladly', and the common people cannot hear this other sort of thing gladly if they do not know what it means. It is words; it is verbiage; it is all so involved philosophically that it is almost impossible to understand what some of them are trying to say. And if the common people cannot hear gladly the message of the preacher, he is not a preacher sent by God, he is not a preacher of the gospel.

Or take the other word of our Lord, when John sent his two disciples to ask the famous question: 'Art thou he that should come, or do we look for another?' [*Matt.* 11:3]. Our Lord's answer was: 'Go and shew John again those things which ye do hear and see: The blind receive their sight, and the lame walk, the lepers are cleansed, and the deaf hear, the dead are raised up, and' – finally, the climax, if you like – '*the poor have the gospel preached to them.*' This is the differentia of the Christian gospel. You see, it is in direct contrast to Greek philosophy. The Greek philosophers had nothing to give to the poor – nothing at all. The poor were 'barbarians' and they called them that. They divided the world into Greek and barbarians, and to the barbarians, the poor, the illiterate, they had nothing to say. Why? Because these poor people did not understand their categories, they could not enter into these involved arguments, and these great thoughts. So the poor were utterly neglected. Nobody had anything to say to them.

But when John's disciples questioned the Lord, He said, 'Go and tell John this is what you have been seeing' – and above everything – '. . . the gospel is preached to the poor'. The poor! That was His emphasis. And the Apostle, of course, takes up this same statement when he writes to the Corinthians dealing with this very point. He puts it like this at the end of 1 Corinthians 1: 'For ye see your calling, brethren, how that not many wise men after the flesh, not many mighty, not many noble, are called: but God hath chosen the foolish things of the world to confound the wise; and God hath chosen the weak things of the world to confound the things which are mighty; and base things of the world, and things which are despised, hath God chosen, yea, and things which are not, to bring to nought things that are: that no flesh should glory in his presence' [*1 Cor.* 1:26–29]. The poor can understand this. This is a message to all. This is a message even to the ignorant and the unenlightened.

And so, when you read at the beginning of the Gospels of how the good news has come into the world, you find that the first man to put it all in a nutshell was old Zacharias, the father of John the Baptist. He had been pretty dull and slow, but now he is inspired. The Holy Spirit has enlightened him, and he cries out, 'He [God] hath visited and redeemed his people' [*Luke* 1:68]! None of your abstruse philosophy, none of your trying to understand the 'spirit of Jesus', no exhortations to men and women to do this or that. No, 'God hath visited and redeemed his people'! Here is the message.

Or take it as we have it in the message of the angels to those poor, ignorant, illiterate shepherds, watching their flocks by night. 'Fear not: for, behold, I bring you good tidings of great joy, which shall be to all people. For unto you is born this day in the city of David a Saviour, which is Christ the Lord.' And then the angelic host burst forth: 'Glory to God in the highest, and on earth peace, good will toward men.' And the shepherds went back from Bethlehem, 'glorifying and praising God', rejoicing in their hearts [*Luke* 2:10–20]. They had heard the good news, they had found their confirmation of it, and they were filled with a spirit of joy and exultation.

You get exactly the same thing in the message of John the Baptist. Immediately before the beginning of our Lord's own ministry, John says, 'I am [nothing but] the voice of one crying in the wilderness.' And he tells us what he is crying: 'Make straight the way of the Lord' [*John* 1:23]. John is quoting Isaiah 40:3 when he says he is nothing but the forerunner. 'Prepare ye the way of the Lord,' wrote Isaiah, 'make straight in the desert a highway for our God. Every valley shall be exalted, and every mountain and hill shall be made low: and the crooked shall be made straight, and the rough places plain . . . and all flesh shall see it together', that is, the salvation of God. It has come over the mountain tops – it has arrived! Here is this tremendous thing! Listen, says John. I am merely the announcer, the voice in the wilderness making a proclamation.

That is the character of the gospel. The essence of this message of the preacher is glad tidings. Why? Because it is not a call to us to do anything. It is a proclamation to us of what God has done about us and our salvation. No human being could do it. 'What the law could not do, in that it was weak through the flesh, God sending his own Son in the likeness of sinful flesh, and for sin, condemned sin in the flesh: that the righteousness of the law might be fulfilled in us, who walk not after the flesh, but after the Spirit' [*Rom.* 8:3–4].

Here it is, you see – what God has done! 'When the fulness of the time was come, God sent forth his Son, made of a woman, made under the law, to redeem them that were under the law' [*Gal.* 4:4–5]. It is God! 'God hath visited and redeemed his people.' This is the great characteristic of the message, and you do not find it in these false gospels. They have no good news, no thrilling joy, no acclamation. It is all human, and human power, and what we are being exhorted to do. But the message of the gospel goes like this: 'By grace are ye saved through faith; and that not of yourselves: it is the gift of God: not of works, lest any man should boast. For we are his workmanship, created in Christ Jesus . . .' [*Eph.* 2:8–10].

You see, this is the very essence of the gospel. When we were considering chapter 3, we spent some time emphasising the tremendous break that comes halfway through that chapter.[1] Here is how the gospel comes: 'Now we know that what things soever the law saith, it saith to them who are under the law: that every mouth may be stopped, and all the world may become guilty before God. Therefore by the deeds of the law there shall no flesh be justified in his sight: for by the law is the knowledge of sin. But now' – oh for the voice of an archangel! – 'But now the righteousness of God without [apart from] the law is manifested, being witnessed by the law and the prophets; even the righteousness of God which is by faith of Jesus Christ unto all and upon all them that believe: for there is no difference: for all have sinned, and come short of the glory of God; being justified freely by his grace through the redemption that is in Christ Jesus' [vv. 19–24].

That is the gospel! It is a gospel that makes men and women shout. In those other teachings there is nothing to shout about, and they mince their words, they are polite. There is no abandon, no liberty; there is no glory, no praise, no thanksgiving; there is no joy. It is not a gospel! It is the antichrist! It is a false gospel. And we must reject it with the whole of our being. The gospel is glad tidings.

[1] See *An Exposition of Chapters 3:20 – 4:25: Atonement and Justification*, 1970.

Twenty-eight

*

> *How then shall they call on him in whom they have not believed? and how shall they believe in him of whom they have not heard? and how shall they hear without a preacher? And how shall they preach, except they be sent? as it is written, How beautiful are the feet of them that preach the gospel of peace, and bring glad tidings of good things! But they have not all obeyed the gospel. For Esaias saith, Lord, who hath believed our report? So then faith cometh by hearing, and hearing by the word of God.*
>
> Romans 10:14–17

I have suggested that we can subdivide the little section from verses 14–17 into two subsections. In verses 14–15 the Apostle tells us of the general call of the gospel which goes out to all people; in verses 16–17 he deals with the effectual call. We are in the process of considering the first of these subsections, verses 14 and 15, and I have suggested that here we have the great missionary charter, the explanation of the missionary enterprise. This is how God has chosen to bring people into the kingdom of His dear Son – by the method of preaching. 'How shall they believe in him of whom they have not heard? and how shall they hear without a preacher?'

We have also dealt with the calling of the preacher and we are now considering his message. We have seen, first, that it is about the Lord Jesus Christ and, secondly, that it is a message of 'glad tidings'. And now that brings us to the third characteristic of this message, and that is the *good things*. The tidings are 'glad tidings' because they are tidings of 'good things'. That is where the whole element of joy comes in. It is the result of the content of the message, and the content is that which is described by the prophet Isaiah, and by the Apostle here, as 'good'.

Now you will remember that in his prophecy in Isaiah 52:7, Isaiah even adds to that. The Apostle gives us the essence of the quotation,

[308]

but here it is in full: 'How beautiful upon the mountains are the feet of him that bringeth good tidings, that publisheth peace; that bringeth good tidings of good, that publisheth salvation; that saith unto Zion, Thy God reigneth!' And in giving us the essence, Paul holds on to this idea of 'good things'.

So what are these 'good things'? Well, in a sense, in using the word *salvation* the prophet summarises it all. The good things of glad tidings are indeed the message of salvation. In other words, the good things about which the Apostle is here speaking in his quotation from Isaiah are simply all that he has already been telling us in the earlier part of the Epistle. This is one of the grand statements of the message of the Christian gospel. The Apostle has announced it at the very beginning, in verses 16 and 17 of chapter 1: 'I am not ashamed of the gospel of Christ' – I exult in it. I rejoice in it. Why? 'For it is the power of God unto salvation to every one that believeth; to the Jew first, and also to the Greek. For therein is the righteousness of God revealed from faith to faith: as it is written, The just shall live by faith.' And Paul has gone on to work that out.

But here – and bear in mind our general analysis of the whole chapter – the Apostle is again summarising the essential content of the gospel. He has got to do it because he is dealing with this problem of the Jews, and here, in chapter 10, in contradistinction to chapter 11, where he is more theological, he is dealing with it from the practical standpoint. He therefore finds it necessary to summarise this glorious gospel once more. Before he finally sums up the position of the Jews, as he will in chapter 11, he is here reminding the Romans, and reminding all Christian people, of what a tragedy this is. How tragic it is that the Jews should be holding on to their works, endeavour and effort, 'going about', as he puts it, taking all this trouble, making all this fuss, using all this energy – 'going about to establish their own righteousness' and rejecting these good things which are offered to them so freely in the gospel of our Lord and Saviour Jesus Christ. And as the Apostle troubles to sum it all up once more, though he has said it all in detail, we must do exactly the same thing.

Now I want to turn aside for a moment just to elaborate this point a little. I feel that often as Christian people, and perhaps even as evangelical people, we are very guilty in this way. When we come to a summary of something that we have already gone over, we have a tendency to say, 'Ah well, of course we have done that, now we go on.' But the Scripture does not do that. Once we have lost the thrill of this great gospel, there is something seriously wrong with us. Once we get into a state in which we say, 'Of course, I know all that,' and go on to something else, we are in a very bad condition.

Let me put it in another way. I often find that there is a type of evangelical Christian who seems to think that a church service which is evangelistic has nothing to say to him. He says, 'I am saved. I believe it all. I know it all already.' And he either does not come to the service at all, or else, if he does come, he spends his time in praying for the unbelievers. That seems to me to be a complete contradiction of what is so plainly taught in the Scriptures themselves. If you – though you may have been a Christian for fifty years – if you do not rejoice as much today as you did at the beginning in the proclamation of these 'good things', then I think you had better examine the foundations once more. You can never become so familiar with these things that you do not want to hear them again or that they do not move or thrill you again. The Apostle keeps on repeating it because to him it is the most glorious thing conceivable, and he cannot repeat it too frequently.

So then, we go into this phrase, 'good things'. What are they? Well, this is the message of the messenger that we see coming away there over the top of the mountains. Here we are in captivity and we can do nothing, but we see the messenger coming: 'How beautiful [upon the mountains] are the feet of them that . . . bring glad tidings of good things.' What has he got to tell us? What are these good things?

So let me try to analyse it once more or, if you like, to give a summary of all the glorious things we have been considering together in the body of this great Epistle. What are they? Well, first of all, they are the things that God has done for us, the things that God has provided for us. The first announcement of the gospel, in a sense, is found in the words of Zacharias, the father of John the Baptist. '[God] hath visited and redeemed his people' [*Luke* 1:68]. That is the good thing! It is all there.

In 2 Corinthians 5 the Apostle says, 'We are ambassadors for Christ' [*2 Cor.* 5:20]. What is our message? What are we to say? Well, we are told to say this: 'That God was in Christ, reconciling the world unto himself, not imputing their trespasses unto them' [5:19]. That is another summary of the message. The New Testament writers, Paul especially, are full of this; they keep on saying it, and always rejoice in it.

We have already seen it in Romans 1:16–17 and also, in a most wonderful way, in chapter 3:21.[1] In Romans 3:20, Paul has said: 'By the deeds of the law there shall no flesh be justified in his sight: for by the law is the knowledge of sin.' Paul then gives this tremendous introduction to the gospel: 'But now' – here come the 'good things' – 'the righteousness of God without [apart from] the law is manifested.' The thing that was 'witnessed by the law and the prophets' [v. 21] has now come, 'Even the righteousness of God which is by faith of Jesus Christ unto all and upon all them that believe: for there is no difference' – the very thing he is saying here in chapter 10. You see, Paul has said it all already, but he is repeating it, he is summing up this great way of salvation in contradistinction to the error of the Jews.

In other words, the first thing we must emphasise under this heading of 'good things' is the great good news which comes to us. It is what men and women had failed to do – 'What the law could not do, in that it was weak through the flesh God [himself] sending his own Son in the likeness of sinful flesh, and for sin, condemned sin in the flesh: that the righteousness of the law might be fulfilled in us, who walk not after the flesh, but after the Spirit' [*Rom.* 8:3–4].

The first note, then, in these good things is that God has intervened; God has entered, as it were, into the fight, and has taken action. He had promised it. The Old Testament is full of the promise. In the Garden of Eden, God told the serpent that the seed of the woman would bruise his head [*Gen.* 3:15]. There is to be an end to this warfare between the serpent and the seed of the women. A seed of the woman is going to come, and will conquer.

The great thing, therefore, at the beginning, is that God has done something, and He has done it in and through His only begotten Son, our Lord and Saviour Jesus Christ.

But, secondly: Why has God done this? Constantly in his Epistles, the Apostle uses the great terms of salvation, the most glorious terms in the whole of the Bible. What are they? Well, you have a wonderful summary of them in Ephesians 2. I turn to that simply because there they all happen to be very close together. We find them scattered about the Epistle to the Romans. But notice them here in Ephesians 2:4 and following: 'But God' – there it is. In the first three verses we have seen ourselves in our utter failure. We were 'dead in trespasses

---

[1] For a full exposition of this verse, see *An Exposition of Chapters 3:20 – 4:25: Atonement and Justification*, 1970.

[311]

and sins' [v.1]; we 'were by nature the children of wrath, even as others' [v.3]; we were completely hopeless. Then, 'But God'!

But why has God done anything? Here is the answer: 'who is rich in *mercy*'. Here are the good things – the mercy of God! Not only that – 'for his great *love*' – mercy! love! – 'wherewith he loved us, even when we were dead in sins, hath quickened us together with Christ (by grace ye are saved;) and hath raised us up together, and made us sit together in heavenly places in Christ Jesus: that in the ages to come he might shew' – what? Oh! – 'the exceeding riches of his *grace*' – here are the words: mercy! love! grace! – 'in his *kindness*' – there is the next – 'toward us through Christ Jesus'.

Now I do not stay with these terms here. We have dealt with them before, but I do rejoice in repeating them. I trust that your hearts are warmed as I remind you of them. God's mercy! That means that He looked down upon our pitiful condition and felt for us. Then His great love! You cannot define, you cannot fully describe, the love of God, all you can say is that 'God is love' [*1 John* 4:8]. 'The love of Christ, which passeth knowledge' [*Eph.* 3:19]! Then, grace! We merit no favour; we deserve nothing but punishment and hell. We deserve nothing but the wrath of God that is upon us all by nature because of what happened to us in Adam – as the Apostle has already told us in Romans 5:12 and following. But God does not deal with us in those terms; He deals with us in grace, unmerited favour, kindness to those who do not deserve any kindness or any mercy or compassion. Grace! Yes, the poet is right. It is 'a charming sound, melodious to the ear'. And one of the tests of our faith is whether that word is to us 'a charming sound'.

These are the good things, you see, that God has been pleased to manifest. Here we are, in captivity, under the condemnation of the law and the wrath of God, but a messenger comes over the mountain tops, and what does he say to us? He tells us that God is not only just and righteous – He is that, but He is not only that – God is love; He is full of mercy and compassion. He says, 'I have no pleasure in the death of the wicked' [*Ezek.* 33:11]. That is why He has done these good and great things.

Then I must emphasise, as the very word 'good' insists upon our doing, the superlative character of these attributes of God that have led Him to do these things for us and for our salvation. And in the quotations from Ephesians 2, notice how the Apostle brings out not only adjectives but superlatives as well; and even they are not enough, so He adds to them in the third chapter.

[312]

But let me remind you of them again: 'God, who is rich in mercy'. Oh, He is full of mercy! He is *rich* in it. Not just a little; God is superlative in everything. All His attributes are absolutes.

And then Paul is not content just with saying, 'For his love wherewith he loved us' – no; it is 'his *great* love' [*Eph.* 2:4]. This is all in this little word 'good'! Little word?! And if the love of God were not a great love, none of us would be Christians; indeed, there would be no such thing as a Christian; we would all be damned and lost for ever. 'Great love'! This messenger is announcing 'good things'! The missionary goes and tells people about this glorious God! They are worshipping their gods, their idols. They do not know the true God; they do not know the living God. Their whole conception of Him is inadequate and unworthy. *This* is God!

And then you come to the next term: 'That in the ages to come he might shew' – not merely His grace but – 'the *riches* of his grace'. But even that is not enough; Paul has to add to that – 'That in the ages to come he might shew the *exceeding* riches of his grace.' Words become inadequate, the thing is so glorious, it is so wonderful. And this is the Christian message; this is what the Christian preacher preaches. He is not just a man who is protesting against atomic bombs or against war, he is not someone who tells people not to do this, that and the other and teaches a little bit of morality and decency and niceness. Out upon the suggestion! How beautiful upon the mountains are the feet of this man who is bringing 'glad tidings of *good things*'. He is telling us about the 'exceeding riches of his [God's] grace'.

But when he comes to the third chapter of Ephesians, Paul finds even that inadequate, for in verse 8 he describes himself as a preacher by saying, 'Unto me, who am less than the least of all saints, is this grace given, that I should preach among the Gentiles the *unsearchable* riches of Christ.' There is no end to them; they are inexhaustible. Paul talks about a love 'that passeth knowledge'. He says that it will be possible, 'to know the love of Christ, which passeth knowledge, that ye might be filled with all the fulness of God' [*Eph.* 3:19]. And he says that the message which he has to give is about One who 'is able to do exceeding abundantly above all that we ask or think, according to the power that worketh in us' [*Eph.* 3:20]. That is the content, and I am emphasising its superlative character. Here we are peeping into some of the content of this goodness which is the goodness of God Himself, the glory of God! And God is good, God is light, God is love – all these glorious attributes of God in all their fulness have come together in order to bless men and women. This is the message of the preacher: 'glad tidings of good things'.

Those, then, are the characteristics of these good things. Oh, I find it difficult to leave this word 'good'. Do you find them good? Are these things moving and thrilling you? Are you more and more amazed at them? I have a feeling that much of the trouble with the church today is that we do not know how to use this word 'good'. We have turned the glories of the gospel into things. The glory somehow is missing. Orthodoxy, even, is not enough. If your orthodoxy does not move your heart, if it does not fill you with praise and rejoicing, there is something wrong. God deliver us from a barren, intellectual belief of these truths, and may He bring them to us with such power that we will always know and feel that they are 'good things', and see something of their glory, until we are 'lost in wonder, love, and praise'.

So, then, what are these things which are so good? Let me just summarise what the Apostle has been telling us. He himself is doing it, I am just following him. The first great thing is justification by faith only, and its consequences. This is why he is not ashamed of the gospel of Christ. 'Therein is the righteousness of God revealed from faith to faith' [*Rom.* 1:17] – by means of faith. This is the way, and this is the most wonderful thing that has ever come into this world, the greatest good news that men and women can ever hear – that they are no longer doomed. They are doomed, of course, as long as their salvation depends upon themselves. If salvation depends upon our good deeds and good life and striving, then every one of us is lost. No one shall ever be justified that way, as Paul has told us in the third chapter: 'Therefore [we conclude that] by the deeds of the law there shall no flesh be justified in his sight: for by the law is the knowledge of sin' – and no more.

In Romans 7:5 the Apostle has shown us how, because of our sinful nature, the law even aggravates our problem and makes us sin all the more: 'For when we were in the flesh, the motions of sins, which were by the law' – they were energised by the law, stimulated by the law. The law cannot save. But here is the message: 'But now the righteousness of God without the law is manifested' [*Rom.* 3:21]. This is the glorious message of justification by faith only. As Paul has put it in chapter 4:5, God 'justifieth the ungodly'. He does not justify us because we have become godly, he justifies the *ungodly*; he justifies the sinner as he or she is. Here is the first great message, the first 'good thing'. And that, as Paul has gone on to point out to us, leads to certain results.

It means that we are freely pardoned and forgiven; it means that our sins are 'blotted out, as a thick cloud' [*Isa.* 44:22] and that God declares us to be just in His sight. It is a declaration; there is this forensic element in justification. God makes the declaration that He regards us as righteous in Christ; our sins are put away altogether. And that, of course, means that we are reconciled to God, and that we have peace with Him.

Paul sums this up at the beginning of Romans 5. Having worked out his argument about justification, he says, 'Therefore being justified by faith, we have peace with God' [v. 1]; we are reconciled to God. In verse 10 he says, 'If when we were enemies, we were reconciled to God by the death of his Son, much more, being reconciled, we shall be saved by his life.' Reconciliation! Peace with God! The old enmity has gone; the enmity between men and women and God. 'The carnal mind', he has told us in chapter 8:7, 'is enmity against God.' But it has gone now. We are at peace with God, and God is at peace with us. God has provided the propitiation Himself, so that the relationship lost in the sin of Adam is now restored. 'We have peace with God through our Lord Jesus Christ.' These are the 'glad tidings'. He comes to me in my utter sinfulness and failure and says: You are forgiven because of what Christ has done for you. 'God was in Christ' – through that – 'reconciling the world unto himself' [*2 Cor.* 5:19].

And further consequences which Paul has outlined and worked out are these. My old nature, the person that I was in Adam, has already been crucified with Christ: 'Knowing this, that our old man is crucified with him' [*Rom.* 6:6]. My old nature is dead, and dead for ever.

But there is more: because of that, I am 'dead unto sin'. 'Likewise reckon,' Paul says, 'ye also yourselves to be dead indeed unto sin' [v.11]. You reckon it because it is true. In the same way, Paul tells me that I am 'dead to the law'. 'The law of the Spirit of life in Christ Jesus,' he says in chapter 8:2, 'hath made me free from the law of sin and death.' He has said it still more plainly and at greater length in chapter 7. Writing to those who know the law, Paul says, 'Ye also are become dead to the law by the body of Christ' [7:4]. These are the consequences of justification by faith only.

But not only am I dead in that way to sin and to the law, I am now

[315]

a new person. I am no longer in Adam, I am 'in Christ'. My life is 'hid with Christ in God' [*Col.* 3:3]. I have a new nature and a new mind – not the mind of the flesh, but the mind of the Spirit; no longer enmity towards, but a love of God. I am alive unto God. 'Reckon ye also yourselves to be dead indeed unto sin, but alive unto God through Jesus Christ our Lord' [*Rom.* 6:11]. Here are the good things that have come to me. Whereas I was dead in trespasses and sins, and an enemy and alien in my mind through wicked works, and having no contact with God – I am now alive unto God! I stand before Him and I can speak to Him.

In other words, it is true of us that: 'Therefore being justified by faith, we have peace with God through our Lord Jesus Christ: by whom also we have access by faith into this grace wherein we stand' [*Rom.* 5:1–2]. I am alive unto God. I can pray to God. We are able to enter even into 'the holiest', says Hebrews 10:19, 'by the blood of Jesus'. Or, as Hebrews 4:16 says, 'Let us therefore come boldly unto the throne of grace, that we may obtain mercy, and find grace to help in time of need.' Because we have this great High Priest, because we go 'by the blood of Jesus', we can pray, we can have access into the presence of God, and can speak to Him as our Father, and make our requests known to Him.

There, then, is a very hurried summary of justification and its main consequences. But it does not stop at that. That is, of course, the first thing I want to know: How can my sins be blotted out? How can I know God? How can I pray? 'How should a man be just with God?' [*Job* 9:2]. And here is the answer: it is a part of the good things He has for me, it is part of the 'glad tidings'.

But, you see, I want more than that. I thank God that my sins are forgiven and that I can pray to God, but I am left in this world, and I have got to fight the world, the flesh and the devil, and how can I do that? It is good to know that I am forgiven, but am I to spend the rest of my life sinning and being forgiven again and again – is there no hope of my being delivered? And the answer is that there is. Sanctification! This new life in the Spirit. 'The law of the Spirit of life in Christ Jesus hath made me free from the law of sin and death' [*Rom.* 8:21]. Or, as Paul has put it in chapter 7:6, 'But now we are delivered from the law, that being dead wherein we were held; that we should serve in newness of spirit, and not in the oldness of the letter.'

So I start out upon an entirely new life. It is a life 'in the Spirit', and I am led by the Spirit. 'As many as are led by the Spirit of God, they are the sons of God' [*Rom.* 8:14]. 'If any man have not the Spirit of Christ, he is none of his' [*Rom.* 8:9]. As the result of this, the Spirit comes to dwell within me and, through the Spirit, the Son and the Father take up their abode within me as a Christian and as a new person. I am living this new life; 'alive unto God'; a life in the Spirit. What was promised in John 14 becomes a reality in the Christian.

And then – this goes on – there is this great process of sanctification: the power of the Spirit within me. In chapter 8:13 Paul has told us, 'If ye live after the flesh, ye shall die; but if ye *through the Spirit* do mortify the deeds of the body, ye shall live.' I cannot do it, but through the Spirit I can. Not only that but, as I am told in Philippians 2:13, 'It is God which worketh in you both to will and to do of his good pleasure.'

And, you see, we are no longer the slaves of sin. Romans 6:14 has told me, 'Sin shall not have dominion over you: for ye are not under the law, but under grace.' And Paul goes on to say: 'God be thanked that ye were the servants of sin, but ye have obeyed from the heart that form of doctrine which was delivered unto you' [6:17]. So I am no longer the slave of sin. I am dead to sin, and now I am 'the servant of righteousness'.

This is the content of the good things – I am indeed no longer under the dominion of Satan. He is still there and I may be fool enough now and again to listen to him, but I am not under his dominion. 'The whole world lieth in wickedness', but 'that wicked one toucheth him not' [*1 John* 5:19, 18]. 'They overcame him by the blood of the Lamb, and by the word of their testimony' [*Rev.* 12:11].

Not only that, and perhaps the most glorious aspect of it all is this: God now looks down upon us as His children and He loves us with an everlasting love. Read again that wonderful statement in Romans 5:9 where Paul says, 'Much more then, being now justified by his blood, we shall be saved from wrath through him.' He goes on, 'If, when we were enemies, we were reconciled to God by the death of his Son, much more, being reconciled, we shall be saved by his life.'

You see, when God has started doing something to me, He will finish it; and if He gave up His Son to the death of the cross that I might be forgiven, He is not going to abandon me now. He will go on with the work until it is complete. If I am reconciled by the death of the Son, how much more shall I be saved by the life of the Son! Or take it as it is put in an argument in Romans 8:32: 'He that spared not his own Son, but delivered him up for us all, how shall he not with him also freely give us all things?'

My friend, here are the good things that the preacher is announcing to you – the 'glad tidings of good things' – that God is your Father; you are His child; He is not going to leave you; He is going on with this until you are absolutely complete. Indeed, if you do not listen to the gospel, He will chastise you: 'Whom the Lord loveth he chasteneth, and scourgeth every son whom he receiveth' [*Heb.* 12:6]. Nothing that is essential to your sanctification and mine is left out, it is all in Christ.

Even when I do not know what to pray for as I ought, I am told in Romans 8:26, 'The Spirit also maketh intercession for us with groanings which cannot be uttered.' Indeed, I am enabled to say quite confidently and assuredly that though hell may be set against me, though day by day I may be led 'as a sheep to the slaughter and be killed all the day long, Nay, in all these things we are more than conquerors through him that loved us' [*Rom.* 8:36–37], 'For I am persuaded, that neither death, nor life, nor angels, nor principalities, nor powers, nor things present, nor things to come, nor height, nor depth, nor any other creature, shall be able to separate us from the love of God, which is in Christ Jesus our Lord' [vv. 38–39].

Here are the good things: Justification! Sanctification! And the end: 'the hope of glory'. Glorification! 'Being justified by faith, we have peace with God through our Lord Jesus Christ: by whom also we have access by faith into this grace wherein we stand, and rejoice in hope of the glory of God' [*Rom.* 5:1–2]. The glory! It is coming. Do you remember the tremendous statement of chapter 8 beginning at verse 17? 'If children, then heirs; heirs of God, and joint-heirs with Christ; if so be that we suffer with him, that we may be also glorified together. For I reckon that the sufferings of this present time are not worthy to be compared with the glory which shall be revealed in us. For the earnest expectation of the creature waiteth for the manifestation of the sons of God.' Glorification! Entire salvation! We are delivered from the fall and all its consequences in every single detail, until we are perfectly glorified, complete and entire, without spot or wrinkle.

'How beautiful [upon the mountains] are the feet of them that . . . bring glad tidings of good things!' These are the good things that Paul tells men and women are possible if they believe, if they 'call' upon the name of this Lord.

There, then, is the content of this great and glorious message. It is all about Him because it all comes through Him; this One on whom we are to call. 'The unsearchable riches of Christ'! That is the message of the preacher, and God raises, calls, sends preachers to bear these glad tidings.

'But they have not all obeyed the gospel. For Esaias saith, Lord, who hath believed our report?' These are the good things that the preacher proclaims. Do we believe them? How can we know that we believe them? Well, that is the question that the Apostle proceeds to consider in verses 16 and 17, and which, God willing, we shall go on to consider.

We have been dealing so far with this general call, this general proclamation; we must now consider how this is made effectual, and how we can know, without any doubt at all, whether it has been effectual in us.

Twenty-nine

※

But they have not all obeyed the gospel. For Esaias saith, Lord, who hath believed our report? So then faith cometh by hearing, and hearing by the word of God. Romans 10:16–17

We have been considering the calling of the preacher and his message and continue to do so in these verses but from a slightly different angle. We need to bear in mind, as we do so, the fundamental object that the Apostle has in writing this chapter, which is, of course, to deal with the case of the Jews. Towards the end of chapter 9, he gave us a key to the understanding of the whole problem of Israel: 'Israel, which followed after the law of righteousness, hath not attained to the law of righteousness.' Why not? 'Because they sought it not by faith, but as it were by the works of the law. For they stumbled at that stumblingstone' [*Rom.* 9:31–32], and thereby proved what had been stated in the prophecy of Isaiah.

Now, as we have seen, chapter 10 is an exposition of that final statement about the Jews given at the end of chapter 9, and Paul has been working it out in detail. They were 'going about' with great fuss and bother to 'establish their own righteousness' and they could not do it. But they were still trying and were refusing this way of salvation that is always by faith. And God has seen to it, therefore, that the message should be proclaimed through His chosen servants in the way that we have considered.

But now the Apostle says that it is obvious that everybody has not believed and is not believing this gospel. There is great discussion among the commentators as to whether Paul is just stating a fact here or whether he is putting up an objection, chiefly from the standpoint of the Jew. There are those who say that the Apostle is imagining a Jew or some objector saying, 'But that cannot really be the way of salvation, because there are only a few who believe it. The masses of the people are rejecting it, the masses of the Jews have certainly rejected it. Is it likely, then, that this is God's way of salvation? You say it is just a question of preaching and of people believing and calling on the name of the Lord, but it does not seem to be working out like that.'

Those who hold that interpretation of these verses may very well be right. Or it may be simply that the Apostle himself is stating a fact – that though the gospel is preached to all, it is only some who believe. 'They have not all obeyed the gospel.' Does this therefore invalidate what the Apostle has just been saying with respect to the way of salvation? But the Apostle deals with that, and gives an immediate answer – 'No, of course it means nothing of the kind.'

But why not? And that is what we must now consider. How, then, does Paul deal with this difficulty? Now, as always, it is very interesting to observe the way in which he does so. As we have seen, we must never forget, as we work through a great Epistle like this, that it behoves us not only to observe the actual teaching, but also to observe the way in which Paul presents it, the way in which he handles a problem. Never have we been in greater need of learning how to handle problems than at the present time. It is not enough that we should be right. We can be right, and yet we can handle our subject or present it in such a thoroughly bad way that we do more harm than good. We must be right, not only in our doctrine and proof, but in our method also.

Now some of us are very concerned about this question of method. Those of us who take the Reformed view of things often criticise other evangelicals because they are wrong in their methods. Well, let us be careful that we ourselves are not wrong in ours, let us learn from the Apostle. I reminded you at the beginning of the chapter how lovingly he writes to people who are some of his most bitter opponents. 'Brethren,' he says, 'my heart's desire and prayer to God for Israel is, that they might be saved.' His heart is breaking for them. And we are very bad exponents of the truth if our hearts do not break for people who are opposed to the truth and opposed to us. We are not truly in the Pauline succession unless we are as careful about our method as we are about our message. So let us watch Paul as he proceeds to deal with this.

The first point he makes is this: the fact that everybody does not believe the gospel is not something surprising; it has all been prophesied. 'But they have not all believed the gospel. For Esaias saith, Lord, who hath believed our report?' And there he quotes the first verse of Isaiah 53. Now you notice that he has a sequence in his mind. He has just quoted Isaiah 52:7 where the prophet says, 'How beautiful upon the mountains are the feet of him that bringeth good tidings, that publisheth peace; that bringeth good tidings of good . . .' Then he goes on with this next quotation from Isaiah, and he is able to show that Isaiah, who had revealed that the way of salvation was to be by this proclamation of the 'good news', had himself also said, 'Lord, who hath believed our report? and to whom is the arm of the Lord revealed?'

So Paul is able, in this way, to show that the children of Israel have always been guilty of this unbelief. They are guilty of it now in his time, but they were equally guilty of it eight centuries earlier, in the time of the prophet Isaiah. Prophecy, you remember, must always be taken in its two senses. It has an immediate and a remote application. The children of Israel were refusing the Word of God as preached by Isaiah. That is the first meaning of Isaiah's statement in chapter 53:1. But Isaiah was given to see that it was not only true in his own day, it was also going to be true in the age of the Messiah.

Now the Apostle, as we have seen, has done this sort of thing quite frequently. He has quoted these statements from the Old Testament just to show that there is nothing surprising about what is happening. He is certainly not surprised himself. He regrets it, he bemoans it, but he is not shattered nor taken aback by it. He does not feel all is hopeless because, as a man who knows his Scriptures, he knows that all this has been prophesied. And that is why you find this statement quoted so frequently in the New Testament. The fact is that the Jews, by not believing, have proved the truth of the prophecy of Isaiah.

But let us turn aside for just a moment or two to glance at what the Apostle is doing here. Notice how he always quotes a Scripture. He was one of the wisest men the world has ever known and he had a great pastoral mind and heart. The Apostle always made his point by quotations from Scripture and you see the wisdom of this. Here were the Jews who boasted of their Scriptures. They had been given the oracles of God; they despised the Gentiles who had not got the Word of God, and they said that nothing mattered but this.

Our Lord dealt with them in exactly the same way, for example in John 5:39, which can be taken in one of two ways. It is translated in the Authorised Version: 'Search the scriptures; for in them ye think ye have eternal life.' Or it can be taken as a statement: 'You do search the Scriptures because you think that in them you have eternal life.' And that is quite right; they were doing that.

And what can be more effective when you are dealing with such people than to take these very Scriptures in which they glory and show that it is their very ignorance of them that accounts for their rejection of the gospel? That is just what the Apostle is doing, and there is no better way of dealing with the Jews than just that.

But remember, it is important for us also. When we are dealing with somebody who is disputing our view of the gospel or of the way of salvation, the best approach is always to take them to the Scriptures. We must, of course, choose the right Scriptures, and show their relevance. It is very much better to quote a Scripture than to say, 'What I say is this,' because, if you put it like that, they are equally entitled to say, 'But I don't say it like that, I say the opposite', and it is one person's opinion against another's. And you can go on shouting at one another for the rest of the time!

No, the thing to do is to go to the Scriptures – 'What saith the scripture?' [*Rom.* 4:3]. And the Apostle had his Scriptures at hand; he knew them. So we do not just shout at one another, we say, 'If you believe the Bible at all, if the Bible is your authority in all matters of faith and conduct, then let us see what it says about this.'

But there is another very astounding thing here, it seems to me, and it is this. There is a sense in which everything about the gospel has been foretold in the Old Testament. Never forget that these Apostles had nothing but the Old Testament. But the Old Testament, you see, if really enough, it is all there. You can find the gospel there if you have a spiritual eye to see it. And thus the Apostles and the others were constantly able to show that what was happening in their day was nothing but a fulfilment of what had been foretold.

But, still more striking, of course, is this point: this one quotation, if we had no others, is enough in and of itself to show the unique, divine and inerrant inspiration of the prophets. Here is a prophet writing eight hundred years before the event and he is able to prophesy it. How could a Jew, how could any man, eight hundred years before the event, ever imagine that the nation of Israel was going to refuse its own Messiah? The whole nation was waiting for him; they were looking for him; it was the biggest thing in their lives. And everybody assumed that when he did come, they would all believe in him, worship him, and follow him. And yet Isaiah was able to say that it was not going to be like that. Indeed, the position would be such that one might almost say, Does *anybody* believe in him? 'Who hath believed our report?' The majority do not believe it. That is the real force of the quotation.

Now there is only one explanation of this kind of thing, and that is what the Apostle Peter tells us in his Second Epistle. 'No prophecy of the scripture is of any private interpretation.' It is not a man's view; it is not a man's teaching; it is not something a man has thought out. That is the meaning of 'private interpretation'. What is it, then? Well, 'Holy men of God spake as they were moved [or carried along, or controlled] by the Holy Ghost' [2 Pet. 1:20–21]. This is an absolute proof of the divine inspiration of the prophets, and therefore of the whole of the Scriptures.

And so we find, in this way, a most amazing demonstration of the truth of the whole of the Bible and of the unity of the Bible. We see that there is this one great message from beginning to end. It is a wonderful illustration, in passing, of the veracity, the inerrancy and the absolute reliability of the Word of God. I am never tired of pointing this out. There is no greater proof, ultimately, of the truth of the Christian faith than fulfilled prophecy. It is one of our most powerful arguments. Let us never forget it.

This, then, is our first comment. The Apostle deals with the problem by the quotation from the Scriptures. But he does not leave it at that. He goes on to elaborate that in verse 17, which is in many ways an exposition of verse 16. While the Apostle is not surprised at the unbelief of the Jews – because it is something that has been prophesied – it nevertheless is a problem, and we are entitled to ask the question: What is it, then, that makes the difference?

So the second point that Paul establishes is that what really matters is 'faith'. 'They have not all obeyed the gospel. For Esaias saith, Lord, who hath believed our report? So then faith . . .' – this is the thing. He has been showing that justification is by faith; it is everyone who 'shall call' on the name of the Lord who is to be saved. Well, they would not call unless they had faith. That is the material thing, that is what really matters in this whole question, and so he takes it up.

Now we can put it like this. All hearing of the gospel does not lead to faith. You can hear the gospel and still have no faith. The offer which is made to all is not effective (or effectual) in all, and this is what the Apostle is now demonstrating. It is offered to all, it is preached to all and sundry, but all do not believe. Everybody may hear the gospel, but everybody does not hear the gospel in the sense of coming to have faith in it. There is a difference between the hearing that does not lead to faith and the hearing that does.

Here, then, is the point that we must examine. The Apostle puts this in terms of the very interesting word *hearing*, which he has used twice in this seventeenth verse; in fact, he really uses it four times in these two verses but not with the same meaning. The first use of the word, with the qualification which I shall mention later, is the word *obeyed* in verse 16: 'But they have not all obeyed the gospel.' The Greek word 'obey' has as its root the word for '*hear*'; it is a particular type of hearing.

Then Paul uses the word again in the word *report*. 'Lord, who hath believed our report?', and the word that is used for 'report' is exactly the same word as the word that is translated twice in verse 17 by 'hearing'. A report, you see, is something that one hears, so you might very well translate verse 16 like this: 'They have not all obeyed the gospel. For Esaias saith, Lord, who hath believed the thing that they have heard?' The translators very rightly used the word 'report', but do not lose sight of the fact that, basically, a report is something you hear.

And then Paul goes on in the seventeenth verse to use it twice. 'Faith,' he says, 'cometh by hearing, and hearing by the word of God.' Now let me just deal with a technical point here. It is agreed by most people that a better translation is, '. . . hearing cometh by the word of Christ'. This is purely a question of early manuscripts. Again, this is not higher criticism, but textual criticism. In the end, of course, the meaning is the same. The gospel is called the gospel of God and it is also called the gospel of Christ, the gospel of the Lord Jesus Christ, and so on.

So the question is: What is the meaning of this word that is translated here twice by 'hearing' and once by 'report'. And the answer is that the word has two meanings. The first is the act of hearing, and the second is the thing that you hear through the act of hearing, the message reported, and it is easy to see how one meaning comes out of the other.

Now we have seen that in verse 16 Paul clearly means the thing that you hear, the 'message'. So it is rightly translated as, 'Who hath believed our report?' You could not say, 'Who hath believed the act of hearing?' It is certainly this second meaning – 'the thing heard', the 'message'. But what about this word 'hearing' in verse 17? You notice that our Authorised translators use a different word here from that in

verse 16. And yet many of the commentators would have us believe
that the word 'hearing' in both these instances in verse 17 has exactly
the same meaning as it has in verse 16. In that case, you might translate verse 17 like this: 'So then faith cometh by the report, and the
report cometh out of the word of Christ.' But I suggest to you that
that is wrong. There are great authorities that I could quote on that
side, but I venture to dissent from them.

I believe that here we are looking at the first meaning of this word.
Remember, the same word in different places carries the one meaning
or the other and you decide in terms of the context. It is not going to
make any difference to the ultimate message, but I think that a shade
of meaning comes out here if we take it as the act of hearing rather
than the thing heard, and I want to try to show you why I take this
particular view.

Now the way to understand this is to go back to another quotation
from the prophet Isaiah, this time to the sixth chapter. This is God
giving His commission to the prophet Isaiah: 'And he said, Go, and
tell this people, Hear ye indeed, but understand not; and see ye
indeed, but perceive not. Make the heart of this people fat, and make
their ears heavy, and shut their eyes; lest they see with their eyes, and
hear with their ears, and understand with their heart, and convert,
and be healed' [vv. 9–10].

Now, our Lord Himself quoted those two verses in His parable of
the Sower. You remember, a problem had arisen in this way. Having
heard our Lord speak in parables in the presence of the Pharisees and
people like that, the disciples had a difficulty in their minds. 'The disciples came, and said unto him, Why speakest thou unto them in
parables? He answered and said unto them, Because it is given unto
you to know the mysteries of the kingdom of heaven, but to them it
is not given. For whosoever hath, to him shall be given, and he shall
have more abundance: but whosoever hath not, from him shall be
taken away even that he hath.'

Then notice this: 'Therefore speak I to them in parables: because
they seeing see not; and hearing they hear not, neither do they understand. And in them is fulfilled the prophecy of Esaias, which saith, By
hearing' – and this is the exact word that we have in our two verses in
Romans 10 – 'By hearing ye shall hear, and shall not understand; and
seeing ye shall see, and shall not perceive: for this people's heart is
waxed gross, and their ears are dull of hearing, and their eyes they
have closed; lest at any time they should see with their eyes, and hear

with their ears, and should understand with their heart, and should be converted, and I should heal them. But blessed are your eyes, for they see: and your ears, for they hear' [*Matt.* 13:10–16].

So, you see, the gospel always causes this division. Incidentally, after the Apostle Paul had arrived in Rome (you will find it in Acts 28) he preached the gospel, and it had exactly the same effect, it divided the Jewish company into two. There were those who believed and there were those who did not. What is the explanation for this? And the Apostle Paul gives there exactly the same explanation as our Lord gave in the parable of the Sower, as God had given to Isaiah when He sent him out to preach, and as the Apostle Paul, I am suggesting, gives us in Romans 10:17.

It is that it is one thing to hear the gospel, but it is another thing to hear in a manner that leads to faith. All hearing is not the same. All people hear the same words, but they do not hear the same message. In effect, our Lord said, 'I am speaking in parables in the presence of these Pharisees in order that they may not understand' – because they are what they are, and because of the state of their hearts.

Now many people hold the foolish notion that parables are just like the stories told by modern evangelists. When the doctrine is a bit difficult, you tell a story and so make it easier. But our Lord said that He did not speak in parables to make it easy, He spoke in parables for the exact opposite reason. Let us never forget that. He did it in order that He might produce two types of hearing: 'Unto *you* it is given to understand,' he said to the disciples, to the believers. Not to the others. The others heard these statements like everybody else. Yes, but they did not understand. So we find our Lord making a most extraordinary exhortation in Luke 8:17–18. He said, 'Nothing is secret, that shall not be made manifest; neither anything hid, that shall not be known and come abroad.' Then: 'Take heed therefore how ye hear', that is, 'Be careful how you listen.' What a text for congregations! Are you careful how you listen? 'You know,' said our Lord in effect, 'you can sit in your seats. You can say, "I heard every word he said." But did you? What did you hear?' 'Take heed how ye hear'! And then he added, 'for whosoever hath, to him shall be given; and whosoever hath not, from him shall be taken even that which he seemeth to have'.

There are people who think that they have the gospel, but they will find one day that they have never had it. That is the kind of person we read of at the end of the Sermon on the Mount to whom our Lord will say, 'I never knew you: depart from me, ye that work iniquity' [*Matt.* 7:23]. They will say, 'Lord, Lord!' They will think they have heard. But they have never heard. He does not know them – 'Depart from me!' 'Take heed therefore how ye hear.'

Now this is the most important point, it seems to me, with regard to this whole matter. There are two types of hearing. There is what you may call a mechanical hearing and there is a hearing of faith. Let me give you another quotation to establish this same point and show you how the Apostle is constantly making it. In Galatians 3 he is dealing with those foolish Galatians who were falling back from faith on to works. He says, 'This only would I learn of you, Received ye the Spirit by the works of the law, or by the hearing of faith?' [v. 2]. Not just 'by hearing', but 'by the hearing of faith' is what he is anxious to emphasise. And then you find the same thing in the fifth verse. 'He therefore that ministereth to you the Spirit, and worketh miracles among you, doeth he it by the works of the law, or by the hearing of faith?' Now that is what Paul is talking about in Romans 10:17. 'Faith cometh by hearing.' Ah, but it is this special type of hearing! It is not ordinary hearing. Everybody hears in one sense, but there are only some people who really hear.

Or take another illustration. There is a difference between seeing and perceiving. You can take a man into an art gallery and point to a painting and say, 'You see that?' And he says, 'Yes!' But he may not be seeing it at all. He sees paint but he does not of necessity see the picture. You can see without perceiving.

So there is all the difference in the world between hearing, even being familiar with the statements, with the words, and with the facts, and really hearing. There is a hearing that leads to faith; there is a hearing that does not. Now that is the distinction, it seems to me, that the Apostle is drawing here in this seventeenth verse.

It is faith, therefore, that matters. The fact that a man says, 'I have been listening to sermons now for fifty years,' does not really tell us anything. What I want to know is: What has he heard in his fifty years? He may have taken a note of every text, he may have taken notes of the sermons, but has he heard the gospel? That is the question. Has he got faith? If he has not, he has not heard.

So, having established that, the next principle is this: How is this faith produced? And the Apostle gives us the answer. Now we bring out this point by again correcting this Authorised Version translation a little. The translators have translated two different prepositions by the same word. The Authorised Version reads, 'So then faith cometh *by* hearing, and hearing *by* the word of God.' But that is inaccurate. They should have put it like this: 'So then faith cometh from' – or, better still, out of – 'hearing, and hearing by' – through, as the result of – 'the word of Christ'. That is the true translation.

Now this true hearing is a very remarkable and wonderful thing. There is a hearing that produces faith; faith comes out of it. What sort of a hearing is this? This, again, is something which is of vital importance. It is of contemporary importance and it has always been important. How do you tell the difference between the two types of hearing? I have said before that preaching is the most amazing thing in the world. It is most romantic, and it is also most responsible, because you know perfectly well, as you are uttering words, that they can have two different effects. And you never know what is happening. What is it that determines this?

Well, the best I can do is to give you some illustrations of this very thing. Let me take you to the book of Acts, to Paul's first preaching on the continent of Europe, at Philippi. We read, 'And on the sabbath we went out of the city by a river side, where prayer was wont to be made; and we sat down, and spake unto the women which resorted thither. And a certain woman named Lydia, a seller of purple, of the city of Thyatira, which worshipped God, heard us' – so did many others, but listen – *'whose heart the Lord opened,* that she attended unto the things which were spoken of Paul' [*Acts* 16:13–14].

That is it! That is what tells us when it is this true hearing, that is, the hearing out of which faith comes – 'whose heart the Lord opened'! And the teaching of the Bible from beginning to end is that you can never get this hearing unless the Lord opens the heart. 'The natural man receiveth not the things of the Spirit of God: for they are foolishness unto him: neither can he know them, because they are spiritually discerned' [*1 Cor.* 2:14]. He hears these words, he hears the gospel, but he dismisses it, he ridicules it. It is utter nonsense to him. Why? Because his heart has not been opened, because the Holy Spirit has not dealt with him. He has heard every word that the preacher has said but he has not heard the gospel.

You see, what happens in this true hearing is, as we are told there about Lydia, '. . . she *attended* unto the things which were spoken of Paul'. She was immediately gripped by them; she laid hold of them. She paid attention, she realised that this was something vital.

Now let me encourage you to examine your own experiences. You may know what it was to be taken to a place of worship when you were a child and you had to listen, and you disliked it, but you had to do it. And then you became an adolescent, and you still went, perhaps because you did not like to hurt or disobey your parents. So there you were, and while the man was preaching, you were thinking of something else or perhaps reading a book surreptitiously. And then you got to a stage in which you felt that that was rather rude, so you just sat and listened and you were hearing words but they meant nothing to you at all.

Then suddenly on one occasion you had a feeling that the preacher was speaking directly to you. You felt he was looking at you, that these words were for you and that they were most vital words, and you began to pay attention as you had never done in your life before. That is what happened to Lydia. That is what always happens in this true hearing. It means a hearkening in the full sense, where all your faculties are engaged because you know it is a word from God to you, and that it is the most vital thing you have ever heard in your life. You are paying heed; you are receiving it; you are accepting it; you are fully engaged. That is the true hearing. Faith only comes out of that sort of hearing, and that is the only type of hearing that ultimately matters.

The second element in the production of faith is this 'word of Christ'. Faith comes out of hearing, and that kind of hearing comes by – through the instrumentality of – this word of Christ, which means the word about Christ. The Apostle is constantly saying this sort of thing. This is how God saves. You have it in 1 Corinthians 1:21: 'For after that in the wisdom of God the world by wisdom knew not God, it pleased God by the foolishness of preaching' – that should be 'by the foolishness of the thing preached', 'the report', 'the message' – 'to save them that believe'.

What, then, is the message? What is this thing that is regarded as 'foolishness' by the world? Well, as Paul tells us, it is the message about Christ. 'The Jews require a sign, and the Greeks seek after wisdom: but we preach Christ crucified' [*1 Cor.* 1:22–23]. It is the word about Christ crucified, who is 'the power of God, and the wisdom of God' – it is the whole message of salvation in and through our Lord and Saviour Jesus Christ.

Now what we draw from that is that faith is always related to that message. It is that message applied by the Spirit to the mind and the heart that produces faith. There are two elements in the production of faith. There is the operation of the Spirit, and there is the 'word of Christ', the message of salvation. You will never have faith without these two factors. You can never have such a thing as general faith. Faith is always specific and it is always about Christ. There is no saving faith unless it is centred on Jesus Christ and Him crucified.

People may think they believe in God, they may think they are being blessed by God, but if their faith is not centred on Jesus Christ and Him crucified, it is of no avail. 'Other foundation can no man lay than that is laid, which is Jesus Christ' [*1 Cor.* 3:11]. This is the only message that the Holy Spirit will ever honour. And it is only when this word about Christ comes to us powerfully in the Spirit, and is made efficacious to us by the Spirit, that we have faith.

So we have the Apostle James telling us what we are as the result of the operation of the Word. 'Of his own will begat he us with the word of truth, that we should be a kind of firstfruits of his creatures' [*Jas.* 1:18]. Yes, but it is the Word applied by the Spirit. The seed is in the Word, and then the Spirit plants it and applies it. He opens our heart, and the result is, new birth!

Or take it as Peter puts it: 'Who by him do believe in God, that raised him up from the dead, and gave him glory; that your faith and hope might be in God. Seeing ye have purified your souls in obeying the truth' [*1 Pet.* 1:21–22]. Then in verse 23: 'Being born again, not of corruptible seed, but of incorruptible, by the word of God, which liveth and abideth for ever.' That is it! This word about Christ. And that, planted, applied by the power of the Holy Spirit, results in faith; faith comes out of this.

Or we can find it all in one verse in 1 Thessalonians 1:5: 'Our gospel came not unto you in word only' – it did come in word, it must, it is the word about Christ, and it is a particular word – 'but also in power, and in the Holy Ghost, and in much assurance.' The Apostle knew, as he was preaching to those Thessalonians, that they were hearing in this 'faith' manner, that the Lord was 'opening their hearts'. He knew it; he had much assurance about it. It came 'in power, and in the Holy Ghost, and in much assurance'. Faith comes out of – is produced by – that Word of God as it is applied and planted in us by the Holy Spirit.

That is why some believe and some do not. It is not enough just to hear the Word. Has the Lord opened your heart? Has the Word come with power to you? Has it come with conviction? Has it come with assurance? That is what decides it. Though the Word is preached to the whole world, all do not believe it. The principle that Paul laid down in chapter 9 of Romans is as definite here in chapter 10 as it was there. It is all of grace! 'By grace are ye saved through faith; and that not of yourselves: it is the gift of God' [*Eph. 2*:8].

Thirty

*

But they have not all obeyed the gospel. For Esaias saith, Lord, who hath believed our report? So then faith cometh by hearing, and hearing by the word of God.   Romans 10:16–17

In our consideration of these verses we have arrived at the point where we have seen that merely to hear the message does not of necessity mean anything at all. It is possible for us to listen to the preaching of the gospel all our lives and still remain unsaved, still be lost and go to hell. We have heard it, in a sense, but we have not heard it in this vital sense that leads to faith; we have not really heard the message of Christ. So I have suggested that the great question which we should all be considering is this: Have I truly heard the gospel? I have listened to it, I have heard it with my outer ear, as it were, but have I heard it with the inner ear? Has it really come to me? Has it led to faith? Or, if you like the question in a different form: What are the marks or the signs of true hearing, the hearing of faith?

Now the Apostle answers the question himself here. He raises it, then he answers it, and he says that there are two main tests which we must always apply to ourselves over this matter of hearing the gospel. So many people assume that, because they have been brought up to go to a place of worship, have listened to preaching, and are familiar with its statements, they are Christians. But clearly they are not. That is the whole point that Paul is making. How can we tell, then, whether our hearing has been a living hearing, a true hearing that has led to faith?

Well, the first test, Paul says, is the test of *obedience*. He puts that in this form: 'But they have not all obeyed the gospel.' He does not say that they have not all heard the gospel, because they have all heard. That is the point he is making and he is going on to repeat that. He will say in verse 18, 'Their sound went into all the earth, and their

[333]

words unto the ends of the world.' But the question is, he says: Have they obeyed the gospel?

Now this is a most important statement. I have mentioned, in passing, that the actual word used by the Apostle, which is here translated as 'obeyed', is very interesting. It is essentially the same word as the word translated 'report' in verse 16, and translated twice by 'hearing' in verse 17. It has the same root, but it is a compound word, something has been added to it. The word that was used by the Apostle means 'to hear under'. But 'hearing under' what? It is hearing under authority, under power; it is hearing with a sense of compulsion. It is a hearing under such authority and power that you are led to submission and to yielding to what you hear.

That is, I think you will agree, most interesting. That is the meaning of this word translated as 'obeyed'. What is it that leads people to obey? It is that they are hearing *under* the authority. It is not mere hearing, there is something more. There is something in this hearing that humbles people, subdues them and renders them ready to yield and thereby, of course, to give obedience. That is the word that the Apostle uses, and you notice that in this way he differentiates between mechanical hearing and living hearing, between hearing words and hearing 'in the Spirit'.

Now in stressing obedience at this point, Paul is not doing anything at all unusual. This is quite the customary thing with the Apostle himself; we have already found him doing it. For instance, in the first chapter, in verse 5, he says – he is talking about himself as a preacher of the gospel – 'By whom [the Lord Jesus Christ] we have received grace and apostleship, for obedience to the faith among all nations for his name.' And when we were dealing with that chapter, we elaborated this point – there is always the element of obedience in true faith.[1] You will find that the Apostle is so concerned about it that he comes back to it twice over in the last chapter of the Epistle. In verse 19 he says, 'For your obedience is come abroad unto all men. I am glad therefore on your behalf.' There are not many people who listen to the gospel. The thing that makes him glad and proud of them is their obedience. And again in verse 26 he speaks of '*the obedience of faith*'.

You will find the Apostle Peter telling the strangers to whom he wrote that they were 'elect according to the foreknowledge of God

[1] See *An Exposition of Chapter 1: The Gospel of God*, 1985.

the Father, through sanctification of the Spirit, *unto obedience* and sprinkling of the blood of Jesus Christ' [*1 Pet.* 1:1–2]. It is exactly the same thing.

Here in Romans 10, then, the Apostle is laying down for us the first great test which we must apply to ourselves and to all our hearing of the gospel. This is the way, if you like to put it in more modern terms, to tell the difference between faith and what we may call 'believism', or 'fideism', or a mere giving of an intellectual assent to the truth. I believe that this is one of the most urgent problems confronting us today. Why is there so much confusion in the Christian church? Why is there so much confusion as to what makes someone a Christian? Why is there so much confusion as to what the Christian message is? Why are so many people unhappy about themselves and uncertain about exactly where they stand?

Now I believe it is very largely due to this very thing: it is that we have not been careful to define, as the Scriptures do, what we really mean by 'faith'. There are so many people who give an intellectual assent to the truth, but that is not faith. We have got to draw the line between merely accepting propositions, merely giving an agreement with our minds to certain things we hear, and a real and a true faith. That is the distinction the Apostle is drawing, and, as I want to show you, it is the same distinction precisely which is drawn by James in his second chapter.

The way, then, to test the difference between these two things is that in faith there is always this element of obedience. You can agree to the truth but if you do not obey it, it is not faith. And that is a terrible reality; it is a terrible possibility. There are people who can accept the Christian doctrine intellectually but it has never made any difference to them. I have known many such myself. This is one of the most subtle and delicate tests of true faith.

So, then, true faith always leads to action. What sort of action? We have many illustrations of this in the Scriptures. Take, again, the case of Lydia in Philippi as it is put before us in Acts 16. 'A certain woman named Lydia, a seller of purple, of the city of Thyatira, which worshipped God, heard us: whose heart the Lord opened' [*Acts* 16:14]. Now that is the vital thing, as we have seen. That is what produces true hearing, this Word of Christ applied by the Spirit, the heart opened by the Spirit. Nobody can have faith unless the Lord opens the heart. It is impossible. 'The natural man receiveth not the things of the Spirit of God: for they are foolishness unto him: neither can he know them, because they are spiritually discerned' [*1 Cor.* 2:14]. So the Lord opened Lydia's heart through the Spirit and by the Word.

But what I want to emphasise now is what that led to, and this is the proof of its being living faith. '. . . whose heart the Lord opened, that she attended unto the things which were spoken of Paul'. In other words, there was a subtle and immediate change in her type of hearing: this 'attention'. Now that is a part of the action, of obedience. Until you are taken hold of and really give your consent to the listening, it is not true listening, it is not faith. But the moment this action on your part comes in, even in your hearing, it is already a part, and a very vital part, of the obedience.

But there are other things that are equally essential. Obviously, this obedience also includes repentance, and repentance means conviction of sin, a recognition and an admission that we have sinned against God and that our natures are sinful. That is a part of repentance. You cease to defend yourself. As long as you are defending yourself, you have not repented and you have not heard in this 'living faith' sense. But when men and women hear in this true sense, they are convicted; they receive it; they recognise it; they acknowledge it; they confess it; and they stop defending themselves in any way.

Not only that, they renounce sin. Seeing what it is, they hate it and are anxious to leave it. Moreover, they turn to God. Their greatest desire is to be right with God. Now you can hear the same gospel as someone else and yet feel none of these things at all; there is no obedience involved. But the moment it becomes this living hearing, you go through these various steps and you are now anxious to know God. So you turn to Him, and want to please Him.

And then a very vital point comes in just at that very stage. In your old days and before this 'living' thing had happened to you, your immediate reaction would have been to decide to do good works and to say, 'I am going to turn over a new leaf. I am going to do this, that and the other.' But the moment there is true repentance, all that stops. You renounce your own works, you admit that there is no good thing in you, that all your righteousness is as 'filthy rags', and that obviously there is no point in your deciding to live a better life, or, by a great effort of the will, to serve God, because all you do will still be polluted and therefore useless.

So you do not do that. You renounce your good works, your self-reliance, and every attempt at self-justification. This is a part of the obedience of faith. You accept the pronouncement of the Scriptures that none of us can ever justify ourselves before God, that 'by the deeds of the law there shall no flesh be justified in his sight' [*Rom.* 3:20]. You accept it completely, and you prove it in action by not attempting to do anything to save yourself.

Then you accept the teaching concerning the Lord Jesus Christ and His way of salvation. You accept, you believe this message concerning the Lord Jesus Christ as your Sin-bearer, as the One sent by God to reconcile you to God. And not only that, you are ready to confess this. You are ready to acknowledge that He is thus your Saviour and your Lord, that He has bought you with a price, that you are not your own, that you have no right to yourself. You confess Him in the glory of His Person as taught in the Scriptures. You have no doubt, no hesitation, about this. A part of the obedience of faith is to say that 'Jesus is Lord', and He alone, that Caesar is not Lord, nor anybody else, but that this Jesus of Nazareth is the Son of God, as the Apostle has already expounded in verses 9 and 10 of this chapter.

So you make this confession that you rely upon Him, and upon Him alone, that there is no way to God except through Him, and that you do not desire any other way. So you submit to Him and to His yoke. He has said, 'Come unto me, all ye that labour and are heavy laden, and I will give you rest. Take my yoke upon you, and learn of me; for I am meek and lowly in heart . . . For my yoke is easy, and my burden is light' [*Matt.* 11:28–30].

In other words, you commit yourself to Him. This is all a part of 'the obedience of faith', and unless we do these things, we have not heard. It is that other external hearing, it is of no value. Faith, true listening, always leads to this. And, of course, it goes further. It means that we become a part of His people. The Apostle says a very interesting thing in writing to the Thessalonians when discussing the effect the gospel had on them. He says: 'ye became followers of us, and of the Lord, having received the word in much affliction, with joy of the Holy Ghost' [*1 Thess.* 1:5–6]. In other words, they had aligned themselves with the Apostles and with the church. You cannot be a Christian in isolation – you want to be with all other Christians.

Not only that, Paul reminds the believers in Thessalonica that they had 'turned to God from idols' [v. 6]. They had renounced the world; they had forsaken idolatry; they had turned their backs upon it and had aligned themselves with the church. They had been baptised, and in the early church that was not an easy thing to submit to. It might cost you your life. It would almost certainly cost you ostracism from your family. But they had done it. 'In much affliction, with joy of the Holy Ghost', they had joined the church and were exposed to all the opprobrium that was cast upon the followers of this teaching, which was regarded as nothing but a new sect.

And not only that, they had gone on with it. It had not been merely a sudden decision which they had forgotten the next morning. They had not merely rushed to some decision in the church and then disappeared in a month or two. The Apostle thanks God for those Thessalonians, especially for their 'work of faith', 'labour of love', and 'patience of hope'. They had gone on! In spite of persecution and all that was against them, they had persisted as Christian people in the Christian church.

There, then, I have tried to give some indication of what is included in this term 'obedience'. Our Lord Himself has said all this perfectly in His famous parable of the man with the two sons in Matthew 21:28–32. Our Lord's point is that an essential part of repentance is actually *doing* God's will. This boy's father told him to go and work in his vineyard. The son first said that he would not do this, 'but afterward he repented' – yes, but it does not stop there – 'afterward he repented, *and went*'. He might have merely changed his mind and said to himself, 'I should not have spoken like that to my father; I should not have said, "I will not" to him. He has a right to command me. I was very wrong indeed to say "I will not".' Now if he had just thought that and even said that, but had done nothing, he would not have repented; but, 'he repented, and went'.

So it was his action of going to the vineyard and doing the thing that the father had told him to do that gives proof of his repentance. That is what is emphasised by our Lord. The other son said that he would go but then he did not; and the fact that he said, 'I will go', was of no value, because he did not. It is a vital part of repentance that we should act upon what we say or what we feel. Now that is what the Apostle is emphasising. The difference between these two hearings is first of all to be measured by this test of obedience.

Two comments, surely, are called for at this point. I cannot leave it like that or I shall be misunderstood. Indeed, this point has very often been misunderstood. What is the danger? The first one is this. Have I now been preaching justification by works or have I not? What does 'justification by faith only' mean? Someone may say to me, 'But if you are telling us that we have got to do all these things in addition to believing, then you are surely teaching justification by works. You are saying it is what we do that saves us, not our faith.' That is the great old question, is it not, and it is very important that we should be clear about this.

Now this is the point that has so often been put by those who try to show a contrast between the teaching of the Apostle Paul and the Apostle James. The answer is, of course, that there is no contradiction whatsoever between them. I say that, not only because I believe that the whole of the New Testament is inspired by the Holy Spirit and that James therefore is as authorised and as divinely inspired as Paul. That is not my only reason. Actually I can show you that they are not saying anything different. Scripture does not contradict Scripture, and there is no question of that arising at this point.

Let us, then, approach it like this. We must be careful to preach justification by faith only. That is the cardinal doctrine. That is the whole point of this Epistle to the Romans. That was the grand re-discovery that came to Martin Luther, revealed to him by the Spirit of God. Justification by faith only. Not by human works, not by the church, not by priesthood, not by anything; faith only. That is central; we hold on to it.

But, then, what about James; what about these extraordinary statements of his? Well, there is obviously only one explanation at this point – it is the way in which James uses the word 'faith'. He means by faith what I have been calling 'believism'. James, you see, had to deal with people who kept on saying, 'Ah, I believe in the Lord', but who were living a life that was the exact opposite. So James says, in effect, 'It is no use your saying "I believe" unless you really do believe. Saying that you believe does not mean faith. Real faith,' says James, 'is something deeper than that.' 'As the body without the spirit is dead, so faith without works is dead also' [*Jas.* 2:26].

Now by that, James is saying exactly the same thing as the Apostle Paul. They have all heard, yes, but have they all obeyed? There is no faith, says Paul, unless they have obeyed. If there is no obedience, there is no faith. That is what they are both saying; it is simply the way in which James puts it. But he clears up the whole thing in the last verse of chapter 2. He is saying – and this is the sum of the whole sub-ject – that true faith always leads to works; true faith always reveals itself through works. And there would be no way of telling whether we have got the right hearing or the wrong hearing if we had not got this way of testing out faith. These things can never be separated.

True faith is always active; it is always operative; it always leads to something; it is never merely intellectual.

Romans 6:17 says it all: 'God be thanked, that ye were the servants of sin, but ye have *obeyed* from the heart that form of [sound words] or doctrine which was delivered you.' There it is again. 'You have obeyed' – there is your will; 'from the heart' – there are your affections and emotions; 'that form of [sound] doctrine that was delivered to you' – to your mind. If the whole person is not engaged, it is not faith. It may be intellectual assent, or it may be a mechanical conformity to some law, but that is not faith. 'They have not all obeyed the gospel.'

So, then, there is no contradiction between James and Paul – and this is a vital part of the preaching of justification by faith only. You are not justified by saying, 'I believe.' You are not justified by saying, 'Lord, Lord!' As we have seen, our Lord Himself says that people will come and say that to Him at the end, and He will say, 'I never knew you: depart from me, ye that work iniquity' [*Matt.* 7:23]. So these are very profound matters which we must always be careful to apply to ourselves.

Now let me put it another way to re-enforce the whole thing. The gospel is a call to obedience. The Apostle Paul preaching in Athens said, 'God now commandeth all men every where to repent' [*Acts* 17:30]. It is a command and it calls for response, for obedience.

The great danger that people fall into is this: they forget that an essential part of biblical teaching in connection with election and predestination is to assert, at the same time, our responsibility. If you preach that doctrine in such a way as to make each person an automaton or a machine, you are doing violence to the Scripture. The Apostle Paul, who preaches the doctrine so powerfully in Romans 9, is equally careful to assert our responsibility.

Paul holds the Jews responsible for the rejection of the gospel. They ought to have known. We shall see that still more clearly when we come to the remaining verses of this chapter.

But, you see, he has really laid it all down in principle in chapter 1. He says, 'For the wrath of God is revealed from heaven against all ungodliness and unrighteousness of men, who hold the truth in unrighteousness' – notice this – 'because that which may be known of God is manifest in them; for God hath shewed it unto them. For the invisible things of him from the creation of the world are clearly seen, being understood by the things that are made, even his eternal power and Godhead, so that they are without excuse' [*Rom.* 1:18–20]. We should believe in God, and creation itself robs us of any excuse. So we are responsible.

'But I thought you said that no man can save himself?' you ask.

You are quite right.

'I thought you said,' says somebody, 'that we are saved as the result of God's election of grace.'

Perfectly right. But that does not mean that we are not responsible. We must always take these two things together. No man can save himself. No man can take pride in his salvation and say, 'I am saved because I believed.' That is wrong. Faith is the gift of God. All who are saved are saved because God has foreknown them, chosen them, predestinated and called them. Yes, but those who hear the gospel and who do not believe it are responsible for their unbelief. And the Apostle is nailing that upon these Jews. They should have obeyed the gospel.

Now modern men and women claim that they have free will. Very well, they are condemning themselves out of their own mouths. If they have free will, why do they not believe the gospel? That will be their condemnation at the day of judgment when God displays His eternal righteousness. So then, all I am concerned to say is that this element of obedience is always a vital part of the preaching of the gospel. We are held responsible, but at the same time we are totally incapable of saving ourselves or doing anything which is righteous in the sight of God. Our salvation is entirely in the Lord Jesus Christ. It is the free gift of God in Him.

'But,' you say, 'I don't understand all this.'

I am not asking you to understand, my friend. It is what we call an 'antinomy', and an antinomy means that there are things taught us in the Scriptures which we, with our finite and fallen minds, cannot reconcile. There is a reconciliation and we will see it in eternity. What we must do in this world of time is to submit ourselves, as little children, to the Scriptures. And if you say to me, 'I do not understand and therefore I do not believe', I tell you that you are guilty of disobedience. The election of God is taught in the Scriptures, it is there in Romans 9, and we have got to believe it. Yes, but individual responsibility is taught equally plainly and we must believe that also. Do not reject one or the other; you must hold the two together. I put it like this, when we were studying chapter 9. No one is responsible for his or her salvation, but all those who are not saved are responsible for their damnation.[1] That is the first comment.

The second is this question of obedience. 'Ah,' says somebody, and very rightly, 'I have known people who have suddenly taken up belief in a cult. They have been unhappy, or have had a problem in their lives. Then they are taken to a meeting and they hear a teaching and they accept it and become devotees of it, and change their lives. What about them? You were saying that the test of true belief and faith is obedience, and here are people whose whole lives have been changed, who have stopped doing what they used to do, and are now very active and very zealous. And yet, I am not quite happy about them as Christians because when we come to talk about the way of salvation, they do not seem to know much about it. What about them?'

Now that is a good question, and I think the answer to it is this. There is all the difference in the world between the practice of an imposed system of life and the obedience that is the inevitable result of a comprehension of the truth.

Let me try to expound that. Take these cults, or even take religion – the Jews' religion and a so-called Christianity that is not Christianity at all. You can become religious, you can become a church member and a very active one, but you still may not be a Christian.

'But,' you say, 'look what I am doing. Is that not obedience? Does that not prove my faith?'

But you must test your belief. I am not saying that obedience alone proves that someone is a Christian. It is an 'obedience of *faith*' and you remember the things that I enumerated. There is involved a belief in the Person of the Lord, in His atoning sacrificial death, in His resurrection, His ascension, His heavenly session and so on. This wrong type of obedience, if I may so term it, always strikes me as being what I would call the 'boy scout' type of obedience. You know, you join an organisation and ask, 'What are the rules?'

'Well, the rules of this society are these . . .'

'Ah, good! I am going to keep them.'

And so you become a good scout. You do your good deeds and you tick them off day by day; you are keeping the system. But that is not the obedience the Apostle is talking about. The obedience he is talking about is this: when the Holy Spirit has brought the Word of God to you, when He has really brought the Word of God to your mind and heart and conscience and will, and you are humbled and

[1] See *An Exposition of Chapter 9: God's Sovereign Purpose*, 1991.

subdued by it, and you really see the truth. Then, out of the very depth of your being, comes this desire to please Him. You see the difference? It is the difference between taking something up and trying to practise it, and something that comes, inevitably, right out of your heart, from the very depth of your being, as your response to the grace of God in Jesus Christ our Lord.

Now this is, I think, most important, for we are living in days of great activism, and there are many people who think that because they are doing things, they are Christians. They are, again, exactly like those people of whom our Lord speaks at the end of the Sermon on the Mount who not only said, 'Lord, Lord', but went on to say, 'Have we not prophesied in thy name? and in thy name have cast out devils?' [*Matt.* 7:22]. They said! They did! But it was no good. It was not this obedience that comes out of the heart.

Go back again to Romans 6:17: 'ye have obeyed from the heart'. If there is not this kind of divine inevitability about our obedience, it is not the obedience of faith. It is not that we decide to live a certain type of life but that we say, 'I can do no other. I must!' Philip Doddridge in his hymn puts it so well:

> My gracious Lord, I own thy right
> To every service I can pay;
> And count it my supreme delight
> To hear thy dictates and obey.

That is obedience from the heart. It is inevitable; it comes out of faith; it cannot help itself. It is not something that one puts on; it is something that moves from within outwards. I think I once compared the difference to the difference between a bought Christmas-tree on which you hang bits of artificial fruit and flowers, and a living tree out in the orchard. That is the difference. They may look very much alike. People are very clever and they can make things that look like fruit and flowers. But actually they are very different. The fruit on one is artificial, on a dead tree, but on the other it grows from the sap, from the life of the tree. That is the difference. And this is the living obedience about which the Apostle is speaking.

Thirty-one

*

But they have not all obeyed the gospel. For Esaias saith, Lord, who hath believed our report? So then faith cometh by hearing, and hearing by the word of God.   Romans 10:16–17

We have begun to look at the two tests which the Apostle gives us to see if we have 'heard' the gospel. We have dealt with the first, which is the test of obedience, and we have seen what that means.

And now that brings us to our second test, which is the test of *joy*. We have seen how the Apostle quotes the words of Isaiah: 'How beautiful upon the mountains are the feet of him that bringeth good tidings, that publisheth peace; that bringeth good tidings of good.' This, again, is a most important matter: not only obedience, but also this further test of joy.

We looked at this, in a sense, when we were dealing with the character of the message. A part of the proclamation is that it is 'good news', and if our preaching is not good news, it is not Christian preaching. It may be morality and many other things, but it is not the gospel. Now we are looking at it from the other side, and it is really one of the most vital tests of all.

When men and women truly hear the gospel, they know exactly what it is to say, 'How beautiful, coming over the mountains, are the feet of this messenger who is bearing this message to me.' Joy is implicit in that. It is good to see the messenger because of the message which he brings. And, of course, Paul further emphasises this in the quotation by talking about 'glad tidings of good things'. Here, then, is a most vital test which we apply to ourselves. What sort of hearing is it? How have I heard this gospel? And the test is: Has it made me rejoice?

Now this is the great characteristic of receiving the gospel in a true sense, and it is clearly seen everywhere in the New Testament. Our

Lord Himself made it very plain. Take the three parables that are recorded in Luke 15. You remember the element that is common to the three? Take the lost sheep. When the owner finds his lost sheep, he invites his friends to join him, and he says, 'Rejoice with me!' The woman whose lost coin is found likewise wants her neighbours to rejoice with her. The father of the prodigal son makes a feast, and there is great rejoicing. This, as our Lord points out there, is ever to be the characteristic of a true hearing of the gospel.

But let me give you a still more specific statement of this from John 16:22: 'And ye now therefore have sorrow: but I will see you again, and your heart shall rejoice, and your joy no man taketh from you.' Our Lord prophesies that that is to be the effect of His gospel upon His people. And, of course, when you turn to the book of Acts, you see that in practice. The moment these early Christians were baptised with the Holy Spirit, they were filled with joy, so much so that some people thought they were drunk! 'These men,' they said, 'are full of new wine' [*Acts* 2:13]. It was this obvious exultation, this happiness. That is how this Christian joy shows itself; it is evident to everybody that you are filled with joy.

And then we find it in specific words at the end of chapter 2 of Acts: 'And they continuing daily with one accord in the temple, and breaking bread from house to house, did eat their meat with gladness and singleness of heart, praising God, and having favour with all the people' [vv. 46–47]. Now that is Christianity. These people had heard the message and that was their response – gladness and praising God.

Then you go on to the next chapter, to the incident of the impotent man who was laid every day at the Beautiful Gate of the temple. The moment this man was healed and received the truth, we find him walking and leaping. 'He walked, and entered with them into the temple, walking, and leaping, and praising God' [*Acts* 3:8]. That, again, is Christianity.

And, indeed, there is a notable instance of this joy in Acts 8 in the story of the Ethiopian eunuch. The man had seen the truth and been baptised. And this is the last glimpse we have of this converted man: 'He went on his way rejoicing' [*Acts* 8:39]. It had been a very brief encounter with Philip, but Philip had opened the Scriptures and preached the gospel to him; and there was the man going on his way rejoicing.

Take also the case of the Philippian jailor. 'And when he had brought them [Paul and Silas] into his house, he set meat before them, and rejoiced, believing in God with all his house' [*Acts* 16:34]. That was the effect of hearing the message. This man had been desperate just a very short time before. He had pulled out his sword and had been on the verge of committing suicide. You cannot imagine a more unhappy and dejected man. But here he was rejoicing and 'believing in God with all his house'.

You find this note everywhere in the Epistles. 'Rejoice in the Lord alway: and again I say, Rejoice' [*Phil.* 4:4]. You will find it in Peter: 'Whom having not seen, ye love; in whom, though now ye see him not, yet believing, ye rejoice with joy unspeakable and full of glory' [*1 Pet.* 1:8]. That is New Testament Christianity. They were a rejoicing people. And, as John writes his First Epistle, he tells those people to whom he is writing, 'These things write we unto you, [in order] that your joy may be full' [*1 John* 1:4]. We are, therefore, entitled to say that, according to the teaching of the New Testament, the great characteristic of true hearing of the gospel is 'rejoicing' – not merely that you know what it says, not merely that you give an obedience to it, but that you *rejoice*! The Apostle says – I quote again Romans 6:17 – 'Ye have obeyed *from the heart*.' You do not merely obey because you are afraid of hell, or because it is the thing to do in Christian circles, you obey from the heart – this element of emotion comes in, the joy. It is glad surrender.

And, of course, as you come to read church history, you find that the same thing is true. Those early Christians, even when they were martyred, were still rejoicing. That was what really shook the ancient world. Whatever you did to these people, they rejoiced. We have seen in 1 Thessalonians 1:6 how the Apostle says that they had received the gospel in great affliction, but 'with joy of the Holy Ghost'. It did not matter what you did to them: you could persecute them, you could malign them, you could abuse them, even if everything went against them, they were still rejoicing. Even those thrown to the lions in the arena were still a rejoicing people.

Now, of course, it is well known that the great characteristic of every period of reformation and true revival is that this element of joy always returns with power. There has never been a revival without great rejoicing, and the greatest hymns of rejoicing have generally come out of such periods. This is a universal principle, therefore, which is to be seen not only in the Scriptures but also in the subsequent preaching of this same gospel by the church, and it makes no difference where, on what continent, or in what clime. Some people think that you can divide up the human race according to the areas of climatic conditions in which they live. The people nearer the Equator are said to be more emotional than those living in the cold north – but you have had as much rejoicing in the Lord in the north as in the south!

This rejoicing is universal. It does not depend upon people's temperament or psychology. Joy is the effect of true hearing. The most stolid is made to praise. I admit that there are variations and that our temperaments remain, but what I am saying is that if the most stolid individual does not know what it is to rejoice, he had better make sure that he has really heard the gospel, that he is not merely an intellectual who says, 'I have heard that before, I know that.'

So what the Apostle is saying is this: The Jews have not rejoiced in it; they have rejected it. You either reject the gospel or else you rejoice in it. It is one or the other, not merely believing but rejoicing! Joy is implicit in a true hearing and in a true believing. And that is the charge that the Apostle is bringing against his fellow-countrymen – that they had not welcomed these messengers of Christ, the Messiah. They had not been delighted to see them coming over the mountains. They had failed to realise that they were bringing 'glad tidings of good things'.

We must examine this, therefore, and I want to do so in a very practical and contemporary manner. I would like to put it in the form of a question. How much of this joy is there in the Christian church today? How much do we know ourselves? We who are familiar with this gospel and have heard it so often, do we respond in this way? Is the church today rejoicing? Is she like the New Testament church? Do we see ourselves in the book of the Acts of the Apostles? They were like that because they had heard this message, they had received this good news. That was their response. Have we so heard the gospel? And if there is an absence of this joy, why is it?

This is a very serious matter. In this country today, why are the masses of people outside the Christian church? For myself, I have no hesitation in answering that they are outside because we have altogether failed to have the impact that the first Christians had upon their contemporaries. We have given the impression that to be a Christian means to be miserable, and to have more problems than anybody else, so the world says it does not want Christianity; it says it has got happiness without it. It has not, of course, but we certainly do not look as though we have happiness.

I am afraid that this is a true charge. So why is this rejoicing absent? I know of no more urgent question than this. To me this is the whole key to evangelism. The early church did not evangelise by mass meetings. They did not have them. The old world was evangelised by individual Christians who had this quality of life that aroused in others a curiosity, perhaps, to begin with, and then a desire to have what the Christians had got.

This has always been the way. When people give this impression that because they are Christians, they are a joyful people, others are immediately ready to pay attention. But if they are just groping their way along, carrying great burdens and are looking glum and unhappy, then it is not surprising that people are not attracted and do not want to listen to the preaching of the gospel. So this is an urgent matter, both from our own experiences and from the standpoint of the spread of the gospel of salvation. Every Christian, in other words, ought to be like a messenger coming over the top of the mountain with good news for people who have not got it.

What, then, is lacking? Or, to put it positively, what are the things that are essential about 'hearing' before it leads to this joy? Now, it seems to me that it is all implicit in the quotation that the Apostle makes [v.15] from Isaiah 52:7. What is it that leads to the rejoicing? The first thing, beyond any question, is this: it is an active realisation of our state by nature.

You see, there are contrasts here. As I have explained, Isaiah puts it in terms of the captivity of the children of Israel in Babylon. There they are, in Babylon, and they cannot sing the Lord's song in a strange land. They have hung up their harps on the willow trees and they cannot sing [*Psa.* 137:4 and 2]. How can people sing in captivity? But, suddenly, here comes a man with a message, and immediately they begin to sing! So what is it that makes people sing? The first thing is negative. It is, I repeat, a realisation of our state by nature.

Now let me remind you of what that is. It is that we are fallen, as the Apostle has been elaborating in the earlier part of this great Epistle. It is that 'All have sinned, and come short of the glory of God' [*Rom.* 3:23]. That knowledge is essential. Not only that. It means a realisation that we have a sinful nature – all that the Apostle tells us in the seventh chapter of this Epistle. This is the sort of thing he says about himself: 'We know that the law is spiritual: but I am carnal, sold under sin' [v. 14]. Then he goes on, 'I know that in me (that is, in my flesh,) dwelleth no good thing' [v. 18]. 'O wretched man that I am!' (v. 24].

That is the sort of thing to which I am referring. It means that we understand that we are 'shapen in iniquity' [*Psa.* 51:5]. And we cannot realise that without being unhappy. We hate this fallen, twisted, perverted, evil nature, this contrast and contradiction within us. 'I delight in the law of God after the inward man: but I see another law in my members, warring against the law of my mind, and bringing me into captivity to the law of sin which is in my members' [*Rom.* 7:22–23]. It is a horrible thing, a hateful thing, a depressing thing. So we must realise that and, furthermore, we must realise that we are under the dominion of Satan and of sin, slaves of the world, the flesh and the devil. As Paul says in Romans 6:17, we 'were the servants [slaves] of sin . . .' Slaves! And the Apostle says in verse 14 of the same chapter: 'Sin shall not have dominion over you.' Everybody born into this world is under this dominion. This 'Peter Pan' notion of life is just nonsense. It is not true – and the world is proving that it is not true.

But still more terrible is the realisation that we are under the wrath of God. This is what the Apostle has been reminding these Romans about with such force. As he says to the Ephesians, we are all 'by nature the children of wrath' [*Eph.* 2:3]. And he says the same thing in the very first chapter of Romans. He rejoices in the gospel, he is not ashamed of it, 'for it is the power of God unto salvation to every one that believeth' [v. 16]. And, especially, he says, 'For the wrath of God is revealed from heaven against all ungodliness and unrighteousness of men, who hold [down] the truth in unrighteousness' [v. 18].

Now that is the realisation that comes to men and women when they truly hear the gospel – that because of their fallen condition, because of their evil nature, because of the sins that they have committed, they are under the wrath of God. That in turn means that when they die, they will have to stand before God in judgment and, because they are sinners, that judgment upon sin is punishment, hell and retribution, which leads to endless misery. The preaching of the gospel brings people to the realisation of that.

In other words, they realise that they are completely hopeless, that they are guilty before God and have the guilt of sin upon them. They see that they are under the power of sin and that they suffer from its pollution. That is the position of every one of us by nature, and it is the gospel alone that brings us to see that. And not only are we hopeless, we are helpless. We think, 'Very well, because of this, I must begin to put myself right.' We take our decisions; we make our resolutions. We are going to live a better life; we are going to be better people. We propose! But then we realise immediately that we can do nothing, that we are paralysed, that we are completely helpless – do what we will, it will avail us nothing.

'Oh dear me,' says somebody, 'this does not sound very much like joy and rejoicing to me!' Of course not! But this is the essential preliminary to that. What I am trying to say is that there is never true joy until there has been a thorough preliminary 'law-work'. It is only those who realise their state who rejoice when they hear the gospel. These things work by contrasts, and I feel that that is what is missing at the present time. Children are coming to the birth too easily, too readily. 'They have healed also the hurt of the daughter of my people slightly [quickly], saying, Peace, peace; when there is no peace' [*Jer.* 6:14].

So the absence of a profound joy is, I suggest, due to the fact that we are in too much of a hurry; we are too anxious to count heads; we are too interested in results. There is not sufficient 'law-work'. Men and women have not realised where they are and what they are and what is going to happen to them. It is those who realise that who rejoice when they hear the gospel. But if it is just a question of taking a decision, or joining a church, or turning over a new leaf, or joining a company – well, you can do that and you never feel much on the one side or the other. We are too ready to repeat formulae; we are too ready to give assent to a kind of 'believism', and this is, of course, the sole explanation of the absence of a deep joy.

Our Lord recalls a very interesting incident concerning a self-righteous Pharisee, Simon, and a repentant sinful woman who anointed Christ's feet [*Luke* 7:36–47]. That Pharisee's need was as great as the need of this notorious sinner. The woman realised she was a sinner and thanked Him for His love and mercy and compassion. But the Pharisee, being a self-righteous man, did not realise his need of forgiveness. Therefore there was no love, and no rejoicing. That illustrates what I am saying. It is the people who realise the depth of their sin, the evil of their nature, the hopelessness of their position, the damnation of hell and all that follows – it is they, when they see the nature of the gospel, who rejoice.

A minister who had won first prize for sweet peas told me that the secret of his success was to dig deep – to a depth corresponding to the desired height of the stalk. And it is exactly the same in this realm.

You have got to have a deep conviction of sin before you will have a great joy, and we all need that deep conviction. You do not get that in terms of the number of sins you have committed, you get it by realising that your relationship with God has been broken. Why do we not rejoice in God? That is the sin. It is not acts of sin, it is my failed relationship with Him. I should live to the glory of God with all my being; I should love Him with all my heart, soul, mind and strength, and my neighbour as myself. God deserves it and God demands it. So if I am not giving it, I am a terrible sinner.

But, you see, we judge sinfulness in terms of particular sins and, like the Pharisee, because we have not been guilty of the sins of this notorious woman we do not think we are sinners at all. There is nothing that so controls the height of joy as the depth of the realisation of our sinfulness, our utter hopelessness as we are by nature. There is never great joy when the preaching is superficial. There is never great rejoicing when there is not much 'law-work', when there is not a deep conviction of sin.

Read the history of revivals of the past and you will find that people used to go through agonies of conviction, not because they were notorious sinners, but because they realised that they did not know God, and that they had not had a desire for Him. They had not read the Bible, they had not prayed, and they saw that that meant that they were dead – dead spiritually – and when their physical bodies died they would go to hell, they would never know God. So they began to feel a terror and an alarm. They would groan; they would weep; they would agonise.

How often have you seen that? No, my friends, in every realm of life today we are such believers in quick returns, that the returns we get are not worth having. You have to 'take time to be holy'. You have to take time to get a conviction of sin. You will never know what it is to be thrilled by the sight of the messenger coming across the top of the mountain unless you know what captivity is, unless you realise the truth about yourself.

In other words, you will never get this joy until you have grasped the teaching of the first five chapters of this Epistle to the Romans, indeed, of the whole of the Bible. It is no accident that the Old Testament comes before the New. It is because of what they were, that the people were longing for the coming of the Messiah. The law of the Old Testament always leads to the gospel. The deeper the law-work, the greater the height of the joy. That is the first great essential.

Then I go on to the second, which follows, of course, by a logical necessity. The second element in the joy is the realisation of the true nature of the salvation. Let me give you the headings only. You say you know them? Well, if you do, shame on you if you are not filled with rejoicing! What does the gospel give? It gives us free forgiveness, complete reconciliation to God. 'Being justified by faith, we have peace with God through our Lord Jesus Christ: by whom also we have access into this grace wherein we stand' [*Rom.* 5:1–2]. All that is given to me immediately I understand the truth of this message. Justification by faith only, and also regeneration, increasing liberation from the power, the tyranny, and the pollution of sin. Is it not wonderful that we need not go to our graves still under the dominion of sin and Satan, always groaning and always failing? Progressive sanctification! No longer under the law, but under grace – dead to the law, dead to sin, dead to all that has kept us down.

That is what Paul has been reminding us of – the new liberty and the new power of the children of God and this mighty work of the Spirit within us, changing us from 'glory into glory, till in heaven we take our place'. '. . . changed into the same image, from glory to glory, even as by the Spirit of the Lord' [*2 Cor.* 3:18]. This is this great and glorious salvation! 'Beloved, now are we the sons of God' [*1 John* 3:2]. Now! And if we do not thrill at that – then, what is the matter with us? If you were told you were left a fortune, you would get excited and you would begin to dance and to shout and you would want everybody to know it. But here we are offered something infinitely bigger and greater! We are not only forgiven and reconciled but are literally made the 'children of God', 'partakers of the divine nature' [*2 Pet.* 1:4], 'heirs of God, and joint-heirs with Christ' [*Rom.* 8:16–17]. My dear people, is there not something wrong with us? Why do we not feel as the children of Israel felt when they saw the people coming with the news that the captivity was at an end and that they were to go back? Here is the message of salvation, here is the content of this great salvation.

And then that leads, of course, to what we shall be. 'Beloved, now are we the sons of God, and it doth not yet appear what we shall be: but we know that, when he shall appear, we shall be like him; for we shall see him as he is' [*1 John* 3:2]. 'We . . . rejoice in hope of the glory of God' [*Rom.* 5:2]. You and I are going to be manifested as the children of God, and the whole creation will see it and will be amazed at it. This is the message of salvation. That is the future to which we are looking, all offered us, promised us, by this gospel.

And then, of course, over and above all that, we know about the certainty of it all, do we not? The Apostle has already said, 'I reckon that the sufferings of this present time are not worthy to be compared . . .' [*Rom.* 8:18]. He has said, 'I am persuaded, that neither death, nor life, nor angels, nor principalities, nor powers, nor things present, nor things to come, nor height, nor depth, nor any other creature shall be able to separate us from the love of God, which is in Christ Jesus our Lord' [*Rom.* 8:38–39]. The thing is certain. Nothing can stop it; nothing can ever rob us of it all. All this glory which is being prepared for us is going to be ours, and no one and nothing can ever rob us of it. That is a part of the message.

And then above all, of course, the Lord Himself, the One who comes. 'He came and preached peace to you which were afar off, and to them that were nigh' [*Eph.* 2:17]. The gospel was first preached by Him, and, 'The common people heard him gladly' [*Mark* 12:37]. Of course! Because they were 'common people', they were poor, despised and neglected. The wise and the mighty did not welcome Him, and He said, 'I thank thee, O Father, Lord of heaven and earth, because thou hast hid these things from the wise and prudent, and hast revealed them unto babes' [*Matt.* 11:25]. The common people heard him gladly! The woman washed His feet with her tears, and anointed them with ointment, the most precious thing she had. Why? Well, He had brought her a message of forgiveness, of hope and renewal, and of wonderful possibilities, and she poured out her thanksgiving, her joy and her praise upon His very feet. She realised who He was!

And it is only as you and I realise that 'God so loved the world, that he gave' – not a prophet, but – 'his only begotten Son' [*John* 3:16], it is only as we are gripped by the thrill and the marvel and the wonder of the incarnation and all that it involved and cost Him, and all He did here on earth in His life and obedience and, above all, in His death, His burial and His rising – it is only as we realise this, that we shall be filled with joy. 'Rejoice in the Lord alway: and again I say, Rejoice,' said Paul [*Phil.* 4:4]. It is He who has made it all possible. You not only look at His feet, as it were, you realise to whom the feet belong, and you see the Son of God coming out of heaven, over the ramparts, down into this world, and the marvel of all His glorious action, and if you are not moved to joy by it, then there is something wrong in the hearing, is there not?

Of course, the devil does not want us to rejoice in these things. He does not want the Lord Jesus Christ to be praised – he will do anything to stop that. But once we really hear these things, once we really know them, then we shall be filled with joy unspeakable and full of glory. But I must ask again: Have we got this joy? Now the devil may try to counterfeit it. So how do we tell the difference between a false joy and a true joy?

There are many tests. The joy of Christian men and women, the joy which is produced by the Holy Spirit, is the joy of those who have looked into hell and who know that they have been saved from that only by the fact that the Son of God came into the world, died upon that cross, was buried and rose again. That is it! It is never glib, it is never artificial, it is never the mere backslapping type of happiness. There is a depth about it; it is the joy of the Holy Spirit. There is something profound about it. There is an element of awe in it. It is a very serious joy. The devil's counterfeit is always glib and easy, but there is never any lightness about the joy of the Lord. Never!

It is the joy that you get in a man like the Apostle Paul. Here is a man who can say, 'We that are in this tabernacle do groan, being burdened . . .' 'We groan, earnestly desiring to be clothed upon with our house which is from heaven' [2 Cor. 4:4, 2]. Here is a man who says in Romans 8:23: 'Not only they' – speaking about creation – 'but ourselves also, which have the firstfruits of the Spirit, even we ourselves groan within ourselves, waiting for the adoption, to wit, the redemption of our body.' Now that sounds contradictory, does it not? How can such a man say to others, 'Rejoice evermore', and 'Rejoice in the Lord alway: and again I say, Rejoice'? You say, 'What right has he got to tell people to rejoice if he says that he himself, and all who have the firstfruits of the Spirit, "groan within ourselves, waiting for the adoption"?'

But there is no contradiction at all. This is the great characteristic of the true joy, the joy of the Lord, the Christian joy. It is a serious joy, a profound joy. It is a rejoicing with trembling, as it were, because you realise that, were it not for the grace of God, you would be without hope. You realise you were so desperate, so evil, so vile, that nothing less than this could ever have delivered you. So it is a sober joy; it is a holy joy; there is nothing carnal about it, nothing glib, nothing superficial. It is not an assumed joy; it is not a false joy; but it is indeed the joy of the Lord, the joy of the Holy Spirit.

So this is the thing by which we test ourselves. Have I heard the gospel? Well, has it led to obedience, and has it led to this joy? You can have degrees of this, I know, but I still ask: Have you really got the elements of this joy in you? Do you know anything about it? It is inconceivable that we can truly have heard and understood the gospel and what it means, negatively and positively, without knowing the joy of the Lord, the joy of salvation, something of that joy which is 'unspeakable and full of glory' [*1 Pet.* 1:8].

God grant that we may know something of this feeling of seeing with rejoicing and wonder, the feet of the messenger bringing us the glad tidings of good things which shall abide for evermore.

Thirty-two

*

> *But I say, Have they not heard? Yes verily, their sound went into all the earth, and their words unto the ends of the world. But I say, Did not Israel know? First Moses saith, I will provoke you to jealousy by them that are no people, and by a foolish nation I will anger you. But Esaias is very bold, and saith, I was found of them that sought me not; I was made manifest unto them that asked not after me. But to Israel he saith, All day long I have stretched forth my hands unto a disobedient and gainsaying people.*
> Romans 10:18–21

We come here to the final subsection of the tenth chapter of the Epistle to the Romans. In these last verses, the Apostle sums up the whole argument of the entire chapter and, in particular, he sums up and concludes what he has just been saying in the previous subsection. So these are very important verses.

We indicated at the beginning that we regard this tenth chapter as a kind of 'excursus', almost a digression, if you like. The main argument of the Apostle with respect to the Jews would, in a sense, be quite complete if we went from the end of chapter 9 to the beginning of chapter 11, but, as is his custom, Paul likes to put a case fully and finally, and so he elaborates it. The main problem, of course, is this particular case of the Jew; this astounding fact that our Lord, when He came into the world, 'came unto his own, and his own received him not' [*John* 1:11]. That is the theme with which the Apostle is dealing, as we have seen in this chapter, he has been bringing out, with particular clarity, the fact that this whole tragedy is because the Jews 'stumbled at that stumblingstone' [9:32] – namely, Christ and justification by faith only. And in their folly, they went about 'to establish their own righteousness', though they could never actually do so.

So Paul has been telling us that God's way of salvation has always been the same, and it has been this: 'Whosoever shall call upon the name of the Lord shall be saved' [v. 13]. And that has led him to say that God has given absolute proof of this by calling preachers. God would never have sent messengers forth to preach were this not His own ordained way of saving men and women. And Paul has dealt with that, as we have seen, in great detail.

Then he raised a further question by means of another quotation, again from the prophet Isaiah. 'But they have not all obeyed the gospel.' And this is the subject that he is finally going to deal with. We have already partially seen the answer to the question as to why people, particularly the Jews, reject the gospel, but the Apostle is now going to take it up in detail, and he does so in this most interesting way. He says, 'But I say . . .' – and, you notice, he writes that twice over, and again in chapter 11.

Now that is one of Paul's favourite ways of conducting an argument. It is, indeed, a very emphatic and effective way of arguing, a very good method for all of us to employ. You put up a rhetorical question and then you answer it. In other words, what the Apostle is doing is this: having argued out God's way of salvation, he is now going to apply it to this particular case of the Jews, and he will go on in chapter 11 to deal with their whole position in a still more thorough manner. So we are leaving the great realm of doctrine pure and simple, and are coming now to Paul's application of it all to the Jews.

Now you may have sometimes wondered why the people who divided up the Scriptures into chapters divided it as they did. And you may have wondered why they did not start a new chapter at the beginning of verse 18. Paul has finished with his exposition of God's way of salvation through preaching. He has finished the doctrine, and now he comes to application. You would have thought, therefore, that they might very well have decided to start a new chapter here instead of later, at the beginning of what is our chapter 11.

But I think they were quite right, because here, in these four verses, the Apostle is primarily dealing with his statement, 'But they have not all obeyed the gospel.' He wants to finish off that particular point and he must do that, for it is only then that he can stand back, as it were, and say, 'Now then let us look at the whole question of the Jews.' He does that in verse 1 of chapter 11 when he says, 'I say then, Hath God cast away his people?' And then he goes on to deal with that in the body of chapter 11. So I believe that the division into chapters in this particular case is more than justified.

I am, incidentally, assuming that you realise that the division into verses and chapters has been done by men. In the original Greek, you do not have this division at all, and let us remember, therefore, that the divisions are not divinely inspired. The words and the matter are, but the division into verses and chapters is not, and we are as competent to decide where to divide them as were the people who originally did it. But it is a matter of interest to notice how their minds worked.

So, then, the Apostle wants to take up this particular point and he does so in this most excellent way. And as we follow what he says, we shall see that he brings here a tremendous, irrefutable indictment against the Jews. He shows that their case is completely indefensible and that their whole conduct with respect to the gospel is entirely inexcusable. The Apostle Paul was a mighty debater and reasoner, and nowhere does he show the brilliance of his debating powers more than he does at this particular point. But let us remember that his ultimate object is not merely to indict the Jews and to show how terribly wrong they are. Do not forget the first verse of this chapter, 'Brethren, my heart's desire and prayer to God for Israel is, that they might be saved.' That is his object. He is not simply setting out to win an argument or to show that he is right. What he really is concerned to do is to show the Jews how tragically wrong they are, hoping that, if they see it, they will repent and acknowledge it and turn to the Lord.

I emphasise that because we should be animated by the same desire. It is not always easy to keep these two things going together, but that is what we are called to do as preachers and teachers and as apologists for the Christian faith. When you are dealing with an individual, you have to show that he or she is wrong, that this is the truth and that you are right. But sometimes it is very difficult to do that in love, by 'speaking the truth in love' [*Eph.* 4:15]. Sometimes, unconsciously, we cross that very delicate line and become more concerned to prove that we are right than to save that person's soul.

But let us remember that, 'A man convinced against his will, is of the same opinion still.' We must not browbeat, and the Apostle never does that. The argument is tremendous, but it is still an argument conducted in love, and with a desire to show the Jews their error in order that, having their eyes opened, they will vacate that position and submit themselves with a willing obedience to the gospel of our Lord and Saviour Jesus Christ. Let us learn, then, from the great Apostle – in this matter, as in every other – and then we shall not go very far wrong.

What, then, is he saying here? Well, here is the argument. 'Faith cometh by hearing, and hearing by the word of God.' All right! 'But they have not all obeyed the gospel.' That is the question, and there is a great discussion among the commentators, both past and present, about this. They argue among themselves, as they are very fond of doing, over this question: To whom is Paul referring here? Some maintain that he is referring to the Jews only, others say he is referring only to the Gentiles. Calvin, for instance, does not hesitate to say that in verse 18 he is referring only to the Gentiles.

Well, my opinion on this matter, for what it is worth, is that I disagree with both parties because I think he is referring to both Jews and Gentiles, that is, to all who have not obeyed the gospel. He has been establishing the point that it is preached to all. 'Well then,' he says in effect, 'it is clear that some believe and some do not. Some obey, some do not. So, the whole question is: Why is it that people do not obey?' This applies to any who do not obey the gospel, but if I were pressed to say one more than another, I would say that he is referring especially to the Jews, because the whole chapter is primarily concerned with their situation. Therefore, the position is: 'They have not all obeyed the gospel.' But why is that? And in these four verses the Apostle answers that particular question. And he does it, as I said, in this interesting way of putting a rhetorical question and then dealing with it.

Now the Apostle here, I want to try to show you, says four things. He deals with both negative and positive reasons. Why is it that the majority of the Jews have not believed the gospel? Let us take the negatives first, and here he has two things to say. The first is that it is not through lack of hearing that they do not believe. Some people may say that they do not believe because they have not heard the gospel. You do not condemn someone for not believing something that he has not heard. And Paul's answer is: 'I say, Have they not heard?'

Now the Apostle puts it in the form of a double negative. It really reads like this: 'Not that they did not hear.' And by putting it in his double negative, he is implying a negative answer. Is that the reason for their unbelief? – 'Not that they did not hear.' Certainly not! Why? Well, 'Verily, their sound went into all the earth, and their words unto the ends of the world.' It cannot be said, says the Apostle, that they do not believe because they have not heard it, for the gospel has been preached everywhere.

And he puts that in this very interesting way by a quotation from Psalm 19: 'The heavens declare the glory of God; and the firmament sheweth his handywork. Day unto day uttereth speech, and night unto night sheweth knowledge. There is no speech nor language, where their voice is not heard. Their line is gone out through all the earth, and their words to the end of the world.' The Apostle appropriates that language about the universe and it makes the point that the gospel is preached everywhere.

This is something that is stated quite often in the Scriptures. The Apostle Paul and Barnabas said the same thing when preaching to the pagan people in Lystra, those people who were about to worship them. But Paul said, 'Sirs, why do ye these things? We also are men of like passions with you, and preach unto you that ye should turn from these vanities unto the living God, which made heaven, and earth, and the sea, and all things that are therein: who in times past suffered all nations to walk in their own ways. Nevertheless he left not himself without witness, in that he did good, and gave us rain from heaven, and fruitful seasons, filling our hearts with food and gladness' [*Acts* 14:15–17]. It is the same idea. The world's ignorance of God is inexcusable because by 'rain from heaven and fruitful seasons' God is giving evidence, He is preaching about himself, and it is very important that we should always bear that in mind. Furthermore, in the first chapter of Romans, the Apostle has been arguing the same thing. In verses 19 and 20 he says, 'Because that which may be known of God is manifest in them; for God hath shewed it unto them. For the invisible things of him from the creation of the world are clearly seen, being understood by the things that are made, even his eternal power and Godhead; so that they are without excuse.'

Now often in preaching one finds oneself doing just what the Apostle does here. You will often find that what you were trying to say, or what you want to say, can be said best of all by a quotation from the Scripture. Though it is not, perhaps, dealing with precisely the point that you are dealing with, the same general statement applies. As there the Psalmist was saying that this knowledge of God the Creator is universal, so here Paul is saying that the knowledge of the gospel is universal.

But somebody probably wants to query this and say, 'Can you say that the gospel of Jesus Christ really has been preached everywhere and universally to all people?'

Let the Apostle answer. In his letter to the Colossians, he says that this truth of the gospel has come not only to them, but to 'all the world' [*Col.* 1:5–6]. He repeats that in the twenty-third verse of the same chapter: 'If ye continue in the faith grounded and settled, and be not moved away from the hope of the gospel, which ye have heard, and which was preached to every creature which is under heaven.'

Now this is where the pedants get into trouble, is it not? They say, 'Fancy the Apostle saying that the gospel has been preached to every creature which is under heaven! Is it true to say that every single person on earth everywhere has heard the preaching of this gospel or had done so in the time of the Apostle Paul?' And the answer is, of course, 'No.' What does the Apostle mean, then? Well, this is hyperbole. It is just a way of saying that the gospel has been disseminated generally. Paul does not mean every single individual. He means that the gospel has not been hidden.

Or let me use the words of Paul himself when he was addressing King Agrippa and others in Caesarea: '. . . this thing was not done in a corner' [*Acts* 26:26]. He meant that the facts were known. So here he is in Romans 10, just bringing out this point that no one can say that he has not heard this, because the gospel is preached everywhere. You remember how our Lord Himself, in giving His commission to the disciples after His resurrection said, 'But ye shall receive power, after that the Holy Ghost is come upon you: and ye shall be witnesses unto me both in Jerusalem and in all Judaea, and in Samaria, and unto the uttermost part of the earth' [*Acts* 1:8].

Now that is another way of saying the same thing – that the gospel is to be preached everywhere throughout the whole world. Our Lord's prophecy began to be fulfilled at Pentecost when there were people up in Jerusalem from most parts of the then known and civilised world. They had that opportunity of hearing it, and they went back to their own countries; so it was spread through them and through other preachers. And here Paul is simply making the same point in a slightly different manner. The expression 'to the ends of the world' is the kind of expression that is quite common in the Scriptures and you must not come with your pedantic mind and say, 'Does this mean, then, that every individual . . . ?' Of course it does not! And we have already dealt with the case of those who have never actually heard the gospel at all and whether they can be saved or not.

So verse 18 is a most important statement. The Apostle is saying that the Jews cannot excuse themselves by claiming they have not heard. 'I say, Have they not heard?' The thing is ridiculous, he says, the gospel has gone everywhere – 'Yes verily, their sound went into all the earth, and their words unto the ends of the world.'

Now in what sense is it right for Paul to say this? How does he really prove that the Jews cannot plead ignorance with respect to the general statement of the gospel? Well, this is a very profound argument of his; this is where he brings it right home to them. Let us start with the way in which our Lord Himself did it. Take what He said in the fifth chapter of John. You see, our Lord really had to face the same question. All that argumentation between our Lord and the Pharisees and scribes was virtually what Paul is arguing in this tenth chapter of Romans.

'Search the Scriptures,' our Lord said – or, if you like the other translation, 'You do search the Scriptures' – 'for in them ye think ye have eternal life: and they are they which testify of me' [*John* 5:39]. He said, in effect, 'You are saying that I am preaching some novelty and that you believe the Scriptures. Very well, read your Scriptures, and if you do, you will find that they are the very statements which tell of me.' Then again, in verses 45 to 47, 'Do not think that I will accuse you to the Father: there is one that accuseth you, even Moses, in whom ye trust. For had ye believed Moses, ye would have believed me: for he wrote of me.' You see, they had heard the gospel through Moses, in their own Scriptures that they were so proud of. '[Moses] wrote of me. Go to your Moses, then,' He said. 'If ye believe not his writings, how shall ye believe my words?'

This is a tremendous statement which we often tend to lose sight of. I hope to take up this point again and deal with it in a more general manner, but if we had nothing else, this would be enough. This is exactly the argument of Paul in Romans 10 – they have heard it. They have been hearing it from Moses; they have been hearing it from the Scriptures.

Or, again, our Lord makes precisely the same point to the two disciples on the road to Emmaus: 'O fools, and slow of heart to believe all that the prophets have spoken: ought not Christ to have suffered these things, and to enter into this glory? And beginning at Moses and all the prophets, he expounded unto them in all the scriptures the things concerning himself' [*Luke* 24:25–27]. Now 'all the Scriptures', you see, does not mean every single verse in the Old Testament, but it means every part of the Old Testament. Christ is there everywhere. That is what he was saying, and it is exactly the same argument.

And, of course, we have it later on again in the same chapter: 'He said unto them, These are the words which I spake unto you, while I was yet with you, that all things must be fulfilled, which were written in the law of Moses, and in the prophets, and in the psalms, concerning me' [*Luke* 24:44]. The Jews had no right to say that they had not heard. They had been hearing the gospel through the teaching of the Old Testament Scriptures. There it is, as our Lord says; it is in the books of Moses; it is in the Psalms; it is in the Prophets, Isaiah 53 and all similar statements.

The Apostle Paul, also, puts exactly this same point in writing to Timothy. 'Continue thou,' he says, 'in the things which thou hast learned and hast been assured of, knowing of whom thou hast learned them; and that from a child' – before Timothy's conversion – 'thou hast known the holy scriptures, which are able to make thee wise unto salvation through faith which is in Christ Jesus' [*2 Tim.* 3:15–16]. You can preach the gospel from the Old Testament, it is 'able to make thee wise unto salvation through faith which is in Christ Jesus'. The Old Testament! That is what Paul means by the 'Scriptures'. And if you and I do not see Christ and His salvation in the Old Testament, it is because we are blind. There are certain foolish Christian people who seem to think we do not need the Old Testament. What terrible ignorance that is, and how unscriptural! What a contradiction of the plain teaching of the New Testament! Yes, Christ is there; salvation is all there. If you have enlightened eyes, you will find it there, and you will find it quite frequently in most glorious terms. So Paul is arguing that the Jews must not say that they have not heard it – they, of everybody, who rejoiced in the Scriptures.

Then, of course, in the New Testament, you have John the Baptist. John was a veritable phenomenon – this extraordinary man who began to preach in the wilderness. And they had crowded to hear this fiery prophetic preaching, this Elijah, as it were, come to life again. All the Jews knew about him, it was noised abroad throughout the whole land of Palestine.

And what was he preaching about? Well, what he said was this: 'I am not the Christ' [*John* 1:20]. 'I indeed baptize you with water unto repentance; but he that cometh after me is mightier than I, whose shoes I am not worthy to bear: he shall baptize you with fire: whose fan is in his hand, and he will throughly purge his floor, and gather his wheat into the garner; but he will burn up the chaff with unquenchable fire' [*Matt.* 3:11–12]. The forerunner! 'Behold the Lamb of God, which taketh away the sin of the world' [*John* 1:29]. That was his message. 'He must increase, but I must decrease' [*John* 3:30]. There was John, pointing to Him, and yet the Jews were trying to defend themselves by saying that they had not heard the gospel. John the Baptist alone was enough to silence them once and for ever. The forerunner pointed to the Messiah; he preached Him. So, you see, the evidence is piling up.

And then, of course, our Lord Himself, the supreme phenomenon! This young man, this apparent carpenter from Nazareth, began to preach at the age of thirty and impressed the people at once, 'For he taught them as one having authority, and not as the scribes' [*Matt.* 7:29]. His understanding! The profundity of His teaching! 'Ye have heard that it was said by them of old time. . . but I say unto you' [*Matt.* 5:27–28]. His exposition of the law in the Sermon on the Mount – this authority! Now the whole of the land of Palestine knew this. It was talked about everywhere and emphasised by the opposition of the Pharisees and scribes.

And then there were His miracles. As He said Himself: Though you do not believe my words, 'believe me for the very works' sake' [*John* 14:11]. Look at the works! He pointed the Jews to the 'signs', as well as to the preaching.

Now all this historical truth is of tremendous importance in this matter. It was the final convicting of the Jews of their utter inexcusability. They could not say they had not heard. They could not help hearing. It was impossible for them not to have heard.

And then, of course, beyond the teaching and the miracles, there was His death upon the cross and, still more amazing, His resurrection. They had not seen that, but they had heard about it. This was the preaching of the early disciples; this was why the Jews persecuted them – because they preached 'Jesus and the resurrection'. And the Jews saw the change in these disciples. In other words, you have the astounding phenomenon of Pentecost. It was impossible for anyone to be a Jew and not to have heard about Pentecost. Everywhere, everybody knew about it. The delegates who had come up from various parts of the civilised world to the feast at Pentecost heard Peter preaching, they heard the teaching about Jesus, and they went back and told what they had seen and heard.

And then, after that, you have the preaching of the Apostles themselves. They travelled abroad, like this man, the Apostle Paul, crossing oceans and continents, preaching, propagating, making this message known. It was an amazing phenomenon in the world at that time, and widely spoken of.

And it was not only the Apostles. You have those other preachers, such as Stephen and the various evangelists who were sent on journeys to preach the message. And not only that, even the devil helped. Because there was a persecution in Jerusalem, the people were all scattered abroad and, as we have seen, 'They that were scattered abroad went every where preaching the word' [*Acts* 8:4]. They made it known; they told people why they were persecuted, why they were having to leave Jerusalem, why they had been evacuated, as it were, and it was all because of this message. The message was carried abroad to all portions of the then known and civilised world.

In other words, the Apostle is making the point that the Christian gospel is not some secret message. It was not like those so-called mystery religions that were so common in that ancient world, it was not an esoteric message. The teachers of these mystery religions did not preach their message from the house-tops, they did not make it known to everybody. No, you had to be 'initiated'. It was a secret message. There are organisations and societies that still do that sort of thing. We do not know what they believe exactly, because we have not been initiated, we do not belong to them. You are not told the message until you go in. It is a secret. But the Apostle's point is that the gospel is the exact opposite of that, not some hidden message but something that at the command of God Himself and the Lord Jesus Christ, through the called, appointed, sent preachers, is to be heard by everybody, everywhere.

In this way, then, the Apostle deals with his first negative argument. The explanation of the Jews and their rejection is not that they have not heard. On that score, they have not got a leg to stand on, because just as the sun proclaims the glory of God throughout the world, so the gospel has been spread abroad in this amazing manner. 'Yes verily, their sound went into all the earth, and their words unto the ends of the world.'

Thirty-three

*

But I say, Have they not heard? Yes verily, their sound went into all the earth, and their words unto the ends of the world. But I say, Did not Israel know? First Moses saith, I will provoke you to jealousy by them that are no people, and by a foolish nation I will anger you. But Esaias is very bold, and saith, I was found of them that sought me not; I was made manifest unto them that asked not after me. But to Israel he saith, All day long I have stretched forth my hands unto a disobedient and gainsaying people. Romans 10:18–21

The Apostle in these verses, you remember, is showing how the whole position of the Jews as unbelievers, and as those who are outside the kingdom of God as rejecters of the gospel, is something which is quite indefensible. He does this first of all negatively. His first argument is that their trouble was not due to lack of hearing, and we have dealt with that.

So we come now to the second negative, which is that their trouble was not due to lack of plain teaching concerning the gospel. You see how the one follows from the other? 'Very well,' someone might say, 'let us grant that this message has gone abroad, but is the message quite plain and clear?' And the Apostle says that it is. He puts that again in the form of this negative rhetorical question: 'I say, Did Israel not know?' Again, it is one of these double negatives. 'Did Israel not fail to know?' The answer is: 'No, they are quite inexcusable.'

What does Paul mean here? Well, he is saying that the gospel is not an innovation. Paul and the other apostles were being charged with spreading some 'new' teaching. The Jews, standing as they thought upon their Scriptures, said, 'But look here, you say you believe in the same God; that you have not turned your back on the God of your fathers, and that you are not denying our Scriptures. You say that, but your message is a blank denial of them, it has nothing to do with them, it is an absolutely new teaching.'

No, says the Apostle, it is not! It is not an innovation which cuts right across everything that you have known in the past.

How can he prove this? Well, he sets out to show that in the Old Testament Scriptures, certain things were made perfectly plain. What are they? Let me list them. Firstly, the way of salvation. Secondly, that the Gentiles were to be included. Thirdly, that the majority of the Jews would reject the gospel. These things have been made perfectly plain in the Old Testament, so that the Jews could not say they did not know. Indeed, by their rejection of the gospel they were fulfilling the Scriptures, they were verifying the prophecies of the prophets! The Scriptures in which the Jews so much delighted convinced them and convicted them of blindness and of sin.

That, then, is the general statement in connection with this second negative argument and the Apostle puts it in terms of Moses and of Isaiah. Why do you think he selects those two? No doubt because, as we have seen in the quotations from Luke 24, it was customary to divide the Old Testament into 'Moses and the Prophets', so you have a quotation from Moses, and a quotation from the major prophet, who is Isaiah, the evangelical prophet. So Moses and the Prophets both condemn the Jews utterly and completely. They had no right to be ignorant; they had no right not to understand. The nature of the way of salvation had been made clear, the calling of the Gentiles had been made clear, and the rejection of the Jews had been made clear.

So, then, we must now examine the evidence. 'First,' Paul says, 'Moses saith, I will provoke you to jealousy by them that are no people, and by a foolish nation I will anger you.' Now here he is quoting from Deuteronomy 32:21: 'They have moved me to jealousy with that which is not God; they have provoked me to anger with their vanities: and I will move them to jealousy with those which are not a people; I will provoke them to anger with a foolish nation.'

Now the whole of the first section of Deuteronomy 32 deals with this very matter, and that is why the Apostle quotes it. But we cannot bypass, as it were, something which is of great interest and, I think, of great instruction to us. I am never tired of reminding you of what a brilliant debater this man was. Apart from his divine inspiration and his thorough grasp of doctrine, no man has ever known better than the Apostle Paul how to present his case. He is anxious to show the indefensible position of the Jews and, of course, if you want to do that, you need only use a quotation from Moses and you have completely undermined them.

The Jews boasted of Moses above everybody else. He was the great lawgiver, the great man who had led the people out of the captivity of Egypt to the Promised Land of Canaan. The Jews always looked back either to Abraham or to Moses and, in many ways, at this time in particular, Moses was even superior to Abraham because he was the man who had been in the presence of God and to whom God had given 'the lively oracles' of the law. So Moses was a man who had a unique position in their history and, therefore, the Apostle is doing a very subtle and very able thing by quoting from him. If he can establish that Moses had prepared them for this, then they have no case at all; and that is exactly what Paul does.

Now the argument of those verses in Deuteronomy 32 can be summed up like this. God, in effect, addresses the nation through Moses and says to them, 'You have been going after idols; you have been worshipping vanities. They are not gods; they are "no gods" and you have thereby aroused my jealousy. I am now going to arouse your jealousy, you who claim that you and you alone are My people, by calling a "no people" and a "foolish nation".' And that is what the Apostle quotes here – though, of course, he just gives us the essence.

God had made it quite plain, when He gave the Ten Commandments to Moses, that He was a jealous God. He had told them, 'Thou shalt have no other gods before me . . . I the Lord thy God am a jealous God' [*Exod.* 20:3–5]. He will not tolerate any other because there is no other, and therefore the greatest of all sins is to be worshipping anything or anybody but God. He alone is to be worshipped and He will not share His glory with any other. But they had been worshipping 'no gods' and they had aroused His anger. 'Very well,' says God, 'I am going to arouse your anger. I will take hold of people whom you regard as "no people", people whom you despise utterly and whom you regard as "dogs". I am going to take people whom you regard as utterly foolish, and it is to them that I am going to give my great salvation.'

This is a most important statement, therefore. Moses had written and taught it. So the Jews must not be surprised; they must not say that they did not know this sort of thing; they must not say that what was happening under the gospel was something absolutely different that cuts across the whole history of Israel – it was not true. Their own great man Moses had been told by God to prophesy this, to pass on this message to them, and here it is actually being fulfilled.

Now what the Apostle is establishing here, quite clearly, is that the Gentiles are to be called, that the gospel is for the Gentiles rather than the Jews, that there will be more Gentiles in the kingdom than Jews. The thing that is happening has been prophesied. The terms that Paul uses are most interesting. The Apostle pinpoints certain things that were of great importance to the Jews. One is this fact that they were the people of God. God had said to the children of Israel through Amos, 'You only have I known of all the families of the earth' [*Amos* 3:2]. What he means by 'known' is that they were the only ones with whom He had been intimate, to whom He had revealed Himself, who were His own peculiar people for His own special possession, and to whom He had given His greatest benefits and blessings. The others were in a different category but now He was going to take them and bring them in, whereas His own people were out.

And then there is the other term *foolish*. That means 'uninstructed', without a knowledge of God's revelation; it is the opposite of 'wise'. The 'foolish' nation is a nation that does not possess the Scriptures, the living oracles of God. So, you see, that is what Moses had been prophesying – that the nation of Israel, for this reason, would be put on one side and God would give His blessings to what He calls 'a foolish nation'. This, of course, is a reference to the church – the Christian church – consisting mainly of Gentiles but also of some individual Jews, as the Apostle demonstrates in chapter 11.

Now all this is but another way of saying what our Lord Himself said at the end of His parable of the Wicked Husbandmen. He puts it like this: 'Therefore say I unto you, The kingdom of God shall be taken from you' – the Jewish nation – 'and given to a nation' – a nation! – 'bearing forth the fruits thereof' [*Matt.* 21:43]. Now that nation is not a nation in the sense of an ethnic nation, like the Germans, or the Japanese, or the Irish, or the Welsh. The nation to whom the kingdom would be given is the Christian church.

And, of course, we find the Apostle Peter also saying the same thing in his First Epistle: 'But ye are a chosen generation, a royal priesthood, an holy nation.' Now who are these? Well, they do not belong to one nation; Peter says he is writing 'to the strangers scattered throughout Pontus, Galatia, Cappadocia, Asia, and Bithynia'. They belonged, in a natural sense, to a number of different nations, but as members of the Christian church, they have become God's nation, God's people, and Peter applies to them the very words that

God had used with respect to Israel in Exodus 19:6. 'That ye should shew forth the praises of him who hath called you out of darkness into his marvellous light: which in time past were not a people [a 'no people'] but are now the people of God' [*1 Pet.* 2:9–10]. It is Christian people who are 'the people of God'. The kingdom has been taken from that foolish nation of the Jews and it has been given to this 'no people' who have now become God's 'holy nation', His 'peculiar people'.

There, then, is the Apostle's case. All this had been anticipated by Moses, it had been prophesied. They must not say that they did not know. Not only have they heard, the thing has been put explicitly to them.

But then the Apostle goes on and, again, it is very interesting to notice the way in which he does so. 'But,' he says, 'Esaias [Isaiah] is very bold, and saith . . .' And what Paul means is that if Moses has put it plainly – well, what can we say about Isaiah? Isaiah has gone even further! Isaiah is much more explicit. Indeed, Paul suggests that in saying what he did, Isaiah was really taking a risk!

And it is not surprising that the Apostle should put it like that. The Apostle himself was offending the Jews. He was a man who had to exercise great boldness and who was persecuted more by his own fellow-countrymen than by anybody else. It was they, in the end, who were even responsible for his death. The records in the book of Acts tell us all about that, and he also tells us here and there in his own Epistles. He knew he was offending the Jews deeply, but that did not trouble him, for he was not afraid of losing his life. With great boldness he spoke. He knew his words would hurt them and offend them – but he did it.

And he says that Isaiah did the same thing. Isaiah was taking a tremendous risk by saying what he did in his prophecy. 'I am sought of them that asked not for me; I am found of them that sought me not: I said, Behold me, behold me, unto a nation that was not called by my name' – you notice 'nation' still? – 'I have spread out my hands all the day unto a rebellious people, which walketh in a way that was not good, after their own thoughts' [*Isa.* 65:1–2].

Now Paul here does something again that is quite characteristic of him. He quotes from the Septuagint, but he not only does that, he reverses the order of the statements in the first verse of Isaiah 65, but it is still the same quotation. Here, in passing, I would remind you of something I have indicated many times before. This is a proof of the divine inspiration of the Apostle Paul. The Spirit who led Isaiah is the same Spirit who leads the Apostle Paul, and if the argument can be brought out more cogently here by reversing the order, then the Spirit leads the Apostle to do so. But it is the same quotation. So what does the statement say? Well, it could not be plainer, could it? Look at it as the Apostle quotes it: 'I was found of them that sought me not; I was made manifest unto them that asked not after me.' And then the contrast with Israel – 'To Israel he saith, All day long I have stretched forth my hands unto a disobedient and gainsaying people.'

So, here Paul is establishing two things. First: that the Gentiles are to be called. The Gentiles are the people who have not sought God. They are this 'other nation', they are outside. But now they are the ones that are brought inside; it is the Gentiles who are going to believe. Isaiah had prophesied it; they are fulfilling the prophecy. But secondly: 'Israel is a disobedient and gainsaying people' who refuse the gospel and to give obedience to it. They hear the word, but they have not all obeyed it.

Isaiah, then, had prophesied exactly these two things. So the Apostle now has made abundantly plain this first point which he is setting out to establish. That is the argument on the negative side – the Jews are, therefore, entirely without excuse. They have heard, and it has been made plain to them. And, therefore, when they are rejecting the gospel, as they are, they are simply confirming the prophecy, the teaching of the Scriptures. Law and Prophets join together in condemning the Jews for their rejection of the way of salvation that is in Jesus Christ our Lord.

There, then, is Paul's negative argument in the two sections, and now we can turn to the positive. Here again there are two sections. If those are *not* the reasons why the Jews are not in the kingdom, then, what are the reasons? You see, the Apostle is not content merely with removing plausible excuses, he wants to bring the things right home. He wants to convict them because, as he has told us at the beginning of the chapter, 'My heart's desire and prayer to God for Israel is, that they might be saved,' and you help to bring people to salvation by convicting them of their sinful state. You expose to them the position that they are in, its falseness, its indefensible character and, indeed, its enormity in the sight of God, and that is what the Apostle is now going to do positively.

Why, then, is it that the Jews have not obeyed the gospel? The answer is implicit in these quotations. The first is this: the trouble with the Jews was their false ideas of salvation and of the way of salvation.

In the first place, they thought of it in terms of nations. Now this, of course, is something which is brought out here quite plainly: 'I will provoke you to jealousy by them that are no people.' The Jews were 'the people of God'. It was the thing on which they prided themselves above everything else. And so the Apostle realises that by using this quotation, he is exposing to them their erroneous view of the way of salvation. They thought that, because they were Jews, because they were God's chosen people, they were automatically saved and they did not need this new way of salvation that was being preached. A Gentile was a 'dog'; he could not be saved because he was not a Jew. Salvation, they thought, was of the Jews only. They relied entirely upon their nationality.

Now the Apostle has already been dealing with this. At the beginning of chapter 9, he reminded them of all the things of which they were so proud. He says there, 'I could wish that myself were accursed from Christ for my brethren, my kinsmen according to the flesh: who are Israelites; to whom pertaineth the adoption, and the glory, and the covenants, and the giving of the law, and the service of God, and the promises; whose are the fathers, and of whom as concerning the flesh Christ came, who is over all, God blessed for ever.' And the whole trouble with the Jews was that they were relying upon that; they thought that nothing mattered but the fact that they were Jews.

In Philippians 3, Paul puts it all perfectly in terms of his own experience. He was a Pharisee and, as a typical Pharisee, he thought he was all right because he was a Jew. So he understood the wrong thinking of the Jew. I know you think that you are all right, he says to them, because you say, We are the circumcision. Those others, they are not circumcised; they are not God's people; they have not got the sign and the seal of the fact that they are God's people. We have it. We are the circumcision. And that is just where you are wrong, says Paul. 'We [Christians] are the circumcision, which worship God in the spirit, and rejoice in Christ Jesus, and have no confidence in the flesh' [*Phil.* 3:3].

But the confidence of these Jews was entirely in the flesh. Why? Here is Paul's answer: 'Though I might also have confidence in the flesh. If any other man thinketh that he hath whereof he might trust in the flesh, I more.' What is this 'confidence in the flesh'? Here it is: 'Circumcised the eighth day, of the stock of Israel, of the tribe of

Benjamin, an Hebrew of the Hebrews . . . a Pharisee' – and so on [vv. 4-5].

And that, you see, is the very thing, according to the Apostle, that explains why the Jews were outside the kingdom of God. It is not that they had not heard; it is not that the knowledge was not made explicit; it is that they had such a wrong notion as to what brings someone to salvation. To them it was nothing but the fact that he was a Jew; it was this confidence in the flesh.

Of course, in saying all this, the Apostle is only repeating what our Lord had to say to the Pharisees and scribes so often during His brief ministry. He told those Jews who believed in Him: 'ye shall know the truth, and the truth shall make you free'. But they were relying on the fact that they were Abraham's seed. They did not need to be set free, they thought. They *were* free, and they were the only people who were, because they were Abraham's seed. They were relying upon this fact of nationality [*John* 8:30-42].

The second way in which they had a false idea of salvation was that they also tended to regard it in terms of learning and knowledge. That is why this quotation about 'a foolish nation' is so important. It so perfectly describes their error. 'I will provoke you to jealousy by them that are no people, and by a foolish nation I will anger you.' What is a foolish nation? We have seen that it is a nation that lacks knowledge and instruction. Again, here was a thing about which the Jew was tremendously proud. The Apostle has already reminded us of it at the beginning of chapter 3: 'What advantage then hath the Jew? or what profit is there of circumcision? Much every way: chiefly, because that unto them were committed the oracles of God.' And we find the same idea in the verses at the beginning of chapter 9.

This was the Jews' proud boast. God has been pleased to give His revelation of Himself to this nation, and to this nation only. The Gentiles were ignorant, they knew nothing. Even the Greeks with all their philosophy did not know God. 'The world by wisdom knew not God' [*1 Cor.* 1:21]. It was only this nation that had the knowledge; it alone was enlightened. The Jews had the Bible, the Old Testament, the 'oracles of God' – nobody else had them – and this, they felt, was going to save them.

Now the Apostle makes this point very frequently. Fundamentally the Jews were absolutely right in all these things, but it was their wrong use of them that constituted the obstacle to salvation. The Apostle reminds the Ephesians that before their conversion they were a foolish people: 'Having the understanding darkened, being alienated from the life of God through the ignorance that is in them, because of the blindness of their heart' [*Eph.* 4:18]. He wrote to the Romans, 'Their foolish heart was darkened' [*Rom.* 1:21].

Those descriptions were true of all the Gentiles. The Gentiles in their utter ignorance and darkness were worshipping the sun and the moon and the stars; they were worshipping Jupiter and Mercury. Some of them were making idols out of wood and stone and silver and precious metals and were building temples to them. The whole thing was madness; it was vanity, emptiness. There was no god there. They had made the gods themselves and had then proceeded to worship them. That is folly.

The Jew, on the other hand, was the only one who knew and worshipped the only true and living God, and the tragedy was that the Jew relied upon that, upon this fundamental difference, and that was his fatal blunder. The Jews said, 'We alone have the Scriptures; it was to us alone that the law of God was given. We are the people of the law; we are the people of the Book; we are the people who have knowledge. Therefore we are saved and all others are lost.' Now the Apostle has already given the answer to that in the second chapter of this Epistle, where he makes a most profound statement: 'For not the hearers of the law are just before God, but the doers of the law shall be justified' [v. 13].

That is the whole thing in a nutshell. They thought that because the law had been given to them and they had heard it, that they had therefore kept it. Paul says, in effect, 'Look, the fact that a man has heard the law does not put him right. The law does not merely say, "As long as you have heard me, you are saved." The law says, "Whosoever puts it into practice . . ."' As the Apostle has been saying earlier in this tenth chapter, 'Moses describeth the righteousness which is of the law, That *the man which doeth these things shall live by them*.' But mere possession of the Scriptures does not save anybody.

And this fallacy is still as true today as it has ever been. There are still people who are foolish enough to call this 'a Christian country', and to say that other countries are 'pagan'. But that is the kind of nonsense that accounted for the position of the Jews.

Then there was a third fallacy in the Jews' false ideas of salvation. It was that they were relying upon their own works. 'I was found of them that sought me not; I was made manifest unto them that asked not after me.' In other words, they said that the thing that saved the

Jew was that he was seeking salvation, that he was asking. The Gentiles, in their ignorance and darkness, were not doing this, and if a man does not seek salvation, he can never be saved. That was the argument; that was their logic. 'But we,' they said, 'are the people who have been seeking.'

Now the Apostle keeps on saying this. Go back to chapter 9:30–32: 'What shall we say then? That the Gentiles, which followed not after righteousness, have attained to righteousness, even the righteousness which is of faith. But Israel, which followed after the law of righteousness, hath not attained to the law of righteousness' – they were following after it, it was their greatest boast – 'Wherefore? Because they sought it not by faith, but as it were by the works of the law. For they stumbled at that stumblingstone.'

Paul puts it again very plainly in this tenth chapter, as we have seen, when he says: 'Moses describeth the righteousness which is of the law, That the man which doeth those things shall live by them. But the righteousness which is of faith speaketh on this wise, Say not in thine heart, Who shall ascend into heaven? (that is, to bring Christ down from above:) or, Who shall descend into the deep? (that is, to bring Christ up again from the dead.) But what saith it: The word is nigh thee, even in thy mouth . . .' [vv. 5–8]. There was the Jew, ascending up to the heavens, as it were, and going down into the depths. Or, as Paul has summed it up so perfectly in one pregnant phrase in the third verse: 'They being ignorant of God's righteousness' – namely, of God's way of righteousness – 'and going about to establish their own righteousness'.

Our Lord said the same thing when he castigated the Pharisees with the words, 'For ye compass sea and land to make one proselyte' [*Matt.* 23:15]. And so they were 'going about' and compassing sea and land in order to work out their own righteousness – up into the heights, down into the depths. Their activity, their keeping the law as they falsely understood it, they thought this was going to save them, and they were entirely wrong.

Thirty-four

*

But I say, Have they not heard? Yes verily, their sound went into all the earth, and their words unto the ends of the world. But I say, Did not Israel know? First Moses saith, I will provoke you to jealousy by them that are no people, and by a foolish nation I will anger you. But Esaias is very bold, and saith, I was found of them that sought me not; I was made manifest unto them that asked not after me. But to Israel he saith, All day long I have stretched forth my hands unto a disobedient and gainsaying people. Romans 10:18–21

We have been considering the positive reasons for the failure of the Jews. The first of these was a threefold error with regard to the way of salvation. Now we move on to the second fact about them, which is that they failed to see the *true* salvation. Of course, this inevitably follows from the first problem, but nevertheless it is something that must be considered in and of itself. Holding their wrong views, they were unable to see clearly and truly the right way of salvation. What is this?

Now the Apostle makes it quite clear in his quotations. The true way of salvation can be summed up like this: it is entirely the result of God's election. Threefold evidence for this is provided by the quotation. Notice, first of all, the emphasis upon the 'I', and the 'I' refers to God. '*I* will provoke you to jealousy' – that is God speaking, through Moses – '. . . by a foolish nation *I* will anger you . . . *I* was found of them that sought me not; *I* was made manifest . . . All day long *I* have stretched forth my hands unto a disobedient and gainsaying people.' The emphasis, you notice, is all along upon the action and the activity of God.

But, secondly, it is made equally plain that salvation is not the result of any activity on our part: 'I was found of them that sought me not.' They had not sought Him. They are the people who find – the ones who had not sought. 'I was made manifest unto them that asked not after me.' You see, it is not the result of our activity. God makes it perfectly clear in these prophetic utterances that had been given through Isaiah so long before, that salvation is not the result of searching or asking. It is entirely the result of God's action. He says: 'This will be the position in the church – the people who are going to find are the people who have never sought. The people who will be given the answer are those who have never asked the question.' So there is the second bit of evidence.

And then, to make it quite clear beyond any doubt whatsoever, you have this tremendous statement, 'I was made manifest' – which really means, of course, 'I manifest myself.' It is God who does the manifesting.

And therefore, you see, we have threefold evidence here to make it perfectly clear that salvation is entirely the result of God's action. 'I'! Not the seeker, not the person who asks but – 'I'! 'I make manifest.'

Now this is the Apostle's summing up, not only of the argument of this tenth chapter, but also of the ninth. Let us never forget that. These chapters 9, 10 and 11 form a section on their own and they all deal with the vital question as to why it is that the Jews of all people are the ones who are outside, while the Gentiles have come in. And the explanation that the Apostle gave us at once, and at such length and with such mighty statements in chapter 9, was that it is all the result of the election of grace. 'That the purpose of God according to election might stand' [*Rom.* 9:11].

Now here the Apostle is saying exactly the same thing but these verses are also a perfect conclusion to the argument of this chapter 10. It must always be the same thing. So we put it like this once more: this is the only explanation of salvation. There is only one explanation of why any single person has ever been saved, and it is the action and the choice of God. There is nothing in us that contributes to salvation – nothing at all! If we have not seen it before, surely we ought to see it in the light of these particular quotations. If salvation were the result of human understanding, or human knowledge, or human works, then the Jews would be in a position of entire advantage, and the Gentiles would be completely hopeless. But in fact it works the other way round. It is the Gentiles who have come in, while the Jews remain outside.

So then, as salvation depends upon the election of God, as it depends upon His grace and on nothing else, as it is entirely of God's good will, then God is free; He is free to choose whomsoever He desires. Nobody deserves salvation in any sense at all, nobody makes any contribution to it. It is God who gives it, and because it is all in His hands and nobody deserves it, then God is as free to give it to the Gentile as to the Jew. And that is exactly what He has done.

The Apostle, then, in this way, is establishing the great case that He is making right through this section and which we have already seen Him making in chapter 8, and even before that. He has put it in greater detail in verses 11 and 12 of this chapter: 'For the Scripture saith, Whosoever believeth on him shall not be ashamed. For there is no difference between the Jew and the Greek: for the same Lord over all is rich unto all that call upon him. For whosoever shall call upon the name of the Lord shall be saved.' The question is: Who is this 'whosoever'? What decides that? Well, as I am showing, it is not nationality, it is not knowledge, it is not searching – it is all of God. The *whosoever* is determined by God, and the promise is that whosoever calls will be saved. And this, of course, is the teaching of the entire New Testament.

But therefore, just in order to establish this in our minds, let us show our blessed Lord Himself teaching exactly the same thing. There is nothing more fascinating and more glorious than the unity of the Scripture! 'At that time Jesus answered and said, I thank thee, O Father, Lord of heaven and earth, because thou hast hid these things from the wise and prudent, and hast revealed them unto babes. Even so, Father: for so it seemed good in thy sight. All things are delivered unto me of my Father: and no man knoweth the Son, but the Father; neither knoweth any man the Father, save the Son, and he to whomsoever the Son will reveal him' [*Matt.* 11:25–27].

Do you want anything beyond that? It is perfectly plain. God withholds these things from the wise and prudent and He reveals them to babes, to the foolish nation, to the 'no people'. It is exactly the same statement. God had revealed this right through the Old Testament. The Apostle has given us this plethora of quotations in chapters 9 and 10 because he is dealing with the Jews and he wants to show them that they have not got a leg to stand on. The whole of the Old Testament is proclaiming this very thing at which they are now stumbling, and therefore they are rendered entirely speechless.

Then we find exactly the same thing in Matthew 22, the parable spoken by our Lord about a king who made a marriage feast for his son. As the guests would not come, the king had them destroyed and their places taken by others [*Matt.* 22:7–10]. And you will find that in many different parables, our Lord made exactly this same point. First, the offer is made to the Jews, but they reject it and then the others are compelled to come in. And you find it wound up very often in this statement, 'Many are called, but few are chosen' [see, for example, *Matt.* 22:14]. That is it! There is a general call of the gospel, and there is a special call. The universal invitation goes out but all do not obey. Who are those who obey? They are the ones who are 'the called of God', those who receive this effectual call, this result of the 'election of grace'.

There, then, is this evidence that is put so plainly before us in the Gospels and in the words of our Lord Himself, and, of course, the Epistles are full of the same argument. In other words, the message is as we find it in 1 Corinthians 1. God has upset all the calculations, everything that the Jews had expected, and that is why the gospel is always a 'stumblingstone' to the Jews; they do not understand it. Why? 'Because the foolishness of God is wiser than men; and the weakness of God is stronger than men. For ye see your calling, brethren, how that not many wise men after the flesh, not many mighty, not many noble are called: but God hath chosen the foolish things of the world to confound the things which are mighty . . .' Why? Well, here is the ultimate reason: 'That, according as it is written, He that glorieth, let him glory in the Lord' [*1 Cor.* 1:25–27, 31]. The glory must be given entirely and only to Him. Yes, says the Apostle in Ephesians 2, 'By grace are ye saved through faith; and that not of yourselves: it is the gift of God . . . we are his workmanship' [vv. 8,10].

Now that is exactly what we are being told here at the end of Romans 10. You see, it is the doctrine of the whole of the Bible and yet it is amazing how people stumble at it still and want to take to themselves some bit of credit here or there. My friends, you cannot. This is the thing that keeps people outside the kingdom. This is why people do not obey the gospel. They do not see that the true way of salvation is this 'election of grace', that it is all of God, and that because it is all of God you must never be surprised at anybody you may happen to see being saved and in the kingdom of God. The Gentile! The foolish person! The ignorant! The nobody! The babe! These are the people whom God calls. It is all of Him. The gospel is 'the power of *God* unto salvation to every one that believeth' [*Rom.* 1:16].

This, then, is the second reason why the Jews were outside. They did not believe the true way of salvation.

And then there is a third reason which is perhaps the most important of all. It was the state of their hearts. We get that, of course, in the last verse: 'But to Israel he saith, All day long I have stretched forth my hands unto a disobedient and gainsaying people.' Here was the trouble. We have been told how God does save: it is all in His power to manifest Himself. Why did Israel not believe, then, why did Israel not give obedience? Here is the answer – the state of their hearts.

Now we must look at these two words – *disobedient* and *gainsaying*. What do they mean? This first word 'disobedient' is very interesting. The obvious meaning, of course, is not to give obedience. But there is a deeper meaning here. The *Grimm Thayer Lexicon* has a most interesting statement to make with regard to the word that was used here by the Apostle. It does not only mean that they did not give obedience to the gospel, it means much more. It means that they were non-persuasible, that they would not allow themselves to be persuaded. They were 'stiff-necked'. It is not merely that they were not persuaded – obviously they were not, otherwise they would have given obedience. But, beyond that, they would not allow themselves to be influenced and persuaded by the truth.

Now as I expound these words and deal with the matter in this way, I take it that we are almost inevitably thinking of what we must have all experienced in handling men and women who are not Christians, and you see the importance of this distinction that I am making. As you talk to people about their souls, you will be with some who do not know, who do not understand and have not believed, and yet it is quite clear that they are ready to listen. But there is another type of person, and people in this second group at once give us the impression – or if not at once, fairly soon – that they are not going to be persuaded. It does not matter what we say, nor how cogently and plainly and lovingly we may put the matter, it will make no difference to them; they are non-persuasible, they are stiff-necked.

Do you not get that impression of the Pharisees as you read the four Gospels? The whole thing was decided beforehand. This, you see, is what is meant by prejudice. It means pre-judging. Prejudiced people do not listen to the evidence; they have brought in their verdict before the prisoner is put in the dock; they have decided the result before they have heard anything at all. That was the trouble, according to the prophecy of Isaiah, with the Jews. It was their

trouble in the Old Testament; it was still their trouble, said the
Apostle Paul. Disobedience! They would not allow themselves to be
persuaded. They were determined not to believe, whatever may be
said to them. And this is still the reason why some people are not
Christians.

But look at the second word – *gainsaying*. What does this mean?
Well, it means 'saying against', 'contradicting'. It means, if you like,
'cantankerous'. Now, of course, this again is important. We can once
more illustrate this from what we all are so familiar with as we talk
with men and women about these matters. You can understand
people who honestly say, 'Well, I just cannot see it. I wish I could. I
would give anything if only I could see that, but I just cannot see it.'
Now they are people whom one can understand. But that was not the
position of Israel, as it is not the position of many people with whom
we have to deal. They are not only prejudiced and non-persuasible,
but they 'speak against'.

Let us put it like this – and I think it is one of the most valuable tests
when you are trying to help another soul to come to a knowledge of
God through the Lord Jesus Christ and to have salvation – the person
who is hopeful is the person who listens and asks questions in order
to be helped and to understand. But you are familiar with the other
type of person, are you not, who always gives you the impression that
they are just waiting for you to stop so that they can disagree. It is a
terrible thing to say, but what the Apostle is really indicating here is
that those people are hopeless; they do not want to hear and they are
waiting for an opportunity to contradict. Their spirit, their heart,
their whole attitude is wrong. That was the final trouble with Israel.
They would not allow our blessed Lord Himself to instruct them.
They were always waiting with their questions, trying to down Him,
as it were, always speaking against. Cantankerous! Contradicting!
Doing their utmost to disprove it! They did not want to be instructed
in the way.

That, then, is the meaning of this quotation from Isaiah 65:2 which
the Apostle gives us here. And as it was the trouble with the Jews with
whom the Apostle was dealing, so it was always the trouble with the
Jews. There it is in our Lord's ministry, clearly standing out before
us. Hear our Lord bringing this charge against the Jews with whom
He had to deal: 'this is the condemnation, that light is come into the
world' – why do people not believe, then? Why does everybody not
submit? Why does everybody not obey the gospel? 'Light is come

into the world, and men loved darkness rather than light, because their deeds were evil' [*John* 3:19]. That is the trouble.

People say it is 'intellect'. But it is not. The trouble is in the heart; it is a moral problem. Ultimately, unbelief has nothing to do with intellect. I could prove that to you very simply for if believing, or not believing, were a matter of intellect, then you would never have an intelligent man who is a Christian. It would be an impossibility, according to this modern argument. But what you actually find, of course, is two things. First, you find that a man with a great intellect was, at one stage in his life, an unbeliever. Then he becomes a believer, but he still has the same brain and the same intelligence and the same powers of argumentation. The same man. He has not suddenly committed intellectual suicide; he is using his brain as much as he ever did. Formerly he rejected the truth, now he believes; obviously it has nothing to do with intellect.

Or take it another way – take two men with equal intellects. It is impossible to decide which is the abler. In their school and college careers, one came top at one time, then the other the next time. There is nothing to choose between them. But one is a Christian, and one is not. It has nothing to do with intellect. No – 'Men loved darkness rather than light, because their deeds were evil.' All the so-called intellectual argumentation is nothing but the excuse and the camouflage that the unbeliever puts up to try to defend himself and to cover his moral refusal. There it is in our Lord's own words: 'Every one that doeth evil hateth the light, neither cometh to the light, lest his deeds should be reproved. But he that doeth truth cometh to the light, that his deeds may be made manifest, that they are wrought in God' [*John* 3:20–21].

But listen to our Lord again in John 5: 'ye will not come to me, that ye might have life' [v. 40]. That is the trouble – they will not come; they do not want to come; they have determined not to come. They decided to down Him from the very beginning, the moment they realised what He was saying. The trouble is in the will, and the will is governed by the heart.

And our Lord goes on saying the same thing: 'How can ye believe, which receive honour one of another, and seek not the honour that cometh from God only?' [*John* 5:44]. 'That is your trouble,' he says, in effect. 'It is not your intellects, it is your pride, your beastly pride. You want honour from one another.' And because He showed them that they were nobodies and could do nothing, they hated Him and that is why they crucified Him. He humbled them; He cast them down; He condemned everybody; and they hated Him for that reason. The trouble is always in the heart.

But, if you want it still more specifically, you will find it in our Lord's exposition of His own parable of the Sower: 'This people's heart is waxed gross, and their ears are dull of hearing, and their eyes they have closed; lest at any time they should see with their eyes, and hear with their ears, and should understand with their heart, and should be converted, and I should heal them' [*Matt.* 13:15]. That is the trouble. 'In them is fulfilled the prophecy of Esaias, which saith, By hearing ye shall hear, and shall not understand; and seeing ye shall see, and shall not perceive' [v. 14]. Why? 'For this people's heart is waxed gross' – it is 'enfattened', as Wycliffe put it; so fat that it cannot function.

So at the end of Romans 10, the Apostle is saying the same thing as our Lord said so clearly in all these passages. And if you want it still more plainly, you will find it in Matthew 23 where our Lord finally turned upon the Pharisees and denounced them in those terrible words, 'Woe unto you!' He pronounced upon them this final sentence of complete hopelessness. 'Woe unto you, scribes and Pharisees, hypocrites! for ye shut up the kingdom of heaven against men: for ye neither go in yourselves, neither suffer ye them that are entering to go in' [*Matt.* 23:13]. They have always been like that and they are still like that, as I hope to show you.

And then the same thing was brought as a charge against these people by the martyr Stephen. In his great address and sermon he finally brought it home to them in these words: 'Ye stiffnecked and uncircumcised in heart and ears, ye do always resist the Holy Ghost: as your fathers did, so do ye. Which of the prophets have not your fathers persecuted? and they have slain them which shewed before of the coming of the Just One; of whom ye have been now the betrayers and murderers: who have received the law by the disposition of angels, and have not kept it' [*Acts* 7:51–53]. That is the truth, and this is exactly what the Apostle is saying here.

And, of course, the writer of the Epistle to the Hebrews says the same thing: 'Take heed, brethren, lest there be in any of you an evil heart of unbelief, in departing from the living God' [*Heb.* 3:12]. And then he warns them about their forefathers' 'hardness of heart' and 'unbelief' [3:15–19; 4:1–2].

There, then, is the third reason given by the Apostle for the failure of these Jews to obey the gospel. They were impersuasible! They were stiff-necked! They were gainsaying! Their whole attitude was such that belief was a sheer impossibility.

And that now brings us to the final cause of the condemnation of the Jews. These are all the particular reasons, but at the back of them there is a final condemnation. And let us remember that this is as true of a modern unbeliever who has heard the gospel as it was of the Jews in the time of the Apostle Paul. What is the final condemnation? It is this: 'To Israel he saith, All day long I have stretched forth my hands unto a disobedient and gainsaying people.' What does it mean? It means that they were utterly and finally without excuse because they rejected the love of God. If it were the case that God simply demanded the impossible and then condemned us because we had not done it, there might be something to be said for the unbeliever, but it is the exact opposite. What is offered to men and women is a gospel of grace. If the gospel really did tell us that we can only be saved if we give a perfect obedience to the Ten Commandments and the whole of God's moral law, then we would all be damned and lost.

But that is what people want it to say. That is what everyone who believes in justification by works really wants the gospel to say. People object to this gospel of the free grace of God, to the fact that salvation is a free gift. 'No, no,' they say, 'what can we do about it?' But the gospel is something that comes to us with outstretched hands. That is the picture that God uses with respect to Himself. He comes with His arms outstretched and His hands pointing to us. He is calling us to Himself. He is pleading with us to come. He is not indicating something, He is appealing. He wants, as it were, to embrace us. 'All the day long I have stretched forth my hands.'

And, of course, this is something we find everywhere right through the Bible. He not only stretches forth His hands and His arms, He does so 'all day long'. You are not merely given one offer and then condemned if you do not accept. He repeats it again and again. In your Old Testament you see this so plainly. Some of the Psalmists put it in a very striking manner. They remind the children of Israel of the whole long story of their history, how God gave them everything and then told them that if they just continued as His people, He would bless them. But they began to turn away and to worship idols and to do various other things, and God withdrew His blessings. Then they came back; they cried and repented. And God took them back and blessed them. Then, after a while, they turned their backs, but God did not give them up. He would go back again and again – 'All day long'! That is the whole story of the Old Testament.

So why did God not blot out this people at the very beginning? It is because He is a God of love and grace, of mercy and compassion. And He puts it in a most extraordinary manner in the mouth of some of the prophets. He turns to these children of Israel and says, in effect, 'You have not got a single excuse. I have sent my prophets unto you, "rising up early"' [*Jer.* 7:13]. As if God says, 'I rose up before the sun rose and sent my messengers, and I have been doing that through this whole day of my relationship to you. Every day I have been working at you from morning to night, before sunrise, well after sunset. I have gone on and on throughout the whole day to the last moment of the eleventh hour.' 'All day long I have stretched forth my hands unto a disobedient and gainsaying people.' Or you remember how He puts it through Isaiah: 'What could have been done more to my vineyard, that I have not done in it?' [*Isa.* 5:4]. As if to say, 'Can you tell me of anything further I could have done?'

Like the fig tree in our Lord's parable [*Luke* 13:6–9], the Jews had had their opportunity and they did not respond – 'Cut them off!' The tremendous and terrible parable of the Wicked Husbandmen [*Matt.* 21:33–45] also teaches the same lesson. But listen to the supreme statement of all this. Here is the tragedy of the Jews, here is their final condemnation. 'O Jerusalem, Jerusalem, which killest the prophets, and stonest them that are sent unto thee; how often would I have gathered thy children together, as a hen doth gather her brood under her wings, and ye would not! Behold, your house is left unto you desolate: and verily I say unto you, Ye shall not see me, until the time come when ye shall say, Blessed is he that cometh in the name of the Lord' [*Luke* 13:34–35]. 'How often would I have . . . but ye would not!' 'All day long I have stretched forth my hands unto a disobedient and gainsaying people.' There is no excuse. God has poured His love out. He has appealed, He has done everything, He has even sent His Son. It is all of no avail.

There, then, you see, the Apostle has summed up once more this case against the Jews, and I would sum it up in a final word like this: what the Apostle is teaching us in Romans 9 and 10 is the election of God, and at the same time, as we have seen, human responsibility. So I put it, as I have put it so many times in studying chapter 9: you are not responsible for the fact that you are saved – that is entirely of God and of His infinite grace. But if you are an unbeliever, and if you ever find yourself in hell, you will have no one to blame but yourself. It is because you were not persuasible; it is because you were stiff-necked; it is because you would not come. You did not want to come and you were determined not to be persuaded. 'All day long I have stretched forth my hands . . .' Why did you not come? That is what God will say to unbelievers at the bar of judgment. They will have no excuse at all. They will realise that they did not come because they were determined not to come, and because they were very proud of themselves for not coming, and because they despised those who did come.

It comes to this. Were it not for the election of God, not a single soul would ever have been saved or ever would be saved. We all of us by nature are hard-hearted; we are a recalcitrant, wicked, gainsaying and disobedient people. It takes the power of the Holy Spirit to soften our hearts and persuade our wills. And nothing less than that power has ever persuaded anybody to believe the gospel. Those who reject are self-condemned. Those who are saved realise that they are saved exclusively by the grace of God. With the Apostle Paul they say, 'By the grace of God I am what I am' [*1 Cor.* 15:10]! I was formerly 'a blasphemer, and a persecutor, and injurious' [*1 Tim.* 1:13]. I was mad in my unbelief, but I am saved.

Why? Well, there is only one answer: it is the grace of God that ever looked upon me and called me, that softened my hard heart, gave me the gift of faith and enabled me to believe. These two things are taught right the way through chapters 9 and 10 of Romans, and they are summed up in these quotations in the last three verses at the end of the chapter: God is found by those who have not sought Him. The revelation is given to those who have never asked. But to those who thought they had got everything and to whom the offer is given, there is only one thing to say – 'All day long I have stretched forth my hands unto a disobedient and gainsaying people.'

We must all examine ourselves in the light of these things. Are you ready with a willing heart to ascribe all the praise, all the honour and all the glory to God in His amazing love and grace? Or are you still trying to hold on to some little bit of credit for yourself? If you hold on to anything, you are like the Jew – that was his whole trouble. He was not ready to be a pauper, he was not ready to become as a little child, he was not ready to be nothing, that God might make him something. It is still the same. It is God who saves, but those who find themselves under condemnation will be faced by the gospel which they refused. If they have got free will, as they say, why do they not exercise it? Why do they not believe? 'Him that cometh to me I will in no wise cast out' [*John* 6:37]. 'Whosoever shall call upon the name of the Lord shall be saved.'

Thirty-five

*

> But I say, Have they not heard? Yes verily, their sound went into all the earth, and their words unto the ends of the world. But I say, Did not Israel know? First Moses saith, I will provoke you to jealousy by them that are no people, and by a foolish nation I will anger you. But Esaias is very bold, and saith, I was found of them that sought me not; I was made manifest unto them that asked not after me. But to Israel he saith, All day long I have stretched forth my hands unto a disobedient and gainsaying people.　　　　　　　　　　　　　　　　　Romans 10:18–21

We have been seeing together how the case against the Jews is unanswerable, and their position inexcusable. Above everything else, it constitutes the greatest tragedy of all human history that God's own, chosen people should be the ones to reject the message and that, on the other hand, the Gentiles, who were not a people and who were foolish and ignorant, should be the ones to come into the kingdom of God and into the Christian church.

Having, then, seen all this, it remains for us now to apply these things to ourselves. Many times in the Scriptures we are told that 'these things . . . are written for our admonition, upon whom the ends of the world are come' [1 Cor. 10:11]. The Apostles say that the Old Testament Scriptures were written not merely that we might have a record of history but that we might learn from that history. And exactly the same is true of these New Testament Scriptures.

In other words, if we fail to apply all this to ourselves and to our present situation, then we shall fall into the very error into which the Jews themselves had fallen. The Jews had got their Scriptures but they never applied them to themselves. They were content with an external relationship and they had never seen how these Scriptures were speaking to them, to their very condition, upbraiding them and, indeed, condemning them. So in order to avoid that, we must now draw certain lessons for ourselves from what the Apostle tells us here.

Here is the first: the unity of the Bible! That is a lesson that all of us, surely, must have learned very plainly. It is quite astonishing to notice the frequency with which the Apostle quotes the Old Testament Scriptures to establish a New Testament principle. And, of course, he does that for one reason only: to show that the same spiritual principles operated under the Old Testament dispensation as in the New and, therefore, we must never be guilty of neglecting the Old Testament. It was the Holy Spirit who led the early church to incorporate the Old Testament with their new documents in forming this book which we now call the Bible; and the reason for that is that there is only one plan of salvation. This is God's eternal purpose, which He purposed before the foundation of the world and which He has been putting into practice ever since Adam and Eve fell in the Garden of Eden.

Now we have seen that developed at great length in Romans 9 and 10. We are all, as children of faith, the children of Abraham [*Gal.* 3:7]. God has one method of salvation and it has always been the method that we have considered – that is, justification by faith only, not by works, not by nationality, not by birth and upbringing. The cases of Jacob and Esau, and so on, settle that once and for ever.

So the way of salvation is the same in the Old and New Testaments, but equally it is true to say that unbelief is also always the same. You get the same principles of unbelief in the Jews under the old dispensation as under the new. That is why the Apostle is able to quote these Scriptures. He says: You are simply behaving as your fathers did. Stephen, in his great address in Acts 7, also says that. And our Lord Himself, in His terrible castigation of the Pharisees at the end of His own ministry, says exactly the same thing. You are filling up, He says, all that the false prophets and others have been doing throughout the centuries [*Matt.* 23:32]. So it is a vital principle, which we must always bear in mind, that the Bible is one, and the great purpose of God is unfolded from the very beginning of Genesis right the way through to the end of the book of Revelation.

There, then, is an obvious lesson which I take it we all have been learning, and I trust we shall be using this as we have to deal with other people. Remember that it is important for us to know our Bibles so that we may be able to find the exact Scripture, give chapter and verse, explain the context, and establish our point. Then nobody can say, 'Ah, that is just your opinion.' You say, 'No, it is not. Here it is in the Scriptures.' Let us learn that lesson, therefore, from the great Apostle.

But, furthermore, I want to emphasise here that the principles with regard to this whole question of salvation, of belief and unbelief, taught here by the Apostle, recur constantly in the whole history of the church and of the human race. What we have here is a pattern which has been repeated many times in different centuries and in different circumstances and, indeed, in different parts of the world. In other words, we are dealing here with a great spiritual principle, and it does not matter, therefore, what age it is, how old people are, nor what part of the world they belong to – it does not make the slightest difference. God's dealings with men and women are always the same; the spiritual principles never vary at all.

What, then, are the great lessons that we learn here? The first is that opposition to the truth of the gospel is always the result of relying on tradition. Now that is the charge that the Apostle brings here against the Jews – that they were falling back on their tradition, on their nationality, on their possession of the Scriptures, on the fact that they had had the prophets and so on.

And the second element is that they were falling back on their own works. They were 'going about to establish their own righteousness', instead of submitting themselves 'unto the righteousness of God'. They were refusing to accept salvation as a free gift of God's grace, and desired to earn it by merit, by their own works.

This is the principle that is laid down here. The Apostle says, in effect, 'Your fathers did that, you are doing the same.' And as I want to show you, the same thing has continued throughout the running centuries. Tradition and a belief in one's own activities have always been the two greatest enemies of the Christian gospel. There are many examples of this. The Christian church started, and all was well at the beginning. The early Christians saw the error of the Jews, and began in purity and simplicity. They believed and they accepted salvation by faith; it was all of grace and they had no confidence in themselves at all.

But in a very short time, things began to change. Indeed, by the beginning of the fourth century, when the Emperor Constantine decided that he would become a Christian and bring the Roman Empire into the Christian church, the situation had already changed. The whole position had hardened and you had this great ecclesiastical body, the Roman Church, incorporating many of the characteristics of the Roman Empire, and there was a rigidity which was quite foreign to the New Testament church. Many ideas had been introduced from Greek philosophy and church leaders were promulgating something that was very remote indeed from the simple teaching of the New Testament. So when you look at the mediaeval church, the Roman Church in the Middle Ages, you find something that is almost the exact opposite of the original Christian church of the New Testament.

And then, from there on you begin increasingly to see the very thing that the Apostle is dealing with here. Certain individuals, even in the Roman Church, would be quickened by the Spirit of God. They would be led back to the Scriptures, and would soon see that the teaching of the Roman Catholic Church was altogether wrong, and they would begin to preach the message of the New Testament. They would agitate for reform, for revival and for reawakening. But what invariably happened was that such people were not only frowned upon, they were bitterly persecuted.

You see, you had a hardened church, exactly like the Jews at the time of our Lord. The people who had the Scriptures, who were religious, who had had the prophets and the teaching, these were the people who opposed the Son of God when He came and preached, and worked His miracles and offered salvation. And they meted out the same treatment to the Apostles. Exactly the same thing occurred in the Middle Ages. It was the church that persecuted a man like Savonarola, this man who had his eyes opened to the truth. The church persecuted him and finally put him to death.

And then you get the Waldensians in northern Italy. They were doing the same thing and they received the same treatment. In this country a man arose called John Wycliffe. He was a priest in the church and a very able scholar. From reading the Scriptures he came to see what a travesty that mediaeval church was of the New Testament church. So he began to preach the truth and to show that no one is saved as a result of the sacraments, or good works, or the intercessions of the church and the priesthood. He saw this doctrine of justification by faith, but you remember what happened to him.

I could go on like this at length. The famous John Huss on the continent of Europe had exactly the same treatment meted out to him; he was put to death. And when you come to the Protestant Reformation you get a re-enactment of what Paul is saying here. Martin Luther was suddenly awakened by the Spirit through the Scriptures to see that there is only one way of salvation, and that is justification by faith only. He saw that 'Whosoever shall call upon the name of the Lord shall be saved'; that a man is 'justified by faith without the deeds of the law' [*Rom.* 3:28]. In other words, he began to preach this very message that the Apostle Paul and the others had preached.

But what happened? Oh, the opposition came not so much from the outside world as from the church. The people who should have welcomed the message, the people who throughout the centuries had been guardians of the Scriptures, appointed to preach them and the gospel, they were the people who opposed this simple, direct evangelical preaching of the gospel – it was a re-enactment of the very thing the Apostle is saying.

And, of course, persecution not only happened to Luther and to John Calvin on the continent, it happened in this country, too. Think of the men and women who were martyred at Smithfield Market, London, simply because they believed this message, and it was the church that persecuted them. Exactly the same thing happened to the Pilgrim Fathers, who were driven out of England and eventually emigrated to America. And it happened to the Methodist fathers of two hundred years ago. Whether they belonged to Whitefield or to the Wesley brothers, it did not make any difference, they were all persecuted; and the thing I am emphasising is that they were persecuted primarily by the church. It was the bishops, the clergy and the prominent people in the church, the squires and others, who persecuted these people just because they were preaching the simple gospel.

So by giving you this very hurried bird's-eye view of the history of the church, I think I have shown you that what happened throughout the centuries has been nothing but a re-enactment of the principle that is taught here by the great Apostle. It is a tremendous and alarming thing, but it is good that we should be aware of it. Persecution has generally come from the people who ought to have been the first to rejoice in the gospel. The people who should rejoice in revival are generally the people who oppose it. The difficulty has been not so much with those out in the world, as with those who are already in the traditional, set, hardened, formal church.

But if that aspect of this message is true, the other aspect is equally true. What does God do when His people become hardened in unbelief, and when their hearts become 'enfattened'? Well, this: 'I will provoke you to jealousy by them that are no people, and by a foolish nation I will anger you.' That is what God has proceeded to do throughout the ages. Look at this history of which I have been hurriedly reminding you, what is it? Well, it simply says that when the church has become not only asleep, but dead and hardened and utterly without understanding, then God has generally revived His work by laying hold upon some most unlikely and unexpected person. It is an astounding thing that, in the whole history of revivals and reawakenings, God has taken hold of some obscure person, not someone in a great ecclesiastical position. It has generally been some nobody whom God has suddenly laid His hands upon and filled with the Spirit, to whom God has given understanding and the power to preach the gospel, thereby angering the church. God's plan has been to 'provoke you to jealousy by them that are no people', by an individual, or a simple group of ordinary, unlettered persons. These are the ones whom God has taken hold of and by means of them He has again brought His truth back before the masses of people. It is a most astonishing thing to notice that, if you want to understand the history of the Christian church from the very beginning up until now, the best way to do so is to know the principles taught us here at the end of Romans 10.

But we must go further. At the time of our Lord and the Apostles, because the Jews would have nothing to do with the message – they who should have received it first and with open arms and should have rejoiced in it because it was a fulfilment of all their prophecies – when they rejected it, God brought a new body, as it were, into being – the Christian church. As He had formed the nation of Israel, so He formed the Christian church. And He has been doing that ever since. What happened in the Protestant Reformation was this: Martin Luther had no intention of leaving the Church of Rome. When he set out, nothing was further from his mind than leaving that church and forming a new church; instead he wanted to reform the Church of Rome. But the old body refused the truth and in the sixteenth century a new body came into being – the Protestant church. And there she stood, filled with truth and with power, preaching the gospel and receiving this persecution from the other body.

And then the cycle started again. The Church of England, which had started so nobly in the sixteenth century in the Protestant Reformation, became hardened. It was because she was opposing the truth as it was preached by the Puritans, that you had the great Ejection in 1662. In that year two thousand clergy were driven out of the Church of England and formed the Congregational and other churches, such as the Baptists, who believed in the congregational principle. 'I will provoke you to jealousy by them that are no people, and by a foolish nation I will anger you.' The old body in its hardness and in its unbelief was left on one side; God produced something new and on the work went.

And you had exactly the same thing in the eighteenth century. Neither George Whitefield nor the Wesleys wanted to leave the Church of England, and in a sense they never did leave it. They died as nominal members and as communicants of that church, but, nevertheless, the main result of their work was that a new body came into being. That was entirely because the Church of England would not tolerate this evangelical message. She made it impossible for these men, and they were driven out of the church.

So you see that on every side the spiritual principle taught here at the end of Romans 10 has been in operation from the very beginning of the church even until this present hour. We must not just read these verses as if they were merely the history of what happened in the first century. We must realise that this has been happening from the very beginning; there has always been this conflict between the spirit and the form. The danger is always that God's people may become hardened, formal and set, and eventually dead, so that when the truth comes, the truth that gave the church her being, she hates it and has to be left on one side.

And so, then, that brings us right up until today. What is the position today? Have these verses anything to say to us who belong to this present generation? I suggest to you that they have a great deal to tell us, and that indeed we are faced with exactly the same situation once more. Speaking generally, what is the position today? Well, I think everybody will agree that the main thing we are aware of is the emphasis upon tradition. You will find that today even the Protestant church, which has always fought the Roman Catholic Church on this very question of tradition, is now beginning to talk again about the importance of tradition. The result of the 'Faith and Order' Conference of the World Council of Churches in Montreal in 1963 was the emphasis on tradition. Protestants, who have always put the Word of God over against tradition, are now accepting tradition; they say we have been too extreme on this. The Catholics have always said, 'The Word of God plus tradition'; tradition and the Bible are held to be equally important. But now in the Protestant church, everybody is talking about the importance of tradition; ecclesiasticism, learning and culture, these are the important things. The church as an institution, that is the big thing that is being emphasised.

What of the doctrine? Well, the main attitude towards doctrine is an entire dislike of it! We are told that doctrine does not matter, that doctrine divides. So we must not be specific in our preaching, we must not be too evangelical. No, the great thing is organisation – a great world church. Do not pay too much attention to what people believe, let them believe almost anything they like, as long as they call themselves Christian. Let there be complete contradiction, it does not matter; the one great institution, that is what matters.

This is the great characteristic of the present time, and with it you always get an emphasis on works. This follows whenever people depreciate doctrine. The popular notion today is that men and women make themselves Christians by living a good life, or by doing good works. The New Testament gospel of salvation as a free gift, the doctrine that Christ bore the punishment of our sins in His own body on the tree, is ridiculed and works and the imitation of Christ are put in its place.

In other words, we are exactly back where the Apostle was, as he faced the Jews of his own age. Indeed, it is unfortunately true to say that those who still adhere to the old evangelical faith and gospel, who try to preach it and who believe it as the Apostle Paul and the first Apostles did, and as these other men whom I have mentioned did throughout the centuries – such people are still being persecuted in this country. The persecution is more polite than it was. People are no longer sent to the stake. But there are other ways of dealing with them which come to very much the same thing in the end. There is active, militant persecution of evangelical people in this country today, leave alone other countries. It is an exact repetition of what we have here.

But let us be quite fair. If that is the position, speaking generally, what is the position among evangelicals? Well, there are some very interesting things happening today. There are certain people who believe that they alone have got the truth. That is why they will not even eat with fellow evangelicals. They think that they alone have the truth, and they will not listen to anyone else. But what they have is the exact opposite of this gospel! They have a legalism of the worst type conceivable. In a sense, they have a reproduction of the whole position of the Roman Catholic Church. They are like the Jews at the time of the Apostle Paul. And those whom the Holy Spirit has enlightened in His grace and has brought out from among them and for whom we thank God – what are they discovering? Well, what they say to us it this: 'We were told that we alone had the truth. We are beginning to see now that we had very little, that we were kept in ignorance. We did not understand; we did not know.'

But let us come nearer home still. What is the condition of the mainstream evangelical churches? Is it not the simple truth that our greatest danger is the danger of deadness, of traditionalism, of self-satisfaction, and of regarding ourselves as the custodians of the faith, despising others? It is the danger, almost, of saying, 'I thank God that I am not like these other people'. And unconsciously, perhaps, there is a tendency even to resist the operation of the Holy Spirit. That is why I say it is vital that we should apply these things to ourselves. It is not enough that a church should be orthodox – is she alive? Is she really being used by God in convicting men and women of sin and bringing them to a knowledge of salvation? Is she attracting people to the Lord Jesus Christ? You can have a dead orthodoxy. We are reminded of that in this very paragraph that we have been examining in such detail. So, you see, we are all involved in this.

What, then, are the ultimate lessons that we should learn? First, we must learn the need for humility. Is it not alarming to realise that these Jews could ever have got into this condition? They were God's people, the people who had the Scriptures, the people to whom the fathers belonged. Look back to the list at the beginning of chapter 9. And these people, of all people, were the ones who rejected the Christ, crucified the Messiah and were opposed to His preaching and the message of salvation.

These were the people who had become blind, of whom Paul wrote that there was a 'veil' over their hearts and eyes [*2 Cor.* 3:13–16]; these were the people who, boasting in the Scriptures, did not understand the Scriptures. I say the first call to us is the call to humility, to pause for a moment and to examine ourselves and to see how things really stand with us. The case of the Jews is a perpetual warning to God's people that we must always be on the alert lest we unconsciously slide into this position which is the exact opposite of that in which we began.

I could have emphasised that point as I did my review of history. As I pointed out, it was the original church that became the Roman Catholic Church. The Church of England came out of that, and yet in a very short time this Church of England was persecuting the people who were preaching that same message. And, I wonder, what has happened to nonconformity by today? Nonconformity came out of the Church of England because of its adherence to the simple gospel message, its adherence to the Scriptures, but I am afraid it is true to say that today the nonconformist bodies are persecuting people who are doing that very thing. They have been hardened in their institutions and it is not surprising that they all want to go back to episcopacy, and perhaps eventually even into the Church of Rome. They have become the exact opposite of what they were when they began.

That is the sort of thing that can happen to all of us. If it happened to the Jews, it can happen to anybody. Therefore I say it behoves us to be humbled. The word that we must apply to ourselves is the word of Paul to the church at Corinth: 'Let him that thinketh he standeth take heed lest he fall' [*1 Cor.* 10:12]. It is right to be orthodox, but make certain that you are alive, or your orthodoxy will avail you nothing.

Then my second lesson is this: we must test everything by the Scriptures. There is no other test apart from that. The Apostle bases his whole argument, as we have seen abundantly, upon the teaching of the Scriptures. He does not just stand up and say, 'I say this to you.' He says, 'Listen, this is what Moses said. Listen to the bold Isaiah.' He proves his teaching from the Scriptures, and unless we establish our position in the same way, we are all wrong. I do not care what experiences you have, or what you think, or what your learning may be – if you are not scriptural, you are wrong! Everything must be determined at the bar of Scripture.

But I want to add to that a third lesson. We must take the Scriptures as a whole, we must take them as they are. We must allow them to speak to us, to search us. We must not merely use the Scriptures to prove our prejudices, or to show that we are right in our position. We must submit ourselves to them in every respect. We must have not only the letter but also the spirit. And perhaps the greatest danger confronting evangelicals is always to stop at the letter and not go on to the spirit; it is the danger of respectability and a fear of the power of the Spirit, a fear of the unusual, a fear of what it might cost. Is not this one of our greatest dangers? We must take the Scriptures as a whole.

If you are priding yourself on your orthodoxy, let me ask you a question: Do you recognise yourself in the New Testament description of the Christian man or woman? You are orthodox – all right, thank God, but is this true of you: 'Whom having not seen ye love; in whom, though now ye see him not, yet believing, ye rejoice with a joy unspeakable and full of glory' [*1 Pet.* 1:8]? Are you filled with the Spirit? Is there a danger that somebody might think that you are filled with 'new wine' because you are so filled with the spirit of praise and of rejoicing? That is the New Testament Christian. Let us be careful, my friends. We must take all the Scriptures. The New Testament church was not only orthodox, she was a church filled with joy and power. Is the modern evangelical church like that? Let us judge ourselves by the Scriptures.

And that brings me, therefore, to an appeal, which is this. Firstly, let us be watchful; let us always examine ourselves; let us not assume that because we were once right, we are still right. Let us not assume that because we are in a certain body, that all is well with us. We must not rely on any one of these things, but we must know our own personal relationship to the Lord.

Secondly, we must keep ourselves open. We must not be in such a rigid position that our first tendency is to down everything or to reject everything; let us examine everything. 'Prove all things; hold fast that which is good,' said Paul [*1 Thess.* 5:21]. But I am afraid that sometimes I detect a tendency on the part of many to down everything. When there is a new movement of God's Spirit, they do not even consider it, but they condemn it because it is new or because it is unusual. We must keep ourselves open. The movements of the Spirit are beyond our understanding. Let us learn the lesson of these Jews. Because things were not happening in their way, they rejected the Christ. Let us be careful.

In other words, let us beware, lest, when God in His grace, and in His mercy and sovereignty, does decide to revive His work in a mighty revival, we be bypassed because of our rigidity, because of our self-satisfaction, because we will not accept that God may be choosing to do things in a way that we have never hitherto known or heard of. The Spirit is a sovereign Lord. Let us be careful that we do not try to limit Him, because if we do, we shall be quenching the Spirit; we shall be resisting the Spirit; we shall be doing the very thing the Jews did, the very things the Roman Catholic Church has done, the Church of England has done, the very things the nonconformist bodies are doing. May God preserve us from such a fate.

There, then, is my appeal, but let me end on a word of hope, and this is our only hope, and we thank God for it. What is our hope? It is that God is still the same! We have seen that God's people tend to be the same. Yes, but the glorious thing is that God is still the same! And the comfort I have is that God's purpose is still the same, that God's work is still the same, that God's power is still the same – and therefore we can be certain of this: whatever you and I may do, whatever you and I may become, whatever you and I may be guilty of by way of failure or obduracy or anything else, God's work will go on. Here is the lesson: 'I will provoke you to jealousy by them that are no people, and by a foolish nation I will anger you . . . I was found of them that sought me not; I was made manifest unto them that asked not after me . . . All day long I have stretched forth my hands unto a disobedient and gainsaying people.' His own people refused Him, but that did not bring God's purpose to an end. God brought His purpose to pass in spite of His people. He brought into being another people out of the 'no people'. He formed a new nation out of a 'foolish people', and He has always done that throughout the running centuries. And I do not see how anybody can look with any degree of hopefulness at the present or the future of the Christian church who does not believe that! In the Middle Ages you would have thought that the Christian church was finished. The Roman Church was dead, completely dead spiritually. It did not matter. Though God's people were failing, God went on. He raised a new people. He has always done that and He always will do that.

You see, it comes back to that tremendous statement that was made by Mordecai to Queen Esther. He begged her to appeal to the king to save the Jews. But she was hesitating, and he pleaded with her and said, 'If thou altogether holdest thy peace at this time, then shall there enlargement and deliverance arise to the Jews from another place . . . and who knoweth whether thou art come to the kingdom for such a time as this?' [*Esth*. 4:14]. 'Go and do it,' he said, in effect. 'It will be wonderful and you will have great honour if you do it. But even if you do not' – and this was a tremendous thing to say in such a situation – 'even if you do not, and if you refuse, God will bring salvation from some other quarter, through some other person.'

God is not dependent upon us and if the message at the end of Romans 10 does not teach us anything else, it teaches us that. That is the thing that stands out most prominently in these verses. God is not dependent on any people, even on His own people, and though the whole of the modern church may become apostate (which God forbid!), God will still carry out His purpose. I almost tremble as I look at the situation and try to foresee the future. What a terrible, what a tragic thing it would be if God should have to carry on His work by bypassing us altogether and perhaps picking up one of these despised people, the outsiders, the hopeless! He has had to do that many times in the long history of the world. He may do it again.

We stand back aghast at such people and, in a sense, we are right in doing so, but, my dear friends, the warning of this passage to me is this. Let us make certain that we are not in the position of the Jews, so that God, as it were, is not driven to raise up those others in order to provoke us to jealousy, and to shame us as He carries on His great and eternal purpose. He pleads with us. He holds out His hands to us. He starts with us – it is always 'beginning at Jerusalem' [*Luke* 24:47].

And I feel that there is a mighty call of the Spirit of God at the present time to those of us who are evangelical, to be God's instruments. God forbid that we should fail because of some hardening of our hearts, or some hardening in our institutions, in our churches, or our movements, or our societies. God forbid that we should have become so hard, so staid, so set, so formal that we cannot tolerate a fresh breeze of the Spirit, that God will have to lay us on one side, as it were, and raise up some nobodies out of the gutters of life to carry on His great and glorious work.

There, then, are some thoughts as the result of our study of these verses at the end of Romans 10. It is, to me, one of the most alarming passages in the whole of Scripture. May God write it deeply on our minds, hearts and spirits in order that we all, examining ourselves, may humble ourselves before Him and allow Him to deal with us as He wills, as He chooses, whatever the consequences – come what may.